The American Teacher

EVOLUTION OF A PROFESSION IN A DEMOCRACY

Ichabod Crane's School

Darley

THE
American Teacher

EVOLUTION OF A PROFESSION IN A DEMOCRACY

 Teachers are employed for purposes "vastly great." They must teach the science of health with all the learning but without the pay of the doctor; they must inculcate the principles of morality with all the impressive sincerity but without the sectarianism of the minister; they must be altogether more patient and discreet than God Almighty himself, for He was "wroth" when He punished the wicked, whereas, if a teacher punishes in anger, he is guilty of an assault and battery; they must invent schemes to invert human nature, and make every good thing and thought enticing and every bad thing and thought abominably disgusting . . . they must tenderly moderate the zeal of the too ambitious, and inspire the dullest blockhead with a manly thirst for fame and knowledge; the incorrigibly uncouth and vicious, they must endow with the tastes, the instincts, and the manners of the refined and virtuous. And in short, they must turn all from the thousand paths that lead to indolence, ignorance, and folly; and prepare them to find infallibly all the ways of pleasantness and all the paths of peace.

Marble, A. P., 1887

BY WILLARD S. ELSBREE
Professor of Education, Teachers College, Columbia University

GREENWOOD PRESS, PUBLISHERS
WESTPORT, CONNECTICUT

Originally published in 1939 by American Book Company,
New York.

Reprinted from an original copy in the collections of Harvard
University Library.

Reprinted in 1970 by Greenwood Press
A division of Congressional Information Service, Inc.
88 Post Road West, Westport, Connecticut 06881

Library of Congress catalog card number 74-104262
ISBN 0-8371-3921-X

Printed in the United States of America

10 9 8 7 6 5 4 3 2

Preface

A number of excellent histories of education have been written, in which the struggles of the American people to establish and support a system of free public schools have been admirably portrayed. For the most part, however, these histories have stressed legislation pertaining to education, modifications in the organization and administration of public schools, curriculum changes, and the various philosophies which have guided educators in their efforts to prepare youth for citizenship in a democracy. Yet in these comprehensive treatises teachers have received relatively little attention. To the author's knowledge, no one has stressed the role of classroom teachers in the development of public education in the United States.

The writer has felt for a long time that every teacher should have some acquaintance with the problems and achievements of those who preceded him in the work of instructing the young; that the conditions under which former pedagogues worked, the kind of persons they were, and the part which they played in society are all matters of interest and concern to modern teachers. It is only through a study of long-time trends that we acquire perspective and insight.

This book is a modest attempt to tell the story of the public-school teacher in America during the last three centuries. It is hoped that it will be of interest and value not only to those engaged in educational work and those preparing for teaching but also to other individuals who see in the evolution of the profession the bases for planning future achievements.

The writer wishes to express his appreciation to all who have assisted him in the preparation of this volume. Among these, five persons are especially deserving of mention: Harriet Shoen, who contributed significantly to the discussion of the colonial period included in Chapter I; the author's wife, Elizabeth Elsbree, who worked intensively on several of the earlier chapters in the book; David Marke, who checked all the sources mentioned in the section on the colonial schoolmaster; Professor Newton Edwards of the University of Chicago, who read the galley proof and offered constructive criticisms and suggestions; and Elizabeth Cunningham, who typed and edited the manuscript.

The author is also grateful to many publishers, societies, and individuals for the quoted materials and illustrations used. Specific credit for these is given throughout the pages of this book.

WILLARD S. ELSBREE

Contents

PART III

THE EMERGENCE OF THE PROFESSIONAL TEACHER

Introduction, 309

List of Illustrations

PART I

The Colonial Schoolmaster

PART I

INTRODUCTION

THE TEACHING PROFESSION in America is what it is today because of forces and circumstances which have been molding it since the establishment of the first school on the New England coast. The practices and procedures inaugurated by the early pioneers in selecting, compensating, and supervising teachers established patterns and set precedents for many of the personnel policies which are now in vogue. Similarly, the attitude of the public toward teachers and teaching, as expressed in colonial laws, local rules and instructions, the minutes of town meetings, and also in local customs, played a significant part in developing traditions which have been both useful and detrimental to public education.

The teaching personnel of the American colonies was not organized into a national society. It published no annual reports of activities. There were no state department records containing detailed information about individual schoolmasters. In fact, in making a study of the colonial schoolteacher the immediate and most striking feature of the entire problem is the distressingly fragmentary character of the source material. Farmers and traders battling the wilderness in a strange new land were naturally more concerned with felling trees, planting crops, building homes, and warding off Indian attacks than with making accurate transcripts of their everyday affairs. Musket, ax, and plow were readier to their hand than pen and paper. Recordmaking depended upon a favorable combination of circumstances: time, opportunity and materials, the none too common ability to write, and an incentive.

Yet the colonial era was by no means unchronicled. Births, marriages, and deaths were recorded from the beginning, but more often than not individually in family Bibles. Land grants, deeds and wills, baptisms, and other church matters were kept officially, and in New England there were town records and selectmen's minutes. The wonder is not that so little was written down, but rather that so much was recorded.

3

Unfortunately, however, much of what documentary material did exist has been lost or destroyed. Town and church records are incomplete. Accounts, bills, indentures, mortgages, contracts, and other business and commercial papers were usually destroyed after they had outlived their immediate uses. Fire, Indian raids, and war took their inevitable toll of property damage. And individual negligence or historical indifference among succeeding generations is responsible for the disappearance of still more data.

On the other hand, we are fortunate in the survival of numerous diaries, letters, and journals, whose quaint pages supplement the official records, filling in gaps and providing a wealth of homely detail which is characteristically absent from more formal documents. The net result of this situation is a striking unbalance in the distribution of source material on colonial life; for certain localities and periods there is a welter of historical data, for other places and times little or nothing.

In studying education we are doubly handicapped. Schools played so subordinate a role in colonial life that only rarely did they achieve a history of their own. Data on education must be winnowed out from a mass of unrelated material in town, church, and court records; in papers, letters, journals, diaries, and other sources. Even in New England, in the few cases where town records are complete, school affairs seem to have occupied the official attention of the founding fathers so seldom and so unobtrusively that references to education are far too infrequent. Apparently school items were entered in the town records and selectmen's minutes only when some situation pressed for concerted action, with the result that whole decades might pass without so much as mention of the business of education.

Source material on the masters and dames who constituted the teaching personnel is still scarcer and more fragmentary. On the one hand, we have such relatively satisfying communities as Boston, Braintree, Dedham, and Dorchester, with a fairly complete set of town records containing numerous references to schools and schoolmasters and occasional reassuring statements that serve as landmarks. Roxbury, for example, affords us a long list of its schoolmasters during the colonial period, and enough additional information concerning these individuals can be gleaned from the town records and other sources to give us a fair picture of the school situation in that village. Dedham, similarly, provides us with the names of sixty-six masters and supplementary details for well over half of them. The Boston and Dorchester school personnel is equally well chronicled.

On the other hand, we have a far from satisfactory situation for many other communities. Ipswich shows large gaps in the chronology of its masters for the eighteenth century. Salem records mention only three masters during the seventeenth century—young Mr. Norris (the minister's son), Mr. Daniel Epes, and Daniel Andrew—and some half dozen between 1720 and the Revolution, leaving several decades unaccounted for. Duxbury, Sandwich, Barnstable, Yarmouth, the entire provinces of Rhode Island and New Hampshire, and the river towns of Connecticut all afford the scantiest possible data on their teaching personnel.

Outside New England, source material on schoolmasters is even more scanty, with notable exceptions in the case of New Amsterdam and New York City, Long Island, Philadelphia and vicinity. Whole counties in Maryland are historical blanks educationally, as is much of northern Jersey and western Pennsylvania, parts of Virginia, and North Carolina. Thus it is that in some communities we do not know when the school was first established, what masters taught there, nor what their qualifications, conditions of life, and compensation were. In a number of cases, indeed, we do not even know whether or not a school was kept.

In addition to the problem of lack of information, we are also faced with the question of the accuracy of the data which we do have. Ambiguity, error, and personal bias inevitably creep into any mass of written material produced under similar circumstances. For example, Governor Berkeley's much-quoted statement concerning Virginia in 1671, "I thank God we have no free schools nor printing," we know to be partially false. Schools of a sort *did* exist in Virginia during the period specified.

Secondary sources are even more prone to mistakes: sweeping generalizations based on insufficient factual evidence, misleading statements, and unjustified conclusions that occasionally can be explained only by the premise that the author was in search of support for a preconceived viewpoint. The Massachusetts Law of 1647, ordering every town of fifty householders to provide a primary school and every community of a hundred families to establish a grammar school, has repeatedly led to the conclusion that schools were established at once, as ordered, and maintained continuously thenceforward—as if the mere passage of a law were equivalent to one hundred per cent enforcement. Yet citations of fines for nonobservance of this regulation and apologetic explanations for inability to comply with it show that there were discrepancies between legislative enactment and actual conditions.

Fortunately, however, we count among our secondary sources the careful scholarship of Seybolt for Boston and Woody for Quaker education, both of whom deal with the teaching personnel specifically, as well as the works of numerous other dependable students of colonial times who treat one or more phases of education for particular localities.

Time has not permitted an exhaustive treatment of the colonial period in this volume. The sheer bulk of the material to be sifted through and the fact that the data are widely scattered among the thirteen original states have made such an objective impracticable. The author will be satisfied if this portion of his study gives a fairly clear bird's-eye view of the teaching group during the early days.

I

The Period

IT would be futile to study a profession as an isolated group of workers. The schoolmaster of the sixteen- and seventeen-hundreds was not a solo actor tricked out in colonial costume, performing against a backdrop of early America, but an integral part of a vigorous frontier life, acted upon by all the stern reality of contemporary circumstance. The warp and woof of the society in which he lived wove him fast to his neighbors and his surroundings, to the pioneer thought and purpose of the time and locality, determining his outline and coloring as certainly as though he were a figure in a tapestry. It seems desirable, therefore, briefly to review the period that formed the matrix for the colonial schoolteacher.

In 1600 eastern America was covered with virgin forest that swept inland from the ocean and up over the Appalachian ranges. Dense, almost unbroken, those dim recesses had for centuries been the home of wild animals and barbarous Indian tribes. Then white sails appeared on the eastern horizon, and before another century had passed the complexion of the Atlantic seaboard was vastly changed.

Singly and in twos and threes little ships came bobbing across the sea, unloaded their cargoes of cattle, horses, swine, poultry, seed, farm tools, firearms, and household goods—and a determined, white-faced people came ashore to stay. The ring of ax and crack of musket echoed up and down the coastline. Forest giants that had stood undisturbed for centuries were hastily hewn into timbers to furnish return cargoes. Hurriedly-dried skins and those procured from trade with the Indians were packed in sturdy hogsheads and stowed in the hold, while whole rooms in the cabins of the ships were filled with dried fish. Then the vessels sailed away, some to deliver their cargoes safely and raise high hopes of profits in the minds of men who had adventured their wealth in plantations in America, others to fall prey to enemies on the sea or to meet a watery grave.

Alone in the wilderness of the New World, the first settlers struggled for existence, often without adequate food, shelter, or goods for trade with the Indians. Of necessity they adopted many of the ways of the red skins. The wigwams of the English settlers in New England differed from those of the savages mainly by the addition of huge fireplaces at one end and great wooden doors at the other. Dugouts, lined with small logs driven vertically into the ground like a stockade, were the first homes of many settlers who later built fine houses.[1] Sturdy homes for all were impossible at first; the building of them would have been too great a strain upon the combined man power of any early settlement, even where the perils of disease that followed the long sea voyage left sufficient men who were able and strong enough to do the heavy work.

A few frame houses were erected by some of the very first settlers of New England and the Southern English colonies, however. Such homes were built by men who either brought with them a number of servants or who, like Sir Richard Saltonstall, sent servants over in advance for the purpose of preparing the way for their master to follow. To build these "faire" houses, logs were squared off and hewn into beams, rafters, lintels, sills, etc., in the usual English style. The outside was covered with weatherboard sawed at a "saw pit."   Later, clapboards or shingles were added. Jasper Danckaerts, who waited for a few weeks in Boston for a ship during the summer of 1680, described the homes of that city thus: [2]

All the houses are made of thin, small cedar shingles, nailed against frames, and then filled in with brick and other stuff; and so are their

[1] The log cabin (with horizontal logs notched at the corners), so much used at a later date all over America, was unknown in early New England. Log cabins of this style were first introduced by the Swedes who settled along the Delaware River.

[2] *Original Narratives of Early American History*, Vol. XII, p. 275. We know that at least one of these houses sheltered a "dame school," because Samuel Sewall wrote in his *Diary;* "This day Dame Walker is taken so ill that she sends home my Daughters, not being able to teach them."   (*Diary of Samuel Sewall, 1674–1729*, Vol. I, p. 164, in Massachusetts Historical Society, *Collections*, 1878.)

churches. For this reason these towns are so liable to fires, as have already happened several times; and the wonder to me is, that the whole city has not been burnt down, so light and dry are the materials.

We can forgive this Netherlander for the air of superiority with which he criticizes the dwellings of Boston when we remember the fine houses of stone and brick that were built in early times in New Amsterdam and along the Hudson River.

The problem of shelter fades into insignificance beside the very grave situation which confronted the first settlers when they sought to replenish their food supply. Sea voyages that lasted anywhere from a few weeks to a few months, during which the passengers had to furnish their own board, usually either consumed or spoiled the greater part of the food supply of the settlers, who only too often landed in the New World sadly in need of provisions. With their scant knowledge of the resources of the new country, they obtained what food they could—fish, game, and Indian corn. Death took its toll from those who failed to make the dietary adjustments that life in the new country demanded, and those who were left alive learned to eat and like the fare of the Indians. There were those who found it hard to drink water instead of ale; but as time passed and they found themselves as "lusty" and full of health as before, they ceased complaining.

Most of the different colonies passed through a "hunger time," the memory of which lasted long in the minds of those who survived. In the Jamestown colony and at Plymouth, conditions grew better only after they abandoned the form of communistic life under which they had first lived and trusted to individual enterprise for the raising of corn. Governor Bradford declared that in Plymouth the "experience that was had in this commone course and condition" proved the "vanitie" of those who believed that "yᵉ taking away of propertie, and bringing in communitie into a comone wealth, would make them happy and florishing" because it did nothing of the sort, but "was found to breed much confusion & discontent, and retard much imployment that would have been to their benefite and comforte." [3]

[3] Bradford, William, *History of Plimoth Plantation* (Boston, 1899), Bk. ii, p. 163.

Times were not so hard for those who came later. The Governor of the Massachusetts Bay Company could write from England to his people in Salem in 1629, saying, "If you want swine, we have agreed with those of New Plymouth that they deliver you six sows." [4] When the first vessel of Winthrop's fleet arrived in the spring of the next year, the physician from Plymouth came to attend the sick after they had been badly treated and put ashore by the captain of the ship, who was anxious to return to England. A few dwellings already existed on the hills around Massachusetts Bay, and their owners, called "old planters" in the ancient records, extended every hospitality to the newcomers. That summer of 1630 witnessed one of the largest organized emigrations of civilized, educated people that the world up to that time had ever known and, although death and disease were no respecters of persons, it is probable that much suffering was alleviated by those who had come before. It is known, for example, that later that summer Indian corn was obtained from Virginia.[5] By the time William Penn planted his colony in the late sixteen-hundreds, the business was carried forward with the greatest efficiency and the settlers suffered comparatively few hardships.

What led these "first planters" to undertake this hazardous experiment, to leave established homes in the Old World for an unknown future in the New? Every schoolboy knows that the first Virginia settlers expected to strike gold in the New World; that the "Pilgrim Fathers" of Plymouth and the Puritans of Massachusetts sought religious freedom in New England; that the first settlers in New Netherland were under the control of a fur-trading company in old Netherlands; that Maryland was a haven for Catholics, Rhode Island for Baptists, Pennsylvania for Quakers; that the Swedes made a brave start along the Delaware, but were forsaken by their Queen and left to take care of themselves in the wilderness; and that various English noblemen were absentee proprietors of estates in the New World which later became North and South Carolina. College students dig deeper into American history and find the narrow intolerance, the per-

⁴ "The Company's Instructions to Endicott and His Council," in Young's *Chronicles of the First Planters of the Colony of Massachusetts Bay* (Boston, 1846), p. 156.
⁵ Roger Clap's *Memoirs, ibid.*, p. 352.

secutions, and the "blue laws" that caused so many upheavals and migrations from one town to another in early New England. Modern students sympathize with the religious liberals who migrated to Connecticut and they are proud of Roger Williams.

Down through the colonial period of American history, Massachusetts was perhaps the most important center of American life. Let us get acquainted with a typical stern New Englander of the early days. First and foremost, he was an Englishman, proud of his rights as an Englishman, and loyal to the laws of England (loyal to the good laws at least!). But his religion was his life and in the old country his church had not been the established church of the land. In New England, his church and his state were one. Here, then, was one of the main reasons for his removal to America. All the prestige and preferment that went with membership in the established church was available to the Puritan in New England. Only by appreciating this situation can one understand the early New England Puritan. He made with his God a stern covenant of works and dedicated his life to its fulfillment. In God's name he persecuted Quakers and others who did not believe as he believed. In God's name he slew the Indians. What seems to us intolerance, to him was righteousness and gave him comfort and pleasure. In such surroundings tolerance rated as a sin and those who professed it were ordered to move on.

William Blackstone was the first Boston liberal. He raised the first house on the peninsula where Boston was later built and had been living there for some years when Winthrop arrived in 1630. How or when he came to America are unknown; he may have come with the Gorges expedition in 1623. Blackstone refused to join with the Boston church, saying, "I came from England because I did not like the lord-bishops; but I cannot join with you, because I would not be under the lord-brethren." [6] He sold his land to the city, bought a herd of cows with the money he received for it, packed his precious one hundred and eighty-three books, and made his way to what was later to become Rhode Island a year before Roger Williams followed the same path for a somewhat similar, although more urgent, reason.

[6] Quoted from Cotton Mather, *ibid.*, p. 170n.

Here was a typical religious independent. He lived alone with his books and spent his days removing tree stumps and picking stone from his land, except for those brief seasons when planting and harvesting gave purpose to the drudgery of the rest of the days. His life differed little from that of other early New England farmers except that most of them married early in life and God gave them many sons to help with the stern task of taming the rocky New England soil.

Thus the business of settlement went on. It was a spasmodic sort of progress, seemingly haphazard. Here a salient thrust suddenly into the wilderness; there the fringe of settlement widened slowly and crept inland. Plantations sprouted like young, green leaves along the stem of a sluggish Southern river, while elsewhere came recession, the swift blight of famine, disease, or Indian massacre.

Life in the Southern English plantations retained some of the characteristics of English manor life; in many ways, in fact, it was similar to life under the feudalism of the Middle Ages. In Virginia, the discovery in tobacco of a staple money crop put the little colony of wrangling planters with their broken dreams of immediate wealth on a firm economic basis which even foreshadowed agricultural prosperity. The introduction of slavery made possible the opening up of more and more land and life for the small group of landowners became increasingly aristocratic. In Maryland, some twenty "gentlemen" came to the newly chartered province provided with from two to three hundred laborers. The lesson of the need for brawn in the laying out of estates and the building of homes in the New World had been learned.

The rigid restraints by which religion dominated the lives of New Englanders were unfelt by men who lived out their lives on Southern plantations. The lone case of dancing round a Maypole that caused so much indignation and furor in the earliest days of New England probably would have passed unnoticed in Virginia. Indeed, it might be quite accurate to assume that similar festivities filled many idle hours in the lives of those who lived on isolated Southern plantations. Even in Maryland, where one might reasonably expect the Catholic Church to have remained forever the established church, religious toleration was early written into the law; and before many years passed, the Church of England became the established church.

By 1700 the English colonies in America extended from the Maine coast to Spanish Florida.[7] An air of permanence pervaded them. Their struggle for existence had passed and men began to turn their attention toward those activities through which a surplus can be accumulated. Already the embryonic commercial activities of the colonists had caused the British Parliament to pass that first "Navigation Act," and already colonial merchants were seeking ways and means of avoiding it. To them it was a "bad" law, which, they declared, violated their rights as freeborn Englishmen. New England religion did not frown upon those who broke "bad" laws.

Shipbuilding was an important occupation in the colonies from the earliest times. Skilled shipwrights had come with the first settlers and shipyards sprang up along the coast in many places. In America, near the supply of lumber, ships could be built for a fraction of their cost in Europe. Many New England merchants and fishermen superintended the building of their own vessels and later became their masters. Some merchants fared forth with their own goods in their own ships and left their children to manage the business in their absence. Others hired a master and crew to sail their ships and prayed for their safe return.

The needs of the American colonists were many. Scythes, needles, knives, and similar items that could not then be manufactured in the New World were required. Cloth and other articles of clothing were also needed, in far greater quantity than the home industry of pioneer women could produce. These things had to be obtained by trade. Fortunately, the colonists had many exports. These included the seemingly inexhaustible supply of lumber and other products of the forest—such as naval stores (tar, pitch, and turpentine) or masts and yards for ships—New England's abundant supply of dried cod, mackerel, fish oil, and whale oil; also tobacco from Virginia, rice and indigo from

---

[7] In 1655 New Sweden surrendered to New Netherland and in 1664 New Netherland surrendered to the British. Thus, without bloodshed, the control of both the Hudson and Delaware river valleys fell to the British.

plantations farther south, not to mention the constantly renewable supply of grain, animals, and meat produced by all the colonies.

If the needs of the colonists could have been supplied by a simple process of barter, value for value, history might have been different and there might have been no United States of America today. The long story of the Trade Acts, the mere mention of which so infuriated colonial merchants, cannot be told here. Not that the colonists obeyed those laws, for they didn't. A Hat Act passed by the British Parliament could not force a colonial backwoodsman (or a Dr. Franklin, either, for that matter) to throw away his coonskin cap and don the fine headgear manufactured in England. The outcome of the Trade Acts was the growth of an enormous illegal commerce in the colonies.

New England sea merchants of the seventeen-hundreds were the grandsons of those staunch, religious Puritans who first peopled New England. They did not especially like to behave like pirates. But continued disobedience of laws which they called "bad" and long experience in trade that knew not the control of any law made many of them into a class of adventurers among whom it was exceedingly difficult to draw a line that would separate honest merchants from pirates. No colonial American ship had any legal right to trade in the West Indies, but there, nonetheless, among pirates and buccaneers, a large volume of the commerce of colonial New England merchants was carried on. For there only could a conveniently reached market be found for the large supply of fish, grain, meat, and animals, and New Englanders soon found a lucrative use for the molasses that was so easily obtained from the West Indies. Thus the vicious molasses-rum-slave-molasses-rum-slave cycle began. Ships left Rhode Island ports loaded with rum, which, in Africa, they exchanged for slaves. Then they made the infamous "middle passage" and traded the slaves in the West Indies for chests of hard Spanish "pieces of eight" and for more molasses to make more rum. Here was freedom, self-appropriated and very much misused.

Englishmen in England knew that this commerce, unsanctified by law, was going on, but for a long time nothing was done about it; it may very well be that they could have done nothing that would have effectively controlled or stopped it. As long as all of Virginia's tobacco was sold only in Britain, at whatever low price British merchants set upon it, and as long as other "enumerated" articles went exclusively to Britain, the British politicians were content to close their eyes while their young and vigorous colonies in America sowed their wild oats. When the time came that Englishmen in England tried to force Englishmen in America to obey their laws, it was too late. What Englishmen in England called "smuggling," Englishmen in America knew to be the established normal channels of their trade and they were ready to fight a war in order to safeguard their economic interests. They wanted to be free to trade, even as freeborn Englishmen who lived in England were free to trade.

There was the political aspect, also, of this curbing of the freedom of American colonists by the British Parliament. In the beginning, the liberal charters that had been granted to the first settlers in America had permitted a degree of self-government that was unknown anywhere in the world at that time. And the English colonies in America had grown and blossomed under that autonomy. Then, side by side with the oppressive Trade Acts, came a gradual process of taking away time-honored charters from the colonies and bringing them under the crown.

During the eighteenth century the population of the American colonies increased by leaps and bounds; and, whether the colonists thought so or not, they were daily growing prosperous. Large families were the order of the day and this meant that many homes grew out of one home in the brief span of a generation. The tide of immigration was continuous. And the newcomers were loud in their praise of their new homes. They took over the opinions of their older neighbors with enthusiasm and gloried in their new-found independence. From a little over a quarter of a million souls in 1700, the population of the American colonies increased to well over two million in 1775, an eightfold gain in numbers. Among the latecomers were the thrifty Palatine Germans, who came to Pennsylvania in response to Penn's advertising, and large numbers of Scotch-Irish, who formed a significant portion of the population of several of the colonies. There were sturdy Scots and not a few Frenchmen also, and the steady stream of English, although reduced in numbers and perhaps in caliber, continued almost down to the Revolution.

The period from 1688 to 1770 in America was a period of gradual flowering of the political principle of federation, union, or what was called in the old days "republicanism," [8] in America. This respect for union came gradually and as a result of the stern demands of necessity. At heart the frontiersman was an individualist, and he disliked to admit that in union there was strength. But the time came when he fought for union. What union probably meant to him, however, was protection for his rights as an individual—never central power.

In this environment the colonial schoolmaster lived and worked.

---

[8] This term was probably derived from the use of the term "republic" by the Romans. An American who lived in the trying days of the Revolution and the making of the Constitution meant by "republic" a representative government by delegates chosen by the people of free states. The term "democracy" was never used by Americans in those days, nor was its modern meaning intended when they spoke of "the republic."

II

The Character of the Colonial Schoolmaster

THE colonial schoolmaster could well be introduced in any one of a number of ways. Some would choose to know first about the nature of his task; others might be curious about his professional qualifications; and still others would like to hear first of all how he fared economically and socially. Perhaps most people, however, would like to know at the start what manner of man he really was. It is here, therefore, that our story about him begins.

Nowhere in educational history has there been a greater tendency to generalize from individual cases than in that concerning the character of colonial schoolmasters—because of the smallness of their total number and the fragmentary nature of existing source material, but more especially because of the disproportionate emphasis given to the picturesque. Since time immemorial, virtue has been characterized by a certain insipidity, while wickedness and evil-doings have been self-illuminated by a phosphorescence of their own. Historical misbehavior, indeed, has had such a fascination for casual readers, and even for students, that striking cases of misconduct lodge in the memory, overshadowing or completely obliterating the commonplace. Statistically more important, but less vivid, the ordinary and the typical pale into insignificance. Thus sporadic examples tend to suffuse a group or locality, an entire profession or period of history, with the opprobrium of a handful of notorious characters, and generalizations spring full-grown from a few specific cases. To secure a fair evaluation of the deportment of our early pedagogues, then, it may be well to marshal the array of damaging evidence against them in some detail and to counterpose it with all the favorable data that can be found.

Mankind being so fallible and human nature remaining relatively constant through the centuries, it is not surprising to discover that the transgressions of the early settlers followed much the same pattern as those of today. Then, as now, we find instances of drunkenness, slander, immorality, and other socially frowned-upon behavior. Since schoolteachers have never been completely above the weaknesses of their fellows, it is not surprising that infractions of the moral code occurred among this group.

DRUNKENNESS

Overindulgence in alcoholic beverages appears to have been a not uncommon failing of the early schoolmasters. Nor is this fault confined to any particular group of colonies nor to any one nationality. Among the Dutch we find that Van Marken of Flatbush, Long Island, was reputed to pay "more attention to the tavern than to the school." [1] Michael Siperus, recently arrived in New Netherland from Curaçao, was considered to be "a good for nothing person" in the eyes of the church because he obtained stores under false pretenses and drank, as well as for other forms of "shameful" behavior.[2] And Jan Tibout of Flatbush was "too intoxicated at times to know what he was doing or saying." [3]

The pedagogic fondness for liquor also existed among the English in New York, as is evidenced by schoolmaster Forster's statement concerning a temporary teacher employed at West Chester, New York, by the Society for the Propagation of the Gospel in Foreign Parts: [4]

Here is one *Edward Fitzgerald* who, during the time I was absent in England which was about twelve months, kept school in this Town.

---

[1] Flatbush Consistory Minutes, p. 30, in Kilpatrick, William H., *The Dutch Schools of New Netherland and Colonial New York*, U. S. Bureau of Education, Bulletin 1912, No. 12 (Washington, Government Printing Office, 1912), p. 170.

[2] Letter of the Classis of Amsterdam to the Reverend Samuel Drisius, December 16, 1661, in *Ecclesiastical Records: State of New York* (Albany, James B. Lyons, 1901), Vol. I, p. 514.

[3] Kilpatrick, William H., *op. cit.*, p. 174.

[4] August 8, 1720, Letter-book, A, 14, p. 120, in Kemp, Walter W., *The Support of Schools in Colonial New York by the Society for the Propagation of the Gospel in Foreign Parts* (New York, Bureau of Publications, Teachers College, Columbia University, 1913), p. 149.

. . . But that you may not be in the dark as to this man's true character I give them this acct. which if desired shall be sufficiently testifyed: He is much given to drink and don't attend the Church. . . .

In other colonies, also, addiction to drink was by no means unheard of in the teaching profession. The first schoolmaster at Francestown, New Hampshire, was a man whom "tradition credits with a rather free use of cider and rum." [5] Luther Martin, who was master of the school in Queen Anne's County, Maryland, from 1767 to about 1769, is reputed to have spent most of his time in drinking.[6]

Alcohol was primarily responsible for the downfall of more than one schoolmaster in Savannah, Georgia. According to the minutes of the Council of Georgia for December 20, 1749: [7]

The Rev[d] M[r]. Zouberbuhler and the Inhabitants of this Town having made repeated Complaints to this Board, that M[r]. Peter Joubert Schoolmaster had for some Time past neglected to give proper Attendance to his Scholars, and likewise that He has been of late so much addicted to Drinking, that He gives great offence to the Inhabitants, and what is more pernicious sets a bad Example to their Children.—The Board being too sensible of this Complaint, and with concern finding that, their repeated Admonitions have not been duly regarded They are now obliged to discharge him.

On the other hand, fondness for strong drink did not prove a serious handicap to Irish John Sullivan. In spite of "habitual intervals of intemperance" he exerted considerable educational and literary influence in Maine for many years as schoolmaster at Thomaston and elsewhere in that vicinity.[8]

The Quaker schoolmasters of Pennsylvania seem to have conducted themselves with a sobriety that was at least above the average. Walter Moor, who taught at Byberry, erred in this respect, however, for in 1753 the Friends "complained of his

[5] Small, Walter H., *Early New England Schools* (Boston, Ginn and Company, 1914), p. 109.

[6] Brown, Edwin H., "First Free School in Queen Anne's County," in *Maryland Historical Magazine*, Vol. VI, No. 1 (March, 1911), p. 10.

[7] *The Colonial Records of the State of Georgia* (Atlanta, Ga., Franklin Printing and Publishing Company, 1906), Vol. VI, p. 303.

[8] Small, Walter H., *op. cit.*, p. 110.

drinking to excess and removing from place to place without giving notice of it." Woody makes the following comment: [9]

An instance of this sort, though not entirely out of keeping with custom in those days, was severely criticized at all times in the meetings. This is the only explicit case of drunkenness, on the part of teachers who were employed by Friends, which has come to the writer's attention. The frequent mention of reproof of members for that offense, in the early years of the century, however, would lead one to believe that such great success in eliminating it from those in the teaching profession was scarcely possible. However that may be, no case has been found (in newspaper reports, where the names were mentioned) in which any Quaker master engaged in disreputable brawling was lodged in jail, which was noted on the part of several other private masters of Philadelphia. This latter source of information is perhaps more reliable than the meeting records.

While Woody's observation is undoubtedly correct, the following condensation of an advertisement in the *Pennsylvania Gazette* seems to further indicate that drunkenness on the part of schoolmasters was not unheard of in Quaker communities:

Broke out of Chester gaol, last night, one James Rockett, a very short well-set fellow, pretends to be a schoolmaster, of a fair complexion, and smooth fac'd . . . he is a great taker of snuff, and very apt to get drunk. . . . Whoever takes up and secures said Rockett in any gaol, shall have two Pistoles reward, paid by

October 27, 1756.   SAMUEL SMITH, Gaoler.

Rockett may not have been a Quaker, or master of a Quaker school, of course; his lodgment in jail may have indicated either the displeasure of this sober sect with his conduct or that he was being held for some other offense. Furthermore, the wording of the advertisement—"pretends to be a schoolmaster"—does not imply conviction on the part of the jailer that he was a bona fide master.

Tippling alone, indeed, if circumspect, seems not to have been sufficiently objectionable even to the Quakers to occasion the dismissal of an otherwise acceptable teacher—or Andrew McMinn,

[9] Woody, Thomas, *Early Quaker Education in Pennsylvania* (New York, Bureau of Publications, Teachers College, Columbia University, 1920), pp. 224–25.

who was so fond of rum that "sometimes its effects partially incapacitated him for his duties," could not have remained for forty
years [10] schoolmaster in Newton, Bucks County, Pennsylvania. [11]

Nor did addiction to alcohol completely impair the usefulness
of a certain indented teacher, since the following public advertisement for him was inserted in the *Maryland Gazette* in 1771:
"Ran away—a servant man, who followed the occupation of
schoolmaster, much given to drinking and gambling." [12]

The foregoing cases are conspicuous because they are rare.
When examined in the light of the customs and practices of the
day, the comparatively small number of instances of drunkenness
among schoolteachers which have come to light suggests that
members of the teaching profession were more sober than
society in general.

SLANDER

Slander appears to have been a shortcoming peculiar to the
Dutch schoolmasters of New Netherland. Several instances of it
have been recorded there, although no mention of teachers with
this failing has been discovered in the records for any of the
other colonies.

Adam Roelantsen, the first schoolmaster of New Amsterdam,
was involved in at least five lawsuits for slander, sometimes as
defendant and sometimes as plaintiff. As defendant in one of
the suits he admitted "in the presence of the court that he hath
nothing to say against the pltff. and knows and esteems him
to be an honest man." In another suit both parties were condemned to pay twenty-five stivers to the poor. A little later he
and a certain woman called "fair Aleeta" were "ordered to cease
slandering one another on pain of being fined." "In a worse
case, 'after defendant had acknowledged that he knew nothing
against plaintiff's wife, and nevertheless had slandered her, he
was condemned to pay fl. 2. 10 to the poor.' " [13]

---

[10] 1772–1812.

[11] Wickersham, James P., *A History of Education in Pennsylvania* (Lancaster, Pa.,
Inquirer Publishing Company, 1886), p. 225.

[12] *Ibid.*, p. 212.

[13] New York Colonial Mss., Vol. IV, pp. 17–18, in Kilpatrick, William H., *op.
cit.*, pp. 51–52.

In 1664 a jail sentence for slander hung over the head of Pelgrom Clocq, at that time schoolmaster at Flatbush, Long Island. A certain Jacob Vis appeared before the court in New Amsterdam and demanded "attachment against Pelgrom Clocq and imprisonment of his person, whenever found here, complaining that he is slandered by him in the highest degree." The request was granted; hence the fact that Clocq finished his school year at Flatbush indicates that he was careful not to be caught in New Amsterdam.[14]

Slander proved to be the undoing of another schoolmaster at Flatbush, Jan Gerritsz Van Marken, who held that post from 1675 to 1680. Never an exemplary character, Van Marken had a quarrel with the minister which was seized upon as sufficient excuse for his dismissal. The reverend, being for no apparent cause "most irreverently and slanderously abused by the schoolmaster," he "called together our consistory and, as is usual here, invited the Magistrates to meet with them." These "all declared that they had long wished for some opportunity to discharge this schoolmaster . . . and his discharge was now affected." But Van Marken continued abusive and insulting, and "no other way being opened, I recommended my case and honor to the Rev. Consistories of all our Dutch villages." Thereupon, after due deliberation, "the honorable consistory, in the presence of the worthy constable and overseers," reaffirmed the decision and decided that Van Marken was "unsuitable and unfit to have charge of the service of church or school in any Christian congregation, and accordingly discharged him." [15]

The prominence of these slander suits in New Netherland and the complete absence of records of similar suits elsewhere in the American colonies inclines one to wonder whether the language of the Dutch schoolmasters could have been relatively so much more abusive or whether it was not that the Dutch populace was supersensitive to verbal insults and more easily ruffled. In this connection Fisher has commented on the prevalence of

[14] Fernow, Berthold (ed.), *Records of New Amsterdam* (New York, City of New York, 1897), Vol. V, p. 47.

[15] Letter of the Reverend Caspar Van Zuuren to the Classis of Amsterdam, June 25, 1681, in *Ecclesiastical Records, op. cit.*, pp. 773 ff., Flatbush Consistory Minutes, p. 30, in Kilpatrick, *op. cit.*, p. 170.

flattering speech and the habitually lavish use of high-sounding modes of address among the Dutch. Such a tendency, of course, would make disparaging remarks more than usually glaring.[16]

PROFANITY

Profanity was a relatively serious offense to the pious inhabitants of colonial America, and more so for schoolmasters than for the general populace. James Cornish of Northampton, Massachusetts, was twice fined for his transgressions in this respect, and the second time the court ordered a fine of twenty shillings, "highly resenting that such an aged man and of his quality and profession, should so dishonor God and give such evil example to youth and others." [17]

The fact that no other specific example of reprimand or chastisement for this offense has come to the attention of the writer points to the conclusion that profanity was conspicuous by its absence in the teaching profession of that day. This supposition is further supported by the frequency with which "sober conversation" is mentioned throughout the records either as a distinct asset or as a necessary qualification for the schoolmaster.

LEGAL COMPLICATIONS

Involvement in lawsuits and legal complications also appears to have been characteristic of the Dutch. The slander suits of Adam Roelantsen and the warrant against Pelgrom Clocq have already been mentioned. Many others appear in the records.

Alexander Carolus Curtius, rector of the New Amsterdam Latin School from 1659 to 1661, was for eight months engaged in a legal wrangle over the price of a hog. In the end he lost the case and the imputation of the court was that he had attempted to cheat. He furthermore objected to paying the excise, claiming the usual exemption accorded professors, preachers, and rectors in Holland, and also that the director general had granted him free excise. But again the court decided against

---

[16] Fisher, Sydney G., *Men, Women and Manners in Colonial Times* (Philadelphia, J. B. Lippincott Company, 1898), Vol. II, p. 57.

[17] Trumbull, James R., *History of Northampton, Massachusetts* (Northampton, 1898), Vol. I, p. 142.

him.[18] In addition, he was called to account by the burgomasters for overcharging his pupils; but just how this case was decided is uncertain, although he was forced to give up his position shortly after.[19]

At New Amstel, in 1660, Jan Juriaanzen Becker was indicted for selling liquor to the Indians, tried, fined five hundred guilders and court costs, degraded from his clerkship in the church and banished from the South River (Delaware River). But when he petitioned for pardon a week later his fine was promptly remitted on the grounds that his offense was a common practice. Some three months later he was again fined, in New Amsterdam this time—thirty guilders because "he entertained people in his tap house after nine o'clock, and tapped during the sermon," and ten guilders "for having behaved offensively to the officer." [20] His subsequent career as schoolmaster in Albany, however, was so successful that Governor Lovelace "thought fitt that y⁰ said Jan Jurians Beecker who is esteemed very capable that way shall be y⁰ allowed schoolmaster for y⁰ instructing of y⁰ youth at Albany & partes adjacent he following y⁰ said Imployment Constantly & diligently & that no other be admitted to interrupt him." [21]

FINANCIAL MISDEMEANORS

Financial complications enmeshed several of the early masters. The burgomasters' objections to the excessive tuition charges of Dominie Rector Curtius have been referred to above. Michael Siperus, also a Dutch schoolmaster, had an unsavory record. Before coming to New Netherland, while connected with the school at Alckmaer, he was "publicly chastised before all the scholars as an example, for many wicked acts, such as obtaining articles from stores in the name of the rector, and taking them to pawnshops." Afterwards he was "sent away" from Curaçao.[22] As schoolmaster in New Haerlem he continued his obnoxious

[18] Fernow, Berthold (ed.), *op. cit.*, Vol. III, pp. 98–99, 103, 133, 201, 253. Fernow, Berthold (ed.), *Minutes of the Orphanmaster's Court of New Amsterdam, 1655–1663* (New York, F. P. Harper, 1907), Vol. II, p. 76.

[19] *Records of New Amsterdam*, Vol. III, p. 344; Vol. VII, p. 257.

[20] *Ibid.*, p. 193.

[21] Munsell, Joel, *Annals of Albany* (Albany, Joel Munsell, 1871), Vol. IV, p. 9.

[22] Letter of the Classis of Amsterdam to the Reverend Samuel Drisius, December 16, 1661, in *Ecclesiastical Records, op. cit.*, Vol. I, p. 514.

habits and "behaved most shamefully . . . drinking, cheating and forging other people's writings, so that he was forbidden not only not to preach, but even to keep school." [23]

An unfortunate propensity for luxury far exceeding the capacity of his modest stipend as schoolmaster led Mr. William Kean, teacher of Latin and Greek in Queen Anne's County, Maryland, to pile up debts so large he had to leave the neighborhood. His dismissal followed shortly, but later he returned and was reinstated pursuant to the following agreement to work off his debts: [24]

The visitors considering that Mr. Kean has closely applied himself since their last meeting has now got lodging in a sober family and has indented himself to serve Messrs. Anthony McCulloh and Nathan Samuel Tyrbutt Wright until by his salary as Master of this school he shall satisfy all his creditors by which means there will be such check upon him as the visitors are in hopes will restrain him from running into any immoralities he may be prone to and the visitors being persuaded that the said William Kean may be greatly useful as master of the said school, provided he can restrain himself determine still to continue him master upon the terms on which he was admitted.

Mr. Barend de Forest, for six or seven years master of the school of the Reformed Dutch Church in New York City, came to financial grief in 1732. On December third of that year "there was presented to the consistory a written request from Mr. Barend de Forest, clerk in the old church, now a prisoner for debt, that the consistory would please become responsible for £50 or £60, and continue him in his office, and . . . take one-half of his salary for debt and pay him the other half for his support." After lengthy deliberation, however, the consistory refused his request, placed his assistant in charge temporarily, and shortly thereafter appointed a successor. [25]

The stony-hearted indifference accorded Mr. de Forest's petition was probably more typical of the colonial attitude toward impoverishment than the concession made to Mr. Kean in

[23] The Reverend Samuel Drisius to the Classis of Amsterdam, August 5, 1664, *ibid.*, Vol. I, p. 555.
[24] Brown, Edwin H., *op. cit.*, pp. 9–10.
[25] Kilpatrick, William H., *op. cit.*, p. 151.

Maryland. In those days of really rugged individualism, with the frontier at every man's doorstep, there was little patience with the needlessly indigent. Yet it is not safe to venture a generalization on this point, since the disposition of each case seems to have been along individual lines. On the one hand, we have Henry Spiller, in 1732, appointed by the selectmen of Ipswich "to keep a school." The year following he was "on the town" but was permitted to establish a private school of his own.[26] On the other hand, we have Henry Herring, in 1763, schoolmaster of Chester, New Hampshire. Two years later the record reads: "Henry Herring, the former master, has become a pauper and warned out of town." [27]

Crimes of Violence

Records of violence on the part of schoolmasters, aside from participation in the rare political riots, are conspicuously scarce. Perhaps wielding the birch rod served to release any smoldering fires of animosity that might otherwise have wreaked havoc in a more vicious form. Or perhaps the extra duties so commonly combined with the position of teacher absorbed so much energy that there was not enough left for dangerous mischief. Whatever the reason, only one case has been discovered that belongs in this category—that of Evert Nolden, a private master in Rensselaerwyck in 1651, who was prosecuted for the picturesque crime of having crushed Adriaen Dirchsz's nose with a pair of fire tongs.[28]

Runaways

Runaways among the indentured servant class were exceedingly common during the colonial period, if we can judge from the number of advertisements for their return which appeared in the newspapers of that day. A number of these were for schoolmasters. Steiner reports that "as late as 1777 a reward of from £10 to £20 is offered for two runaways, one of whom is 'a school-

---

[26] Felt, Joseph B., *History of Ipswich, Essex and Hamilton* (Cambridge, Charles Folsam, 1834), p. 88.

[27] Small, Walter H., *op. cit.*, pp. 108–9.

[28] Kilpatrick, William H., *op. cit.*, p. 120.

master, of a pale complexion, with short hair. He has the itch very bad, and sore legs.' " [29]

Whether this propensity for running away among the indentured servant class in general, and among schoolmasters in particular, indicates weakness of character and a disposition to disregard contractual obligations or whether it is attributable to intolerable conditions of servitude is an open question. It would be hardly fair, at least, in view of our meager information concerning them, to condemn this group wholesale.

Nor can the fact that a number of schoolmasters were indentured servants be considered as derogative of their character *per se*. It is true that this class comprised many convicted felons, rogues, rascals, villains, and others of low degree, but it is equally true that it included political prisoners, captives of war, debtors, and adventurers who had voluntarily bound themselves over in order to pay their passage to the New World. There is no reason to believe that those who were, or who became, pedagogues were drawn from the baser segment of this group rather than from its better portion. And it is unfortunate, though natural, that the more respectable element of the group shared in the infamy attaching to the more vicious members.

IMMORALITY

The records also show that a few of the early schoolmasters overstepped the bounds of propriety in their relations with women. Adam Roelantsen, the first schoolmaster of New Amsterdam, already notorious for his slander suits, added attempted adultery to his other misdemeanors. In 1646 he was arrested for trying "forcibly to violate Harck Sybaltsen's wife in her own house" and was subsequently condemned by the court "to be scourged with rods and then to be banished from the country as an example to others." [30] Because of his four motherless children and the imminence of winter, however, the execution of

---

[29] Steiner, Bernard C., *The History of Education in Connecticut* (Washington, Government Printing Office, 1893), p. 34. (Contributions to American Educational History, U. S. Bureau of Education, Circular of Information No. 2 [1893].)

[30] New York Colonial Mss., Vol. IV, p. 277, in Kilpatrick, William H., *op. cit.*, p. 56.

this sentence was postponed and then for some reason never carried out.

During his second period as schoolmaster in Flatbush (1681–1682), Jan Tibout also "behaved himself unseemly" with respect to women. The women concerned, when called upon to testify against him, accused him of "very scandalous and entirely indecent deeds, viz, that Jan Thibaud (Tibout) had approached them with dishonorable words and acts and that they in self defense had pursued him with blows." [31] In attempting to deny the charges, his admissions and explanations only served to incriminate him further. "By his own confession he was grossly obscene in addressing the women, and was besides too intoxicated at times to know what he was doing or saying. By the explicit testimony of several women he had made most improper advances upon their persons, and according to one he had been in her presence inexpressibly indecent." [32]

As a result, although he was allowed "one month to investigate his case and search his heart to find out the truth," court and consistory voted unanimously that in the meantime he be "suspended from service in the church and deprived of the participation in our Lord's holy supper." At the end of this period, since no new evidence was forthcoming that might serve to clear him, he was dismissed from both his school and church offices. It is pleasant to be able to report, however, that apparently the disgraced schoolmaster reformed, for in 1685 he was offered the joint office of voorlezer and schoolmaster in New Haerlem. On the strength of a testimonial from the dominie of that vicinity, ". . . wherein it was stated that during the two years that Jan Thibald had passed under the ministry of N. York, nothing was heard of him except what beseemed an honorable man," [33] the Flatbush consistory was prevailed upon to remove the censure they had laid upon him, in order that he might accept the position.

Mr. Griffin of North Carolina also strayed from the straight

[31] Flatbush Consistory Minutes, pp. 53 ff., in Kilpatrick, William H., *op. cit.*, p. 173.

[32] Kilpatrick, William H., *op. cit.*, p. 174.

[33] Flatbush Consistory Minutes, p. 62, in Kilpatrick, William H., *op. cit.*, p. 164.

and narrow path in his relations with the fair sex, as is evidenced by the following passage: [34]

I wrote to you formerly of one Mr. Griffin, who had behaved himself very remarkably in the office of a reader and schoolmaster: he has fallen into the sin of fornication, and joined with the Quakers' interest, which has proved great stumbling-block to many of our persuasion.

The ambiguity of this passage, however, leaves the reader in doubt as to whether the schoolmaster's religious heresy was not regarded by the orthodox as more serious and more disturbing than his moral laxity. It is further significant that discovery of this sexual delinquency seems not to have resulted in his immediate dismissal.

The description of Mr. William Kean as "a sporting gentlemen" [35] and the expressed hope of the visitors that a change of lodging plus temporary indenture "will restrain him from running into any immoralities he may be prone to" [36] raises the unanswerable question of just what sort of immoralities he *was* prone to. Perhaps nothing more reprehensible than extravagant expenditures of any and every sort.

It would be a mistake to suppose that the misconduct pictured on the preceding pages was typical of colonial schoolmasters, or even common among them. For every schoolteacher who was a rogue, scoundrel, defamer, souse, or knave, there must have been a dozen, yes, a score or more who were sober, upright, virtuous, and God-fearing. Doubtless it is because misbehavior is inherently alluring and picturesque, because colonial life—especially in Puritan New England—may have been so dull and toilsome that colorful escapades were a welcome diversion, and because the trouble occasioned by these roisterers necessitated community action that these accounts have lived to come down to us and have thus tended to overshadow the general run of cases.

Probably a truer and more typical picture is that given by Crippen in his study of the colonial schoolmasters in Dedham,

[34] Letter of Mr. Adams to the Secretary, October 4, 1709, in Saunders, William L. (ed.), *The Colonial Records of North Carolina* (Raleigh, P. M. Hale, 1886), Vol. I, p. 721.
[35] Brown, Edwin H., *op. cit.*, p. 9.   [36] For the full agreement see page 25.

Massachusetts, from 1644 to 1757.   During that period of one hundred and thirteen years, Dedham had sixty-six schoolmasters, all of whose names are known and concerning whom considerable other information is extant. Yet the records show that only four of them provoked censure of any kind, while praise is much more frequent. Crippen tabulates the praise accorded them in the records as follows: "as teachers 7; as to character 11; as to learning 9; as preachers 6; general praise of some kind 6." [37] Even allowing for some overlapping, where the same individual was lauded on more than one count, we see that favorable comment was more common than unfavorable, and are justified in concluding that this group of teachers must have been of unusually high caliber when compared to the population at large. This is further supported by the fact that thirty-one, or nearly half of the total number, entered the ministry after teaching. [38]

Nor should too much weight be given to the censure meted out to the four.   Even the famous and revered Ezekiel Cheever, easily the most outstanding schoolmaster of colonial America, at one time in his long teaching career (1649) drew a rebuke from New Haven colony in the form of a formal church censure for "his contradicting, stiff, and proud frame of spirit." [39] In a civilization which severely punished even the mildest of transgressions, which sternly forbade many innocent pastimes and all forms of work or pleasure from Saturday evening till Monday morning; where a harmless Sunday afternoon walk was penalized by a five-shilling fine, where a Sunday kiss cost the perpetrator two hours in the stocks, where picking apples on the Sabbath cost a fine of five shillings, while wringing and hanging out clothes on the Lord's Day cost ten [40]—in such a civilization it would be strange, indeed, to find sixty-six men so submissive to this legislated asceticism, or so consistently discreet in their behavior, that they never once overstepped the narrow confines of prescribed comportment. The wonder is that records of censure

[37] Crippen, John H., *Character of the School Master in Colonial Period* (New York, Teachers College, Columbia University, unpublished Master's thesis, 1907), p. 104.
[38] *Ibid.*, pp. 103–4.
[39] See "The Trial of Ezekiel Cheever before the Church at New Haven, 1649," in *Collections of the Connecticut Historical Society*, Vol. I, pp. 22–51.
[40] Crippen, John H., *op. cit.*, p. 9.

are so few and that cases of chastisement or legal penalties are completely lacking.

Nor is Dedham unique among New England towns for the virtuousness of its schoolmasters. Dorchester, Braintree, and doubtless several other Massachusetts villages could also point with pride to a succession of blameless instructors of youth. Pennsylvania, too, could no doubt boast a notable preponderance of virtue over vice, at least among the Quaker masters.

Furthermore, in colonial New York, among the schools supported by the Society for the Propagation of the Gospel in Foreign Parts, the records indicate a considerable period during which favorable comments about individual schoolmasters were much more frequent than criticisms. In fact, the succession of exemplary characters in the group was scarcely broken from 1706 to the Revolutionary War. Lest it be objected that the New York schools were church enterprises, where higher standards of conduct might logically be expected than in the secular schools, it should be pointed out that other sects and other nationalities also had church schools, including the Dutch, whose masters could scarcely be claimed to achieve a moral tone so consistently high. Moreover, in those days, religion and education were so intertwined, both in popular thought and in actual instruction, that it would be difficult indeed to draw a sharp line between church schools and secular schools.

This array of evidence all seems to point to the fact that the colonial schoolmaster was at least as "good" as his contemporaries and probably better.

III

Qualifications of Teachers during the Colonial Period

RELIABLE generalizations cannot be made about the professional competence of schoolmasters in the thirteen colonies. Wide differences existed in their academic training, their religious affiliations, and their general cultural background. To gain any real appreciation of the fitness of these teachers for their tasks, it is necessary to study the qualifications of schoolmasters in those communities and districts for which school records are available. Even after these data have been examined, one must be exceedingly cautious in drawing conclusions for the somewhat larger number of teachers in the colonies for whom no biographical facts have as yet been unearthed.

The academic qualifications of schoolmasters during the colonial period ranged from bare ability to read and write to the scholarly attainments of a college graduate. The younger the children to be taught and the more rural the community, the lower were the requirements exacted of the master. In the most unfavored areas, mere willingness to "keep" school often constituted the necessary qualifications for teaching. Those responsible for engaging teachers in the rural sections of Pennsylvania expected the master to be able to "read, write and cipher as far as the double rule of three." [1] Similarly in the parish schools of Virginia, the requirement for teaching in the reading and writing schools was the "ability to read and write." According to one observer, all the qualifications needed in Springfield as late as 1800 were "the knack to continue in the schoolroom the discipline of the kitchen, and being a good mender of quill pens." [2]

---

[1] Creigh, Alfred, *History of Washington County* (1870), p. 53. Compound proportion; *e.g.*, if three men can dig a ditch 20 feet long in two days, how long will it take seven men to dig a ditch 30 feet long?

[2] Small, Walter H., *op. cit.*, p. 93.

Comparable conditions were reported for individual communities in other sections of the country. In fact, there is considerable evidence pointing to the conclusion that every colony had some ignorant and poorly educated teachers. One writer of these early days, commenting on the abysmal ignorance of schoolmasters, said: "It is a general plague and complaint of the whole

MENDING QUILL PENS

land that for one discreet and able teacher you shall find twenty ignorant and careless." [3]

While John Trumbull's poem "Progress of Dulness" was not aimed especially at the colonial schoolmaster, the description fits the less competent of these pioneer pedagogues perfectly. Trumbull satirically depicted the early schoolteacher as follows: [4]

> He tries, with ease and unconcern,
> To teach what ne'er himself could learn;
> Gives law and punishment alone,
> Judge, jury, bailiff, all in one;
> Holds all good learning must depend
> Upon his rod's extremest end,

[3] In Beard, Charles, and Carr, William, "Colonial School Days," in *Journal of the National Education Association*, Vol. XXIV, No. 43 (February, 1935).

[4] *Poetical Works . . . Containing . . . The Progress of Dulness*, etc. (Hartford, For Samuel G. Goodrich, 1820), Vol. II. (Reprinted from the original edition in *The Colonnade*, 14:423 [1919–1922].)

Whose great electric virtue's such,
Each genius brightens at the touch;
With threats and blows, excitements pressing,
Drives on his lads to learn each lesson;
Thinks flogging cures all moral ills,
And breaks their heads to break their wills.

There seems to be some reason for believing that cripples were occasionally favored in the appointment of schoolmasters. In 1673 three men were chosen schoolmasters in Albany. They were to be the sole teachers of the village, but shortly after, according to the records, Luykas Gerritse was also appointed schoolmaster because "he was impotent in his hand." [5] Gerritse was a baker by trade, but sympathy for him on account of his affliction weighed more heavily in his appointment than his qualifications as a teacher.

Apparently the Quakers, too, were disposed to give preference to the physically handicapped in appointing teachers. In one of their reports, in which the major emphasis was the encouragement of schoolmasters through the provision of more generous living arrangements, they point out as one by-product to be realized through their recommendation "the opportunity they would have of training up lame children and such, who in other respects may be incapable of supporting themselves by labor, to be educated and qualified to serve as schoolmasters." [6]

Considering the loosely knit governmental structure existing in the several colonies, together with the scarcity of able individuals who wanted to teach, it is not surprising that the requirements for schoolmasters in many localities were relatively low.

However, in spite of the absence of state certification laws and of other central agencies for the maintenance of scholastic standards, many individual communities insisted on high qualifications for their teachers. In Dorchester, Massachusetts, the schoolmaster was almost always a college graduate. As early as 1648 Henry Butler, the teacher there, was a graduate of Cam-

[5] Pratt, Daniel J., *Annals of Public Education in the State of New York from 1626 to 1746* (Albany, The Argus Company, 1872), p. 62.

[6] "Observations relating to the establishment of Schools," in *Minutes, Philadelphia Yearly Meeting*, 1778, pp. 410 ff., in Woody, Thomas, *Quaker Education in the Colony and State of New Jersey* (Philadelphia, The Author, 1923), p. 25.

bridge University, England, holding the master's degree. Of forty-five colonial masters of the Dorchester school mentioned by William A. Mowry more than forty were graduates of Harvard College.[7]

Of sixty-six schoolmasters who taught in Dedham, Massachusetts, between 1644 and 1757, thirty-three were graduates of some college and eighteen of these had their master's degrees.[8] Seybolt tells us that in Boston all except four of the masters and ushers of the South Grammar School during the colonial days were graduates of Harvard College or English universities and that all the masters and ushers at the North Grammar School were Harvard College graduates.[9] In the case of the Boston writing schools during this same period, six masters and three ushers were college graduates. The other writing-school masters were evidently men of considerable scholastic ability, for, following their teaching career, many of them became well-known figures in Massachusetts. Only one master in this latter group was dismissed for incompetence.[10] It seems safe to infer from these facts that the communities at the doorstep of Harvard gave preference to college-trained men for the position of schoolmaster and that this background came early to be almost a requirement in that region.

Massachusetts, however, was not the only colony to boast of teachers with high qualifications. In Pennsylvania, we find the Quakers laid great stress on the competence of the candidate to teach the subjects included in the school program. This was particularly true of the Latin schoolmasters, many of whom were imported from England. Notable examples are found in the neighborhood of Philadelphia. Francis Daniel Pastorius, the first schoolmaster in Germantown (1701), was a very learned man. He had command of seven or eight different languages, ancient and modern, and was well versed in science and philosophy. Christopher Taylor was another highly educated teacher

[7] Historical Address in Mowry, William A., *Dorchester Celebration; Two Hundred and Fiftieth Anniversary of the Establishment of the First Public School in Dorchester, June 22, 1889* (Boston, Rockwell and Churchill, 1890), pp. 36–41.

[8] Crippen, John H., *op. cit.*, pp. 102 ff.

[9] Seybolt, R. F., *The Public Schools of Colonial Boston, 1635–1775* (Cambridge, Harvard University Press, 1935), p. 31.

[10] *Ibid.*

in Pennsylvania around 1684. Wickersham says of him: "This gentleman was a man of great learning, well versed in the ancient languages and a minister among Friends." [11]

Apparently college degrees did not weigh so heavily in Pennsylvania as in Massachusetts, for the references to college graduates are fewer in number. Furthermore, the Quakers were undoubtedly less impressed by formal conferments of this sort than were other colonial groups. The history of Quaker education, however, would lead one to conclude that the quality of their schoolmasters was rather uniformly high. The Lutherans in Pennsylvania were fortunate in having as teachers, at least for a time, the services of a small group of unusually capable and well-educated men, most of whom had received their training at the University of Halle and had been sent over primarily as catechists. [12]

Similarly, the school of the community of Seventh-Day Baptists at Ephrata, Pennsylvania, was noted for the learning and skill of its teachers. Mathematics and the ancient languages, as well as the common branches, were included in the curriculum, and such was the reputation of the school during the period of its prosperity that it drew pupils from Philadelphia and Baltimore. The most noted of its teachers was Ludwig Hocker, who took charge shortly after 1739 and continued in that office for more than forty years. According to Wickersham, "he was a good scholar, fond of children, ingenious and progressive in his methods and entirely forgetful of himself in his devotion to the service of God and man." [13]

The qualifications of grammar-school teachers were everywhere superior to those possessed by elementary-school teachers. The records show that a Reverend Leonard Cutting kept the grammar school at Hempstead, Long Island, in 1764; he was educated at Eton and Cambridge and had acted as a "public tutor" at King's College. Ministers were often sought for these positions, since a command of Latin was a major requirement for schoolmasters in the secondary schools. However one may feel

[11] Wickersham, James P., *op. cit.*, p. 81.

[12] Maurer, Charles L., *Early Lutheran Education in Pennsylvania* (Philadelphia, Dorrance and Company, 1932), p. 228.

[13] Wickersham, James P., *op. cit.*, p. 175.

about the religious complexion of these early teachers, it is significant that their academic qualifications for those days were of a high order.

The Society for the Propagation of the Gospel in Foreign Parts was responsible for a degree of favoritism toward college graduates when employing schoolmasters. They adopted in 1743 a plan whereby it was "agreed that in appointing Catechists and Schoolmasters, a principle regard ought to be had to such persons as are in Holy Orders, or intend to offer themselves for it." [14] This was done as an encouragement to prospective ministers during the interval between graduation from college and final ordination as missionaries. Teaching was a steppingstone to what was then deemed a higher calling. There were not enough of these prospective divines available as schoolmasters to supply all types of schools, but the grammar schools were not infrequently taught by men of this character.

It appears then that the grammar schools throughout the colonies were, for the most part, taught by individuals of ability and learning; that the smaller children were less fortunate generally in the qualifications possessed by their instructors than the more advanced pupils; and that the rural areas usually found it difficult to attract and retain competent schoolmasters. In almost none of the communities was consideration given by prospective employers to the special fitness of those teachers for their work. Even in the grammar schools, strength to apply the rod constituted the chief pedagogical consideration outside of a knowledge of subject matter.

Religious, Moral, and Character Traits

Of even greater importance to the colonists than scholastic preparation as a prerequisite for teaching was religious orthodoxy. Not to adhere to the prevailing religious tenets of the colony was to disqualify oneself for a profession which was regarded as the half brother of the ministry. In New England, the law in 1654 stipulated: [15]

---

[14] Kemp, William W., *op. cit.*, p. 55.

[15] *The Colonial Laws of Massachusetts* (Boston, Published by Order of the City Council of Boston, 1889), p. 191. (Reprinted from the edition of 1660.) Italics ours.

For as much as it greatly Concernes the welfare of the Country, that the youth thereof be educated not only in good Literature, but in sound Doctrine. This Court doth Therefore Commend it to the serious Consideration, & special care of our Overseers of the Colledg, & the Selectmen in the several townes, not to admit or suffer any such to be continued in the Office or place of teaching, educating, or instructing youth or children in the Colledg or Schools, that have manifested themselves *unsound* in the *faith*, or *scandalous in their lives* & have not given satisfaction according to the Rules of Christ.

In New York, in 1711–1712, the Society for the Propagation of the Gospel in Foreign Parts set the following standards for their schoolmasters: [16]

That no person be admitted as Schoolmasters till he bring certificate of the following particulars.

1. his age. 2. his conditions of life, whether single or mary'd. 3. his temper. 4. his prudence. 5. his learning. 6. *his sober & pious conversation.* 7. *his zeal for the Xtian Religion* & diligence in his calling. 8. his affection to the present government. 9. *his conformity to the doctrine & discipline of the Ch. of England.*

That no person shall be sent as a Schoolmaster by Soc. till he has been tryed & approved by three members appointed by the Soc. or Comm^ee who shall testify by word or writing *his ability to teach reading, writing, & the Catechism of the Ch. of England* & such exposition thereof as the Soc. shall order.

Actually, according to Kemp, these requirements were not always met, particularly in the case of those teachers who were selected from the plantations and not sent out directly from England. This is easily understandable in light of the limited facilities for communication which must have interfered markedly with the carrying out of these orders. On the other hand, they represent the prevailing point of view regarding the qualifications that should be exacted of schoolmasters in New York.

As late as 1760, Governor Thomas Boone of New Jersey issued a proclamation that all schoolmasters must obtain a license to teach. The qualifications imposed were *good character*, loyal principles, and *professed protestant faith.*[17] In the neighboring colony

[16] Kemp, William W., *op. cit.*, p. 59. Italics ours.
[17] From the report of a Proclamation in the *New York Mercury*, November 4, 1760.

of Pennsylvania the Quakers, in addition to competency to teach subject matter, laid great stress on (1) *morality* and (2) membership in the *Society of Friends*. According to Woody, "The recommendation of well-known Friends was the best pass a teacher could have." This and a certificate of removal from his home meeting indicating that he was "clear" of entangling alliances and might be received into full membership were the only certification requirements the teacher needed.[18]

The Scotch-Irish in Pennsylvania required schoolmasters to be intelligent and possessed of sufficient piety to teach the principles of the Calvinistic faith. In the German parochial schools, which comprised a rather large percentage of the school population in several counties in Pennsylvania, great emphasis was placed upon religious instruction and schoolmasters were expected to be God-fearing, virtuous men, of exemplary character.

The following contract, quoted by Wickersham and dated 1750, indicates the attitude of the Pennsylvania Lutherans toward schoolmasters: [19]

That the schoolhouse shall always be in charge of a faithful Evangelical Lutheran schoolmaster, whose competency to teach Reading, Writing and Arithmetic, and also to play the organ (Orgelschlagen) and to use the English language, has been proved by the pastor; special regard being had at the same time, to the purity of his doctrine and his life. He shall be required to treat all his pupils with impartial fidelity, and to instruct the children of other denominations, and of the neighborhood generally. He shall not allow the children to use profane language either in or out of school; but shall carefully teach them how, both in church and in school, and in the presence of others and upon the highway, to conduct themselves in a Christian and upright manner, and "not like the Indians."

The extent to which these Lutheran teachers were able to "live up" to their contracts is not known, but it is certain that their ability to indoctrinate children in the principles of the Lutheran faith was a primary consideration in their appointment.

Among the Swedes in New Jersey and Delaware, education was largely determined by the church and its ministers. Em-

[18] Woody, Thomas, *Early Quaker Education in Pennsylvania*, p. 209.
[19] Wickersham, James P., *op. cit.*, p. 140.

phasis, therefore, was placed upon the religious zeal of the candidate in the appointment of teachers. Earnest and conscientious schoolmasters were almost universally sought in these colonies and the ministers themselves frequently served in the double role of teacher and preacher.[20]

In Virginia, the qualifications of teachers of the reading and writing schools seem to have been that they be orthodox, "of good life and conversation," and able to read and write.[21] According to one writer, "The state [Virginia] gave little concern to literary education except to exact a guarantee from communities that all teachers should be sound in the doctrines of the church and safe subjects of the Crown." [22]

Church affiliation in the Carolinas was also a prerequisite for holding a teaching position. The Act of Incorporation of the Edenton School in North Carolina charged the trustees never to employ a teacher who was not a member of the established church. This was a common requirement for teaching in both North and South Carolina prior to 1776.[23]

Innumerable statements can be found in the literature of this period which suggest that the schoolmaster, in the eyes of the public, must be a man of high moral character, free from the vulgarities common to lower callings. Such phrases as "a man of sober conversation," "a fit person," "a sober person of good morals," "a man of pious, exemplary life and conversation" appeared frequently in the advertisements for schoolmasters and in the specifications given to selectmen and school visitors for their guidance in employing teachers.

The insistence today by the public in many sections of the United States that teachers maintain a standard of morality and conduct considerably above that expected of all other vocational groups save the ministry had its origin in the early beginnings of our educational system. This sentiment, therefore, is not a twentieth-century product; it was almost universally accepted in

[20] *Ibid.*, p. 15.

[21] Wells, Guy F., *Parish Education in Colonial Virginia* (New York, Bureau of Publications, Teachers College, Columbia University, 1923), p. 20.

[22] Maddox, William A., *The Free School Idea in Virginia before the Civil War* (New York, Bureau of Publications, Teachers College, Columbia University, 1918), p. 6.

[23] Noble, M. C. S., *A History of the Public Schools of North Carolina* (Chapel Hill, N. C., University of North Carolina Press, 1930), pp. 13, 27.

the colonies during the seventeenth and eighteenth centuries. Education was designed to aid the church in the work of salvation—to enable the masses to read the catechism and to study the Scriptures. The opportunity in the schools for inculcating religious beliefs and moral principles was so great that ministers were sometimes persuaded to accept the responsibility of teaching in addition to their regular church offices. Whenever ministers were not available, other earnest and pious individuals were sought for this work who subscribed wholeheartedly to the doctrines of the church and whose character and habits were above reproach. That schoolmasters occasionally did not measure up to the above specifications has been pointed out in an earlier chapter.

OTHER QUALIFICATIONS

Disposition toward Government. In recent years we have heard much about schoolteachers and patriotism. Progressive organizations and educational leaders have protested against laws requiring teachers to take oaths to support the Constitution and to pledge allegiance to the government. The Ives Law [24] in New York State is an illustration of the insistence on the part of certain elements in the population that those entrusted with the education of children shall profess loyalty to the United States of America and to the state in which they teach. Many teachers and educators have considered this requirement somewhat alarming in nature. There is little new, however, in this public concern for the disposition of teachers toward their respective governments. We find the Society for the Propagation of the Gospel in Foreign Parts, as early as 1711–1712, setting as one item among the qualifications for schoolmaster "his affection to the present government." That this remained an important consideration is evidenced by the following letter of recommendation addressed to the society in 1744 by Commissary Vesey in behalf of Basil Bartow: [25]

[24] L. 1934, c. 862, in effect August 10, 1934. This law requires schoolteachers to take the following oath of allegiance: "I do solemnly swear (or affirm) that I will support the constitution of the United States of America and the constitution of the state of New York, and that I will faithfully discharge, according to the best of my ability, the duties . . . to which I am now assigned."

[25] Kemp, William W., *op. cit.*, p. 153, and his authorities. Italics ours.

Mr. Bartow is 23, a single man, of good temper, prudent, and sober & pious in life and conversation, *well affected to the present Government*, conformable to the doctrine & discipline of the Church, and in his opinion, exceedingly well qualified for teaching children.

As was mentioned earlier, Virginia exacted a guarantee from communities that all teachers should be *"safe subjects of the Crown."* [26]

Likewise in New Jersey, in 1760, Governor Boone included in his proclamation regarding schoolteachers a statement concerning their qualifications, and mentioned among others "loyal principles." The proclamation is reported as follows: [27]

New York, November 5. On the 21st Instant, his Excellency Thomas Boone, Esq., Governor of New Jersey, issued a proclamation setting forth, that whereas the Education of Youth is a Matter of great Consequence, and ought not to be trusted but to Persons of good Character, and loyal Principles, and professed Protestants; therefore he requires all Magistrates to inform themselves sufficiently of the Character of the School-Masters in the Province; to administer the Oaths to them, and give them, under the Hands of two, a Certificate of Approbation, by which they may obtain a License; and forbidding all Persons, after the 31st of December, to execute the Office of a School-master without such License first obtain'd.

Judging from these requirements, considerable emphasis was given in these early days to the loyalty of teachers toward their government. The records do not show that any teachers rebelled against taking oaths of allegiance, nor is there any evidence that as a group they were disloyal.

Experience, Age, Marital Status, and Residence. There seems to have been no uniform policy regarding such qualifications as experience, age, marital status, and residence of teachers. Preference was undoubtedly given to experienced teachers whenever a community had a choice in the matter. Frequently, however, the only alternative to taking an inexperienced master was to be without a school. A more important factor in the selection of teachers in colonial days appears to have been the character of their recommendations. The following advertisement for a

[26] Maddox, William A., *op. cit.*, p. 6. Italics ours.
[27] The *New York Mercury*, November 4, 1760.

schoolmaster, taken from the *Pennsylvania Gazette*, September 25, 1755, stresses this point: "A Sober person, that writes a good copy hand, and comes well recommended for a schoolmaster, may hear of encouragement in that calling, by applying to William Foster, of Burlington County."

This request implies teaching experience as one qualification, but it does not stipulate any amount nor is it perfectly clear that this will be insisted upon.

The beginning age at which teachers taught varied so widely that no general conclusion seems warranted. Crippen found that the average age at which thirty-four Dedham, Massachusetts, masters began their teaching was twenty-three and seven-tenths years. The range for this group, which perhaps more perfectly portrays the situation, extended from sixteen to seventy years.[28] Occasionally communities specified as a qualification "a young man," which was probably the result of economic considerations rather than any preconceived notion that age had any relation to competency. Such an advertisement appeared in the *New York Gazette revived in the Weekly Post-Boy* for August 24, 1752, and read as follows: "*A Young man*[29] qualified for a School-Master, is wanting at Rariton, in the Township of Bridge-water, in the County of Somerset, and may hear of Encouragement, by applying to John Broughton, Esq. of said Township."

One can only speculate as to the reasons for specifying youth in these advertisements. Unfortunate experience with a super-annuated master may have prompted some communities to incorporate this age factor in their requirements but, as stated above, it is more likely that it was a matter of economy.

Paralleling this qualification as to age is one adopted by some colonial communities to the effect that "single men" were more acceptable as masters than married men. Several advertisements carried this requirement. One which appeared in the *New York Mercury* for July 31, 1758, read as follows: "*A Single Person*,[30] with a Recommendation capable of teaching Children to read, write, cypher, is wanted at Raritan-Landing, in the County of Middlesex, in New-Jersey, where he'll meet with suitable Encouragement."

[28] Crippen, John H., *op. cit.*, p. 102.   [29] Italics ours.   [30] Italics ours.

A similar request was printed in the *Georgia Gazette*, May 11, 1774. It read: "*A Single Man*, qualified for a Schoolmaster, will meet with encouragement by applying at Midway to John Baker, St. John's Parish, May 2, 1774." [31]

Without question, the basis for this qualification was economic. Many of these schoolmasters were "boarded around" and the added expense of a wife and children would have greatly augmented school costs. In those towns where married men were employed, the locality frequently provided a house and several acres of land over and above the regular salary. Single men, however, were unpopular in some communities because they were transient or itinerant, and there are instances where towns seriously attempted to attract married men, so they could retain them longer. An interesting illustration of this is found in a report prepared by a committee of Friends in 1777–1778, which undoubtedly expressed sentiments held by many people long before the American Revolution. The first recommendation in the report was as follows: [32]

. . . that within each meeting where the settlement of a school is necessary, a lot of ground be provided, sufficient for a garden, orchard, grass for a cow, etc., and that a suitable house, stable, etc., be erected thereon. . . . Such a provision would be an encouragement for a staid person, with a family, who will be likely to remain a considerable time, perhaps his whole life in the service.

This would make it unnecessary to bargain with transient single men of doubtful character; and it would not be necessary to "board the master from one house to another." . . .

Unfortunately there are no statistics for this period indicating the proportion of married and single men employed as teachers. It is certain that the unmarried group was relatively much larger among the temporary schoolmasters than among those who followed teaching as a career.

Local residents were more frequently employed in the ele-

[31] In Boogher, Elbert W. G., *Secondary Education in Georgia, 1732–1858* (Philadelphia, University of Pennsylvania, 1933), p. 294. Italics ours.

[32] "Observations relating to the establishment of Schools," in *Minutes. Philadelphia Yearly Meeting, 1778*, pp. 410 ff., in Woody, Thomas, *Quaker Education in the Colony and State of New Jersey*, p. 25.

mentary schools than in the grammar schools. Scarcity was usually the determining factor and the importation of school-masters occurred chiefly when qualified local candidates were not available. Difficulties of transportation and communication were obvious barriers to the mobility of teachers, though they were by no means insuperable, as is evidenced by the fact that New York masters are reported as teaching in Philadelphia and Boston, and some Northern teachers actually accepted positions as far south as Georgia.

IV

Certification and Appointment of Teachers

CERTIFICATION OF TEACHERS

NO elaborate methods of certification such as are now common in the forty-eight states were in existence during the colonial period. Educators had not yet developed a system of teacher training calling for a high degree of specialization in methods and subject matter, and therefore the problem of licensing was a relatively simple one. There were, in most of the colonies, some governmental regulations bearing on the rights of individuals to establish schools and teach. In some instances the provisions were largely ignored, while in others the requirements seem to have been adhered to rather consistently.

As early as 1637, Adam Roelantsen was authorized to teach in New Netherland. He was examined and approved by the Classis of the Reformed Dutch Church in Holland and was the first schoolmaster sent over by the West India Company to New Amsterdam to serve in the multiple role of schoolmaster, reader, and preceptor. There is some evidence suggesting that the Dutch continued this general procedure in licensing their official schoolmasters in New Netherland. A number of private teachers also established schools among the Dutch before 1664 but whether or not a formal certification plan existed for this group is problematical. One writer, in commenting on the matter of licensing these Dutch private schoolmasters, says: [1]

It is an enlightening commentary on the inadequacy of our records that in no instance do the record of licensing and the known fact of teaching concur; that is, of those known to have been licensed we do

[1] Kilpatrick, William H., *op. cit.*, p. 118.

not know that they taught, and of those known to have taught we do not know that they were licensed.

When the English took over New Amsterdam in 1664 they introduced a requirement to the effect that all schoolmasters be licensed. Down to 1686 the Governor alone granted the certificate. After that date, by special instructions from the Crown, the Archbishop of Canterbury and later the Bishop of London licensed those teachers coming from England. It is the opinion of Kilpatrick that the requirement was not rigidly enforced, especially as it affected the Dutch schoolmasters. The purpose of this certification plan was not primarily, as one might suppose, to protect children against an illiterate or incompetent teacher, but rather to guard against the employment of religious dissenters.

This practice of licensing schoolmasters through the Bishop of London if they came from England, and through the royal governors when they resided in the colony or came from other parts, appears to have been the commonly accepted procedure followed in nearly all the royal colonies. Thus the Governor of New Jersey in 1758 received instructions from the English government as follows: [2]

65. *We* do further direct that . . . no Schoolmaster be henceforth permitted to come from England and to keep School in the said province without the License of the said Bishop of London, and that no other person now there or that shall come from other parts, shall be admitted to keep School in that Our said province of New Jersey, without your License first obtained.

Similar instructions were given to Governor Thomas Boone in 1759 and were reflected in the proclamation he issued in 1760, which "required all magistrates to inform themselves sufficiently of the character of the schoolmasters in that Province; to administer the oaths to them . . . forbidding all persons after the 31st of December, to execute the office of schoolmaster without such license first obtained." [3]

---

[2] "Instructions to Our Trusty and Well Beloved Francis Bernard Esqr," etc., in *New Jersey Archives* (1st series), Vol. IX, p. 68.
[3] The *New York Mercury*, November 4, 1760.

The provisions for licensing schoolmasters in New Hampshire were identical with those of New Jersey. Likewise in Virginia, schoolmasters were required to hold licenses either from the Bishop of London, in whose diocese Virginia was included, or from the colonial governor. This rule was rather strictly adhered to. It was usually necessary, also, for the applicant to submit to an examination by the minister of the parish in which the school was located and to produce a certificate of his capacity. The first step, according to Heatwole, in securing a teaching post was for the master to petition the county court to obtain the necessary license from the Governor. In this way the magistrates largely determined who should be allowed to teach.[4]

When the first public school was established in Newbern, North Carolina, in 1766, the following provision was included in the Act of Incorporation:[5]

III. . . . That no Person shall be admitted to be Master of the said School, but who is of the established Church of *England;* and who, at the Recommendation of the Trustees or Directors, or the Majority of them, shall be duly licensed by the Governor, or Commander in Chief for the Time being.

South Carolina stressed specific qualifications for schoolmasters in 1712 in an act for establishing a free school at Charlestown. Among other things was this provision:[6]

. . . that the person to be master of the said school shall be of the religion of the Church of England, and conform to the same, and shall be capable to teach the learned languages, that is to say, Latin and Greek tongues, and to catechise and instruct the youth in the principles of the Christian religion, as professed in the Church of England.

It is altogether probable that masters of these free schools had to obtain some kind of certificate and be licensed. Georgia practice appears less certain, although the records show that John

4 Heatwole, Cornelius J., *A History of Education in Virginia* (New York, The Macmillan Company, 1916), p. 51.

5 "An Act for establishing a School House in the Town of Newbern," Chap. XIX, in *A Complete Revisal of All the Acts of Assembly, of the Province of North Carolina* (Newbern, James Davis, 1773), p. 359.

6 "An Act for Founding and Erecting of a Free School in Charlestown, for the use of the Inhabitants of This Province of South Carolina," in Cooper, Thomas (ed.), *The Statutes at Large of South Carolina*, Vol. II, p. 393.

Burnside in 1734 petitioned for a license to keep a writing school in Savannah.

The procedure in Massachusetts differed, apparently, from that followed in the other royal provinces. An act in 1701 included, among other provisions, a clause to the effect that every grammar-school master was "to be approved by the minister of the town, and the ministers of the two next adjacent towns, or any two of them, by certificate under their hands." Furthermore, the justices of the peace in each town were directed to see to it that this regulation was observed.[7] In 1712 another act was passed, which extended the authority over grammar-school masters to include all teachers and limited their employment to those that "are of sober and good conversation, and have the allowance and approbation of the selectmen of the town in which any such school is to be kept." This law provided a fine for those who established a school without the permission of the selectmen.[8]

In 1742 Connecticut passed a law which forbade any one "to erect, establish, set up, keep or maintain, any college, seminary of learning, or any publick school whatsoever, for the instruction of young persons, other than such as are erected and established or allowed by the laws of this Colony, without special lycence or liberty first had and obtained of this Assembly." As was the case in Massachusetts, a fine was imposed upon anyone violating this mandate.[9]

Pennsylvania seems to have been rather lax about the matter of licensing teachers, although certificates of character, ability, and "clearance" of all entangling alliances were universally required among the Friends before a schoolmaster was appointed to a position. These perhaps served the purpose of a licensing system fairly well, for in the absence of an oversupply of teachers

[7] "An Act in Addition to an Act for the Settlement and Support of Schools and School-Masters," secs. 2, 4, passed and published June 28, 1701, in *Acts and Resolves of the Province of the Massachusetts Bay* (Boston, Wright and Potter, 1869), Vol. I, p. 470.

[8] "An Act against Intemperance, Immorality and Prophaneness, and for Reformation of Manners," secs. 17, 18, in *ibid.*, Vol. I, pp. 681–82.

[9] "An Act relating to, and for the better regulating Schools of Learning," in Hoadly, Charles J. (ed.), *Colonial Records of Connecticut, 1735–43* (Hartford, Case, Lockwood and Brainard Company, 1874), Vol. VIII, p. 501.

a more formal certification plan would have added little if anything to the general efficiency of the profession. With its heterogeneous population and variety of religious sects, Pennsylvania as a colony could scarcely have successfully imposed any uniform system of teacher licensing during the colonial period, particularly as it pertained to church affiliation.[10]

Judging from the results of an inquiry put by Governor Hart in Maryland to the Episcopal clergy at Annapolis in 1714 concerning the demoralization of the established colonial church, licenses there, though theoretically required, had been sorely neglected. One of the Governor's questions was: "Are there any schoolmasters within your respective parishes that come from England and do preach without the Lord Bishop of London's license? or that come from other parts and teach without a license from the Governor?" The answer framed by twenty-one clergymen indicated that the requirement of a license by the Governor or Bishop of London had been entirely neglected.[11]

The forms used in licensing schoolmasters were not uniform throughout the colonies. They usually indicated the types of subjects to be taught but beyond this they varied according to the stipulations which the Governor of the Province or the Bishop of London saw fit to include.

The license granted to John Shutte in 1665 for teaching the English tongue in Albany contained the following authorization: [12]

Whereas, the teaching of the English tongue is necessary in this government; I have, therefore, thought fitt to give license to John Shutte to be the English Schoolmaster at Albany; And, upon condition that the said John Shutte shall not demand any more wages from each Schollar than is given by the Dutch to their Dutch Schoolmasters, I have further granted to the said John Shutte that hee shall bee the onely English Schoolmaster at Albany.

Given under my hand, at Fort James in New York, the 12th day of October, 1665.

RICH'D NICOLLS.

[10] Woody, Thomas, *Early Quaker Education in Pennsylvania*, p. 209.
[11] Clews, Elsie, *Education in the Colonies* (New York, Columbia University Press, 1899), p. 425.
[12] Pratt, Daniel J., *op. cit.*, p. 57.

In 1706 the records disclose the provisions of a license granted to Mr. James Jeffray by Governor Edward Cornbury. The certificate read as follows: [13]

To Mr. James Jeffray Greeting.

I do hereby authorize and Impower You to Keep and Teach School within the city of New York and to Instruct all children with whom you Shall be intrusted in the art of Writing and Arithmetick for and During my Pleasure.

Given under my hand and Seal at ffort Anne in New Yorke this Seventeenth day of Aprill—in the fifth Year of the Reign of our Sovereign Lady Anne, by the Grace of God of England, Scotland, ffrance and Ireland Queen Defender of the faith, etc.—Annoque Domini 1706

CORNBURY.

These attempts at licensing schoolmasters in the colonies met with partial success only. The scarcity of qualified candidates, the physical difficulties encountered in supervising all school arrangements, and the religious differences prevalent in many of the colonies seriously complicated the task of licensing. It is significant, however, in the development of the teaching profession in America, that the civil authorities established entrance standards almost from the beginning of our public-school system and that the church exercised a powerful influence on appointments.

APPOINTMENT OF TEACHERS

The selection of schoolmasters during the seventeenth and eighteenth centuries was a relatively simple process when compared with the complicated procedure followed by present-day boards of education. In an era when one schoolmaster was expected to serve all the educational interests in the community, and when certification procedures involved no complicated evaluation of college and university credits nor appraisals of scores of letters of recommendation, the matter of teacher appointment was one requiring but little professional knowledge or skill on the part of the appointing agency. It consisted largely of bargaining with individuals professing competence as schoolmasters.

It is true that this job of selecting teachers was not always

[13] *Ibid.*, p. 92.

an easy one, especially in those colonies where the demand was greater than the supply. Occasionally, it was necessary for some selectman to travel to a neighboring town in search of a schoolmaster or even to write abroad for one, and the difficulties involved in arriving at a satisfactory arrangement were frequently serious. There were no teachers' agencies to whom governing boards of schools and local town committees could look for assistance in filling positions. This absence of appointment bureaus was as inconvenient for schoolmasters looking for positions as for employers seeking suitable candidates.

In New England, it was a fairly common procedure, early in the colonial period, to appoint teachers at regular town meetings. It was also customary on these occasions to state the conditions of the contract, including salary, period of employment, and the general nature of the work to be done. This method of selection, however, proved cumbersome and was supplanted in many towns by delegating the responsibility of teacher appointment to the selectmen with instructions from the town. This latter group occasionally found it desirable to delegate responsibility and would appoint one of their members or a committee of individuals to "treat" with some parishioner or townsman to keep the school. In a few instances, the selectmen were instructed to recommend a schoolmaster to the town and the actual choice was made by the voters. What the town was perhaps most concerned about was the wage to be assigned and the conditions of employment. These were legislative matters and were generally reserved by the town in New England, whereas the executive functions were frequently delegated.

The approval of the local minister was often necessary before grammar-school masters could be appointed. Such a stipulation was incorporated in the law passed in Massachusetts in 1701.[14] This practice was extended to other colonies in New England and seems to have been rather generally accepted. The following is a typical certificate of approbation signed by three ministers of Medfield in 1723: [15]

[14] See *supra*, note 8.
[15] Small, Walter H., *Early New England Schools* (Boston, Ginn and Company, 1914), p. 42.

These may certify whom it may concern, that we the subscribers, understanding that the selectmen of Medfield have procured Mr. Jabez Wright to teach the grammar school in Medfield, & being desired by the said selectmen to signify our approbation of him as the law directs, do well approve the said Mr. Wright as a person suitably qualified according to law for that service, & some of us do know that he is now engaged in that work in Medfield.

New England practice in the appointment of teachers, then, may be summarized as follows: Selection by the selectmen, election by the inhabitants in open town meeting, and approbation by the ministers. Outside of New England, employment procedures relating to schoolmasters were not so uniform. In New Netherland, in the more important Latin schools, the matter of appointing teachers was largely under the control of the city burgomasters and selection was apparently made by them without reference to the church. Elementary schoolmasters were appointed by the magistracy but the appointments were often influenced by the consistories.[16]

The foregoing statement comes as near describing the method of appointing schoolmasters in the Dutch communities prior to the Revolution as any that can be made without a lengthy discussion of exceptional cases. The differences in method which are reported concern chiefly the relative parts played by the Dutch Reformed Church and the magistracy in the selection of schoolmasters and are principally differences in degree rather than in kind.

The English schools in New York were frequently manned by masters appointed and supported by the Society for the Propagation of the Gospel in Foreign Parts. The rules of the society were very explicit regarding the qualifications of schoolmasters and considerable supervision of their selection was exercised by the home office of the organization, which was located in England. Although distance made it impracticable for the headquarters' staff to interview all applicants for teaching positions, the relationships which the S. P. G. maintained with the New

---

[16] Kilpatrick, William H., *op. cit.*, p. 104. The consistory was the lowest court of the Dutch Reformed Church, corresponding to the Presbyterian session, but not to be confused with the present-day use of the term. Today it is more closely identified with the Senate or College of Cardinals over which the Pope presides.

World enabled them to control pretty largely the type of individual who was chosen for this work. Each applicant was supposed to submit to examination by "three members appointed by the Soc. or Com^ee who shall testify by word or writing his ability to teach reading, writing, & the Catechism of the Ch. of England & such exposition thereof as the Soc. shall order." [17]

Special deputies were appointed by the society to supervise their undertakings and advise the home office regarding its affairs in the colonies. The official appointment always rested in the hands of the parent organization. Local schoolmasters who showed signs of success in operating a private school frequently made application to the S. P. G. for appointment and support. The following petition from some residents in Westchester County is illustrative of this practice: [18]

To the R^t Reverend Father in God Henry Lord Bishop of London— The humble address of several of the Inhabitants and Freeholders of the Towns of Rye & Mamaroneck in behalf of Themselves & ye rest of the S^d Inhabitants.

We the Inhabitants and Freeholders of the Towns of Rye and Mamaroneck in ye Province of N. York out of the deep sense we have of that unparallel'd care & Tenderness yor Lordship has been pleased at all times to manifest for the Prosperity and welfare of this Province, are hereby emboldened to become most humble Supplicants to yor Lordship in behalf of Mr. Joseph Cleator ye Presenter hereof who did make a beginning to teach School in our Towns, but his own private Affairs requiring his immediate Attendance in England he could not continue long amongst us to our inexpressible grief he being a very sober man and good schoolmaster and not only indefatigable in Teaching our Children but in Catechising and otherwise Instructing them to our wonderful Satisfaction.

We therefore most humbly pray yor Lordship to endeavour the procuring him such an allowance from ye Society wch with what we are able to give him might encourage his Return, amongst us, And as in Duty bound we shall ever pray for yor Ld^ps long life and Happiness.

In Philadelphia and the territory occupied by Friends, the matter of appointing teachers was in the hands of the meeting. General qualifications for teachers were formulated and circular-

[17] Kemp, William W., *op. cit.*, p. 59.   [18] *Ibid.*, p. 123.

ized throughout the Quaker settlements and the actual selection was made by a committee of the local meeting. Several of the Friends' schoolmasters were obtained by communication with John Fothergill and John Hunt in England. These two gentlemen evidently served as a sort of teachers' agency and furnished the Quakers with many excellent schoolmasters. In the rural areas of Pennsylvania, the schoolmaster was not selected in any formal way. He usually "hung out his shingle," as it were, and gathered about him a few pupils at whatever fee he could exact. Teachers in these sparsely populated sections stood or fell on the basis of their popularity. If they failed, they moved on to other parts or changed their vocation; if they succeeded, they were encouraged and made welcome. Selection here was mostly by trial and error.

The Maryland procedure in appointments was, apparently, relatively simple. The school visitors, a group comparable to our local board of education, selected the schoolmaster and established the conditions of employment. In the extreme Southern colonies, where tutors were frequently employed, the matter of selection was almost wholly a private arrangement between the head of the family and the tutor. The public took no official steps to dictate the conditions of appointment. While the church in the South expressed some interest in the attitude of teachers toward the established religion, there is little evidence of their exercising any significant control in the matter of appointment.

A common means in the colonies of securing candidates for teaching vacancies, especially during the last half of the eighteenth century, was by advertising. A few illustrations will indicate the nature of these early efforts to secure schoolmasters:

Maryland Gazette, 1747: [19]

Whereas there is a vacancy for a master in Queen Anne's County School, any person properly qualified upon applying to the visitors will meet with such encouragement as the law relating to free schools will support them in.

Signed by order   Nathan Wright, Register.

[19] Brown, Edwin H., *op. cit.*, Vol. VI, p. 5.

The Virginia Gazette, March 5, 1752:

NOTICE is hereby given, That *Symes's* Free School, in *Elizabeth-City* County, will be vacant on the 25th of *March* Inst. a Tutor of a good Character, and properly qualified, may meet with good Encouragement, by applying to the Trustees of the said School.

N.B. The Land Rent of the said School is 31 £ *per Ann.* besides Perquisites.

The Pennsylvania Gazette, November 22, 1759:

This is to give NOTICE,

That the Subscribers hereof, living in the Township of Evesham, Burlington County, and Province of West New-Jersey, do want a Schoolmaster, and choose to have a single Man, such Person applying, qualified for the said Service, may expect good Wages, and good Treatment by us.

ABRAHAM HAINES, and THOMAS SMITH, Senior.

The Virginia Gazette, August 20, 1772:

WANTED IMMEDIATELY,

A Sober diligent Schoolmaster capable of teaching READING, WRITING, ARITHMETICK, and the *Latin* TONGUE. The School is quite new, has a convenient Lodging Room over it, is situated in a cheap Neighbourhood, and its Income estimated at between sixty and eighty Pound a Year. Any Person qualified as above, and well recommended, will be put into immediate Possession of the School, on applying to the Minister of *Charles Parish, York* County.

Sometimes, as in the following illustration, the schoolmaster advertised *his* qualifications and indicated the type of position which he was seeking:

Georgia Gazette, September 23 and October 7, 1767:[20]

A single man of good character who Teacheth the Principles of the Latin, and French as accented in Paris, the right Spanish Castellans, and children to Read and Write English, would be glad of employment in a Latin School as an assistant, or in a private family in town or country. Any gentlemen or ladies desirous to employ him in such capacity may hear of him by applying to the printer.

[20] Boogher, Elbert W. G., *op. cit.,* p. 291.

The appointment of teachers in these early years, then, consisted in most communities of locating, either through hearsay or by advertisement in the paper, someone who was both qualified and willing to teach and who would accept the salary which had been voted for this purpose. At no time during the colonial period does it appear that the supply of well-qualified schoolmasters was so large as to necessitate the introduction of any involved machinery for eliminating the weak applicants.

V

The Schoolmaster's Tasks

THE teacher's task during colonial days varied widely in scope from colony to colony and even from district to district. There was a little uniformity in the length of the school day and almost none in the number of pupils enrolled in each school or in the number of subjects taught by each teacher.

In New England, in 1667, a six-hour teaching day was fairly common during September, October, March, and April; a four-hour day during November, December, January, and February; and during May, June, July, and August school was kept eight hours, from 7 A.M. until 5 P.M. with a two-hour lunch period.[1] The variations from this practice were numerous. Thus the Dorchester "rules and orders concerning the school," in 1645, contained among others these regulations:[2]

2ly: that from the begiñing of the first moneth untill the end of the 7th he [the schoolmaster] shall evy day begin to teach at seaven of the Clock in the morning and dismisse his schollers at fyve in the afternoone. And for the other five moneths that is from the beginning of the 8th moneth untill the end of the 12th mõth he shall evry day beginn at 8th of the Clock in the morning and [end] at 4 in the afternoone.

3ly: evy day in the yeere the usuall tyme of dismissing at noone shalbe at 11 and to beginn agayne at one, except that

4ly: every second day in the weeke he shall call his schollers togeither betweene 12 and one of the Clock to examin them what they have learned on the sabbath day prceding at which tyme also he shall take notice of any misdemeanor or disorder that any of skollers shall have

---

[1] Crippen, John H., *op. cit.*, p. 91.
[2] "Dorchester Town Records," in *Report of the [Boston] Record Commissioner, 1880* (Boston, Rockwell and Churchill, 1880), Vol. IV, pp. 55–56.

Committed on the saboath to the end that at somme convenient tyme due Admonition, and Correction may bee admistred. . . .

7ly: evy 6 day of the weeke [Saturday] at 2 of the Clock in the afternoone hee shall Chatechise his schollers in the principles of Christian religion. . . .

The school day in New Haven, in 1684, as specified in rules for the Hopkins Grammar School, was from "6 in ye morning to 11 a clock in ye forenoone and from 1 a clock in the afternoon to 5 a clock in the afternoone in Summer and 4 in winter." [3] In Boston, the school day apparently was seven hours long until 1802, when it was reduced to six.[4]

The practice in neighboring colonies did not differ significantly from that reported for New England. Thompson, in his *History of Long Island*, reproduces the agreement between Johannes von Eckkellen, schoolmaster, and the town of Flatbush, Long Island, in which the length of school day is stipulated. Article 1 reads as follows: "The school shall begin at 8 o'clock, and go out at 11; shall begin again at 1 o'clock and end at 4. The bell shall be rung before the school commences." It would appear from this that a six-hour day was considered adequate there, whatever the season. The same agreement called for the teacher's keeping "his school nine months in succession, from September to June, one year with another; and shall always be present himself." [5]

In Queen Anne's County, Maryland, it was required that the hours of teaching be from 7 to 11 A.M. and 1 to 5 P.M. from April to October 1, and from 8 to 11 A.M. and 1 to 4 P.M. for the balance of the year. No mention is made of vacations or holidays until 1775.[6] Practice in the other Southern colonies was equally varied. The community schools in Virginia, which were sometimes taught by women, were open in the summer months from April

---

[3] "Annual Catalogue of the School for 1857," in Steiner, Bernard C., *op. cit.*, p. 26.

[4] Martin, G. H., "Boston Schools One Hundred Years Ago," in *New England Magazine* (1902), pp. 630–31.

[5] Thompson, Benjamin F., *The History of Long Island from Its Discovery and Settlement to the Present Time* (New York, Gould, Banks, and Company, 1843), Vol. I, pp. 285–86.

[6] Brown, Edwin H., *op. cit.*, p. 4.

to September. Apparently this custom prevailed pretty much throughout the colony. In discussing the tutorial system of instruction among the planters in Virginia, Heatwole states that the school day was divided into three parts, from six to eight in the morning, from nine o'clock until noon, and from three to six in the afternoon.[7] In Georgia, according to Bowden, the school day began at sunrise and continued until five o'clock in the afternoon and the successful master taught the entire year.[8]

Standardization in time was not so important nor so easily achieved during these days as at a later period. Schoolhouses were not equipped with clocks and only a few schoolmasters owned watches. Hourglasses and sundials gave rough approximations of the time of day and, as Littlefield observed, "each school was sure to have a noon mark on a southern window sill." [9] The range in the school year extended from two months or less to nearly the full calendar year. Schools were apparently open longer in certain New England communities during this period than now. According to one writer, referring to a somewhat later date (1802), the holidays and vacations were only those in which the public shared. There was no school on Thursday and Saturday afternoons, nor on Fast and Thanksgiving Days, April 1, June 1, Christmas, and the Fourth of July. Vacations consisted of the four afternoons of Artillery training, six days in election week, the four last days in Commencement week, and general training days.[10] These conditions were probably fairly characteristic of the late colonial period in Boston, for it is recorded that when Daniel Munson was engaged to teach the Hopkins School in 1729 it was agreed that he should "keep the gramer scholl . . . about 7 hours in the day in the winter season and about 8 hours in the summer season in each day and *not to exceed twelve play dayes in the year*. . . ." [11]

---

[7] Heatwole, Cornelius J., *op. cit.*, p. 57.

[8] Bowden, Haygood S., *Two Hundred Years of Education* (Richmond, Va., Dietz Printing Company, 1932), p. 102.

[9] Littlefield, George E., *Early Schools and School-Books of New England* (Boston, The Club of Odd Volumes, 1904), p. 93.

[10] Martin, G. H., *op. cit.*, p. 631.

[11] Bacon, Leonard W., *An Historical Discourse on the Two Hundredth Anniversary of . . . Hopkins Grammar School*, etc. (New Haven, Thomas J. Stafford, 1860), p. 57. Italics ours.

SIZE OF CLASS AND NUMBER OF DIFFERENT SUBJECTS TAUGHT

Colonial records show a wide variation in the size of school and the number of pupils for which the teacher was responsible. Except in the larger towns, there was usually only one free school in each community and its size depended upon the number of children in the neighborhood. One is not surprised, therefore, to find enrollments of fifteen and others of one hundred or more under a single master. When the teacher's work became too arduous and the number of scholars reached a point where he seemed justified in petitioning for assistance, an usher was sometimes employed to give whatever help his qualifications permitted.

To a modern classroom teacher, eighteen or twenty pupils may seem to be an unusually light load but it must be remembered that the colonial schoolteacher had to cope with the additional problems of classification and grading. Under his jurisdiction were children of various ages and achievement levels. To keep all these individuals profitably occupied during a seven- or eight-hour day was like juggling as many balls simultaneously. Furthermore, he could not sweeten the process of education by providing children with attractive textbooks, to say nothing of lantern slides or moving pictures. In the grammar schools, the variety of subjects taught by a single master would be considered quite beyond the competence of most secondary-school teachers of modern times. Greek, Latin, English, Good Manners, and the principles of the Christian Religion constituted the offering of the Salem Grammar School in 1667.[12] Nor was the Salem curriculum unique. A Hingham contract of 1670 reads as follows: ". . . Henry Smith engageth that with care and diligence he will teach and instruct, until a year be expired, in Latin, Greek & English, in Writting and Arithmetik, such youths . . . as shall, for the fore mentioned Sciences, be sent into their Schooll." [13]

The situation was not significantly different in the colonies south of New England, where a relatively wide knowledge of subject matter was commonly professed by schoolmasters. Thus

[12] Small, Walter H., *op. cit.*, p. 5.
[13] *History of the Town of Hingham, Massachusetts* (By the Town, 1893), Vol. I, p. 85.

William Thorne, a Philadelphia master in 1766, was either very versatile or extremely conceited as is evidenced by his advertisement in the *Pennsylvania Gazette* to teach "writing, arithmetic, geometry, trigonometry, navigation, mensuration, surveying, guaging, and accounts." [14]

An equally wide knowledge of subject matter was professed by James Farrill, whose advertisement in the *New York Mercury* on July 12, 1756, read as follows:

This is to notifie the public, that James Farrill, *late of* New-Jersey, *purposes by God's permission, to open school in* Broad-street, *on monday the 12th day of this instant* July, *at the house of Mrs.* Elizabeth Witt, . . . *and purposes (God willing) to teach reading, writing, arithmetic, vulgar and decimal logarithmatical and instrumental, merchants accompts, navigation, surveying, dialing, &c, &c, carefully and expeditiously, by*

JAMES FARRILL.

The teachers of today, however, probably work just as hard as the masters of the seventeenth and eighteenth centuries. The latter had few examination papers to mark and but little, if any, homework to do. Furthermore, they were relatively free from close supervision and the standards achieved were largely those set by the masters themselves. These were the days before lesson plans, diagnostic tests, elaborate attendance records, and refined techniques. There was some compensation, therefore, for the long day, the heterogeneous school population, and the variety of subjects to be taught in the degree of freedom accorded the master in the management of his school.

EXTRA DUTIES

Teaching in colonial days was not usually considered a full-time occupation. Many and various were the extra tasks either expected of the schoolmaster or assumed by him to help eke out his miserly wage. Of the additional responsibilities required of teachers, the most prevalent were religious or semireligious in character. In some communities, indeed, the same man was both preacher and teacher, the latter office no doubt taking secondary rank to the more highly regarded calling. In Virginia

[14] Woody, Thomas, *Early Quaker Education in Pennsylvania*, pp. 223–24.

and Maryland, in the Dutch and Swedish settlements along the Delaware, and in a number of villages in New England, several of the early schoolmasters were also clergymen. When teachers were not ordained ministers they were commonly found assisting in the church in various capacities, taking a prominent part in religious services and officiating in the pastor's absence. Among the early Swedes and the Dutch, the schoolmaster was frequently the minister's assistant, reading for him, leading the singing, visiting the sick, and in his absence "taking the vacant place at the sacred desk." Evert Pietersen served in such a capacity in New Castle, Delaware, in 1856. In addition to the responsibility for a school, he was also employed as *zieken-trooster*, to read God's word and lead the singing until the arrival of a clergyman. Five years later, we find him in New Amsterdam as a combination consoler, clerk, chorister, and schoolmaster.

The New England schoolmaster was also required to perform various duties in connection with the church, which included conducting ceremonial services and leading the Sunday choir. Less-exalted religious duties, chiefly sweeping out the meeting-house, ringing the bell for public worship, and digging graves, were equally common. Thus, throughout the colonies, the position of schoolmaster was more likely than not to embrace that of reader, chorister, psalm setter, and sexton as well.

The agreement referred to earlier between Johannes von Eckkellen and the town of Flatbush, Long Island, in 1682, shows the extra duties which were considered appropriate for the schoolmaster in that town and illustrates the church chores and tasks which were sometimes exacted of pedagogues: [15]

Art. 5. He shall be chorister of the church, keep the church clean, ring the bell three times before the people assemble, and read a chapter of the Bible in the church between the second and third ringing of the bell; after the third ringing, he shall read the Ten Commandments and the twelve articles of our faith, and then set the psalm. In the afternoon, after the third ringing of the bell, he shall read a short chapter or one of the psalms of David, as the congregation are assembling; afterwards he shall again sing a psalm or hymn.

[15] Thompson, Benjamin F., *op. cit.*, p. 286.

Art. 6. When the minister shall preach at Brooklyn or Utrecht, he shall be bound to read twice before the congregation, from the book used for the purpose. He shall hear the children recite the questions and answers out of the catechism on Sunday, and instruct them therein.

Art. 7. He shall provide a basin of water for the administration of holy baptism and furnish the minister with the name of the child to be baptized. He shall furnish bread and wine for the communion, at the charge of the church. He shall also serve as messenger for the consistory.

Art. 8. He shall give the funeral invitations, dig the graves, and toll the bell. . . .

CIVIC AND OTHER DUTIES

Other additional duties assigned to schoolmasters were civic in character. In 1661 the regulations for teachers in Portsmouth, New Hampshire, specified that they act as court messengers and serve the summonses.[16] Samuel Corbett, who taught in Bristol,[17] was also an appraiser and a grand juryman. Daniel Rogers of Ipswich was town clerk and register of probate.[18] Private-school masters often served as public accountants, scriveners, and translators. Others were popular lecturers or readers.[19]

John Thelwell, a famous schoolmaster in Wilmington, Delaware, in Revolutionary times, had so many outside duties that one chronicler says of him: "It would be easier to say what he did not than to recount his numerous duties." Among his various tasks was that of clerk of the market, and the office of bellman had been his from time immemorial. As town crier, Daddy Thelwell and his big bell were a familiar sight in the streets, warning the burgesses to attend their meeting or announcing auction sales of goods and property.[20]

[16] Grizzell, Emit D., *Origin and Development of the High School in New England before 1865* (New York, The Macmillan Company, 1923), p. 24.

[17] Small, W. H., *op. cit.*, p. 113.

[18] *Ibid.*, p. 113. Felt, Joseph, *History of Ipswich*, p. 86.

[19] Seybolt, Robert F., *The Private School*, Source Studies in American Colonial Education, Bulletin No. 28 (Bureau of Educational Research, University of Illinois, 1925), p. 85.

[20] Powell, Lyman P., *History of Education in Delaware* (Washington, Government Printing Office, 1893), p. 41. (Contributions to American Educational History, No. 15, U. S. Bureau of Education, Circular No. 3 [1893].)

SUPPLEMENTING THE JOB OF SCHOOLTEACHING

Various other vocations were also united with schoolkeeping. The records show that William Turpin, the first schoolmaster of Providence, Rhode Island, combined instruction of children with innkeeping; that Roger Sherman of Milton was an itinerant maker and mender of shoes when not engaged in teaching; and that many of the Dover masters added surveying to school-keeping.[21] John Woolman, the Quaker schoolmaster, learned tailoring, and many other Quaker educators were carpenters or followed some other vocational "art" or "mystery."[22]

Most of the early teachers in Maine were small farmers. In addition to a salary of thirty pounds for his educational labors, Richard Norcross, a New England teacher, received two shillings a head for tending the dry herd, resulting in the quip that "he wet-nursed the brains of the children and dry-nursed the bodies of the cattle."[23]

This common assumption of other duties by colonial school-masters seems odd to our twentieth-century eyes, but it was not unusual for that period nor was it peculiar to teachers as a class. In the agricultural society and economy of the day, specialization was the exception rather than the rule. Indeed, the greater majority of small farmers throughout all the colonies lived a multifold life and were generally butchers, coopers, joiners, carpenters, shoemakers, and general handy men.

[21] Small, W. H., *op. cit.*, p. 113.
[22] Woody, Thomas, *Quaker Education in New Jersey*, p. 304.
[23] Small, W. H., *op. cit.*, p. 113.

VI

Men and Women Teachers in Colonial Schools

IN the literature of the colonial period the term "schoolteacher" seldom appears. This expression came into use later, when women began to command an important place in the business of education. During these early days there were few educated persons except men. It is not surprising, therefore, that the colonial teacher was almost always a schoolmaster rather than a schoolmistress. In the public mind, woman's place was in the home, not in the classroom. The reliance upon the "rod of correction" for curbing the fractious spirits of boys was a further reason for limiting the personnel of the teaching profession to the male sex. Still another consideration was the character of the extra duties assigned to the pedagogues of the seventeenth and eighteenth centuries. Females could scarcely be expected to fulfill the function of sexton and gravedigger—tasks which were sometimes allotted to the teacher in New England.

While the relative insignificance of women as teachers in colonial days is a clearly established fact, some educational historians have fallen into the error of denying that they played any part whatsoever. Statements such as the following are quite unwarranted in light of the numerous exceptions: [1]

The teacher of the schools in early days *was always a man*, frequently the minister, or a candidate for the ministry. It is only within recent years that a woman has been considered competent to preside over a grammar school, a high school, or a college. It was many years before she could teach a common school, and then only during the summer term.

Even for New England, this statement is too strong. The Wallingford records in Connecticut, for example, reveal the fact

[1] Littlefield, George E., *op. cit.*, p. 87. Italics ours.

that in 1695 "the town authorized the Committee to employ a
woman to teach in summer; and a man in winter." [2] This same
practice prevailed in Windsor where it was voted in 1718 that
the "schools shall be kept by women [in] the summer until
October." [3] In Norwich, Connecticut, in 1745, one finds the
following provision which suggests further that women teachers
were not unknown: "If any of these schools should be kept by a

A NEW ENGLAND SCHOOL DAME

woman, the time was to be doubled, as the pay of the mistress
was but half that to the master." [4] Moreover, it is clearly established that dame schools existed in many New England towns
during this period and that schooldames performed the functions
now commonly assigned to primary teachers. In many instances
they were paid partly out of public funds.

[2] Davis, Charles H. S., *History of Wallingford* (Meriden, Conn., The Author,
1870), p. 311.

[3] Stiles, Henry R., *History of Ancient Windsor, Connecticut* (New York, Charles B.
Norton, 1859), p. 452.

[4] Caulkins, Frances M., *History of Norwich, Connecticut* (The Author, 1866),
p. 275.

The names of a few women teachers appear in New York records. Among these were Goody Davis, who kept school at Jamaica in 1685 in a "little house" soon after used "as a shoppe." [5] Rachel Spencer is also reported as having taught school at Hempstead, Long Island, prior to 1687, and in 1739 a Presbyterian schoolmistress was established in Rye, Westchester County, New York.[6]

Women teachers were commonly employed by the Quaker communities in Pennsylvania. Woody comments on this practice, pointing out that "encouragement was at all times given to women as teachers, mention having already been made to their employment as early as 1699." [7] It must be remembered, of course, that the Quakers did not discriminate against women to the same degree that other religious sects did. The religion of the Friends was an important factor in freeing women from the fetters of ignorance and in elevating them to a comparable plane with men. The fact that the Quaker religion required no clergy, no readers, no psalm-setters, nor many of the other church officials commonly combined with the position of schoolmaster in other colonies, may also account for the relatively large proportion of women teachers in Pennsylvania. Even among the Friends, however, tradition must have played a powerful part, for, judging by the relative wages paid to men and women and the apparent neglect in recording appointments and dismissals of women, the genus male teacher appears to have been clearly dominant.

Nor were men exclusively employed as teachers in the Southern colonies. Edward McCrady, in his *History of South Carolina under the Royal Government, 1719–1776* points out that there were many female teachers for the girls in South Carolina.[8] In the tobacco colonies, particularly Virginia, the wives of planters sometimes taught in the "Old Field Schools," [9] which were

[5] *History of the County of Albany, 1609–1886* (New York, W. W. Munsell and Company, 1886), p. 257.

[6] Kemp, William W., *op. cit.*, p. 132.

[7] Woody, Thomas, *Early Quaker Education in Pennsylvania*, p. 58, and his authorities.

[8] Page 491 (New York, The Macmillan Company, 1899).

[9] The term "Old Field Schools" refers to those schools which were erected and maintained on fields temporarily abandoned for raising tobacco or cotton. The

private neighborhood schools located in the country.   That women were in the minority as teachers in the South is clearly evident, but illustrations of the type reported here can be found in every colony to prove that they occasionally taught school even during the colonial period.

Like most generalizations, then, the conclusion that the teachers of colonial days were men is only partially true and needs some qualification. On the other hand, it is certain that women played a relatively small part in the formal education of children. They were more often assigned to teach during the summer months (April to September) than men; they taught chiefly the younger children and, in many of the colonies, the children of the poor. Furthermore, they received but little recognition either in terms of compensation or in the position accorded them in the community.

expense of operating them was commonly shared by the planters in the immediate neighborhood.

VII

School Supervision in the Seventeenth and Eighteenth Centuries

TEACHERS in American schools financed partially or wholly at public expense have never been completely free from supervision and control. In all the colonies, the schoolmaster's work was appraised by laymen. Most of this supervision was casual and informal at best, and the teacher was perhaps more nearly his own boss at this time than at any subsequent period.

In New England, the schools were visited or inspected by the ministers, by the selectmen accompanied by prominent citizens, or by special committees. The specific purposes of the inspection varied from place to place and from time to time but usually included the following:

1. To appraise the progress made by children in mastering the principles and doctrines of the Christian religion.
2. To hear the younger scholars read.
3. To appraise the performance of the scholars in writing and arithmetic.
4. To examine the writing of the masters.
5. To report on the number of scholars in attendance.

Accounts of school visiting are perhaps most completely recorded for the Boston schools. One report made by a committee in that city in 1710 suggests rather clearly the supervisory procedures which were considered desirable. The following item is taken from the committee's report: [1]

We further propose and recommend, as of Great Service and Advantage for the promoting of Diligence and good literature, That the

---

[1] "Boston Town Records," *Report of the [Boston] Record Commissioners*, Vol. VIII, p. 65.

Town, Agreeably to the Usage in England, and (as we understand) in Some time past practised here, Do Nominate and Appoint a Certain Number of Gentlemen, of Liberal Education, Together with Some of Yᵉ Revᵈ Ministers of the Town, to be Inspectors of the Sᵈ Schoole. . . . To Visit yᵉ School from time to time . . . to Enform themselves of the methodes used in teaching of yᵉ Schollars and to Inquire of their Proficiency, and be present at the performance of Some of their Exercises, the Master being before Notified of their Comeing, And with him to consult and Advise of further Methods for yᵉ Advancement of Learning and the Good Government of the Schoole.

This suggestion was accepted as a sound policy to guide the school committee and undoubtedly influenced later practice considerably. As the above recommendation implies, these visits by the selectmen and other prominent citizens were apparently not surprise visits to the schoolmasters. This is further substantiated by a Boston record of June 24, 1761, in which it was "Voted, that the Selectmen visit the Publick Schools. . . . Ordered that Mr. Williston . . . acquaint the several schoolmasters therewith" of the intended visit.[2]

The town was not always satisfied to leave the matter of supervision wholly to selectmen or to the committee, as is evidenced by the fact that in Boston it was voted on March 29, 1734, "that the several Writing Masters in the Town, do present, at the next General Town Meeting, Some of their own performances in Writing, for the Town's inspection."[3]   Other New England towns were equally sensitive to the need of supervising the work of schoolmasters. In the Dorchester rules of 1645, instructions were given by the town to the wardens of the Grammar School to ". . . take care that the Schoolemʳ for the tyme beeing doe faythfully p'rforme his dutye in his place, as schoolmʳˢ ought to doe." . . .   In addition to this general responsibility for the schoolmaster, which the wardens were advised to appraise, was a list of specific items sufficiently objective in character to be easily observed. They included such things as the hour of opening and dismissing school, the basis for the admission of scholars,

---

[2] "Boston Records," *op. cit.*, Vol. XIX, pp. 152–53.
[3] *Ibid.*, Vol. XII, p. 75.

the religious instruction to be provided, and the character of the discipline to be maintained.[4]

Although in Connecticut the directions to selectmen or visitors were apparently not so specific as those listed above, the schoolmasters in this colony were not entirely free from supervision. In the records of the town of Wallingford, in 1713, there is a note to the effect that John Moss and Samuel Culver were appointed "to see that the teacher keeps his hours." [5]

A function closely allied to supervision in some New England towns was that of inducting the new masters into the schools. A Charlestown record of August 20, 1764, describes this procedure as follows: [6]

This day the selectmen, accompanied by the Rev. Mr. Prentice and some other gentlemen of the town, visited the school, and after good advice given the children and solemn prayers to God for his blessing, they gave Mr. William Harris the care of the Writing School.

Similar practices are reported by Seybolt for Boston, where it was the custom for two or more of the selectmen to introduce newly appointed schoolmasters into their schools.[7]

Massachusetts was probably more advanced in educational organization than the other colonies; at least the provisions established by the towns for inspecting and overseeing the work of schoolmasters were more universal. It would be unfair to assume, however, that the supervision provided in the colonies south of New England was always less adequate than that reported for the Bay Colony. Wherever public moneys were made available or even private donations, there was an accounting made, and in several instances the interest and time spent by laymen in the management and supervision of schools was equal to that of the New England towns.

Some supervision was evidently exercised over the work of the Dutch schoolmasters in New Amsterdam. The records are not complete on this subject but, judging from the following rules

---

[4] "Dorchester Town Records," *op. cit.*, Vol. IV, p. 55.
[5] Davis, Charles H. S., *op. cit.*, p. 314.
[6] Small, Walter H., *Early New England Schools* (Boston, Ginn and Company, 1914), p. 336.
[7] Seybolt, Robert F., *The Public Schools of Colonial Boston, 1635–1775*, pp. 57–66.

drawn up by the civil authorities, the schoolmaster's task was rather well defined for him: [8]

Instructions and Rules for Schoolmaster Evert Pietersen, drawn up by the Burgomasters of this City with advice of the Director General and Council.

First. He shall take good care, that the children, coming to his school, do so at the usual hour, namely at 8 in the morning and one in the afternoon.

2. He must keep good discipline among his pupils.

3. He shall teach the children and pupils the Christian prayers, commandments, baptism, Lord's supper, and the questions with answers of the catechism, which are taught here every Sunday afternoon in the church.

4. Before school closes, he shall let the pupils sing some verses and a psalm.

5. Besides his yearly salary he shall be allowed to demand and receive from every pupil quarterly as follows:

for each child, whom he teaches the a b c, spelling and
   reading   30   st.
for teaching to read and write   50   "
"   "   to read, write and cipher   60   "
from those who come in the evening and between times pro rata
   a fair sum
the poor and needy, who ask to be taught for God's sake he shall
   teach for nothing.

6. He shall be allowed to demand and receive from every body, who makes arrangements to come to his school and comes before the first half of the quarter preceding the 1st of December next the school dues for the quarter, but nothing from those, who come after the first half of the quarter.

7. He shall not take more from anybody, than is herein stated. Thus done and decided by the Burgomasters of the City of Amsterdam in N. N. November 4, 1661.

These detailed instructions would seem to imply some kind of an accounting or check upon teachers. In all probability it

[8] Fernow, Berthold (ed.), *Minutes of the Orphanmasters Court*, etc., Vol. II, pp. 115–16. A stiver is the equivalent of two cents in United States money.

was not systematic, for the records are quite silent on the procedure that was followed.

The position of schoolmaster among the Dutch in America was almost as ecclesiastical as it was academic. The fact that the Classis and Consistory determined, in connection with licensing, whether or not schoolmasters possessed the necessary religious qualifications and, furthermore, the fact that the Classis maintained an interest in the general welfare of its schoolmasters, might lead one to expect the church to have maintained close supervision over the schools. Despite this interest, however, the church officially had relatively little to say about the control and supervision of the school. To what extent schoolmasters in New Amsterdam were influenced unofficially by the ministers is not known. Since the two vocations were so closely related, it is highly probable that the clergy exerted an appreciable influence over those aspects of education and school life which were concerned with religion. No radical change in policy occurred in the matter of supervision and management of the Dutch schools following the occupation of New Amsterdam by the English in 1664.

The Society for the Propagation of the Gospel in Foreign Parts exercised considerable control over the teachers of the English schools whom it employed, and also provided for supervision. The latter usually consisted of a call by the minister or one of the missionaries in the neighborhood, who was officially requested to "visit these schools at least once a year to see that the Masters are not remiss in duty." New teachers were always provided with a copy of the "Society's Instructions to Schoolmasters," which embraced every particular that seemed necessary for their guidance.[9] The existence of an interesting supervisory relationship is suggested in one section of these instructions, in which the schoolmasters were advised to consult frequently with the minister of the parish in which they dwelt about the methods of managing their schools. Not only were these masters accountable to the minister, but they were also expected to send to the secretary of the Society, once in every six months, "an Account of the State of their respective Schools, the Number of their Scholars,

---

[9] Kemp, William W., *op. cit.*, p. 58.

with the Methods and Success of their Teaching." In 1738 a special form for reporting, known as the Notitia Scholastica, was provided every schoolmaster working under the society and it was required that this be filled out and attested by the missionary and by some of the principal inhabitants.

A COPY OF THE NOTITIA SCHOLASTICA

The extent to which these particular forms were used is not known. In any event there is evidence which suggests that the information called for on the blank was sent regularly to the society.

The Friends in Pennsylvania laid considerable stress upon the deportment of children and established a number of rules for both the guidance of masters and the observance of the pupils. Among these were the following: [10]

1. Pupils must be at school promptly.
2. No pupil shall absent himself from school without a permit from parents.

[10] Woody, Thomas, *Early Quaker Education in Pennsylvania*, pp. 182–83.

3. The monitor is to be strictly obeyed; but if there is a real grievance, complaint may be made to the master.
4. Pupils must be orderly in coming to and leaving school.
5. The plain language must be used to all persons; pupils must be civil to all.
6. During hours of leisure, pupils must avoid all "ranting games" and quarreling with one another.
7. Pupils shall not play or keep company with rude boys of the town, but shall play with their own schoolfellows.
8. Pupils shall come to school on 5th day prepared to go to the regular meeting.

In Philadelphia, general supervision was entrusted to school overseers or trustees, but frequently among the Friends committees of visitors were appointed by the monthly meetings to inspect and report on the condition of the schools. There were in Pennsylvania many schools which were not under the supervision of the Friends. Some of these were financed by the Society for Propagating Christian Knowledge among the Germans in America. This organization provided in its resolutions for a certain number of the most reputable persons residing near every particular school to "be appointed deputy trustees, to visit that school, superintend the execution of the scheme of education in it, and use their interests in the support of it." [11] In the Wyoming Valley, in northern Pennsylvania, the settlers from Connecticut brought with them advanced ideas about school organization. They elected a school committee of three members to exercise general supervision over the schools. This committee not only employed the schoolmaster but, in some degree at least, attempted to evaluate the instruction provided.[12]

Education in Delaware was almost as diverse as the three racial groups which made up the greater part of the population, namely, the Swedes, the Dutch, and the English. What little is known of the practices common to the Dutch schools in Delaware would lead us to believe that they did not differ radically

[11] Wickersham, James P., *op. cit.*, p. 69.
[12] Miner, Charles, *History of Wyoming* (Philadelphia, J. Crissy, 1845), p. 144; *The Historical Record: The Early History of Wyoming Valley* (January, 1889), Vol. III, p. 1.

from those prevailing in New Amsterdam. It also seems probable that the English schools were managed much after the fashion of the Quaker schools in Pennsylvania, since Delaware was a part of this colony until 1702. Among the Swedes, the minister appears to have exercised the greatest amount of control over the schoolmaster's work whenever the two jobs were not held by one and the same person. The following interesting description of the last day of school in Christina, April 8, 1718, shows the nature of the appraisal made of the schoolmaster's success and, in the absence of modern achievement tests, the examination procedure reported would seem to have been exceedingly comprehensive: [13]

The pastor met with Mr. Gioding and all the scholars in the house of Johan Stalcop, in presence of most of the parents of the children, to have a formal closing of the past schoolkeeping, which began June 17, 1717, and had been sometime since ended, that it might be known by a proper examination how much improvement the children had made, and, according to the wish of the parents, dismiss Mr. Gioding from his school work. The pastor opened the exercises with a godly prayer and appropriate remarks, after which Mr. Gioding, in his praiseworthy manner, according to the method of His High Worthiness, Bishop Swedberg, in the beginning of his catechism, asked questions regarding the most important Christian doctrines requiring proof from Holy Scripture, to which questions of Mr. Gioding, to the surprise and gratification of all, they answered promptly and boldly, and so quickly confirmed their answers by a text of Holy Scripture that all the company present could not refrain from glorifying God with tears of joy and gladness for their children's quick memory and attainments and the schoolmaster's diligence and circumspection, who all that, only by conversation and without any book, had impressed upon the memories of the children, and that there had been no fault in teaching them reading the pastor proved by having them read portions of the psalms selected by him, and found to his great satisfaction that they could read Swedish well.

The supervision of education in the "tobacco" colonies was not significantly different from the general type prevailing in New England. It was in many instances more casual, but what-

[13] Powell, Lyman P., *op. cit.*, p. 18.

ever management of schools existed, apart from that assumed by the schoolmaster, was in the hands of local citizens. Here again clergymen were prominent in the affairs of schools and were usually active members of visiting committees or held responsible positions as overseers or trustees. In Queen Anne's County, Maryland, the visitors of the school were the leading men of the county. They were constituted by law into a body politic and given the power to appoint their successors in office and to make such bylaws as were necessary to carry on the activities of the free school. They concerned themselves with matters of attendance, teaching methods, and the moral welfare of pupils. Because one of the assistants in Queen Anne's County "taught dancing two days a week in the school house which the visitors apprehended, must necessarily tend to the hindrances of teaching reading, writing . . ." they threatened to discharge the master. In this same school the visitors individually exercised supervision over both master and pupils. The following incident reported by Brown is indicative of the nature of this supervision: [14]

Upon one occasion the "visitor observing the scholars shooting at marks with guns had them called together and admonished and ordered them not to bring guns to school again and also in their presence order the master to have strict attention to them during their playtime, and to punish any who shall be catched contrary to this order." At the same time "observing most of the scholars pronounce badly" they "order the master to be particularly attentive to make them express their words and syllables as distinct and clear as possible" and they "advise and admonish the scholars to use their utmost endeavors to break themselves of the bad habit which they have heretofore contracted in uttering their words in a thick confused manner."

It would appear from this that the visitors considered themselves fully competent to advise not alone on disciplinary measures but even on such professional matters as the technique of teaching reading.

The educational records of Virginia are not particularly informative about supervisory procedures there. We do know that trustees were appointed to look after the interests of the endowed schools, that they were frequently remiss in their duties, and that

[14] Brown, Edwin H., *op. cit.*, p. 4.

the improvement of instruction was not considered a major part of their work. Since the endowed schools were established largely to provide opportunities for poor children to improve their unhappy state rather than to further the interests of any religious sect, the concern of the clergy for the success of the enterprise was undoubtedly secondary. There is also little to relate about the supervision of the parish schools in Virginia. It was apparently unorganized and ineffective. As for the remaining Southern colonies, it is safe to infer that they did not contribute to the development of supervision and management.

The underlying purposes of supervision in the more progressive areas during the colonial period were similar in some respects to those prevailing today; namely, to appraise the general achievement of pupils in subject matter, to evaluate the methods used in teaching, to observe the general management of the school and the conduct of the pupils, and to ascertain as far as possible whether or not the money appropriated for the educational enterprises was being properly expended. Of equal importance to supervisors were the amount and character of the instruction given in the principles and doctrines of the Christian religion. Judging from the prominent part played by the clergy in the supervision of schools, one is tempted to infer that this last motive was probably the dominant one in school visitation and inspection. Such a conclusion, however, needs qualification. The clergy were among the few well-educated persons in the colonies and it is only natural that they should have been selected to evaluate the work of the schoolmasters by passing on the quality of instruction provided and examining the pupils in the various subjects taught.

At best, supervision of the schoolteacher's performance during these days amounted to a superficial appraisal by ministers, selectmen, and school committees. The hierarchy of officers common to our present city school systems was foreign to the minds of the early settlers, and professionalized supervision, with emphasis upon the improvement of instruction, was a far cry to a civilization that could scarcely provide schools and schoolmasters.

VIII

The Tenure of Early Schoolmasters

T HE tenure of the typical schoolmaster of the colonial period was relatively brief. Not only did he remain but a short time in any given community, but his career as a teacher was frequently of short duration. There are numerous individual exceptions to this generalization, the most famous of which, perhaps, is Ezekiel Cheever, who was a teacher for seventy years and taught continuously in Boston for thirty-eight years.

In Massachusetts, there are several records of schoolmasters who remained as teachers in their respective communities for twenty years or more. Prominent among these were Richard Norcross, who began teaching in Watertown in 1650–1651 and was the only teacher there for twenty-nine years; [1] Richard Rogers, who taught in Oxford for twenty-two successive years; [2] and John Lovell, who served as master of the Boston Latin School for forty-two years. [3] Several other cases of schoolmasters whose tenure exceeded a score of years could probably be cited.

As a general rule, however, the turnover of teachers was high. The average length of time taught by sixty-six schoolmasters employed in Dedham, Massachusetts, between 1644 and 1757 was one year and ten months. [4] Seybolt, in discussing the private schoolmaster in colonial America, points out that teachers were itinerant. He traces William Elphinstone as follows: In 1753 he taught in New York City. In 1754 he moved to Philadelphia,

[1] *The Watertown Records* (Watertown, Mass., Fred G. Barker, 1894), pp. 21–138.
[2] Freeland, Mary de Witt, *The Records of Oxford, Mass.* (Albany, N. Y., Joel Munsell's Sons, 1894), pp. 308–9.
[3] Winsor, Justin (ed.), *The Memorial History of Boston* (Boston, James R. Osgood and Company, 1881), Vol. II, p. 401.
[4] Crippen, John H., *op. cit.*, p. 102.

returned to New York City in 1755, left for Boston the middle of the year. In the spring of 1756 he was established in New York again; two years later he was in Philadelphia. Returning to New York, he remained there for almost twenty years.[5]

In Delaware, we have a record of Arvid Hernbohm, who taught in Wicaco for some years and then went into the ministry. In the same colony we read that Herr Nils Forsberg taught in Christina but retired the next year because of ill health and lack of support. Likewise, Evert Pietersen was teaching in New Castle, Delaware, in 1657 but in 1662 he was teaching in New York.[6] Transiency appears to have been the rule rather than the exception. Many Harvard graduates taught school for a year or two and then entered some other profession, frequently the ministry. Trask points out that "of seventy teachers whose names have been found connected with the Dorchester schools, during the time above mentioned,—nearly a century and three quarters—fifty-three, or three-fourths of the whole number graduated at Harvard College. . . . Thirty-one . . . or nearly one-half, were ordained ministers, the most of them subsequent to their teaching school."[7] Others went into law and medicine; one became a distinguished judge, and one a lieutenant governor of the colony.[8] Teaching was only a temporary vocation to these ambitious men.

In Pennsylvania, conditions were not significantly different from those just reported. Judging from the tenor of the complaints of the yearly meetings and their recommendations that better and more permanent accommodations be afforded so that teachers might be more easily kept, it would seem that the tenure of the early Quaker schoolmaster was short.[9] Several cases are cited from Philadelphia showing a wide range in length of stay, from which the conclusion is to be drawn that conditions in the country were undoubtedly much worse than those existing in

[5] Seybolt, Robert F., *The Private School*, pp. 84–85.

[6] Powell, Lyman P., *op. cit.*, pp. 17, 19, 25.

[7] "Brief Notices of the Early Teachers in the Public Schools," in Dorchester Antiquarian and Historical Society, *History of the Town of Dorchester, Massachusetts*. (Boston, E. Clapp, Jr., 1859), p. 480.

[8] Mowry, William A., *op. cit.*, p. 41.

[9] Woody, Thomas, *Early Quaker Education in Pennsylvania*, p. 207, and his authorities.

Philadelphia.[10] Teacher turnover in the tobacco colonies was also high and records in Chatham, Georgia, show that teachers were transient and taught sometimes in as many as three communities a year.[11]

The causes of this instability among schoolteachers varied somewhat among the colonies. In most instances, wages were low and teachers were scarce.[12] These two factors tended to produce instability and to stimulate change. Furthermore, in some communities a master's success was sometimes conditioned by his political and religious affiliations, depending upon whether he were a Tory or a Whig, a Baptist or a Methodist, a Catholic or a Protestant. In others, the public oral examinations of pupils worked great hardship on schoolmasters. In Georgia, for example, those witnessing these exhibitions were so critical that no schoolmaster remained with the same group of patrons longer than four years.[13] In fact, conditions surrounding the employment of schoolmasters generally throughout the colonies tended to make the position a steppingstone to other "more respectable" professions, especially the ministry; and even for those who planned to make teaching their vocation the hope of larger rewards and an improved social life were dominant factors in producing transiency.

[10] *Ibid.*, p. 208.　　　　　　　[11] Bowden, Haygood S., *op. cit.*, p. 68.
[12] This seems like an inconsistency, *viz.*, low wages and scarcity of labor, but in education this phenomenon still occurs.
[13] Bowden, Haygood S., *op. cit.*, p. 170.

IX

Teachers' Salaries in Colonial Days

NO single statement can adequately portray the economic status of schoolteachers during the colonial period. To say that they were poorly paid is to ignore such conclusions as Seybolt's concerning the salaries of Boston schoolmasters to the effect that they "were usually higher than those of the various town officials." [1] Furthermore, there is some reason to believe that at least a few of these early teachers acquired considerable property.

On the other hand, there is plenty of evidence that schoolmasters complained a good deal about their wages and that teaching was frequently thought of as a steppingstone to more respectable or remunerative positions. The high rate of turnover, especially the migrations into the ministry, which offered greater financial rewards than teaching, is one evidence of this generalization. Efforts to secure food, clothing, and shelter seemed vastly more important to the colonists than education. In fact, the task of providing just these bare necessities of life demanded the services of nearly every able-bodied person. Under pioneer conditions, therefore, it was only natural to value more highly than schoolmasters such productive workers as agricultural laborers or artisans. Indeed, in none of the middle colonies in the eighteenth century did the schoolmaster occupy an exalted position. The average colonial teacher was considered to be "a cheap commodity," an "unproductive worker," "a tolerated necessity, maintained by free subsistence and little, if any, wage." [2]

---

[1] Seybolt, Robert F., *The Public Schools of Colonial Boston, 1635–1775*, p. 56.
[2] See Geiser, Karl F., *Redemptioners and Indentured Servants in the Colony and Commonwealth of Pennsylvania* (New Haven, Little, Morehouse and Taylor **Company,**

Salary policies were by no means uniform in the various colonies. Nor did they remain constant in any single colony throughout the whole of the colonial period. Wide variations were produced by a number of influences, many of which continue to affect wages to this day. Other things being equal, the larger the community the greater the salary. The economic welfare of the Boston and New York City schoolmasters was vastly superior to that of teachers in the smaller communities in the surrounding regions. The newer settlements ordinarily paid teachers less than the older and more established towns. The relationship of the church to colonial development was an important factor bearing upon the amount and kind of support which was provided for schools. In those colonies where the church was unusually powerful and active, generous treatment of schoolmasters was not uncommon. Ability to pay was equally as important a determiner of salaries then as now. Needless to say, scarcity was a factor, although the absence of standard qualifications made it possible for communities to create readily a supply of teachers. The relative immobility of schoolmasters, because of primitive transportation facilities, made competition somewhat less significant than it is today and, finally, the wide range in length of school year resulted in corresponding variations in annual salaries. In short, the same general factors which are responsible for the differences in salaries of schoolteachers during the twentieth century were also present during the colonial period.

Even though it is risky to attempt a generalization for any one or all of the colonies regarding the annual salary paid to teachers, the picture would not be complete without examining the wages actually paid by some of the communities during these early days. It must be remembered that the amounts listed represented only a part of the total remuneration of schoolmasters, since it was customary, as will be shown later, for communities to grant teachers certain perquisites in addition to the stated wage. Facts for the early years of the colonial period are available for several communities in New England. The records show that

1901), p. 108. Dix, Lester, *The Economic Basis for the Teacher's Wage* (New York, Bureau of Publications, Teachers College, Columbia University, 1931), p. 6.

Hartford [3] paid thirty pounds to the schoolmaster in 1642; Dedham,[4] twenty pounds in 1644; Roxbury,[5] twenty pounds in 1645; Hampton,[6] twenty pounds in 1649; Watertown,[7] thirty pounds in 1650; Essex,[8] fourteen pounds in 1651; Dorchester,[9] twenty-five pounds in 1655; Dover,[10] twenty pounds and Wethersfield,[11] twenty-five pounds in 1658.

Salaries did not change significantly in most of these communities for a number of years. Watertown, for example, continued to pay the schoolmaster about thirty pounds a year for some seventy consecutive years. In Dedham, Crippen found that if the currency had been constant between 1644 and 1755 the rate of pay for teachers would have been between twenty and twenty-five pounds a year.[12]

Boston was a good-paying town and was the goal of ambitious schoolmasters throughout the colonial period. Ezekiel Cheever was receiving sixty pounds per annum there in 1693 and his grandson, who assisted him, was paid forty pounds in 1699. Salaries rose gradually in Boston during the eighteenth century and in 1758 the sum of one hundred and twenty pounds was allowed for the yearly compensation of a schoolmaster and his assistant. Since the assistant, commonly known as usher, received anywhere from thirty-five to fifty pounds of this amount as his share, the regular salary of the master was at least seventy pounds.[13]

Grammar-school masters were usually better paid than

---

[3] "Hartford Town Votes," in *Collections of the Connecticut Historical Society* (Hartford, The Society, 1897), p. 63.

[4] *Early Records of the Town of Dedham [Mass.], 1636–1659* (Dedham, Mass., 1892), Vol. III, p. 105.

[5] Ellis, Charles M., *The History of Roxbury [Mass.] Town* (Boston, Samuel G. Drake, 1847), p. 35.

[6] "Hampton Town Records, ' in Dow, Joseph, *An Historical Address, Delivered at Hampton, New-Hampshire*, etc. (Concord, Asa McFarland, 1839), p. 44, note F.

[7] *Watertown Records* (Watertown, Mass., Fred G. Barker, 1894), p. 21.

[8] Felt, Joseph B., p. 83. See also Crowell, Robert, *History of the Town of Essex 1634–1700* (Boston, C. C. P. Moody, 1853), p. 55.

[9] "Dorchester Town Records," *op. cit.*, Vol. IV, p. 74.

[10] "Dover Town Records," in Scales, John (ed.), *Historical Memoranda Concerning Persons and Places in Old Dover, N. H.* (Dover, N. H., 1900), p. 50.

[11] Stiles, Henry R. (ed.), *The History of Ancient Wethersfield, Connecticut* (New York, The Grafton Press, 1904), Vol. I, p. 357.

[12] Crippen, John H., *op. cit.*, p. 106.

[13] Seybolt, Robert F., *The Private School*, p. 48.

writing-school masters, although the policy regarding this matter was never clearly defined. Whether the public considered the task of teaching the higher branches more difficult, calling for both greater ability and greater effort on the part of teachers, or whether the salary differential favoring grammar-school masters arose out of other considerations cannot be finally answered here. In all probability the colonists accepted the practice common in the Old Country without inquiring seriously into the merits of the case. Brown sums up the salary situation in New England as follows: [14]

In the seventeenth century, the salary of the masters of grammar schools commonly ranged from twenty to sixty pounds per annum. Twenty pounds is so frequently mentioned that it may almost be regarded as the standard, or perhaps the minimum rate, especially in the earliest times. . . . In the eighteenth century we find salaries mounting sometimes to one hundred pounds a year.

Conditions in the middle colonies were not so uniform as those found in Massachusetts and her New England neighbors, although the differences are no greater than might be expected from such a heterogeneous population. Perhaps the greatest variant was New Netherland, because of the Dutch influence. The salaries reported by Kilpatrick for New Netherland schoolmasters indicate that three hundred to five hundred florins [15] a year were commonly allotted to the Dutch teachers in New Amsterdam, Brooklyn, and Flatbush.[16] Pratt lists the salaries of fifty-five schoolmasters and catechists employed in the province of New York by the Society for the Propagation of the Gospel in Foreign Parts. Twenty-seven, or approximately half, of these teachers received ten pounds per annum.[17] Salaries as high as fifty pounds, however, were paid in some of the more prosperous communities in New York, although the usual amount assigned was much lower.

In Pennsylvania, salaries differed as widely as those paid teachers in New York and New England. Woody gives the

[14] Brown, Elmer E., *The Making of Our Middle Schools* (New York, Longmans, Green and Company, 1905), p. 123.

[15] A florin was worth approximately forty cents.

[16] Kilpatrick, William H., *op. cit.*   [17] Pratt, Daniel J., *op. cit.*, pp. 111–14.

salaries of several Quaker schoolmasters, extending over the period of a century. From his data one might classify the compensation of teachers as follows: between 1680 and 1700, 10 to 120 pounds; between 1700 and 1750, 20 to 150 pounds; and between 1750 and 1775, 10 to 200 pounds.[18] While there was a substantial increase noted in teachers' salaries in Pennsylvania during the century (1675–1775), the most striking fact with regard to the remuneration of schoolmasters was the great variation in the amounts paid them at any one time. In some of the rural areas of Pennsylvania, one can only speculate as to the actual compensation received. The congregation at New Providence, Trappe, Montgomery County, in 1750, allowed the schoolmaster seven shillings and sixpence and one half bushel of grain every six months for each scholar; in addition, he was permitted to live in the schoolhouse free of rent and to have the collections taken in the church on two of the chief festivals of the year, together with other perquisites.[19] It appears from this provision that the master's remuneration was a variable and dependent upon his popularity and the generosity of church members.

Wage rates similar to those obtaining in New England and the middle colonies prevailed in the Southern colonies. Generally the amount of cash salary was small and the total income difficult to estimate accurately because of the varying perquisites accompanying contract salary. In Queen Anne's County, Maryland, in 1724, David Davis, the schoolmaster, was allowed twenty pounds for ten foundation scholars and, in addition, he could charge tuition for pupils beyond the ten specified. Above this amount he could try to eke out a precarious existence by cultivating the few acres of cleared land which belonged to the school farm.[20] Thomas Johnson taught in this county in 1747 and was allowed twenty pounds current money and was promised an addition of ten pounds if he behaved well.[21] Twenty years later Luther Martin was receiving twenty pounds in this same school and the last schoolmaster in Queen Anne's County

[18] Woody, Thomas, *Early Quaker Education in Pennsylvania*, Chap. X.
[19] Wickersham, James P., *op. cit.*, p. 140.
[20] Brown, Edwin H., *op. cit.*, p. 3.   [21] *Ibid.*, p. 5.

before the Revolution, Joseph Potter, was granted a salary of twenty pounds and a promise of more if the school flourished.[22] This amount, besides the benefit and use of a plantation, was specified in the Act of 1723 as the schoolmaster's salary. The provisions of this Act applied to all the twelve counties in Maryland.[23]

Georgia appears to have pursued about the same policies regarding salaries. In 1743 the Common Council in Savannah passed a resolution to maintain a free school and voted a salary of twenty pounds sterling a year for a master.[24]

The salaries of pedagogues in the foundation schools in Virginia were frequently dependent upon the rental of lands left by the donor. On March 5, 1752, an advertisement in the *Virginia Gazette* contained the following statement: "The land rent of the said School [Symes] is 31 £ *per Ann.* besides Perquisites." Since the master's salary was about the only fixed charge which the school had, it is probable that thirty-one pounds was approximately his wage for the year.

In the establishment of the Winchester school earlier in the century (1702), it was agreed that the schoolmaster's compensation should consist of "dyett, lodging and washing, 500 pounds of tobacco & a horse, Bridle and Saddle to ride on during his stay." [25]

One of the most generous salary arrangements which has come to the author's attention is the provision made for the teacher of the free school in Charlestown. The Act for founding the school provided that besides perquisites the schoolmaster "as a further encouragement unto him, shall have and receive out of the publick treasury of this Province, the full sum of one hundred pounds per annum, to be paid to him half-yearly." [26]

From these citations it is clear that the salaries of schoolmasters were by no means uniform and in many instances consisted only in part of money. One must keep in mind that the responsibil-

---

[22] *Ibid.*, p. 10.　　　　　　　　　　　[23] Clews, Elsie W., *op. cit.*, p. 432.
[24] Bowden, Haygood S., *op. cit.*, p. 47.
[25] Maddox, William A., *op. cit.*, p. 8. Tobacco was worth about twopence, or approximately two cents, a pound at that time and was the commonly accepted medium of exchange in Virginia.
[26] Cooper, Thomas, *op. cit.*, p. 393.

ities of these early teachers differed widely and that their qualifications ranged from very poor to excellent.

Comparisons of Schoolmasters' Salaries with Wages Paid Other Workers

Actual salary amounts by themselves are almost meaningless
when attempting to understand the economic position of a group
of workers. Comparisons with wages paid in other lines of endeavor are necessary if the relative position of schoolmasters is
to be determined. While information concerning the salaries
and wages paid to professional workers during the colonial
period is rather meager, there are a number of references which
afford us sufficient information to enable us to make some tentative generalizations. In the first place, it is evident that ministers,
as a class, were much better paid than schoolmasters and that
communities were more generous in their support of religion
than of education.

An examination of New England town records and of the
proceedings of the S. P. G. indicates something of the disparity
which existed between these two professions in the matter of pay.
New England schoolmasters rarely received a salary one half
that paid to the minister [27] and the S. P. G. usually paid its

[27] Hope Atherton, the schoolmaster in Dorchester in 1669, received 30 pounds
per annum. While here, he received a "call" to the ministry in Hatfield, where he
was to receive a suitable house and a salary of 50 to 60 pounds. "Dorchester Town
Records," *op. cit.*, Vol. IV, p. 159. Wells, Daniel W., and Reuben, F., *A History of
Hatfield, Massachusetts, 1660–1910* (Springfield, F. C. H. Gibbons, 1910), p. 55.
Judd, Sylvester, *History of Hadley* (Northampton, Metcalf and Company, 1863),
p. 92.
  In 1683 Braintree was paying its schoolmaster 25 pounds (10 pounds in cash and
15 pounds in town land rent), while its minister was receiving 90 pounds plus
house and land. Bates, Samuel E. (ed.), *Records of the Town of Braintree, 1640–1793*
(Randolph, Mass., Daniel H. Huxford, 1886), p. 21.
  In 1742 the schoolmaster at Harwich, Mr. Selew, received a salary of 100 pounds,
one half the amount paid to the minister. Small, Walter, *op. cit.*, p. 134.
  In Easton, about 1726, it was proposed that the salary of the schoolmaster be
made equal to that of the minister's. It was voted down instantly and the final
salary agreed upon was so small (3 pounds) as to be relatively insignificant by
comparison. *Ibid.*
  The minister of the Episcopal church in Philadelphia in 1698 received 50 pounds
per annum for his services and the schoolmaster 30 pounds. Wickersham, James P.,
op. cit., p. 96.
  In 1759 the schoolmasters in Lancaster received 8 pounds; Kreutz Creek, 3
pounds; Conewago, 1.10 pounds; and the minister in these places about ten times
as much. *Ibid.*, p. 134,

schoolmasters one third the amount allotted to clergymen.[28]

The Dutch ministers also fared much better than school-masters. The report of the Board of Accounts in New Nether-land for 1644 gives an estimate of the expenses which the West India Company would have to bear in New Netherland for the following persons, to be rationed at their own expense: [29]

1 Director	3000 florins or approximately	$1200
1 Clergyman	1440 florins or approximately	576
1 Schoolmaster, pre-centor, and sexton	360 florins or approximately	144

While the above disparity is perhaps extreme, the superiority of the minister's salary is so great as to leave no doubt that clergy-men occupied a preferred position.

Apparently the Southern teacher stood in about the same relative position to the minister as his Northern colleagues. A detailed report of taxes and disbursements for changes of gov-ernment made in South Carolina in 1710 contains the following item: "Stipends to ten ministers of the Church of England, 1000 pounds." [30] This would indicate that one hundred pounds was the average salary paid to ministers in South Carolina at this time. While, as previously reported, the free school in Charles-town made equally as generous provision for the schoolmaster, it is doubtful if many teachers in this colony received annually as much as half this amount during this period. This is cor-roborated by the fact that schoolmasters in this colony appar-ently looked upon the ministry as the preferable vocation. One interesting instance of this was the case of Mr. McCrallen, master of the provincial free school, who in 1767 resigned his position to become assistant minister of St. Phillip's church. The commis-

[28] The financial reports of the S. P. G. for the years 1716 to 1758 show that salaries paid to ministers in the colonies averaged 50 pounds per annum while those of the schoolmasters averaged between 10 and 15 pounds. See *Abstracts of Proceedings of the S. P. G.* for the years 1716–1758.

[29] O'Callaghan, E. B. (ed.), *Documents Relative to the Colonial History of the State of New York*, 1603–1656. (Albany, Welch, Parsons and Company, 1856), Vol. I, p. 155.

[30] *A Description of South Carolina*, etc. (London, 1761), in Carroll, B. R. (compiler), *Historical Collections of South Carolina* (New York, Harper and Brothers, 1836), Vol. II, p. 259.

sioners of the school complained "that this is not the first instance of a master quitting the school for an ecclesiastical bene-
fice which affords a more-comfortable maintenance." [31]

Conditions in Virginia were not unlike this. As early as 1649
the author of *A Perfect Description of Virginia* estimated the minister's living as worth one hundred pounds. This was several
times the amount paid to the typical schoolmaster in this colony
prior to the Revolution.[32]

Valid comparisons of teachers' salaries with the earnings of
professional groups other than the ministry are scarcely possible,
since the conditions of work differed so widely. Certainly numerical differentials cannot be calculated accurately. The physician
had some capital outlay to consider, medicines to dispense, and
equipment to maintain. Fluctuating factors of this type were
not present in such vocations as the ministry or teaching. It
may be significant to note, however, that the charges of physicians were occasionally considered to be grossly immoderate.
Writing of doctors in Virginia, Bruce says: "So excessive were
their rates previous to 1630, that masters were tempted to suffer
a servant to perish for want of proper advice and medicines
rather than submit to their exactions." [33]

Quite a different situation is reported for New England at a
somewhat later date. Weeden characterizes the physician there
as a great benefactor of mankind, generously devoting his time
and skill to his patients. He emphasizes the moderate fees of
doctors, pointing out that: [34]

Even in Boston prior to 1782, the ordinary visit was charged at one
shilling six-pence to two shillings. Half a dollar was only charged
"such as were in high life." In that year a club of the leading physicians fixed the common fee at fifty cents, in consultation at one dollar.

---

[31] McCrady, Edward, *The History of South Carolina under the Royal Government,
1719–1776* (New York, The Macmillan Company, 1899), p. 449.

[32] Force, Peter, *Tracts and Other Papers* (Washington, Peter Force, 1838), Vol. II,
p. 8.

[33] Bruce, Philip A., *Economic History of Virginia in the Seventeenth Century* (New York,
The Macmillan Company, 1895), Vol. II, p. 233.

[34] Weeden, William B., *Economic and Social History of New England, 1620–1798*
(Boston, Houghton Mifflin Company, 1894), Vol. II, p. 863. See also " Dr. Eph-
raim Eliot's Account of the Physicians of Boston," in *Proceedings of the Massachusetts
Historical Society,* 1863 (Boston, The Society, 1864), Vol. VII, p. 181.

What Weeden considers modest fees for physicians would undoubtedly have appeared large for schoolmasters and it seems probable that the former was the more lucrative position of the two.

Small cites the case of Dr. Return Johnson of Medfield, who was simultaneously schoolmaster and practicing physician. According to the report, it was found that, "being much abroad out of town" on account of his medical demands, the two occupations did not go well together. Johnson, therefore, consented to the cancellation of his contract. It is significant that it was teaching which he relinquished rather than his medical practice.[35]

Judging by the number of individuals who used teaching as a steppingstone to the legal profession, the latter seemed to be a preferable vocation from the standpoint of financial rewards. Willis cites the case of two graduates of Harvard College who were teaching in Portland, Maine, in 1761—Mr. David Wyer and Theophilus Bradbury. These young men were studying law while keeping school. Both of them remained but a short time in teaching and as soon as they were admitted to the bar they abandoned the classroom for their legal practice. Similarly Theophilus Parsons, afterwards the Chief Justice of Massachusetts, came to Falmouth, Maine, in May, 1770, to take a school. He stayed three years, during which he pursued the study of law. After being admitted to the Cumberland Bar, in 1774, he devoted himself exclusively to his new profession. According to Willis, "It was very much the custom of that day for young men on their leaving college to sustain themselves while studying their professions by keeping school."[36]

The wages paid to common laborers and artisans constitute another basis for comparison. Here again, unfortunately, the large number of variables leads one to be exceedingly cautious in drawing final conclusions. Labor conditions were vastly different then from those which prevail today, particularly in cities. The average workman of the twentieth century has no income apart

---

[35] Small, Walter H., *op. cit.*, p. 98.
[36] Willis, William, *The History of Portland from 1632 to 1864* (Portland, Bailey and Noyes, 1865), pp. 372, 374–76.

from his wages. This situation was not so universally true in colonial days.

Wages carefully husbanded then could be invested in ways that were certain to bring handsome returns. William Bullock has left an interesting opinion as to how a hired laborer, in 1649, earning three pounds a year should dispose of his earnings. He believed that a part of the sum received should go to the purchase of a heifer, and twenty shillings of it into buying three or four flitches of Virginia bacon for exportation to England, where they could be easily disposed of for two pounds, three shillings, and fourpence. This amount was to be invested in pins, laces, and combs "for the maids," which commanded in Virginia double the price current in England, insuring the owner upon his original investment in bacon not less than five pounds sterling. In the meantime his cow would probably give birth to a calf, and his wages for the second year become due. At the end of four years, Bullock estimated, the laborer, by following this course in his trading, ought to have accumulated sixty pounds sterling, and if he had been allowed by his employer to cultivate a patch of tobacco of his own, this sum would be very materially increased.[37]

One of Bullock's contemporaries says of laborers, in 1642, that "there are many hundreds of labouring men, who had not enough to bring them over, yet now worth scores, and some hundreds of pounds."[38] It is certain that the laborer of colonial days frequently possessed land, raised cows, cultivated tobacco or other produce, owned oxen and rented them to the town for use in construction and repairing roads. Many with business acumen lifted themselves out of the lower economic levels and attained a degree of leisure and prosperity. Free mechanics in seventeenth-century Virginia, according to Bruce, probably did not enjoy even a moderate degree of prosperity from their trades. There are many evidences, however, that numerous persons belonging to this class possessed considerable wealth, probably the result of cultivating tobacco on their own account as much as

[37] Bullock, William, *Virginia* (London, John Hammond, 1649), pp. 53–54.
[38] Johnson, Capt. Edward, *Wonder-Working Providence of Sions Saviour in New England*, etc. (London, Nath, Brooke, 1654), p. 175.

through the earnings from their mechanical work.[39] This happy condition of affairs must not be interpreted as characteristic of common labor in all the colonies, but it is true that the highly industrialized state of today is far more rigid as regards the vertical movement of labor than was true of the seventeenth and eighteenth centuries.

In view of these opportunities for labor to supplement the regular established wage in the early development of America, comparisons of the earnings of labor with those of professional workers must be made with caution. Fortunately, in the case of the schoolmaster there is good reason to believe that his salary is not a fair measure of his income. As a group, teachers were even more favorably situated with regard to land ownership and outside earnings than common labor.[40] Some of the better schoolmasters in the larger communities undoubtedly acquired property. Ezekiel Cheever of Boston is reported to have left an estate valued at eight hundred and thirty-seven pounds, nineteen shillings, and sixpence. While this sum is relatively insignificant when contrasted with the estates of some of the successful merchants of Cheever's time, it is improbable that he accumulated this property solely out of his modest salary. Heatwole, in commenting on the Virginia pedagogues, says: "There are a number of records, particularly among deeds of transfer, that indicate that these Virginia schoolmasters accumulated enough money to purchase considerable estates." [41] While land in Virginia was undoubtedly cheap, the ownership of tillable soil made it possible for the teacher to increase his annual income by whatever amount of tobacco or other commodity he could produce.

The wages of skilled and unskilled labor during the colonial period varied somewhat from time to time and from place to place. Between 1690 and 1713 common laborers could earn two shillings a day in New England and between two shillings threepence and three shillings in New York and New Jersey.[42] A skilled laborer like John Marshall earned about four shillings

---

[39] Bruce, Philip A., *op. cit.*, p. 418, and his sources.
[40] Crippen, John H., *op. cit.*, p. 59.
[41] Heatwole, Cornelius J., *op. cit.*, p. 53.
[42] Weeden, William B., *op. cit.*, p. 400.

or sixty-six and two thirds cents a day at Braintree from 1697 to 1711. In addition to farming on a small scale, Marshall made laths in winter, was painter and carpenter, acted as messenger, burned bricks, and bought and sold stock.[43] Carpenters were apparently paid a little more generously than Marshall, for they received between five and six shillings a day in Pennsylvania in 1698 and those who worked on the Boston Town Hall were paid five shillings (83.3 cents) a day "all cash." The bricklayers on this same job received six shillings.[44]

In a few instances the wages paid to teachers and laborers are reported for the same community or region. At Leicester, for example, in 1739, Mr. Samuel Coolidge, the schoolmaster, received the equivalent of one dollar and thirty-two cents a week plus board, while laboring men in this same general area were paid the equivalent of thirty-three cents a day for their services, and in addition one half this amount for the use of a yoke of oxen on the highway.[45]

Occasionally, the salaries of schoolmasters were no higher than two shillings a day, although, as a previous discussion indicates, the rate of pay was generally larger than this. The teacher's wage was usually fixed by the year and was not dependent upon weather and other unpredictable factors which affected many types of skilled and unskilled laborers. The total yearly salary income of the schoolmaster was probably greater in most instances than that of the skilled laborer, who was paid on a daily basis and presumably was unemployed a number of days during the year.

The comparisons which have been made in this chapter refer only to school*masters* and no attempt has been made to appraise women teachers' wages. The salaries of schoolmistresses and schooldames were consistently lower than those awarded men. Since the number of women teachers in the colonial period was relatively insignificant, however, and in no way representative

[43] Charles F. Adams, Jr., Memorandum on John Marshall's Diary, in *Proceedings of the Massachusetts Historical Society*, 1884 (Boston, The Society, 2d series, 1885), Vol. I, pp. 148–49.

[44] *History of Wages in the United States from Colonial Times to 1928*, U. S. Department of Labor, Bureau of Labor Statistics (1929), Bulletin No. 499, p. 51,

[45] Small, Walter H., *op. cit.*, p. 144.

of the profession as a whole, this omission seems amply justified.

From the fragmentary data just discussed, it appears that colonial teachers were probably paid higher wages than common laborers in most sections of the country; that the total yearly wages of teachers, including perquisites, were not greatly different from those of skilled carpenters, bricklayers, and other craftsmen; that clergymen usually received two or three times as much salary as teachers; and that physicians and lawyers also fared better than pedagogues. The most striking fact in the data which have been assembled is the wide variation in the wages assigned teachers, both among the several colonies and within individual provinces.

FORM OF PAYMENT

The reader will undoubtedly have deduced from the preceding discussion on teachers' salaries that money represented only one form of compensation. Currency was scarce in those days and it was much easier to exchange services and commodities than it was to collect and pay out actual cash money. Therefore, in the several colonies, we find interesting practices growing up pertaining to the payment of schoolmasters.

Prior to 1700, the most widely used mediums of exchange in New England were beaver skins and "country pay." The latter consisted of agricultural products and livestock. Massachusetts made corn [46] legal tender in 1631 for all debts, unless money or beaver had been expressly stated in the contract. Thus we find that Dedham in 1685 engaged a schoolmaster for the space of half a year for seven pounds in corn pay and five pounds in money.[47]

The fluctuations in the prices of corn, tobacco, and livestock frequently worked serious hardship on schoolmasters, the shrinkage amounting in some cases to fifty per cent of their salaries. In Virginia, wages were quoted in pounds of tobacco and the schoolmasters in this colony were frequent losers by the depreciation in the value of their pay from year to year. Presumably

---

[46] Corn also included "several species of grain and even peas." *History of Wages in the United States*, p. 14.

[47] "Dedham Town Records," *op. cit.*, Vol. V, p. 170.

they sometimes profited, although the records are strangely silent on this point.

In New Netherland, the schoolmaster's pay consisted variously of wampum, beaver skins, the coin of Holland, and wheat. Silver apparently replaced commodity equivalents for the most part after 1700, and not until the Revolution was "country pay" resorted to again to any great extent in the payment of wages.

A Dutch Schoolmaster Receiving His Pay in Wampum

In addition to the payment of schoolmasters in some form of commodity, such as corn, wheat, livestock, and tobacco, it was fairly common to provide them with a dwelling and a few acres of land for cultivation as a part of their wage. While the management of the Dutch schools differed in many ways from the procedure followed by the English, the arrangement described below for paying schoolmaster Joosten illustrates the type of practice reported in many of the colonies of furnishing dwellings and providing for use of land. Jacob Joosten was employed to teach in Flatbush in 1670. Among the articles in the contract regulating his school and stipulating the sources of his remuneration is this one: [48]

To receive in addition an annual salary of 300 gl. in wampum, or grain, to be delivered at the ferry; in addition a house free of rent, with a garden and use of lands belonging to the school and annually from each farm one load of manure and one load of firewood or the value thereof, and next summer a new and proper dwelling house on the school lot.

In Boston, in 1652, according to Seybolt, "Dwellings, owned by the town, were provided for some of the masters" and in other instances the town appropriated a flat rent allowance which permitted the master to choose his own house. [49]

This same practice was followed in Maryland and in South Carolina. The visitors in Queen Anne's County held out the following inducement to those interested in finding a school to "keep": [50]

Whereas a master is wanted in Queen Anne's County free school, any gentleman who can teach the English, Latin and Greek languages, reading, writing, and arithmetic will meet with encouragement by applying to the visitors of said school; 100 acres of land belong to said school, about 60 whereof are under good fence with a good dwelling house, 40 x 22 feet, two rooms below stairs and as many above, a cellar under one half of the house and two small outhouses besides the school house which is large and commodious, situate in a thick settled neighborhood where are a good number of children.

While the above advertisement was scheduled to appear shortly after the Revolution, the perquisites promised were typical of earlier arrangements.

There were many other emoluments and favors available in the larger communities which enabled schoolmasters to supplement, in some small measure, their relatively low cash wages. The colonial schoolmaster was granted a sort of concession on the ink business, the manufacture and sale of quill pens, and the

[48] Kilpatrick, William H., *op. cit.*, p. 168.
[49] Seybolt, Robert F., *The Public Schools of Colonial Boston, 1635–1775*, pp. 50, 52.
[50] Brown, Edwin H., *op. cit*, p. 11. (Prepared for the *Pennsylvania Journal*, December 11, 1782.)

sale of copy books; he was also frequently allowed to use the school building for his own private tutoring outside of school hours.   Many communities in the North made it possible for him to make a little money out of fuel transactions, although some schoolmasters perhaps lost money on this proposition.   In Boston, for example, the master was allowed to collect not more than five shillings apiece for "firing."   Some teachers used special scholarship pupils for cultivating their gardens and working around the dwelling.[51]   Occasionally, pupils from a distance boarded at the schoolmaster's, thus providing an additional source of revenue.

In the smaller communities, certain other privileges beyond those just cited were sometimes extended.   In 1677, for example, Daniel Epes, the schoolmaster at Salem, was to have, in addition to a minimum salary of sixty pounds, the right to commonage (feeding his cattle on town land).[52]   A few cases suggest that the schoolmaster received his board as a part of the consideration for teaching school.   In 1683 this was the situation in Dorchester, where William Deneson was allowed twenty pounds and his accommodation and diet.[53]   Similarly a New Haven agreement of 1651 with the schoolmaster, Mr. Thomas Hanford, provided for twenty pounds a year and the town to pay for his chamber and diet.[54]   It is impossible to say to what extent the practices just reported are typical for the various colonies, because of the infrequency with which they appear in public records.

Tuition—A Part of the Salary

Until education became free, schoolmasters in nearly all the colonies were privileged to collect tuition (the amounts usually having been stipulated in the agreement) and to appropriate some or all of the money collected from this source.   As the importance of public education became more firmly established in the minds of governing bodies, the practice of allowing tuition

[51] The term "benefit of scholars," to which schoolmasters were frequently entitled, sometimes implied, in addition to fees, light manual labor.

[52] Felt, Joseph B., *Annals of Salem* (Salem, W. and S. B. Ives, 1845), Vol. **I**, pp. 434–35.

[53] "Dorchester Town Records," *op. cit.*, Vol. IV, p. 262; see also *ibid.*, p. 271.

[54] New Haven Historical Society, *New Haven Town Records, 1649–1662*, Vol. I, p. 99.

charges to be retained by the schoolmaster gradually disappeared and a flat sum was voted for his salary regardless of the number of tuition pupils. Throughout the colonial period, however, tuition charges constituted an important item in the compensation of schoolmasters. Illustrations of this practice are legion. A few will suffice to show the type of procedure followed.

In 1671 in Charlestown, Benjamin Tompson, a celebrated poet, physician, and teacher, was engaged by the selectmen to keep school for thirty pounds a year and he was to receive twenty shillings from each particular scholar.[55] In Newbury, the records of 1687 show that the master received "twenty pounds . . . in good country pay, besides what the schollers shall give." [56]

Malden records mention the case of Ezekiel Jenkins who was employed there in 1702–1703. He was "to have 3 pounds for ye yeer: and ye befitit of ye scollars." The next year he agreed to serve "for thirty shilings money and he to have ye benifit of ye scholars." He enjoyed these terms until he died in 1705. His gravestone at Sandy Bank bears the unusual inscription: "Mauldens Late School Master From A Painful Life Is Gone To Take His Rest His Lord Hath calld Hi^m Who^me." [57] Whether or not the "painful life" mentioned in his epitaph resulted from the difficulties he encountered in trying to balance his budget is not clearly indicated but that problem undoubtedly contributed to his troubled existence. Similarly in New York, in 1705, Andrew Clark was paid fifty pounds by the government, plus the usual quarterly fee from each scholar.[58]

The tuition of poor scholars was often borne by the church. Thus the Parochial School of the Dutch Reformed Church in Philadelphia (around 1760) provided for the schoolmaster's salary in the following way: "Each child shall pay five shillings per quarter for tuition. But in case the parents are poor, the

[55] See *Charlestown Archives*, Vol. XXI, p. 59, in *New England Historical and Genealogical Register*, Vol. XV, under "Cheever."

[56] *Town of Newbury Records*, 1680–1692, Vol. II, p. 71, in Currier, John J., *History of Newbury, Massachusetts, 1635–1902* (Boston, Damrell and Upham, 1902), p. 400.

[57] Corey, Deloraine P., *The History of Malden, Massachusetts, 1633–1785* (Malden, 1899), p. 603.

[58] Kemp, William W., *op. cit.*, p. 72.

Elders may pay the schoolmaster three shillings out of the church treasury." [59]

Some communities varied the tuition rate according to the subject taught. In Northampton, for example, the master received ten pounds from the town and, in addition, pupils paid "ffowre pence [5.6 cents] per weeke for such as are in the primer & other English books and Six pence [8.4 cents] per weeke to learne the Accidence [Latin grammar], Wrighting Casting Accounts." [60]

EXEMPTIONS

Teachers were exempt from taxation in some of the colonies, although the rule was by no means universal. Prior to 1700, Massachusetts had provided for the exemption of grammar-school masters from poll taxes, from watch and ward taxes, and from taxes on their personal estates.[61] No mention, however, is made of writing-school masters in the statute on exemptions. If Boston practice is any guide, the tax collectors were exceedingly generous in their interpretation of the intent of the statute and it was frequently extended to include schoolmasters in the lower grades.

Kilpatrick reports the following interesting incident which occurred in Bergen, New Netherland, about 1661, from which it appears that the matter of taxing schoolmasters was a disputed one in this colony: [62]

It seems that about fifteen months after the school had been in operation [in Bergen] certain soldiers were quartered in the town. Each family was to maintain one. Steenhuysen, the schoolmaster, declined to receive one, whereat the "majority of the community" complained, feeling that since Steenhuysen was the "owner of a house and lot and of a double bouwery in the jurisdiction of the village," he should pay his part. "This," in the words of the plaintiffs in the suit, "has aggrieved the said Englebert Steenhuysen so much that he has resigned

---

[59] Wickersham, James P., *op. cit.*, p. 141.

[60] Johnson, Clifton, *Old-Time Schools and School-Books* (New York, The Macmillan Company, 1917), p. 5.

[61] Clews, Elsie W., *op. cit.*, p. 65.

[62] Kilpatrick, William H., *op. cit.*, pp. 137–38. A "bouwery" is a farm or plantation.

his office, asserting that a schoolmaster should be exempt from all village taxes and burden, as it is customary, he says, everywhere in Christendom."

The Schout and Schepens demurred to this plea, conceding that it might be valid if the schoolmaster had only the school lot but not when he owned a lot and double bouwery. Professors, preachers, and rectors were exempt from taxation in Holland, and Steenhuysen evidently assumed that this practice should be followed in New Netherland as well. In Virginia, around 1686, county courts sought to attract schoolteachers within their counties by offering them the added inducement of exemption from taxation for a period of time.[63]

Just how extensive this practice of excusing teachers from paying taxes really was is not evident from the researches available in colonial education. It seems probable that conditions of supply and demand, rather than any fundamental belief in the efficacy of the principle, determined the policy of the early settlers regarding it in most of the colonies. To the degree that colonial schoolmasters were exempt from paying property taxes, their stipulated salaries were an inadequate measure of their compensation, since exemptions constitute "free income."

Sources of Salary Revenue

Teachers' salaries were derived from several sources. In Massachusetts, each town was permitted to "appoint" its own method of supporting schools. This policy of leaving to each local community the matter of providing for the master's wage was typical of nearly all the colonies.

As reported elsewhere in this chapter, schoolmasters were frequently paid directly by the parents of the children attending school. Tuition rates were almost universal and only the poorer families were exempt from payment. An important qualification for success as a schoolmaster in many colonial communities was the ability to collect money, and the responsibility of making a going concern out of the school frequently rested heavily on his shoulders. Additional funds for salaries were often secured from the rental of town lands. It was quite common in

[63] Heatwole, Cornelius J., *op. cit.*, p. 52.

New England, for example, to set aside a parcel of land, the rent from which was earmarked for maintenance of schools. As early as January 10, 1641, Boston provided "that Deare-Island shall be Improoved for the maintenance of a free schoole for the Towne, and such other Occasions as the Townsmen For the time being shall thinke meet, the sayd schoole being sufficiently Provided for." [64]

Later, Boston applied the rentals from its wharf and dock toward the support of schools. Plymouth Colony "farmed its fisheries of bass and mackerel on the Cape coast and gave the proceeds to the support of the public schools." From 1684 to 1693 the rental from these fisheries was thirty pounds (one hundred dollars) per annum.[65] The foundation schools in Virginia were financed almost wholly by rentals of tobacco land and in Savannah, Georgia, in 1760, market stalls were leased to pay the teacher. Rentals, therefore, constituted an important source of revenue and made the payment of teachers' salaries relatively easy in those communities where the demand for the use of land or other property exceeded the supply.

Support was also derived from legacies, voluntary contributions, semicompulsory contributions such as those provided by the Quakers in Pennsylvania, and from general tax levies or rates. In Queen Anne's County, Maryland, in addition to a county levy, the schoolmaster's salary was derived from "an additional duty of 20 shillings current money per poll on all Irish servants being Papist, to prevent the growth of popery by the importation of too great number of them into the province and an additional 20 shillings per poll on all negroes imported into the province." Beyond this, certain fines when collected were due the school—such as the fines for killing deer and the fines imposed for a white person marrying a colored person. In case the fines were not paid, the guilty persons were sold and the money received from the sale made available for the school.[66] In fact, nearly every money-raising device known to man was tried out by the colonists in their efforts to raise funds for the support of schools.

---

[64] "Boston Town Records," *op. cit.*, Vol. II, p. 65.
[65] Weeden, William B., *op. cit.*, p. 247.   [66] Brown, Edwin H., *op. cit.*, p. 11.

OTHER SALARY PROBLEMS CONFRONTING THE SCHOOLMASTERS
OF THE COLONIAL PERIOD

Time of Payment. The twentieth-century teacher expects to receive her salary in ten or twelve installments, at regular scheduled dates during the year of her service. This practice is so uniform in the United States that it has long ceased to be considered a matter of concern.

The colonial schoolmaster was not so fortunately situated. Frequently he was paid twice a year, and in the more advanced communities four times. In Dedham, in 1653, the selectmen agreed with Jacob Farrow to keep the school for twenty pounds per annum and to be paid at the end of each half year.[67] Similarly, in 1668, John Prudden, schoolmaster at Roxbury, was promised his salary of twenty-five pounds in two installments, half on the twenty-ninth of September and the other half "to be payed on March 25." [68] Ezekiel Cheever in Boston (1693) was paid quarterly. Seybolt reports: "The town did not establish a 'pay day,' on which all schoolmasters received their stipends. Each salary was 'to be paid quarterly as it shall become due.' The quarters began with the dates of appointment." [69] Boston probably represented the best practice in New England, for in one case at least, in Dorchester, a three-year contract with Ichabod Wiswall called for the salary to be paid annually at or before the first of March.[70]

Delinquency. More discouraging to the early schoolmasters than the long intervals between salary payments was the tendency for communities to be in arrears in the payment of salaries. Sometimes teachers waited for a year or more after the regular scheduled date of payment for their salaries. That this situation was not unique is evidenced by the fact that even in Boston, in 1671, a full year's salary was owing "Capt. Daniell Hinksman" after he left the "Free Schoole." [71]

Under these conditions it was necessary for the schoolmaster

---

[67] "Dedham Town Records," *op. cit.*, Vol. III, p. 213.
[68] Ellis, Charles M., *op. cit.*, p. 52.
[69] Seybolt, Robert F., *The Public Schools of Colonial Boston*, p. 44.
[70] "Dorchester Town Records," *op. cit.*, Vol. IV, pp. 73–74.
[71] "Boston Town Records," *op. cit.*, Vol. VII, p. 63.

to borrow from his friends, ask for long-term credit at stores, or sometimes, with the permission of the collectors, to receive money direct from those taxpayers who were willing to pay part or all of their obligations to the teacher (especially if they happened to be friendly with him). Complaints because of arrears in payments were fairly common and it is doubtful if teachers achieved any immediate relief from them, since the money simply wasn't available. Small apparently believed this condition was due to the inability of the communities to pay rather than to any disposition on their part to withhold the money, for he says: "People and towns were poor, but everywhere there seemed to be the desire to deal fairly with the schoolmaster." [72] Seybolt, on the other hand, in writing of Boston practices, indicates that "the town considered other obligations more pressing and at times gave them preference." [73]

Sick Leave and Retirement Provisions. Most progressive school systems today make reasonably generous provisions for the absence of teachers on account of illness. While considerable variation exists with regard to the specific practice followed, the principle of payment during illness is sufficiently well established now to command the support of many boards of education. A typical provision is ten days' sick leave annually with full pay. The colonists were not unmindful of this problem of providing for disabled teachers and we find individual instances of generous provision such as the following one: [74]

The Town took into consideration the Petition of M[r]. John Vinal, Usher to the South Writing School, that an allowance may be made him, in consideration of the Straits and Difficultys he has been reduced to by means of the Small Pox—After debate had thereon

Voted, that the Sum of Fifteen Pounds be and hereby is allowed the said M[r]. Vinal, for the reasons above mentioned. . . .

Unfortunately, illustrations of sick-leave provisions during the colonial period are too few in number to warrant the assumption

[72] Small, Walter H., *op. cit.*, p. 156.
[73] Seybolt, Robert F., *The Public Schools of Colonial Boston*, p. 45.
[74] "Boston Town Records," 1764, *op. cit.*, Vol. XVI, pp. 118–19.

that they were at all common. It is interesting to note, however, that they were not altogether unheard of.

In a similar fashion, gratuities were occasionally provided to care for superannuated teachers. In the case of schoolmaster Peleg Wiswell of Boston (1766), the town voted a sum of one hundred pounds for his support the year after his retirement and in answer to his request for aid replied "that the disposition of the Town was such that we could not doubt he would be provided for during the remainder of his Days." [75]

Salem was generous with Edward Norris, who taught the grammar school there for more than thirty years. When he retired in 1671, he received a pension of ten pounds a year from the town.[76] A few instances are recorded where widows of schoolmasters received either a pension or some other gratuity from the governing body of the school. Widow Woodmansey of Boston (1669), whose husband had been a schoolmaster, was allowed by the town eight pounds per annum for house rent during her widowhood.[77] Kilpatrick reports that after the death of Mr. Welp, a teacher in the Dutch school in New Netherland around 1770, the church (Dutch Reformed) "canceled a debt against his estate of 5 pounds, paid his funeral expenses, allowed the family to continue in the church house for some months without charge, and gave the widow an annual pension of 20 pounds." [78]

That these cases were not typical of practice in all the colonies is indicated by the neglect shown to a Philadelphia pedagogue, as revealed in the following news item taken from the *Pennsylvania Gazette* of November 29, 1733:

On Monday evening last, Mr. Thomas Meakins fell off a wharf into the Delaware, and before he could be taken out again, was drowned. He was an ancient man, and formerly lived very well in this city [Philadelphia], teaching a considerable school; but of late years was reduced to extreme poverty.

While the isolated provisions described here were a far cry from the teachers' pension and retirement arrangements of mod-

[75] *Ibid.*, Vol. XX, p. 243. [76] Felt, Joseph B., *Annals of Salem*, p. 433.
[77] "Boston Town Records," *op. cit.*, Vol. VII, p. 53.
[78] Kilpatrick, William H., *op. cit.*, p. 157.

ern times, they nevertheless indicate that early recognition was given to the principle of providing for public servants who had devoted their life energies to the affairs of the community. Precedents such as those established in Boston, Salem, and the Dutch school in New Netherland were instrumental, in later years, in securing a more generous and certain allowance for the sick and retiring members of the profession than their progenitors had been able to secure.

X

Social Status of Colonial Schoolteachers

EDUCATIONAL historians of the colonial period give us varying impressions of the social status of the early schoolteacher. Some would have us believe that the master was a low, coarse fellow, an adventurer, rogue, or ne'er-do-well, often an indentured servant who was given to running away and was retrieved through an advertised reward like a slave or a criminal. Others picture him as a man respected and honored in the community.

Davis, in his *History of Wallingford*, assigns him a place in the minds of the people close to that held by the minister, pointing out that:[1]

In New England, ever since the first free school was established amidst the woods that covered the peninsula of Boston in 1636, the schoolmaster has been found on the border line between savage and civilized life, often indeed with the axe to open his own path, but always looked up to with respect, and always carrying with him a valuable and preponderating influence. Next to the minister, ruling elder and magistrate, he was regarded with the profoundest respect, and when he walked through the village, or rambled in the fields, with his head bowed down in meditation upon some grave moral question, or solving some ponderous sum, the boys never dared pass him without pulling off their hats. He was among the few who received the title of "Mr." and stood next to the minister in the minds of the people; just as he does in Goldsmith's inimitable description in "The Deserted Village."

For the most part, however, these conflicting impressions are more confusing than contradictory and can be accounted for in several ways. In the first place, there were notable geographical

---

[1] Davis, Charles H. S., *op. cit.*, p. 308.

differences. The schoolmaster's prestige varied greatly from colony to colony, and sometimes even from settlement to settlement within a given colony—hence no generalization can be made for America as a whole. Also, a master's social status might be governed by the type of school he taught. The rector of a Latin school was considered to be on a distinctly higher plane than one who taught in the English school and was much more nearly equal in position to the clergymen. Moreover, the time element is not to be ignored. The colonial period lasted well over a hundred years, and during this time there grew up distinct social and economic cleavages between the frontier groups and the rising middle class. These were sufficient to permit many changes in attitude on the part of the populace toward education and the social position of schoolmasters. And, finally, the school-teachers of that day did not constitute a caste in which the social status of one member is the same as that of every other member; on the contrary, they must be thought of as individuals whose prestige was affected by their respective characters, person-alities, wealth, and cultural backgrounds as well as by their vocation.

One must proceed cautiously, then, in discussing the relative position of the schoolmaster in the social hierarchy of colonial society. For colonial society was by no means democratic. Seventeenth-century America resembled seventeenth-century England in consisting of a succession of well-marked social planes. The early settlers brought over from the Old Country strong traditions of rank and privilege, which they conscientiously strove to maintain; and while the extremes were absent in the new country, a number of different levels were rather sharply distinguished.

The great body of the people were those known as "Goodman" or "Goodwife" So-and-so. Generally they were yeomen and owners of land. Below these was the servant class, which included farm and houseworkers, apprentices, and indentured laborers performing widely varied types of service. Above were the more distinguished families, whose lords were entitled to the designation "Mr." At the top were the magistrates and ministers.

Seating in the Meetinghouse

One of the clearest indications of the stratification of society in early New England was the manner of seating the congregation in the meetinghouse (church) according to their adjudged rank. Particular seats were assigned to the more prominent individuals in the community and the people were admonished not to press into seats already allotted. Some pews belonged to the congregation and were assigned to individuals, and some were built and owned personally, according to the vote of the society. Men and women were commonly segregated on opposite sides of the church. So jealous, indeed, were these respectable worthies of the distinction conferred upon them by the pews in which they sat that a public apology or a heavy fine might be exacted from those who trespassed upon the more "honorable" precincts reserved for others.

A formal seating list was usually drawn up by a special town committee, sometimes by the selectmen or elders, or was voted on by the whole congregation. Frequent revisions and rearrangements were necessary to keep abreast of changes in social status or to appease the beruffled pride of those who felt themselves slighted. For even after the most minute consideration had been given to nice distinctions of dignity, office, age, property, and at a later date to the relative amounts contributed to the minister's salary, there was much dissatisfaction among the congregation, which not infrequently culminated in a serious disturbance.

Thus the official seating list of the meetinghouse represented New England's social register. Unfortunately, we know in all too few instances what seats were occupied by the schoolmaster and his wife. Perhaps this is significant in itself. If the schoolmaster had been universally, or even very commonly, a socially prominent personage, would not some general indication of this fact have crept into the town records, letters, and diaries which have survived to modern times, in connection with the assignment of seats in the meetinghouse? The few direct statements we do have, however, accord the schoolmaster a decidedly "honorable" social position, as the following excerpts show.

"Dr. Bentley notes from records in 1699 that . . . the school-master's wife was voted a seat in the 'Women 2ᵈ Pew.' This was probably in the Salem parish." [2]

In Salem, "to show proper respect to the schoolmaster in placing the families in the meetinghouse, the wife of the grammar schoolmaster was to be accommodated in the pew next to the wives of the magistrates." [3]

In New York, it was "ordered that a New Gallery be built over the West Gallery if the charge thereof can be defrayed by Subscriptions and when built the front pews to be appropriated to Housekeepers & their wives, Masters of Vessels and their wives and Schoolmasters & their wives." [4]

In 1721 Wallingford, Connecticut, "gave Mr. Bates, the schoolmaster, liberty to sit in the first pew in the front gallery of the new meetinghouse." [5] With reference to the position accorded the master of another Connecticut town is this: "And as evidence of this respect, it may be mentioned that in the bill for fitting up the first meetinghouse in Windsor there is a separate item for wainscoting and elevating pews, to be occupied by the magistrates, the deacon's family, and the schoolmaster." [6]

While these references to the seating of schoolmasters are obviously too few in number to constitute any proof positive that teachers occupied a rung high up on the ladder in American colonial society, they do point consistently in that direction.

TITLES

A second objective gauge of the social status of the colonial schoolmaster is the prevalence with which he is accorded the title of "Mr." or "Sir" in town records and other documents. In the early days most of the colonists were addressed as "Goodman." The word "Mr." betokened respect and was a badge of social distinction which was not conferred on everybody. Indeed, only one freeman in fourteen was so designated in the Massachusetts of 1649.

[2] Dr. William Bentley ms., in Weeden, William B., *op. cit.*, pp. 417–18.
[3] Small, W. B., *op. cit.*, p. 115.
[4] Trinity Vestry Minutes, September 15, 1718, Vol. I, p. 116, in Kemp, William W., *op. cit.*, p. 91.
[5] Davis, Charles H. S., *op. cit.*, p. 315.   [6] Small, W. H., *op. cit.*, p. 115.

SCHOOLMASTER BATES'S SEAT IN THE MEETINGHOUSE

The corresponding term "Mistress," or "Mrs.," was at first applied to both wife and daughter of a "Master" or "Mr." In later documents this appellation seems to have been reserved for married women of good social position, while single women of similar rank were mentioned without title. An inferior social status was indicated by the term "Goodwife," or "Goody." The use of "Miss" to designate any young female did not appear until after 1720. The general application of "Mr.," "Mrs.," and "Miss" was a reflection of a slowly emerging recognition of personal rights, which did not become apparent until a much later date.

A careful examination of town records, letters, diaries, and other documents of the colonial period, with the significance of such titles in mind, would thus throw much light on the social status of the schoolmaster. Crippen made such a study for Dedham, based on the contracts of employment quoted in Slafter *The Schools and Teachers of Dedham, Massachusetts.* He found that at least thirty-two, or nearly half of the sixty-six schoolmasters who taught in that community between 1644 and 1757 were addressed either as "Mr." or "Sir." Even this is not exhaustive, however, as Crippen admits "that by a careful study of the Town Records of Dedham this number would be increased from thirty-two to between forty and forty-five, as many of the contracts of employment were not given by Mr. Slafter." [7]

Out of a list of twenty-one names recorded in 1660 as "creditor to the towne" of Watertown, only three, including schoolmaster Norcross, received the distinction of having the word "Mr." before their names. One person was regularly called "Lieutenant," which was probably a mark of respect. [8]

The number of individuals who were entitled to use the designation "Mr." is not known. Felt, in his *History of Ipswich, Essex, and Hamilton,* says:

The title of *Mr.* was applied to captains and sometimes to mates of vessels; to military captains; to eminent merchants; to schoolmasters, doctors, magistrates, and clergymen; to persons who had received a second degree at college, and who had been made freemen. The wives and daughters of such individuals were called *Mrs.* To be deprived of this address was deemed a serious degradation.[9]

Limited in scope as this evidence is, it definitely tends to place the schoolmaster in the upper crust of New England society, at least in the vicinity of Boston.

One caution should be observed, however, in inferring from this that the office of schoolmaster always carried with it sufficient social prestige to earn for its occupant the title of "Mr." There is another possible interpretation. It is conceivable that the term "Mr." as used in New England is a corruption or abbreviation of the academic degree of "Master" conferred by a college or university, and that it came to be used loosely by the populace as a deferential mode of address for those with a considerable educational background. Thus it may be merely a coincidence (although a natural one, since it is not to be wondered at that the better-educated should frequently gravitate into the teaching profession) that so large a percentage of the Dedham schoolmasters were accorded the title "Mr." and that the Watertown schoolmaster should have been one of the few townsmen to be similarly designated in that community.

This interpretation of the situation is supported by the following quotations from authors who were familiar with the customs of the colonial period:

In the town records of 1638 four persons have Mr. prefixed to their names, to indicate that they had taken the Master's degree at a University.[10]

The schoolmaster had local dignity, especially if he were a college graduate; "sir" was his usual title under that condition. Many records are found in which "Sir" is prefixed to the surname and the first name omitted, as, for example, "Sir Fox."[11]

That he [schoolmaster Norcross] was respected for his education is shown by the use of the word "Mr." when he is first mentioned.[12]

[9] Felt, J. B., *op. cit.*, p. 23.
[10] Slafter, Carlos, *The Schools and Teachers of Dedham, Massachusetts, 1644–1904* (Dedham, Mass., Dedham Transcript Press, 1905), p. 6.
[11] Small, W. H., *op. cit.*, p. 115.   [12] Crippen, J. C., *op. cit.*, p. 67.

This deduction is further reinforced by the fact that not *all* schoolmasters in any given community were accorded the term "Mr.," which would be an inexplicable inconsistency if the office itself were the sole determining factor. The typical New England schoolmaster *did* have considerable social prestige, but probably by virtue of his superior education rather than because of his vocation.

In New Netherland, the title "Mr." is so regularly accorded the schoolmaster that Kilpatrick, in working out his chronology of Dutch teachers, relies on it as a positive means of identifying the master. Further study of Dutch customs would be necessary to determine what social significance this title carried with it— whether it was a badge of social distinction, a mark of respect accorded one with a superior formal education, or merely a convenient abbreviation for "Master" or "Schoolmaster."

Unfortunately, the author has been unable to locate any source material or any discussion by secondary authors dealing specifically with the subject of titles and mode of address in Pennsylvania, New Jersey, Delaware, or the Southern colonies. Social distinctions of any kind were abhorrent to the Quakers, so that group is automatically eliminated, and for the rest of the colonies other indications will have to serve as the straws that show the direction of the social current.

COLLEGE PLACEMENT

Still a third clue to the social status of the New England schoolmaster is found in the manner of listing students at Harvard and Yale universities. In the catalogues of graduates of Harvard College down to 1772 and in those of Yale down to 1767, the names of the students in each class, instead of being listed alphabetically as at present, were arranged in an order intended to correspond with the rank of their respective fathers or families. Ancestral prestige and also the economic wealth and professional or official standing of his father were the chief criteria used in appraising the relative social position of each student.

The successive classes were usually "placed" toward the end of their freshmen year. Once determined, the arrangement of names stood virtually unchanged ever after, except when an individual was punished for a misdemeanor by "degradation," or change of place, a penalty second only to expulsion in severity. Certain practical advantages accompanied high standing on the class list, such as choice of rooms and precedence at table, but it was chiefly the honor that counted.

That the order of prestige represented by these class lists was a matter of serious concern is evident from the furor created each time a class was "placed." Often the students were enraged beyond measure with disappointment in their relative standing, and there are instances of pique on the part of parents also, at the recognition, or rather the lack of it, accorded their sons. It was only gradually and reluctantly that each class resigned itself to acquiescence in their allotment. Dexter says of this hierarchy:

Probably the general expectation of those who have not looked into the matter would be that with a little study an exact order of precedence, to cover nearly all cases, could be evolved,—somewhat perhaps like this: first sons of Governors, then in due succession sons of Deputy-Governors, of Councillors or Assistants, of ministers, of judges, of lawyers, of doctors, of members of the General Assembly, of justices of the peace and quorum, of militia officers, of merchants, of farmers, of mechanics, and so on. But . . . in practice the arrangement was governed by no such simple formula. Considerations of ancestral distinction, of family estate, of paternal position, and the like, entered into each case in ever-varying combinations, precluding the possibility of any cut-and-dried system.[13]

This passage is noteworthy because of the implication that *if* the students *had* been listed solely according to paternal vocation the above order is the one which would have been approximated. It is significant, therefore, that although the occupations cited descend to civilians of so lowly a rank as merchants, farmers, and mechanics the vocation of teacher is nowhere mentioned. The only conclusion to be drawn is that schoolmasters rated even lower in the social scale.

[13] Dexter, Franklin B., "On Some Social Distinctions at Harvard and Yale, before the Revolution," in *Proceedings of the American Antiquarian Society*, new series, Vol. IX, p. 50 (October, 1893).

This impression is further confirmed by a direct statement of Dexter regarding them:

Next to the three learned professions ought to come that of the teacher; but not so in the regard of these college authorities. At least we find such examples as that of Henry Rust, son of a schoolmaster in Ipswich, Mass., who is allowed to stand last in the class of 1707 at Harvard.

At first glance the implications concerning the social status of New England schoolmasters, gained from the relative rank of their sons at Harvard and Yale, appear to contradict those drawn from their prominent seating in the meetinghouse and the deferential mode of address accorded them. How can it be that the son is typically assigned a decidedly inferior place in college while the father is honored with a front pew and the title of "Mr."? This situation will not seem so paradoxical if it be remembered that the student body of Harvard and of Yale was a highly selected group—more so during the colonial period than at present, and even today it is by no means a typical cross section of the general population. Thus the schoolmaster might easily rank well toward the social top of his own small community and at the same time have a negligible standing among the fathers of college students.

No inferences concerning the relative social standing of schoolmasters' sons can be drawn by this method for the other colonies, however, since this system of cataloguing does not appear to have ever been used in any other American college. And since the student bodies of Harvard and Yale were recruited almost entirely from New England stock, this technique has only a sectional application.

WEALTH

A fourth clue to the social prestige of the colonial schoolmaster is his proportionate share of this world's goods. Since time immemorial, wealth has invested its possessor with a social prestige that cannot be ignored, no matter how greatly it may be despised. To a greater or lesser degree, money, then as now, has always been social as well as legal tender. Our early American forebears were no exception to this general rule. Their deference to wealth is too evident to be disputed. It can be seen in the allotment of seats in the meetinghouse, as in Brookhaven, Long Island, where Pew No. 1 was reserved for those who subscribed twenty shillings toward the minister's salary, while contributors of a mere nine shillings were relegated to Pew No. 6.[14] One can be certain that such a hierarchy was not prompted by an appreciation for financial self-sacrifice, but rather by a recognition that the heaviest contributions came from those who could best afford them and thus constituted a fairly reliable index of the wealth of the populace.

Many New England communities (notably Windsor, Wethersfield, and Waterbury, Connecticut) in their directions to the seating committee specifically mention wealth ("estate") as one of the major attributes to be considered.[15] Certain towns even devised a scale for equilibrating the respective claims of age and money. Thus, in 1719, Waterbury, Connecticut, ordained that four pounds on the tax list should be the equivalent of one year in age,[16] while later in the century the adjacent town of Southington decreed that fifteen pounds were necessary to counterbalance each additional year of age.

Dexter's discussion of college placement further reveals the importance attached to possession of property. The authorities at Yale and Harvard were not insensible to the social significance of tangible wealth as evidenced by the arrangement of the early class lists of students: [17]

In estimating family rank, I believe also that an ample fortune was taken prominently into account, and that some of the perplexing cases, where persons of undoubted family claims are placed low in the class-lists, may in part at least be explained by straitened paternal circumstances. . . .

I may quote also . . . a memorandum made repeatedly by President Clap of Yale in his notebooks, in the times of a greatly depreciated cur-

---

[14] *Records: Town of Brookhaven* (Patchogue, 1880), *op. cit.*, pp. 94–95.

[15] Stiles, Henry R., *History of Ancient Windsor, Connecticut*, p. 356. Stiles, Henry R., *History of Ancient Wethersfield, Connecticut*, p. 222. Bronson, Henry, *History of Waterbury, Connecticut* (Waterbury, Bronson Brothers, 1858), p. 223.

[16] *Ibid.*, p. 223. In other words, a man one year younger but paying four pounds more of taxes than another would be entitled to an equally good seat.

[17] Dexter, F. B., *op. cit.*, pp. 40 ff.

rency [about 1753–1754] where he described the parents of certain students, low in grade, as "of middling estate, much impoverished."

Aside from general family rank, then, in estimating the claims of a student, the comparative wealth or poverty and the professional or official standing of his father were mainly to be regarded.

These college authorities should not be condemned too harshly for their deference to economic wealth. Probably they were not mercenaries with an eye cocked only toward possibilities for future endowment. More likely they reflected the spirit of their times.

The relative wealth of the schoolmaster cannot even be estimated accurately, since the available data are exasperatingly fragmentary. We know that Ezekiel Cheever left an estate valued at eight hundred and thirty-seven pounds, nineteen shillings, and sixpence. This legacy is insignificant when contrasted with the estates of successful merchants and businessmen of the time. The records tell us also that schoolmaster Evert Pietersen of New York was assessed one florin for billeting soldiers, which was the median rate. Kilpatrick concludes from this that "evidently the schoolmasters were about of medium wealth and income." [18] But, in other sections of the same research, he points out the repeated efforts of Pietersen to collect his salary, apparently in vain, despite the fact that he continued to teach year after year. It would seem that he must have had some outside income to sustain himself during this period—real-estate dealings perhaps, or a wealthy wife. "In 1674 his name appears on a list of the sixty-two 'best and most affluent inhabitants' of the city, with 2000 guilders to his credit." [19]

Mr. Aegidius Luyck, of New Amsterdam, also seems to have been a man of substance. In a tax list dated 1674 he was assessed at five thousand guilders, the median being between four thousand and five thousand. For the same year the average wealth of the sixty-two most affluent inhabitants mentioned above was eighty-four hundred guilders. This gives a rough indication of the relative position of two of the most prominent schoolmasters of the period. It should be pointed out, however,

---

[18] Kilpatrick, W. H., *op. cit.*, p. 143.   [19] *Ibid.*, p. 146.

that Luyck was a *Latin* schoolmaster and, furthermore, that he added to that position the offices of minister and magistrate. His case is, therefore, not typical.

It is interesting, and undoubtedly significant, that these are the only two cases, which have come to the author's attention, of schoolmasters who were reckoned as well-to-do men by their contemporaries. Therefore, they mark the all-time high during the colonial period in the matter of wealth, and should be regarded as rare exceptions singled out from the mass of their fellows by virtue of their very dissimilarity in this respect. All the evidence by implication points to the conclusion that economically the *typical* schoolmaster occupied a rather lowly position in the general population.[20] In the Southern colonies, those schoolmasters who were not clergymen must have had an unenviable lot financially. The very ease and frequency with which Southern planters "bought" schoolmasters for a period of years from the captains of incoming vessels bespeaks the relative economic status of the two groups. In fact, schoolmasters did not even rate so high on the commercial scale as skilled artisans, as is clearly indicated by Boucher's oft-quoted statement of 1678: [21]

Not a ship arrives with either redemptioners or convicts in which schoolmasters are not regularly advertised for sale, as weavers, tailors, or trade; with little other difference that I can hear of except perhaps that the former do not usually fetch so good a price as the latter.

As the foregoing discussion implies, the social status of teachers in provincial society cannot be certainly depicted because of the limited and sometimes controversial data which historians have thus far uncovered. When judged by the number to whom the prefix "Mr." was used in addressing them, colonial schoolmasters ranked well in the vanguard of the general population in social prestige. This favorable position of pedagogues in the hierarchy

---

[20] The wealth and social position of schoolmasters undoubtedly were related closely to their annual incomes. As was reported in the chapter on salaries, the pedagogue in colonial days received a much smaller salary than the minister and was about on a par economically in most colonies with the skilled craftsman.

[21] Crippen, J. H., *op. cit.*, pp. 111–12.

of colonial society is further substantiated by the preference shown to schoolteachers in assigning them seats in the meeting-houses. While the number of cases in which schoolmasters are clearly identified in the seating arrangements of the meetings is too small to warrant our drawing a final conclusion about the deference shown them, the little evidence which does exist points consistently to the generalization that grammar-school masters, at least, were accorded a high rank among the churchgoing set.

On the other hand, there is the inference to be drawn from the examination of catalogue lists that schoolmasters' sons were not recognized among the aristocracy at Harvard and Yale, and that their social rank was low in the eyes of the college author-ities at least. Moreover, the economic status of schoolmasters, when judged in terms of their wealth as revealed through either taxation or wills, suggests by implication that as a group they were numbered among the proletariat.

Until historians delve more deeply into the records pertaining to early schoolmasters, one can only speculate as to the true position which they occupied in colonial society. Further study will probably disclose wide differences among the colonies, and even within colonies, in the esteem with which they were held and it seems likely that the prestige which individual teachers enjoyed was attributable more to the personal and professional qualities which they possessed than to their position as peda-gogues.

The colonial schoolmaster is unclassifiable. He was a God-fearing clergyman, he was an unmitigated rogue; he was amply paid, he was accorded a bare pittance; he made teaching a life career, he used it merely as a steppingstone; he was a classical scholar, he was all but illiterate; he was licensed by bishop or colonial governor, he was certified only by his own pretensions; he was a cultured gentleman, he was a crude-mannered yokel; he ranked with the cream of society, he was regarded as a menial. In short, he was neither a type nor a personality, but a statistical distribution represented by a skewed curve.

Suggested Readings for Part I

BOWDEN, HAYGOOD, S., *Two Hundred Years of Education* [*in Georgia*] (Richmond, Va., Dietz Printing Company, 1932).

CURTI, MERLE E., *The Social Ideas of American Educators* (New York, Charles Scribner's Sons, 1935), Chaps. I, II.

EARLE, ALICE M., *Colonial Days in Old New York* (New York, Charles Scribner's Sons, 1896).

FISHER, SYDNEY G., *Men, Women and Manners in Colonial Times* (Philadelphia, J. B. Lippincott Company, 1898), Vols. I, II.

HEATWOLE, CORNELIUS J., *History of Education in Virginia* (New York, The Macmillan Company, 1916).

JOHNSON, CLIFTON, *Old-Time Schools and School-Books* (New York, The Macmillan Company, 1917).

KEMP, WILLIAM W., *The Support of Schools in Colonial New York by the Society for the Propagation of the Gospel in Foreign Parts* (New York, Bureau of Publications, Teachers College, Columbia University, 1913).

KILPATRICK, WILLIAM H., *The Dutch Schools of New Netherland*, U. S. Bureau of Education, Bulletin 1912, No. 12 (Washington, Government Printing Office).

KNIGHT, EDGAR W., *Education in the United States* (New York, Ginn and Company, 1929), Chaps. IV, XI.

LITTLEFIELD, GEORGE E., *Early Schools and Schoolbooks of New England* (Boston, The Club of Odd Volumes, 1904), pp. 55 ff.

SEYBOLT, ROBERT F., *The Public Schools of Colonial Boston, 1635–1775* (Cambridge, Mass., Harvard University Press, 1935).

————, *The Private School*, Source Studies in American Colonial Education, Bulletin No. 28 (Bureau of Educational Research, University of Illinois, 1925).

WEEDEN, WILLIAM B., *Economic and Social History of New England, 1620–1789* (Boston, Houghton Mifflin Company, 1890), Vol. I.

WELLS, GUY F., *Parish Education in Colonial Virginia* (New York, Bureau of Publications, Teachers College, Columbia University, 1923).

WICKERSHAM, JAMES P., *History of Education in Pennsylvania* (Lancaster, Pa., Inquirer Publishing Company, 1886).

WOODY, THOMAS, *Early Quaker Education in Pennsylvania* (New York, Bureau of Publications, Teachers College, Columbia University, 1920).

————, *Quaker Education in the Colony and State of New Jersey* (Philadelphia, The Author, 1923).

PART II

The Public-school Teacher during the Early Years of the Republic

INTRODUCTION

THE HISTORY of American education between 1776 and the Civil War can scarcely be appreciated without at least some knowledge of the social and economic changes which took place during this eventful period. A number of excellent treatises dealing exclusively with these topics have been written. The author directs the attention of those readers whose acquaintance with early American history needs reviving to such books as *The Rise of American Civilization* by Beard and Beard and Carman's *Social and Economic History of the United States*.[1]

By way of orientation, however, a few significant developments in the early life of our forefathers need to be mentioned here, since they were directly related to the activities and status of the teaching profession. Perhaps the most important single factor was population change. In 1790 there were approximately 4,000,000 people in the United States, 90 per cent of whom lived on the Atlantic seaboard from Maine to Georgia. The most populous state at this time was Virginia, followed in order by Pennsylvania, North Carolina, and New York. There were only five cities in 1790 with a population of more than 8000, and less than 4 per cent of the inhabitants lived in these more densely populated districts. During the next seventy years several remarkable changes occurred. The first was the phenomenal growth in population due to immigration, the number of people increasing on an average of 35 per cent during each succeeding decade and reaching a total of 31,443,321 by 1860. The second spectacular change was the shift from rural to urban areas, the percentage of the population in towns of 8000 inhabitants or more rising from 3.97 in 1800 to 16.13 in 1860. During this period the population of New York City had grown

[1] The reader may also wish to consult Faulkner, Harold U., *Economic History of the United States* (New York, The Macmillan Company, 1937); the same author's *American Political and Social History* (New York, F. S. Crofts and Company, 1937); and Shannon, Fred A., *Economic History of the People of the United States* (New York, The Macmillan Company, 1934).

from 60,510 to 813,669, and that of Philadelphia had increased from 41,220 to 565,529.

A third transformation in the population map resulted from the westward movement. Whereas 90 per cent of the people in 1790 lived along the Atlantic seaboard, only 55 per cent of the inhabitants lived east of the Alleghenies in 1850. This tremendous shift had far-reaching effects on education, many of which were immediately disturbing. The group who migrated to the West from New England and the Middle Atlantic States were replaced to a large extent by immigrants from abroad, and this perpetual change in population created a confusion in school programs which drove the pedagogues nearly to distraction. Pupils were here today and gone tomorrow.

The increase in the foreign-born population also presented unique problems. Between 1830 and 1860 no less than 5,000,000 foreigners were added to the population of the United States. Included in this group were the Irish, Germans, English, Welsh, Scotch, Dutch, Swiss, and French Canadians. The task of assimilating these widely different racial stocks and absorbing the children into the primitive schools of early America was a gigantic one.

Related to the population problem and carrying with it equal implications for education was the effect of the industrial revolution on American life. While farming and agriculture continued to hold first place among the occupations, their prestige was challenged by the development of factories and the establishment of manufacturing enterprises. The invention of machinery and the demand for industrial labor drew thousands of men, women, and children from the farms into the towns and cities, and the unprecedented growth of the latter created new problems and stimulated business activities which had enjoyed only a modicum of prosperity heretofore. Living conditions resulting from the congregation of people into cramped urban quarters were frequently deplorable.

Capitalists bent on establishing new records of wealth and power resorted to exploitation and commonly required factory workers to put in from twelve to fourteen hours a day for what scarcely amounted to a subsistence wage. Children as well as adults were practically enslaved to boost the profits of ruthless manufacturers. As a defense against these greedy business lords, labor began to organize and to substitute collective bargaining for the inadequate individual methods which had been used in the past. Strikes interrupted the normal activities of the factory in many cities and towns and disturbed the populace generally. While the caste system of the Old World was never paralleled in America, distinctive economic classes had existed in various degrees since the landing of the Pilgrims and were much accentuated by the industrial revolution.

The labor movement was a boon to public education and, indirectly, to the development of the teaching profession. Through the political strength which labor was soon able to demonstrate, it exercised an influence over the aristocratic tax dodgers which eventuated in a broad extension of educational opportunities. It was in the towns and cities, where economic and social problems were most perplexing and where labor was strong, that many of the ideas for improving public schools originated and the teaching profession made its greatest progress.

Along with the introduction of the factory system and the growth of cities went the improvement of transportation and communication. This story is so familiar that it needs no elaboration. Railroads, canals, steamboats, and the telegraph extended the horizon of businessmen, stimulated trade and commerce, and provided avenues of unification and education heretofore undreamed of. Whereas in the beginning of the century there was relatively little exchange of ideas between professional workers in various parts of the country, by 1860 all sorts of national associations and societies had been formed and met annually for mutual improvement.

The invention of the power press and the subsequent reduction in the prices of printed material stimulated the publication and distribution of books, magazines, and daily newspapers. Not only did this affect the number and variety of textbooks available to school children and teachers, but it resulted also in a flood of educational periodicals which served to keep both the public and the teaching personnel abreast of improved theories and schoolroom procedures.

The progress made in other professions was used by educational statesmen to direct the attention of the public and schoolmasters to needed reforms in the vocation of teaching. Medical science at the close of the Revolutionary War and extending well into the nineteenth century was in a highly undeveloped stage. There were only a few medical schools, and the training of doctors consisted chiefly in an apprenticeship served in the offices of members of the medical profession. Knowledge of the causes and cures of disease was for the most part lacking. The lay public were extremely superstitious, resorting to patent medicines and quack prescriptions for the alleviation of their ills. Doctors were ignorant, overworked, and poorly paid. By 1860, however, medical schools had increased in number and the proportion of graduates who became practicing physicians had multiplied severalfold. Significant discoveries, such as the use of anesthetics, had been made. Surgery had been improved, and doctors enjoyed a reputation far in excess of that held at the turn of the century.

The legal profession experienced a similar metamorphosis. While lawyers were respected at the time the Constitution was drafted because of their contribution to the reorganization of the government, they lost much of their prestige during the next few decades. This was due partly to the fact that some of their abler members forsook the profession for politics, but chiefly because they were associated in the public mind with the imprisonment of debtors. In their capacity of counsel for the creditor class they were held responsible for filling the jails with unfortunate farmers, speculators, and investors, whose assets were unequal to the indebtedness incurred in their experimental ventures. As Carman says, "Everywhere throughout the land lawyers were denounced as banditti, charlatans, demagogues, bloodsuckers, windbags, smooth-tongued rogues, and political tricksters." [2] In the latter part of the period (1840–1860), however, the practice of law again became respectable and attracted many competent individuals into the ranks of the legal profession.

[2] Carman, Harry J., *Social and Economic History of the United States* (Boston, D. C. Heath and Company, 1930), Vol. I, p. 435.

Engineering also made great strides during this period and contributed significantly to internal-improvement projects, including the construction of railroads. The ministry, which vied with the legal profession for first honors, did not experience any great changes between 1776 and the Civil War. Many ministers had no special preparation for their work but, in general, they exercised a great deal of influence upon public opinion. The orthodox religion remained the dominant faith although liberalistic tendencies cropped out, particularly in New England among the intellectual classes. The growth and influence of the Unitarian Church with its humanitarian emphasis became a serious threat to the orthodox creed. Questioning, as the former group did, the doctrines of original sin and predestination, they brought down a storm of criticism upon their own heads and stirred their enemies to preach even more vigorously against intemperance, immorality, profanity, skepticism, and Sabbathbreaking. While the American people as a whole continued in the orthodox camp, the penetrating logic of the more liberal evangelists, with their emphasis upon the "improvability" of mankind, modified indirectly the attitude and conduct of people and served to increase tolerance.

A less tangible influence on the teaching profession was the struggle which raged between the political parties in their efforts to promote their own peculiar philosophies of government. Jefferson's pronouncements on the place of education in a democracy and his efforts to secure a greater equalization of opportunity focused attention upon reforms which were destined to take place within the next half century. While many historians believe that the American public-school system was a product of Jacksonian principles, it cannot be denied that the way had been paved earlier for the launching of this great institution.

This sketchy portrayal of certain important conditions and developments in early American life can scarcely do more than direct the attention of the reader, as he peruses the chapters which follow, to their implications for the teaching profession.

XI

Educational Developments during the Early Days of the Republic

THE period from the dark days of the American Revolution to the close of the Civil War marks the beginning of epoch-making changes in public education in general and in the teaching profession in particular. It was during the latter half of this historical era that the great process of professionalization began and that public-school teaching was recognized as an occupation which demanded specific training in addition to native talent. Before the Revolution, individuals here and there had already advocated specialized preparation for teachers,[1] sporadic attempts at initiating apprentices into the calling of teaching had been made, and isolated experiments in improving the methodology of schoolmasters were not unknown. It remained, however, for men like Horace Mann and Henry Barnard in the thirties and forties to crystallize the sentiments of the more intelligent and farseeing citizenry before the real achievements of this period were realized.

As has already been suggested, this evolution in educational processes was closely related to developments in the economic, social, and political realm of the period under discussion. The Revolutionary War was a costly adventure from the standpoint of the man power lost, the property destroyed, and the indebtedness incurred from maintaining an army in the field for six long years. In a society where at least seventy-five per cent of the inhabitants made their living from tilling the soil, where brawn ranked with brain in providing mankind with food, clothing, and shelter, a war of such magnitude as the

---

[1] Franklin's Academy in Philadelphia (now the University of Pennsylvania) laid emphasis upon the training of teachers and was an attempt to meet a need which Benjamin Franklin early recognized.

American Revolution was bound to leave its imprint upon the lives of the inhabitants and particularly upon those institutions which were classed as nonessential in the struggle for survival. During the war two of the ten colleges (Columbia and Pennsylvania) which had been established before the beginning of hostilities were forced to close their doors, a majority of the one hundred or more academies suspended their sessions, and those that remained open were badly crippled. The elementary schools also received severe setbacks despite heroic efforts in many areas to keep the candles of knowledge burning.

It should be borne in mind that the Northern colonies, particularly Massachusetts and Connecticut, contributed more generously of their male population in order to further the cause of the Revolution than did the middle and Southern colonies. More than half of the American soldiers (155,000 of the 218,000) were from New England, and the two states mentioned above sent 130,000 men. While the proportion of the total population actually engaged in military activities during the American Revolution was at no time large and while all the colonies were exceedingly apathetic about providing troops and funds for carrying on the war, the fact still remains that publicly and semipublicly supported institutions were seriously neglected during these trying days. The war had a further significant bearing on education, because those colonies which were in the vanguard, as far as educational achievements were concerned, provided the largest proportion of their man power for war. Such diversion of energy and thought away from cultural and intellectual pursuits left its mark upon the schools and colleges and impeded professional progress generally.

Alleviation of poverty, rehabilitation, realignment of taxation, and provision for the physical needs of the people were matters of primary importance and occupied the foreground of American thought and effort. Despite Benjamin Franklin's observation in 1787 that "the prosperity of the nation was so great as to call for thanksgiving," there are undeniable facts supporting the conclusion that the problems of reconstruction were of such magnitude as to force into the background, at least temporarily, any wide expansion of educational projects.[2] It is scarcely to be wondered at, then, that the period immediately following the Revolution was less fruitful educationally than later years.

Not only was America forced to direct the energies of her people toward the material things of life in order to survive, but the stupendous problem of political reoganization presented itself immediately. The feeble efforts of the Continental Congress to cope with issues which heretofore had been left almost wholly to the individual colonies or to European dictators brought home to Washington and to other statesmen of the day the necessity for strengthening the whole governmental structure. Failure to do so would most certainly spell disaster, and there were times when the staunchest supporters of the newly established republic were extremely pessimistic about the probable success of the venture of self-government. The best brains were, therefore, drafted for public service to secure some kind of order out of chaos and to start the great experiment in political democracy upon which were focused not only the eyes of America but also those of the world.

That education was early acknowledged to be the foundation stone of the democracy does not in any way alter the fact that the machinery for introducing our public-school system and for lifting it to a high level of efficiency was markedly slow in developing. The famous ordinance of 1785,[3] which gave expression to a national principle of education (federal support), was most significant as a forerunner of public policy but it alone could not bring about an educational millennium. The federal lands set aside for the support of schools provided relatively little revenue during this period, because land was plentiful and rents were small.

Also the states were slow to put into practice what their constitutions permitted or provided. Between 1776 and the War of 1812, only ten of the states had placed in their new con-

[2] An exception to this generalization is the academy movement, which flourished during the seventy years following the Revolutionary War. However, there were few innovations even in the case of the academy—the old models persisting for decades.

[3] This law reserved the sixteenth section of each township, containing 640 acres, for public education.

stitutions a recognition of the obligation of an American common-wealth to educate all its future citizens. Educational ideals were frequently expressed in legal documents and loudly acclaimed, but the action of political bodies was delayed. New Jersey, for example, did not provide for a school fund in its statutes until 1816 and no distribution of funds occurred until 1829. In most of the states there was a great lag between statutory regulation and practice, between permission and execution, and despite marked progress in isolated communities the onward march of education and the systematic development of the teaching profession were painfully slow.

EDUCATIONAL TRENDS AND INNOVATIONS IN TEACHING METHOD

It would be unfair to this period, however, to dismiss it without mention of certain far-reaching trends. The seeds of our public education system were being sown immediately following the Revolution. Men like Manasseh Cutler, Benjamin Rush, Thomas Jefferson, George Washington, Benjamin Franklin, Robert Coram, and a host of others repeatedly emphasized the need of lifting the masses from ignorance and illiteracy to a high level of culture and citizenship if the Republic were to succeed. Articles, pamphlets, and books on the function of education in a democracy poured from the presses. The American Philosophical Society for Promoting Useful Knowledge, a creation of Benjamin Franklin and his friends, offered a prize for "the best system of liberal education and literary instruction adapted to the genius of the United States; comprehending also a plan for instituting and conducting public schools in this country on the principles of the most extensive utility."

Private individuals bent on reform proposed elaborate systems of education from the elementary school to the university. Practically every important controversial topic known to modern students came up for consideration in the writings of these early educators. Lecturers were imported from abroad to discuss the application of the theories of Rousseau and Pestalozzi to a democratic system of government. Interest in public education ran high.

Certain innovations were introduced. The Lancasterian

method of teaching—by which one teacher, with the assistance of monitors, was able to instruct large numbers of children without undue cost to the taxpayers—was brought to New York in 1806 and adopted in the schools operated by the Free School Society of that city. Joseph Lancaster, the author of the plan, came over himself shortly after the above date (1818) and lent aid to the extension of his system. That he proved to be something of a disappointment, particularly in Massachusetts, and that his system was destined to crumble because it was inefficient and inadequate does not alter the fact that it stimulated unusual interest in the possibilities of public education and hastened the day when children of all classes would be provided with some kind of educational opportunity. The model schools established to demonstrate the merits of the Lancasterian method were, in many respects, the forerunners of the American normal school. The significance of these model schools in promoting the preparation of teachers is well illustrated in the following excerpts taken from the *Fifth* and *Eleventh Annual Reports* of the Controllers of the Public Schools of the First School District of the State of Pennsylvania. The first of these says: [4]

It is with pleasure the controllers observe the establishment of a school in the city of Lancaster upon the same system as that adopted here, the Teacher of which was instructed in the Model School. During the last year, several other persons were qualified for instructors on this system under the auspices of the controllers.

Six years later the controllers were still enthusiastic about the teacher-training activities of the newly established system of instruction and announced that: [5]

The principal of the Boy's Model School has compiled an Epitome of Geography, especially adapted to Seminaries of Mutual instruction, the publication of which the controllers encouraged, and have supplied each school in the district with the requisite number of copies.

Several persons of both sexes, have recently availed themselves of the privilege of acquiring a knowledge of the Lancasterian plan of instruction, by attending the Model and other schools, and some of the in-

[4] *Fifth Annual Report* (Philadelphia, 1823), p. 8 n.
[5] *Eleventh Annual Report* (Philadelphia, 1829), p. 6.

dividuals thus qualified are candidates for employment in Pennsylvania; in many of the interior Counties of which an increased degree of attention has lately been manifested, for providing the means of elementary instruction to a large number of Youths now destitute of that blessing.

Houghton Mifflin

A LANCASTERIAN SCHOOLROOM

The Lancasterian system reached its highest point in Pennsylvania, and the enthusiasm of the leading educators of the Keystone State was in no small degree responsible for the spread of this radical departure in educational theory. Robert Vaux, President of the Pennsylvania Society for the Promotion of Public Schools and also President of the Board of Controllers of the Public Schools, sent out a circular letter in 1829, addressed to the "Citizens of Pennsylvania," offering to "furnish well qualified teachers at reasonable salaries."[6]

TEACHER-TRAINING PROPAGANDA

Perhaps the high point in the achievements of these early years of the nineteenth century was the establishment of a seminary for the preparation of teachers in Concord, Vermont, in 1823 by the Reverend Samuel R. Hall. While private in nature, this seminary possessed many of the characteristics of the public normal school of a later date. In 1830 Hall moved

[6] Wickersham, James P., *op. cit.*, p. 610.

to Phillips Academy at Andover, where he directed a similar experiment; it was at this institution that Horace Mann gleaned some of his ideas about teacher training which were soon to bear fruit in Massachusetts. That other individuals also recognized the need for such preparation is evidenced by the speeches and writings of ministers and educators of the period. In 1816 Denison Olmstead made an appeal in a commencement address at Yale for seminaries that should be designed especially for the preparation of teachers. Likewise, James T. Kingsley of Yale College wrote an article in 1823 for the *North American Review* in which he expressed a similar point of view. Two years later the Reverend Thomas Gallaudet outlined in the *Connecticut Observer* (January 4, 1825) "A Plan of a Seminary for the Education of Instructors of Youth." This article was reprinted in other newspapers of the time and received considerable attention by educators and others interested in the improvement of teaching. James G. Carter, sometimes referred to as the "father of normal schools" because of his work in Massachusetts, urged the establishment of normal schools in that state. His "Essays on Popular Education" which appeared in the *Boston Patriot* aroused public interest not only in Massachusetts but throughout the United States.

Similarly Walter Johnson, principal of the Germantown Academy in Philadelphia, published a pamphlet in 1825 in which he strongly recommended the establishment of teachers' seminaries and argued for their creation as follows: [7]

We have theological seminaries, law schools, medical colleges, military academies, institutes for mechanics, and colleges of pharmacy for apothecaries; but no shadow of an appropriate institution to qualify persons for discharging with ability and success the duties of instruction, either in these professional seminaries or in any other. Men have been apparently presumed to be qualified to teach from the moment they passed the period of ordinary pupilage—a supposition which with few exceptions must of course lead only to disappointment and mortification.

Travelers to foreign countries reported their observations upon returning to America. Henry E. Dwight, at the completion of

[7] *Ibid.*, p. 220. See Johnson, Walter, *American Journal of Education*, Index.

a tour of northern Germany, published in 1829 an account of his experiences, including his reactions to the seminaries for the training of teachers. It was a period of agitation which, in America at least, seemed necessary for the launching of any important change in educational practice. Europe had experimented with teacher training for a century or more but the people of the United States were not yet alert to the importance of developing a specialized profession of teaching comparable to that of law, medicine, or the clergy. It was first necessary for some educational evangelists to spread the gospel.

The Academy Movement

It was during this period following the Revolution that the academy movement flourished in America, and despite the fact that these secondary schools were far less democratic in character than the high schools of a later date they played an important role in developing a favorable mind-set toward public education. The rapid increase in the number of academies created a demand for schoolmasters and tended to focus attention upon the professional needs of those engaged to teach in these schools.[8]

One of the arguments advanced for the support and extension of academies in America was that they would furnish the elementary schools with a supply of well-trained teachers. In 1821 the Board of Regents in New York recommended state aid to the academies in the hope of encouraging better prepared teachers for the common schools. No real provisions, however, were made in New York academies for teacher training until relatively late in the thirties (1835–1836) and the experiment proved to be somewhat disappointing. New England was also experimenting with the idea of training teachers in the academy. A catalogue of the Bristol Academy at Taunton, Massachusetts, dated 1837, contains the following announcement: " A department for the training of teachers is opened in this institu-

---

[8] The academy was a secondary school of a semipublic nature offering a much broader course of study than the Latin grammar schools which preceded it. It was often open to girls as well as boys and aimed to prepare for practical life and for teaching as well as for college.

tion. Instruction is given in the art of Teaching and the use of Apparatus." [9]

The American academy of this period was extremely conservative and the curriculum provided for those students who planned to become elementary teachers did not vary significantly from the general program available to regular students. The graduates of these schools were perhaps superior in ability to the individuals commonly appointed to teaching posts heretofore, but as far as their knowledge of pedagogy was concerned they were equally as ignorant.

It is perhaps fruitless to speculate upon the relative status of the teaching profession in America in 1776 and in 1836, but if one were to judge solely by the qualifications required of teachers he would have to be something of an optimist to conclude that the public-school pupils of Andrew Jackson's day were markedly better prepared to face the world upon graduation than those whose schooling antedated the Revolution. The special preparation of teachers, with emphasis upon methodology and pedagogical principles, had not yet received any general or widespread consideration.

EDUCATIONAL AWAKENING

In contrast with the period just discussed are the events and achievements recorded during the years 1836 to the close of the Civil War. As mentioned previously, this was an era of great educational change and, from the standpoint of the teaching profession, these years were probably the most significant ones in our whole history. There were at least nine educational or professional developments which make this twenty-eight-year period especially noteworthy. They are as follows:

1. The establishment of public normal schools for the training of teachers.
2. The rise and development of the teachers' institute as a means of improving teachers in service.
3. The provision of county and state supervision of schools,

---

[9] In Agnew, Walter, *The Administration of Professional Schools for Teachers* (Baltimore, Warwick and York, 1924), pp. 18–19.

resulting in a greater unity among members of the teaching profession and a vastly improved educational program.

4. The widespread use of examinations as a basis for certifying teachers and as a consideration in their appointment to positions in city school systems.

5. The inauguration of the graded system of schools, with marked changes in the scope of the teacher's responsibility. Prior to this time, pupils of all sizes, ages, and achievements had been thrown together rather heterogeneously under one teacher.

6. The organization of teachers into local, state, and national associations for purposes of improving education and, especially, the status of the teaching profession.

7. The extension and improvement of textbooks, courses of study, materials of instruction, and educational literature generally.

8. The substitution of female for male teachers in the public schools.

9. The lengthening of the school year, thereby making teaching more nearly a full-time job than it had previously been.

Each of the above topics will be discussed in detail in the chapters which follow.

SUGGESTED READINGS

BEARD, CHARLES, and BEARD, MARY, *The Rise of American Civilization* (New York, The Macmillan Company, 1927), Vol. I, pp. 437–506.

KANDEL, I. L., *History of Secondary Education* (Boston, Houghton Mifflin Company, 1930), pp. 391–462.

MAYO, A. D., "Public Schools during the Colonial and Revolutionary Period in the United States," in *Report of the Commissioner of Education, 1893–94* (Washington, Government Printing Office), pp. 708 ff.

"Schools as They Were Sixty Years Ago," in *American Journal of Education*, Henry Barnard (ed.), (new series, No. 5), No. XXX (March, 1863), pp. 123–44.

XII

The Rise of the Public Normal School

THERE has been considerable controversy among students of education over the origin of the American normal school. Certain recognized authorities have insisted that it was lifted bodily from the Old World and transplanted to American soil. They point out that the Prussian influence was great in New England during the years just prior to the establishment of the first normal school at Lexington, Massachusetts, in 1839 and indicate that it is reasonable to suppose that American educators learned about teacher training from those countries which had experimented most with the idea. Germany had been operating teachers' seminaries for about a hundred years when they were first being considered in the United States. France and England had both organized them early in the nineteenth century.

Furthermore, as evidence of their foreign origin, it was argued that certain American travelers had written extensively about European normal schools before they were instituted in the United States. Among these authors was Henry E. Dwight who, in 1829, wrote his impressions of the teacher-training institutions of north Germany.[1] Two years later William C. Woodbridge gave an account of the Prussian system of training teachers in his *Annals of Education.* It was during this period that the Reverend Charles Brooks devoted considerable time to a study of teachers' seminaries in Europe and became an active promoter of teacher training in Massachusetts. Henry Barnard also went abroad in the late thirties and studied a number of the educational systems in Europe rather thoroughly. His writings were directed toward winning public support for normal schools in New England. At about this same time (1837) Calvin E. Stowe's

[1] Dwight, Henry E., *Travels in the North of Germany in 1825–26.*

Report on Elementary Education in Europe appeared, and in 1839 Professor Alexander D. Bache published his *Report on Education in Europe*. These two documents, and especially the latter one with its strong endorsement of the German teacher-training program, aroused great interest and discussion in America. Our early educational leaders, therefore, among whom were several clergymen, were well informed on comparative education.

Those who oppose the theory that our normal schools are of European, and especially of German, origin point out that the American normal school grew up like Topsy and was the logical outgrowth of the academy and of those private institutions which had been experimenting quite independently of foreign influence. They insist that the need for trained teachers was more apparent in the thirties and forties than it had previously been and hold that it was only natural that the states should look to some public institution to help meet this demand. Moreover, they maintain that the normal school in this country was more like the academy than like the Prussian training schools and show the great dissimilarities between the early normal schools here and those seminaries which existed at the time in Germany, concluding that relatively few, if any, ideas were copied from abroad. And, finally, some of them claim that Americans were much prejudiced against the importation of foreign institutions and cite the unfavorable reaction of New Englanders toward Horace Mann's efforts to promote German educational ideas in Massachusetts.

The preponderance of evidence appears to be against the contention that America reproduced the German system, lock, stock, and barrel. To deny, however, that American educators were influenced by their observations of Prussian training schools and other European experiments, and that these schools had at least an indirect effect upon the character and program of those established in America, seems unreasonable. In all probability, Americans learned much from foreign experience and gathered many ideas which assisted them in the establishment of similar institutions here. On the other hand, while some of the characteristics underlying our early normal schools were European in origin, many of them were rooted deeply in American institutions. It is significant, for example, that the first normal school at Lexington was referred to by the students as the Lexington Academy. In the minds of the public, the early normal schools were largely adaptations or extensions of the American secondary school. The term "normal school," which was used by the French and derived from the Latin noun *norma*—meaning "a carpenter's square, a rule, a pattern, a model"—was not common in the United States until rather late in the period under discussion.

Because of the apathy of the public generally toward the training of individuals for an occupation which had previously been assumed to require no professional knowledge, it was necessary to spread propaganda widely before the normal school became a fixture. In the meantime private and semipublic academies, seminaries, and colleges provided the vast majority of trained teachers for the schools. It must be remembered that most of the teachers of this period still remained untrained and continued to use trial and error methods of imparting instruction. As late as 1833 Samuel R. Hall stated in a lecture on the necessity of educating teachers that "there is not in our whole country one seminary where the educator of children can be thoroughly qualified for his important work."

Private and Semipublic Experiments in Teacher Training

The private seminary led the way in experimenting with the novel idea of training teachers. As was mentioned earlier, Hall, in 1823, had opened a private seminary with a model school attached at Concord, Vermont, and later had directed a similar venture at Phillips Academy at Andover. At about this same time (1827) James G. Carter, with the aid of some local citizens, established a teachers' seminary at Lancaster, Massachusetts. Western states pursued a similar course during these days when teacher training was looked upon as something of a luxury. In 1826 James N. Neef founded the New Harmony Community School in Indiana, where he introduced the Pestalozzian methods of teaching. During this whole period Ohio depended chiefly upon private institutions for the preparation of teachers for the common schools. Strange as it may seem to us now, only a few of the more thoughtful citizens during these early years of the

Republic realized that private institutions did not possess the necessary resources to provide adequately for the teacher-training needs of the country and that the state must lend a helping hand. This latter fact became increasingly obvious as time went on.

An intermediate step in the evolution of the normal-school movement in several of the states, therefore, was the state-aided seminaries and academies. Unwilling to take over the full responsibility, the state compromised and gave financial support to already existing institutions. New York, for example, provided funds for teachers' classes in academies in 1834 and began distributing moneys for this purpose in 1835–1836. The appropriation was discontinued in 1844 but resumed again in 1849. Other states, notably Pennsylvania, Indiana, and Wisconsin, pursued a similar policy of assisting private and semipublic schools in the preparation of teachers. Unfortunately, the efforts of these early training institutions were not always crowned with success. The preparation of teachers was too frequently subordinated to the other objectives of the school. Notwithstanding this limitation, state aid to academies and seminaries constituted a long step forward in the development of the teaching profession and focused the attention of intelligent laymen as well as of educators upon the need for normal schools entirely supported and operated by the state.

STATE NORMAL SCHOOLS

As has already been indicated, Massachusetts was the first state to launch out on the great experiment of public normal schools. This was achieved through the combined efforts of several educational statesmen, of whom Horace Mann was the most prominent. It was Mann who was instrumental, in 1837, in getting his friend Edmund Dwight to contribute ten thousand dollars toward the support of teacher training in Massachusetts, on the condition that the legislature would provide an equal sum, and it was largely through Mann's efforts that this body passed a resolution accepting the proposition. As a result of much labor and discussion, the first public normal school in America was opened at Lexington on July 3, 1839. This was followed by the opening of a second school at Barre on September 4, 1839, and a third at Bridgewater the following year. It was nearly ten years after the establishment of the Lexington enterprise that the board of education formally resolved "that the schools heretofore known as normal schools shall be hereafter designated as State Normal Schools."

Worcester Museum

THE FIRST PUBLIC NORMAL SCHOOL IN AMERICA

The nature of these first attempts at teacher training is well described in the Journals of Cyrus Peirce, the principal of the Lexington Normal School.[2] If the reader can imagine himself teaching ten subjects in a single term and seventeen different subjects in the course of a single year, and at the same time supervising a model school of thirty pupils, acting as demon-

[2] Peirce, Cyrus, and Swift, Mary, *The First State Normal School in America; The Journals of Cyrus Peirce and Mary Swift*, Harvard Documents in the History of Education, Vol. I (Cambridge, Harvard University Press, 1926).

stration teacher, developing the professional materials to be taught in the normal school, and serving as janitor of the building, he will begin to appreciate the difficulties confronting the principals of our early state normal schools. While this picture was modified somewhat as a result of the first great experiment by Cyrus Peirce, lack of funds and the general skepticism of the public about the project imposed unbelievable tasks upon the shoulders of those in charge. Despite the small number of students who attended (approximately forty), the scope of the educational program made the work inordinately difficult. The studies included in the one-year program at Lexington were (1) a review of the "Common Branches"—spelling, reading, writing, grammar, and arithmetic; (2) advanced studies (except ancient languages) as time permitted (*e.g.*, geometry; algebra; natural, intellectual, and moral philosophy; political economy; and natural history); (3) the physical, mental, and moral development of children; (4) the science and art of teaching each of the common branches; (5) the art of school government; and (6) practice in teaching and governing a "model" school. Peirce's heroic efforts were watched carefully by admiring educators everywhere and gave impetus to the establishment of other normal schools both inside and outside of the state.

It took another decade, however, before Connecticut, under the leadership of Henry Barnard, was able to organize similar institutions in that commonwealth. Through articles in the *Connecticut School Journal* and the *Annual Reports* of the Secretary of the Board of Commissioners of Common Schools, considerable favorable sentiment was first created. Then a voluntary course for teachers was inaugurated at Hartford in 1839, in which special lectures were offered on academic subjects and methods of teaching. Through experience with this project and the investigation of the whole question of teacher training by a committee appointed by the legislature in 1845, the public was convinced that some provision should be made. It was the report of a second committee in 1848 which finally brought the matter to a head. This committee visited the Massachusetts normal schools and the teacher-training classes in the academies in New York and brought back definite recommendations for the establishment of normal schools in Connecticut. The culmination of the ten years of study and experimentation was the opening of the New Britain Normal School in 1850.

New York, as implied previously, relied for a long time upon the training departments in academies for the preparation of teachers. The plan was only partially successful, since the emphasis in all these schools continued to be upon the general academic rather than upon the professional subjects. Teacher training continued to remain nobody's business as long as it was "farmed out" to the academies. It did not require great insight (although it was not clear to the average citizen) to realize the futility of trying to meet the teacher-training needs of the Empire State through these makeshift institutions. After some debate and investigation, a bill was passed authorizing the establishment of a state normal school at Albany. This was opened in 1844. The number of graduates were so few in number, however, that they left but little imprint upon the teaching personnel of the state as a whole. Some appreciation of the situation can be had by examining the statistics pertaining to the graduates of the Albany Normal School for the four years immediately following its inauguration.

Date	Number Graduated	
1845	Males	29
	Females	5
1846	Males	67
	Females	43
1847	Males	64
	Females	44
1848	Males	42
	Females	54
TOTAL	Males	202
	Females	146
GRAND TOTAL		348

No other training schools appeared in New York until 1861 when the Oswego Normal School was founded. This school did not become a state institution, however, until 1866.

Pennsylvania struggled along, looking first to the academies and later to the county normal schools as agencies to provide teachers for the common schools. The history of these institutions up to 1857 is one of trial and error, disappointment and defeat, with the inescapable conclusion arrived at very late that the task was one of such magnitude as to require the supervision and support of no smaller unit of government than the state itself. Many leaders in the Keystone State had recognized, early in this period, the great problem which confronted the advancement of education, but they were required to wait patiently for a confused citizenry to see the light. The state superintendent in his annual report for 1836 said: [3]

Teaching should be a profession—the business of life—and should be prepared for and paid for accordingly. One year or six months, or even three months, spent by a person of common acquirements in an institution for the preparation of common school teachers, under well-qualified professors, would work wonders. $10,000 a year appropriated to the establishment of two such institutions, would soon produce a complete revolution in the art of teaching. Such an appropriation is most earnestly and respectively recommended.

It is an interesting fact that practically every state superintendent in Pennsylvania from 1834 to the Civil War pleaded in similar fashion for the support of teacher-training institutions. Unfortunately, they were not so clear or influential in their declarations as some of the leaders in New England. With the advent of county superintendents in Pennsylvania, in 1854, came county normal schools and a greater emphasis upon the improvement of teaching. Because of limited funds, however, and the temporary character of many of the schools, the results obtained were far from satisfactory. Fortunately, the issue was kept alive and agitation for state normal schools continued. Meetings were held in various cities in the state and the teachers themselves were stirred up to the point of petitioning the legislature for action. In the meantime the academies, the county normal schools, and the colleges were carrying the load with some subsidies from the state. That the job was rather badly done must be admitted and that Pennsylvania was slow to accept

[3] *Pennsylvania School Report*, **Annual Report of the Superintendent, 1836.**

state responsibility for teacher training is evidenced by the fact that normal schools remained in private or local hands until 1913.

Other states faced problems similar to those met in Pennsylvania and experimented with halfway measures. In most instances, however, the process was faster and less painful. Rhode Island first looked to Brown University as the base of supply for trained teachers and in 1850 the superintendent of schools in Providence, Samuel S. Greene, was invited to accept the chair of Professor of Didactics at Brown. He did this without resigning his job as superintendent; and after a brief experience with the venture, he joined some other educators in setting up a private normal school. This new school received some financial support from the city of Providence in 1854, and later in that same year the state assumed the major responsibility for its operation and made it a state normal school.

The superintendent of schools in Maine recommended a state normal school in his annual report for 1855 and estimated the cost at three thousand dollars. It was not until 1862, however, that the legislature took successful action and established two normal schools. In the meantime the academies there struggled rather half-heartedly with the problem of teacher training.

During this period of experimentation there were many adherents of the so-called New York academy plan as opposed to the Prussian normal-school system of preparing teachers, and it was only after years of unsuccessful experience with the former that the public awakened to the need for specialized institutions supported by the state to perform this task. The Board of Regents in Wisconsin as late as 1857 distributed moneys, derived from the sale of swamplands and earmarked specifically for normal schools, to the colleges and academies maintaining teacher-training classes. That educators were disappointed in the results is evidenced by the fact that in 1863 the Wisconsin State Superintendent pointed out in his annual report that "they have not satisfactorily met the necessity."

Eastern educators carrying ideas from their native states moved into the *then* Northwest and exerted tremendous influence on educational practices there. The struggle for free schools and trained teachers was of relatively short duration. Illinois State Normal University was established in 1857. Through the efforts of the Reverend John D. Pierce, a native of New Hampshire and an ardent supporter of education, Michigan founded a normal school in 1849. Minnesota made similar provision in 1858. The Southern states moved more slowly and their achievements during this period were not especially noteworthy.[4] The issue of training teachers for the common schools was constantly before the people, however, and it remained only a matter of time before the acceptance of state-supported teacher-training institutions became a reality. The extent of the normal-school movement during this period is well illustrated in Table 1, showing the dates of establishment.

Table 1. American Normal Schools Established before the Civil War [1]

Location	Date of Opening
Massachusetts, Lexington	July 5, 1839
Massachusetts, Barre	September 4, 1839
Massachusetts, Bridgewater	September 9, 1840
New York, Albany	December 19, 1844
Connecticut, New Britain	May 15, 1850
Michigan, Ypsilanti	March 29, 1853
Massachusetts, Salem	September 12, 1854
Rhode Island, Providence	September 12, 1854
New Jersey, Trenton	October 1, 1855
Illinois, Normal	October 5, 1857
Minnesota, Winona	September 3, 1860
New York, Oswego (made state school, 1866)	May 1, 1861

[1] Adapted from Agnew, Walter, *op. cit.*, p. 31.

THE MUNICIPAL NORMAL SCHOOL

It was obvious from the beginning that state institutions were not going to furnish enough teachers to meet the requirements of all the schools, and enlightened communities were impatient with the slowness of legislatures in satisfying this need. Therefore, with the rapid growth of cities there developed a demand for local training schools for teachers, which in most respects

[4] According to Knight, North Carolina provided for teacher training in 1853 at Union Institute, later named Normal College. This experiment ended in 1859, after which no other provision was made until 1876.

would resemble the state normal schools of this period. These institutions were created by municipalities and financed by local taxation.

As early as 1852 Boston established a normal school, the purpose of which was to train girls who had graduated from the local grammar schools for positions as assistant teachers in the common schools of Boston. This normal school was combined with the girls' high school in 1855 and attempted to serve a twofold purpose for several years. In 1856 the New York City Board of Education organized what was known as the "Daily Normal School for Females." Saturday normal schools had been in existence in New York, Newark, and Brooklyn for several years.[5] The purpose of the latter, however, had been the improvement of teachers already in service in the city schools rather than the preparation of new teachers. By the early sixties Philadelphia, San Francisco, Baltimore, St. Louis, Trenton, and several other towns had established full-time teacher-training institutions. The programs of these city normal schools did not include formal instruction in methods of teaching, although opportunities were usually provided students to practice their art under the direction of instructors. The emphasis was placed on mastering subject matter, in spite of the importance which a few early educators attached to the study of methodology. Considering the inadequacies of teacher-training facilities in 1860, however, the municipal normal schools of pre-Civil War days rendered a genuine contribution to the improvement of teaching. As a later discussion points out, they flourished during the last decades of the nineteenth century and only in recent years have they been superseded by state institutions.

From the standpoint of teachers, the creation of normal schools was by far the most significant contribution of the period from 1836 to 1860. Without special training the teaching personnel in America could never have commanded the respect and atten-

[5] In New York City these schools were established by the Public School Society about 1834. The first one was a school for female auditors, which was later supplemented by one for male monitors and a school for colored monitors. (Eckelberry, R. H., *The History of the Municipal University in the United States*, U. S. Office of Education, Bulletin 1932, No. 2 [Washington, Government Printing Office, 1932].)

tion which their important work warranted, nor could they have hoped to win a place in the sun in any way comparable to the professions of law and medicine. While these early attempts at teacher training appear crude when judged by present-day standards of instruction for prospective teachers, they established a precedent which was destined to have far-reaching consequences for public education and for the members of the teaching group. One can estimate only roughly the influence of training on the economic and social status of teachers, but it seems clear that without this important step the public would never have accorded them the protection and respect which they have subsequently enjoyed.

Suggested Readings

Agnew, Walter, *The Administration of Professional Schools for Teachers* (Baltimore, Warwick and York, 1924).

Bunker, F. F., *Reorganization of the Public School System*, U. S. Bureau of Education, Bulletin 1916, No. 8 (Washington, Government Printing Office, 1916).

Carnegie Foundation for the Advancement of Education, Bagley *et al.*, *The Professional Preparation of Teachers for the American Public Schools*, Bulletin No. 14.

Eckelberry, R. H., *The History of the Municipal University in the United States*, U. S. Office of Education, Bulletin 1932, No. 2 (Washington, Government Printing Office, 1932).

Knight, Edgar W., *Education in the United States* (New York, Ginn and Company, 1929), Chap. XI.

"Normal Schools in America," in *American Journal of Education*, Henry Barnard (ed.), Vol. XIII (1863), pp. 756–57.

XIII

Teachers' Institutes

WHILE the advent of the public normal school was unquestionably the most significant milestone in the evolution of the teaching profession prior to the Civil War, it was preceded in many states and paralleled in others by an agency whose influence in stimulating professional growth and solidarity has frequently been underestimated—the teachers' institute.

This agency is wholly American in origin and credit is usually given to Henry Barnard for the establishment of the first one at Hartford in the autumn of 1839. Barnard's experiment consisted in providing for twenty-six young men a six-week period of instruction in pedagogics together with the opportunity to review the usual topics taught in common schools. A number of prominent educators, including Charles Davis, the well-known author, and Thomas H. Gallaudet, assisted Barnard in the instructional program and the Hartford schools were made available for observation and classroom visitation. Apparently the results were encouraging, for the institute was repeated the following year and an additional class provided for female teachers.

At about this same time Samuel N. Sweet was struggling with the idea of temporary normal schools in New York State and projected a plan which closely resembled the experiment carried on by Barnard. The term "institute" was first used in connection with a convention, composed of twenty-eight teachers, held at Ithaca in the spring of 1843. The institute lasted for two weeks and was conducted by J. S. Denman, the Tompkins County Superintendent of Schools. Within the next two years similar institutes were held in thirty-nine counties in the Empire State and more than one thousand teachers received instruction. Other states were quick to adopt similar arrangements.

In the year 1844 William B. Fowle, Esquire, of Boston visited several of the institutes in New York State and published an interesting account of their proceedings in a Boston newspaper. Almost immediately following this report, Horace Mann laid the subject before his friend, Edmund Dwight, and secured a fund (one thousand dollars) for their support in Massachusetts. In this latter state four towns were designated as places of meeting and the number of teachers who might attend any one of these institutes was limited to one hundred, fifty of whom were to be males and fifty females. Public interest in this new experiment must have been marked, for the governor of the state attended the first meeting in Pittsfield in the autumn of 1845 and was reported to be one of the most attentive and interested observers throughout the session. In 1846 the legislature of Massachusetts made an appropriation of twenty-five hundred dollars for their support.

Other states arranged for institutes soon after their introduction into New York and Massachusetts. Rhode Island, in the law of 1845, made it the duty of the commissioners of public schools to establish institutes "where teachers and such as propose to teach may become acquainted with the most approved and successful methods of arranging the studies and conducting the discipline of instruction of public schools." [1] New Hampshire, in June, 1846, passed permissive legislation whereby any town in the state might raise money for the support of institute work not to exceed five per cent of the amount required for the support of common schools. In 1847 Connecticut appropriated one hundred and twenty-five dollars to each county for this purpose, and New York sixty dollars. In this same year Maine voted twenty-six hundred dollars for institutes, and each county was the recipient of aid from this general fund. Pennsylvania, Ohio, Michigan, and Illinois had all established institutes by 1846.

These assemblies were commonly held once or twice a year for two or four weeks; and in some instances, six or eight weeks. They were not intended to serve as a substitute for academic training but were established as a supplementary agency to pro-

[1] *New Jersey School Report, 1857*, pp. 42–45.

vide a brief course in the theory and practice of teaching adapted to the common schools. At first they were purely voluntary and their expense was borne by the teachers themselves. Then interested citizens came to the rescue and private contributions relieved the burden of cost to teachers. This policy was soon supplanted by public support in many states as the appropriations, referred to above, indicate.

Some notion of the primitive character of the early institutes can be had from the following materials which applicants were advised to bring to the meetings: [2]

Each applicant must be provided with a Bible or Testament; with a slate and pencil, with pen, ink, and paper; with geography and atlas, and with the reading book for the first class which is most generally used in the neighborhood whence he comes. Each one must also have an English dictionary, and a small blank book, or common-place book.

Despite the intention of some of the founders to stress instruction in methodology and in the general principles of school government, many of these early institutes were conducted in the manner of a public school, with considerable emphasis placed upon subject matter. Arithmetic, grammar, geography, and reading constituted the core subjects during the day. Horace Mann, in a circular letter to school committees in Massachusetts in 1845, emphasized the academic training available at institutes by pointing out that: [3]

It is the design of a Teachers' Institute to bring together those who are actually engaged in teaching common schools, or who propose to become so, in order that they may be formed into classes, and that these classes, under able instructors, may be exercised, questioned and drilled, in the same manner that the classes of a good Common School are exercised, questioned and drilled. Thus, during their attendance on the Institute, the future teachers become scholars. They are expected to prepare and recite lessons, in the same way they would expect their own scholars to do.

In some institutes a public examination was held at the close of the session and students were tested on the subject matter learned.

[2] Sweet, Samuel N., *Teachers' Institutes* (Utica, N. Y., H. H. Hawley and Company, 1848), p. 47.
[3] *Ibid.*, pp. 45–46.

The evening exercises were devoted to more general subjects, of interest both to teachers and the public. Some of the most distinguished educators of the time lectured at these evening meetings. Louis Agassiz, the great naturalist; Professor Arnold Guyot, the geographer; Professor William Russell, the master of elocution; Henry Barnard, the educator; and other equally notable leaders were commonly engaged for institute work.

As the movement advanced, there was a tendency to introduce more educational theory and to assume that those in attendance had already acquired the basic subject matter requisite for teaching, or at least to leave this problem for other agencies to solve. The institute furnished an opportunity, incidentally, for spreading propaganda and for unifying and solidifying the teaching profession. As the forerunner of teachers' organizations, it proved to be a great force in initiating reforms in the teaching profession. Opportunities were provided for the discussion of resolutions and for the reports of committees. In the Chenango County Institute, held in September, 1846, in New York State, a resolution was adopted which was apparently one of the earliest attempts to secure equal pay for men and women. It read as follows: [4]

Whereas, The education of a lady is obtained at no less expense than that of a gentleman, and as it is generally admitted that they can impart instruction with equal facility and success, therefore,

Resolved, That ladies and gentlemen of equal qualifications, should receive equal compensation.

Special committees reported at this institute on "school-houses and sites, vocal music, Teachers' Institutes, school celebrations, school associations, school apparatus and teaching penmanship."[5]

While a large amount of institute time was devoted to "actual progress in the various branches of education," all kinds of matters related to the schools and to the activities of pupils were discussed. At the Chautauqua County Institute, held at Maysville in 1847, the following two questions received considerable attention: [6]

---

[4] *Ibid.*, p. 95.   [5] *Ibid.*, p. 95.   [6] *Ibid.*, p. 85.

1. What is the best method of preventing whispering?
2. What is the best method of teaching morals?

At the Mercer and Crawford Institute held at Jamestown, Pennsylvania, later in this period (January 14, 1858), the following questions were discussed: [7]

Is it better for teachers to board around?

Should the teachers encourage pupils to chew tobacco?

Should teachers open their schools in the morning by reading a portion of the scripture?

Should the door be closed against pupils, who are not present at 9 o'clock in the morning?

Should the rod be used in school?

Should the wages of females be equal to those of male teachers?

The nature of the topics considered depended to a large extent upon the imagination and wisdom of institute leaders. There was a noticeable tendency to broaden the subject matter as the movement developed and to include in the programs a discussion of philosophical principles as well as detailed methods and procedures. Samuel P. Bates,[8] one of the most influential institute workers, prepared a handbook in 1864 which was designed to serve as a guide to organizers of institutes. Among other suggestions he included a list of recommended topics for discussion. A few of these are worth examining, since they reveal the nature and scope of the better programs during the latter years of the period under discussion. Outside of the questions pertaining primarily to method, Bates suggested the following: [9]

Is it necessary that the laboring class in a nation should be educated?

Should a military spirit be encouraged among the pupils of our common schools?

Does the pecuniary prosperity of a nation depend upon its intelligence?

[7] *Pennsylvania School Journal*, Vol. VI, No. 9 (1858), p. 268.
[8] Bates, Samuel P., *Method of Teachers' Institutes and the Theory of Education* (New York, A. S. Barnes and Burr, 1864).
[9] *Ibid.*, pp. 53–55.

Do the good morals of a community depend upon its intelligence?

Does the stability of a nation depend upon the universal diffusion of intelligence?

What are the prominent causes of failure in teaching?

Should prizes and rewards be offered for superiority of scholarship?

What are the causes of the declining health of pupils, and the remedies?

How can the cordial cooperation of parents be best secured?

Can teaching be reduced to a science?

What are the prominent defects of textbooks?

Are our courses of study and methods of teaching sufficiently practical?

What disposition should a teacher make of his time out of school hours?

What is the true philosophy of school government?

What motives and incentives to study ought to be appealed to?

Are public school examinations and exhibitions advisable?

Should physical culture be made one of the regular branches of instruction in our common schools?

Should singing be one of the regular branches taught in school?

The variety of topics chosen for institute programs increased as this agency grew and developed. It is significant, however, in light of the recent interest of teachers in social problems, to note how few fundamental and practical issues were discussed during the early history of institutes. The assemblage of teachers and other school officials for mutual improvement incidentally offered an opportunity for textbook and supply salesmen to display their wares and further the commercial interests of their respective concerns. That the book representatives were characteristically aggressive in promoting sales and that their enthusiasm was sometimes resented by institute organizers, is evidenced by the following criticism proffered by James M. Milne: [10]

The highest efficiency of Institutes will never be reached until so-called book-men, or pedagogical missionaries, shall be relegated to their

[10] Milne, James M., "Teachers' Institutes; Their Past and Their Future," in *History of Educational Journalism* (Syracuse, C. W. Bardeen, 1893), p. 17.

proper place in the Institute room. They should be taught to know that they have a place in the Institute for the benefit of the teachers, while often from their practice one would judge that teachers are gathered together for their special advantage, and that the rest of the Institute work is purely perfunctory and incidental. An institute is not a book fair, no matter how desirable or attractive such a place may be. Sometimes, the book tables are placed in front between the conductors and the teachers. The book men seated at these tables often use the period given to Institute work in casting up their accounts, writing letters, or making out their reports. Sometimes, the tables are placed in a wide aisle in the centre of the room, thus breaking the audience into two parts, where the assiduity of the agents at work diverts and distracts attention. Even when the tables are in the rear of the room, these missionaries, during an Institute period, will often carry on a conversation with some reluctant buyer, or will chaff each other on their success or failure.

Despite the difficulties just reported, it was the judgment of most prominent educators that teachers' institutes were highly profitable, that they gave impetus to inquiry and earnest thought, and that they served as an agency for educating untrained teachers. While it was never seriously felt that they were an adequate substitute for normal schools, they were supported and promoted as the only quick means of lifting the general level of teaching.

It is difficult to appraise the significance of teachers' institutes during this period because they were paralleled by many other important educational innovations. The introduction of normal schools, the establishment of the office of county and city superintendent, the increase in the number of professional books and educational journals, all tended to awaken the interest of both the teachers and the public in improving the schools. It seems clear that the growth of the population during this period much surpassed the establishment and maintenance of normal schools and that thousands of prospective teachers had no other means of securing even the most elementary training for their posts outside of the institute. Of equal significance was the stimulation provided by this agency toward the professional growth of those individuals who had entered the teaching profession before the advent of any kind of teacher-preparatory institution. The infusion of new ideas of teaching and of classroom management was made possible through institute sessions, and incalculable value was derived if the comments of state superintendents and county school officers can be relied upon.

A further contribution was the arousal of public sentiment in favor of schools. The general sessions of the institutes were open to the public and some of the ablest educators and friends of education participated in these meetings, thus bringing to the local districts and counties new ideas and encouragement for improved programs of education. Perhaps of greater importance was the unification of the profession itself through the spread of propaganda. Institutes went on record as favoring supervision, state normal schools, equal pay for men and women teachers, higher salaries, and state aid for institutes. Teachers became active in political matters related to the schools. Where hitherto they had been relatively powerless as individuals, they now became articulate as groups and were occasionally able to exert pressure on state legislatures.

SUGGESTED READINGS

American Journal of Education, Henry Barnard (ed.), Vol. VIII (1860), pp. 673–78; also (new series, No. 15), No. XL (1865), pp. 387–414.

BATES, SAMUEL P., *Method of Teachers' Institutes and the Theory of Education* (New York, A. S. Barnes and Burr, 1864).

DICKINSON, JOHN W., "Proceedings of the Department of Superintendence of the National Education Association [Washington Meeting] State Teachers' Institutes," U. S. Bureau of Education, Circular of Information, No. 2 (Washington, Government Printing Office, 1889).

MILNE, JAMES M., "Teachers' Institutes; Their Past and Their Future," in *History of Educational Journalism* (Syracuse, C. W. Bardeen, 1893).

SWEET, SAMUEL N., *Teachers' Institutes or Temporary Normal Schools* (Utica, N. Y., H. H. Hawley and Company, 1848).

XIV

The Development of Supervision

THERE were no noteworthy changes in the supervision of schools immediately following the Revolutionary War. The public still looked to laymen to manage school affairs, and committees and visitors continued their surveillance of teachers and pupils in much the same fashion as they did in colonial days. Evidences of inefficiency and neglect on the part of school boards in the fulfillment of their supervisory responsibilities are numerous and extend well past the turn of the century. As late as 1839 the Connecticut Board of Education, in their annual report, were lamenting this situation and described conditions as follows:

But the present mode of discharging this duty [supervision] is, in many places, inefficient, irregular, and formal at best. Schools are not unfrequently visited "twice," as required by law, in the same week, and sometimes in the same day. In many cases it is done not so much to encourage the teacher, or stimulate the pupil, as to secure a title to the school money. Until the past year it was not customary for any one of the Visitors to examine all the schools. Hence, no one could compare their relative progress. It is the practice to allot different schools to different members of the committee, and thus to make the labor less to each individual, if not as profitable to the school.

This condition was by no means peculiar to Connecticut. Other states suffered equally from the inattentiveness of school committees. Not only were the lay supervisors generally remiss in the matter of visiting schools, but the quality of the supervision which they were able to provide was uniformly poor. It was apparent to the more discriminating statesmen that members of school boards who were engaged eight hours a day at the task of making a living could never hope to raise the instructional level of the public-school system to celestial heights. In fact, in spite of the educational innovations for which this period (1776–1860) is especially noted, the quality of supervision showed scarcely any appreciable improvement over that of pre-Revolutionary days. There were many obstacles that stood in the way. Schooling still remained, actually, a local function despite the persistent efforts of educational leaders to weld together the heterogeneous parts into some semblance of a whole. Tradition favored the laissez-faire policy. State and county aid to local schools, even as late as 1850, constituted such a small proportion of school budgets as to be unimpressive. Distance and the limited facilities for travel made unification difficult if not impracticable. The science of pedagogy was in its infancy and normal schools were just being established. Teachers were transient, untrained, and ignorant. Only a few members of the profession were competent to appraise the practices of teachers and it was generally conceded that the latter were "born," not "made." In view of these limiting factors, it is not surprising that the art of school supervision remained undeveloped for such a long period of time in America.

Despite this apparent static condition, there were forces at work during this period which presaged the advent of a new era in school supervision. The physical changes which were taking place in American life itself—such as the growth of cities, inventions that displaced or relieved manual labor, and the development of roads and intercommunication improvements generally—hastened the arrival of a coordinated program of education. It was during this period, as Chamberlain so aptly put it, that "the trail was expanding into the turnpike; the canal-boat was fitted with a boiler and a steering gear; the stage coach took on the form of the railway car. The mail pouch, carried by weary rider on faithful horse, was now conveyed by steam. The telegraph had come to tie the East and the West, the North and the South. The modern printing press had placed the weekly, and later the daily, paper upon the reading table. The sewing machine; the kerosene lamp, that connected the tallow dip with the arc light; the magazine; the cotton gin; the perfected lathe; the milling machine; the dredge, were the forerunners of the electric car, the telephone, the bicycle, and the gas engine." [1] These improvements and inventions increased the complexity of life, lured people into the cities, and created both wealth and leisure time for a larger proportion of the population than had ever enjoyed them before. Schools grew rapidly, the curriculum was expanded to care for vocational and cultural needs hitherto neglected or unknown, and educational leadership became imperative.

Perhaps the greatest impetus to school reform came from the reorganization of our national and state governments. As the colonies were about to enter into the conditions of statehood, the Congress of the Confederation in 1785 passed legislation which laid the foundation for state support of schools. The setting aside of land from the public domain as a fund whose sale was to be controlled by state authority and the proceeds invested for use in the development of schools gave rise to a form of state supervision which was destined to have far-reaching effects upon local educational projects. State officers were given supervision over the sale of these lands, and conditions were attached to the distribution of the proceeds of the fund which involved supervision by county, township, and district officers. At first this surveillance applied only to the "material appliances" of public education but it suggested a pattern which was later carried over to matters more closely related to the teaching process.

THE OFFICE OF STATE SUPERINTENDENT OF SCHOOLS

The acceptance by the individual states of the responsibility for popular education and the organization of a state system of schools with the constitution of the state as its basis necessitated the appointment of a public officer to administer and supervise the work. [2] At first the job was treated as incidental to the other work of the state and the duties attached to the office were added to those of an already existing officer, whose chief responsibilities lay in some other direction. Illinois, for example, in 1825

---

[1] Chamberlain, Arthur H., "The Growth of Responsibility and Enlargement of Power of the City School Superintendent," in *Education*, Vol. III, No. 4 (May 15, 1913) (University of California Publications), p. 318.

[2] New York was the first state to create a state officer to exercise supervision over its schools. This office was established in 1812.

instructed its secretary of state to act, ex-officio, as state superintendent of schools. Similarly in Vermont, Louisiana, Pennsylvania, and Tennessee, one officer (the secretary of state) performed this dual task. By 1861, according to Cubberley, "there were ex-officio officers in nine and regular officers in nineteen of the then thirty-four states." [3]

It was obviously impossible during the era of horse-drawn vehicles for a state superintendent of schools to personally visit and supervise the work of all classroom teachers even in the rural areas. [4] By dint of unusual strength and effort he sometimes managed to visit selected schools in each county and thereby gained firsthand impressions of educational conditions. In some states the commissioner was required by law to spend several weeks in the different counties of the commonwealth each year.

Because of its magnitude and scope, however, the task soon took on the character of broad supervision. It was the state superintendent's responsibility to gather statistics, to awaken public interest, to advise regarding legislation, to unify the school work of the state, to supervise the use of school funds, and to exercise leadership generally with respect to educational matters. Cubberley summarizes the functions of these early officers as "clerical and exhortatory." [5]

Conscientious state superintendents were overladen with work. Horace Mann, on retiring from the office after having held it

[3] Cubberley, Ellwood P., *The History of Education* (Boston, Houghton Mifflin Company, 1920), p. 688.

[4] The state superintendent of schools in Indiana stated in his *First Annual Report* (1852) that "it would be impossible for him however he might desire it to make personal visitations to the public schools, and to exercise over them any direct influence. Should he attempt to go into every school district of the state, as some seem to suppose he ought, it would require for him to get once around spending a day in each district, full *sixteen* years" (pp. 29–30).

The clerical demands of the office apparently prevented many state superintendents from devoting needed attention to the improvement of instruction. William H. Powell, the state superintendent in Illinois in 1857, describes conditions as follows: "The undersigned has frequently gone to his office in the morning, after having devoted the entire day previous to letter writing, with the hope of spending a single hour in the investigation of some interesting educational topic, and found fifty and not unfrequently as high as an hundred letters awaiting his attention, and all demanding immediate answers." (*Second Biennial Report of the Superintendent of Public Instruction in the State of Illinois, 1857–58*, p. 28.)

[5] Cubberley, Ellwood P., *State School Administration* (Boston, Houghton Mifflin Company, 1927), p. 274.

eleven years, said that he had labored in the cause an average of not less than fifteen hours a day, that from the beginning to the end of the period he had never found a single day which could be spared for relaxation, and that months and months together had passed without his being able to withdraw from working time to call upon a friend.[6]

State Agents and County Superintendents

Educational leaders early recognized the inability of a single official to cope successfully with the great problems of administration and supervision which presented themselves in every state. There was need for greater unification and solidarity among the various units and districts within the states. The educational achievements of one community were unknown to others and improvements were by no means universal. Teachers were ignorant and local school committees were unable, even though willing, to supply helpful suggestions with respect to classroom teaching. The solution lay in part in a more direct and close supervision of teachers and curricula. Various experiments were tried. Some states sent out agents or school visitors to work in the field, to study local conditions, and assist wherever possible.[7] While these temporary measures were helpful, it was evident that some permanent machinery needed to be created to extend the services of these agents. The most promising solution pointed in the direction of a county school officer who would serve as a liaison between the state and the local districts.

The basic foundation for this new office had already been laid in some states in the form of school-land commissioners, township superintendents, board of county commissioners, or other county officers. In certain states where the county constituted the local political unit, the office was evolved as a result of the increasing state need for oversight and control of the schools. It was the duty of these new officers to look after the sale and preservation of school lands, to assemble and report statis-

---

[6] *Indiana School Report, 1852*, p. 33.

[7] In 1850 the state board of education in Massachusetts sent out several agents to visit the schools of the commonwealth and instructed them to do all that a body of eminent educators, without administrative authority, could do for the schools of the state.

tical data to the state office, to apportion the income from school funds and the proceeds of taxation, to approve changes in district boundaries, to settle disputes between districts, and to exercise general supervision over the schools.

Unfortunately, in most of the states, the office was an elective one, following the pattern already established for other county officials, and the term was limited to one year. The direct result of this process of choosing a county superintendent by popular vote and for such a short duration of time was to throw the office into politics. The candidates were frequently men without any educational qualifications whatsoever, whose sole interest lay in the small salary provided. To further aggravate the problem, the county superintendency was frequently a part-time job and the incumbent carried on his former vocation as usual, devoting only his spare time to the duties of his newly acquired post. Since their reelection and, consequently, their tenure were dependent upon the will of the people, the decisions and policies of these administrators were colored by the immediate reactions of their constituents rather than made for the ultimate good of the school system. Charged with the responsibility of examining teachers for licenses, county superintendents held the key to the most important door of the educational house and frequently unlocked it for incompetents. As supervisors, many of them were ineffective and unable to provide teachers with either inspiration or suggestions.

The Nature of Supervision in the District Schools

Present-day teachers can scarcely appreciate the difficulties confronting both supervisors and teachers of these early days. Not only was the physical equipment of the classroom meager in amount and crude in quality, especially in the rural districts, but the infrequent visits of superintendents, coupled with the absence of any well-defined program of studies, could not conceivably result in any appreciable improvement in teaching.

Some notion of the nature of supervision [8] and the conditions

---

[8] The following report of procedure is fairly characteristic of that employed by the more intelligent group of county and town superintendents: "During my stay in the school-room, I would note the teacher's method of instruction, his manner

prevailing in the district schools of the eighteen-fifties can be gathered from the following comments of the county superintendent of schools of Bucks County, Pennsylvania, about his experiences in school visiting: [9]

In one school, where I had drawn the map of Pennsylvania on the black board, the same diagram had remained for a year, the board never having been used in the interim.

In another, not a scholar in the school could tell me in what country he lived, and when I held up Holbrook's five inch globe, the oceans on which were painted blue, and asked what it was, a large boy, at least seventeen years of age, replied, "a bird's egg!"

At one school, where I called, the teacher came to the door; it was storming severely; without any salutation or token of recognition, he hastily withdrew, and by the time my horse was tied and blanketed, and my school apparatus placed in the door-way, he had roughly sketched a map of his own state on each of two black-boards, which the directors had recently procured for him. Divesting myself of my wet hat and over-coat, I stepped to one of the boards, and expressing my pleasure at the interest thus manifested in the study of geography, commenced pointing with a ruler to the boundaries and rivers, inquiring of the scholars at the same time, what they were. I was unable to get a single answer from any of them, because this was their first "drill." They interchanged sly looks with each other, as much as to say, "Our foxish teacher has been holed this time."

At the time of my visit to another school, with eight good windows in the room, three of them only had the shutters open. The mephitic atmosphere was very oppressive and offensive; but it was not long before the sashes of all were raised and a free circulation of pure air admitted. Although this was late in the summer, the house had not been whitewashed this season, nor the desks, benches and floors scrubbed and

---

of school government, the deportment of the pupils, the degree of interest they appeared to manifest, and the general condition of the school house, &c. Before leaving I would generally give a short address to the pupils, endeavoring to impress upon their minds the necessity of an education, the propriety of improving the present opportunity by close application &c. My remarks were usually listened to with profound attention and deep interest. I would also make suggestions to the teacher, as presented themselves to my mind, or the nature of the case seemed to require." (*Report of the Superintendent of Common Schools of Pennsylvania, 1856,* Beaver County, pp. 59–60.)

[9] *Report of the Superintendent of Common Schools of Pennsylvania, 1856,* Joseph Fell, County Superintendent of Schools, Bucks County, pp. 76–77.

cleaned. The room might be fairly characterized as filthy and un-healthy, and but little wonder need be expressed that a child, *compos mentis*, should be, as was here the case, twelve months learning its letters! This teacher asked me if I thought the schools throughout the county were any better than before the County Superintendency. Judging by things about him, the question was natural enough.

Despite these discouraging conditions, the work of county su-perintendents contributed significantly to the unification and im-provement so urgently sought by the state authorities. This was reflected in the examinations of teachers and in the supervi-sion of instruction. Annual reports to the state throughout this period are filled with specific recommendations from county school officers for the advancement of the profession and with illustrations of crude pioneer experiments in the field of teaching. It seems clearly evident from the literature that under this form of administration conditions were improved over the local efforts which preceded them.

The Advent of the City Superintendent

The greatest advances during this period in the improvement in both teachers and curricula occurred in the cities. There were obvious reasons to account for this. The tasks confronting city school boards were so time-consuming and so difficult that dele-gation of the instructional phase of school administration to professional educators seemed expedient. Increase in population called for the erection and maintenance of a large number of schools. Teachers had to be employed, examined, and super-vised. The program of studies required considerable attention if any degree of uniformity were to be secured. Such an avalanche of problems descended upon the heads of board members that many of them resigned their posts or refused reelection because of the demands which the schools made upon their time. Reller describes this situation graphically, pointing out that: [10]

The short tenure of school committee members was not due alone to annual elections, however; resignations and declinations were fre-

[10] In Reller, T. L., *The Development of the City Superintendency in the United States* (Philadelphia, The Author, 1935), pp. 34–35. (From *Worcester School Committee Report*, 1855, pp. 11–12.)

quent. Resignations often followed the year's service in Worcester, which was described as being "with some the mission of the first two months to reform abuses, the experience of the next two to cool down and become conservative, the work of the following six to walk reluctantly at the heels of a routine, and the conclusion of the matter . . . an unspeakable disgust at the whole transaction."

The Detroit board of education, acting upon a law of 1842, provided in its rules and regulations that a fine not exceeding five dollars be imposed upon any member neglecting "to perform any duty required by the preceding regulations as a committeeman or otherwise or who shall be absent from any regular or from two successive special meetings of the board." [11]

The occasion for such drastic action indicates the degree to which private business interests were competing with school-board affairs for the time of committee members. While many cities continued to "muddle" along with their cumbersome machinery, others looked for a way out of their dilemma by employing an agent to represent and advise the board about educational matters. It is difficult to say with certainty just when the first superintendency in the United States was established. Most authorities agree, however, that Buffalo was the first city to provide officially by enactment (May 15, 1837) for the position, giving to the encumbent "the duties and obligations" generally borne by the "inspectors of the common schools of the different towns" of the state. Louisville, St. Louis, Providence, Springfield, Cleveland, Rochester, and New Orleans were not far behind Buffalo in setting up this office,[12] although it is doubtful if any one of these cities was seriously influenced in this matter by the experiences of the others. There were peculiar forces at work in each of these communities which hastened the creation of the superintendency.

The superintendent was usually elected either by the city council or by popular vote in these early days and the term of office was commonly limited to one year. In many cities no qualifications for the office were specified by law, ordinance, or

[11] *Ibid.*, p. 37. (From Detroit *Rules and Regulations*, Board of Education, 1842.)
[12] Louisville established the office of superintendent in 1837; St. Louis and Providence, in 1839.

resolution. This did not prevent members of the electing body from devising and applying their own standards.

Contradictory generalizations about the competence and character of these new educational officers can be found in the literature of this period. One commentator says that the announcement of the decision to establish the superintendency with a liberal salary had a "wonderful effect. Lawyers, whose business could not 'wane' because it had never 'waxed'; doctors, whose patients were not troublesomely numerous; clergymen, afflicted with bronchitis or some other malady, or not overburdened with hearers; office-seekers of various kinds, and all sorts of 'do nothings' all became suddenly and wonderfully impressed with the importance of common schools, accompanied by a sort of feeling that in themselves was the only power for truely elevating those schools." [13]

This dismal picture is considerably overdrawn, as is evidenced by the fact that experienced schoolmen constituted by far the largest proportion of appointees to the superintendency throughout the nineteenth century. That politics sometimes entered into the selection and that poorly qualified persons gained admittance to the office must be acknowledged. It seems clear, however, that despite considerable public skepticism, which nearly always accompanies an innovation of this nature, the affairs of the schools were better managed in the cities under superintendents than ever before. As can readily be understood, boards of education did not entrust superintendents with all the work which logically might have been centered in this executive office. They clung tenaciously to much of the business administration of the schools and were particularly jealous of those functions which involved patronage, such as the appointment of teachers and janitors.

SUPERVISORY TECHNIQUES

The work of supervision, however, was left almost entirely in the hands of the superintendent. The two methods most commonly employed by him in improving teachers were classroom

---

[13] Reller, T. L., *op. cit.*, p. 124. (From *Connecticut Common School Journal and Annals of Education*, Vol. VIII [August, 1860].)

observation and teachers' meetings. Superintendents devoted almost all their time to visiting schools and observing teachers. In some cities a required number of visits was imposed by law. The state superintendent in New York reported that "the schools of the state were visited during the year 1854 by the several town and city superintendents 22,082 times." [14]

Just how much good resulted from this practice of visiting schools will always remain a matter of speculation. In view of the absence of any standardized measuring rods for appraising either the methods of instruction or the achievements of pupils, and with supervisors so poorly equipped by preparation for the task as were the superintendents, it seems highly improbable that the technique of teaching was vastly improved during this period. On the other hand, intelligent superintendents learned a great deal from their observations, which contributed to the ultimate improvement of instruction. Outstanding achievements of teachers were brought to the attention of those who were less successful and the whole problem of method became a subject of discussion and study.

Teachers' meetings were frequently held. In most cities the meetings were held on Saturday and attendance was compulsory. General meetings, grade meetings, and special subject meetings provided an opportunity for teachers to share experiences and develop unified programs of study. Outside lecturers were often invited to participate in these gatherings and to bring new ideas and modes of teaching to the attention of the staff. The effect of these meetings was most salutary. They provided a medium by which leaders could direct and stimulate the thinking of those upon whose shoulders the real task of education rested.

The student of education can well record the establishment of the city superintendency as one of the greatest educational achievements of the nineteenth century. Not only did it place the leadership for public schools in the hands of men experienced in the work, but it also gave impetus to the scientific study of education, hastened the gradation of schools, resulted in an

[14] Reller, T. L., *op. cit.*, p. 196. (From New York, *Annual Report of the State Superintendent of Public Instruction*, January 28, 1856, p. 8.)

enriched curricula, encouraged teacher growth, and consolidated and unified the educational programs in cities. Perhaps of less significance, although not to be discounted, was the influence which the achievements of these early superintendents had on instruction in rural areas. Many of them were "trail blazers."

THE SCHOOL PRINCIPAL

A discussion of supervision would be quite inadequate without mention of the part played by principals. This office developed rapidly during the first half of the century as villages and cities expanded and one- and two-room schools were enlarged to care for the phenomenal increases in pupils. As "head teachers," this group was expected to keep a vigilant eye on discipline and to lend a hand to assistant teachers whenever occasion demanded. Prior to the advent of the superintendent, the principal was the direct representative of the board of education. He was frequently present at board meetings and advised this body about material as well as instructional matters related to the schools. In the smaller communities, his time was occupied chiefly in teaching the upper grades so that the amount of classroom supervision provided was relatively insignificant. Supervision was, at best, only incidental and took the form of planning and revising courses of study, regrading and classifying pupils, arranging schedules, and occasionally demonstrating method.

Even in the larger cities, principals were not freed of teaching duties until late in the period under discussion. They apparently knew relatively little about the work in the lower grades of the school system, as the following discussion of supervision by principals in the Cincinnati schools in 1858 indicates: [15]

The most efficient agency in the improvement of the schools has been the constant and active supervision of the Principals over the labors of their Assistants. *They were, till within the last two years, only teachers of the highest classes of their respective schools.* Though nominally the Principals, they were almost as ignorant of the classification and instruction administered in the lower grades of their own schools, as of the schools

[15] *Cincinnati School Report*, 1858, p. 35.

in the adjoining districts. By a regulation of your Board, which I had the honor of submitting for your consideration, the Principals are now, with one or two exceptions, relieved of the personal charge of any one department, and almost all of them have small recitation rooms assigned to them, where they may keep the records, examine classes, and transact the general business of their schools.

Despite the slow development of this office of principal as distinct from head teacher, many of the educational leaders of the generation both preceding and following the Civil War were recruited from this group. Experience as a principal became a big consideration in qualifying for a school superintendency, and even today the largest proportion of our chief school executives come into office by this route. Perhaps the greatest gain derived from this separation of the principalship from teaching was the impetus which it gave to the study of method and curriculum content. The concentration of a large number of excellent minds on the improvement of instruction was bound to leave its imprint upon the schools and pave the way for a more scientific approach to the problems of teaching.

THE ATTITUDE OF TEACHERS TOWARD SUPERVISION

This review of the history of supervision from 1776 to the Civil War includes much of the machinery designed for improving teachers and teaching but touches only incidentally upon the effects of it all on the classroom teacher. Unfortunately, her testimony is not included either in the local annual reports along with that of school committees and superintendents or in the reports that incorporate statements of county and town supervisory officers. Only isolated reactions of teachers to the whole program of administration and supervision are available, preventing any broad generalizations from being drawn regarding their point of view about its merits and limitations.

There is some evidence and much good logical argument in support of the notion that many teachers were opposed to the idea of the city superintendency. One teacher, writing for the *Rochester Daily Democrat*, showed her opposition to the supervisory machinery by saying that the system "needs not much trial to secure its abandonment at once." She remarked that "more than $1000 is annually expended for the payment of salaries of superintendent and expenses which, if added to the tuition fund would place the schools on a sure foundation and free them from many embarrassments." [16]

Whether or not this teacher represented any substantial number of his or her associates is a matter of conjecture. It seems reasonable that teachers who had become accustomed to the visits of laymen and whose only superior officer was a teaching principal would be somewhat fearful of a program of supervision which promised to be more critical. If the reports of county and town superintendents can be relied upon, a large body of teachers were not only untrained but were in the classroom for lack of something better to do. It would be surprising, to say the least, in view of these conditions, to find teachers enthusiastic about reforms of this nature.

During the campaigns for establishing county superintendencies in the various states, resolutions were sometimes passed at teachers' institutes and associations in favor of this office. At the Pennsylvania state education convention at Harrisburg in 1850, the teachers went on record in support of the office of county superintendent. [17] Similarly the Conemaugh Teachers' Institute [18] in Pennsylvania passed a resolution in 1852 (October 25) commending to the consideration of the legislature the office of county superintendent. It is extremely unlikely that teachers originated these resolutions. Institutes and associations were usually organized by administrators, and in all probability this support for improved supervisory machinery came as a result of the persuasive oratory of lay leaders and superintendents.

The great contribution of this period was not the improvement in the techniques of supervision but rather the establishment of an administrative structure which made professional supervision possible at a later date. The dearth of professional knowledge

[16] Reller, T. L., *op. cit.*, p. 65. (From *Rochester Daily Democrat*, June 12, 1848.)

[17] Wickersham, James P., *op. cit.*, p. 496.

[18] Taylor, William S., *Development of the Professional Education of Teachers in Pennsylvania* (Philadelphia, Lippincott, 1924), p. 67.

generally and the abysmal ignorance of principals and county superintendents in the area of child psychology continued to focus the attention of supervisors upon such relatively unimportant matters as arrangement of rooms, ventilation, discipline, dress, Bible reading, speech, and punctuality. It remained for another generation of educators to develop the science of teaching to the stage where the important objectives of education were clearly appreciated and where principles of teaching were understood.

SUGGESTED READINGS

CHAMBERLAIN, ARTHUR H., "The Growth of Responsibility and Enlargement of Power of the City School Superintendent," in *Education*, Vol. III, No. 4 (May 15, 1913) (University of California Publications).

CUBBERLEY, ELWOOD P., *Public Education in the United States* (Boston, Houghton Mifflin Company, 1934), pp. 212–30.

MAYO, A. D., "The Organization and Reconstruction of State Systems of Common-School Education in the North Atlantic States from 1830–1865," in *Report of the Commissioner of Education, 1897–98* (Washington, Government Printing Office).

RELLER, T. L., *The Development of the City Superintendency in the United States* (Philadelphia, The Author, 1935).

XV

Teachers' Examinations and Certification

IN modern times an individual who plans to enter the field of public-school teaching must be prepared to undertake an extended period of training and to meet the requirements laid down by institutions whose main business is to supply the state with teachers. The law requires that candidates for teaching positions shall possess not merely knowledge of the specific branches to be taught but, in addition, the mastery of a number of subjects commonly designated as "education." Graduation from state institutions frequently carries with it permission or license to teach in the field in which the prospective candidate has done his major work. For the majority of these graduates, no special examinations are required beyond those taken in the regular course of their college or normal-school program.[1] For those who have not attended state institutions, teaching certificates are granted on the basis of meeting specific course requirements in recognized colleges or universities.

No such training institutions existed in the early history of our country to serve as a selective agency for recruiting and preparing teachers. During the colonial period and well into the nineteenth century, the selection of teachers and the determination of their qualifications rested almost entirely in the hands of selectmen and school committees. Education was a local rather than a state matter, supported by the residents of the various districts, sometimes generously and sometimes niggardly, depending upon community wealth and cultural development. The only safeguards which the citizen had against incompetent teachers were the qualifications which his representatives on the school committee established for eligibility to teach. These requirements

[1] Certain large cities are exceptions to this rule.

usually consisted of three types: a good moral character, capacity to govern a school, and suitable academic attainments.

CHARACTER QUALIFICATIONS AND ABILITY TO GOVERN

Because of the emphasis placed upon religion, particularly in New England, the character of the applicant received most careful scrutiny. Traditionally, the New England schoolmaster had been a God-fearing, virtuous man who could have substituted for the local minister almost any Sunday without disturbing the equanimity of the congregation. He was expected, therefore, to be a man of sober conversation, of exemplary character, and addicted to no bad habits whatsoever. That the schoolmaster's perpetual responsibility of serving as a model sometimes induced repressions which were expressed in punishments meted out to fractious spirits in the classroom gave the school committee but little concern. Since our educational inheritance sprang in no small measure from New England practice, this emphasis on character was extended to other sections of the country and therefore became a fairly common requirement of school boards.

To assume, however, that all the teachers of New England, not to mention those in other divisions of the United States, were exemplary characters as a result of the emphasis placed by school committees upon the conduct of applicants would be quite erroneous. The state superintendent of schools in Vermont, in his *Annual Report* of 1851, deprecated the activities of some of his teachers as shown by the following comment: [2]

In some of our larger towns, I have been informed that men have been employed for years as the instructors of youth who tarry long at the wine press . . . and are not infrequently incapacitated in the after part of the day to proceed even with the ceremonies of the school.

While this perhaps represents an extreme situation in the matter of personal conduct, it was by no means peculiar to Vermont. A New Jersey superintendent in 1851 bewailed the fact that one of his associates, a town superintendent, had granted a

---

[2] *Report of the State Superintendent of Schools, Vermont, 1851,* p. 35.

license to a man who "had fallen into very gross habits of profanity" in spite of the fact that everybody involved was acquainted with the facts of the case.[3]

That every state admitted into the profession a number of individuals whose character qualifications were below those intended in the law is an acknowledged fact. This situation is, of course, not peculiar to this period but was exaggerated somewhat by the scarcity of good applicants.

The character of the applicant was not always easily discernible. Testimonials of former employing boards, ministers, and prominent citizens were given proper weighting and, coupled with the committee's general impression of the candidate's demeanor, constituted the chief basis for judging his moral fitness for the post.

To the degree that suggestions of state school officers were carried out, the prospective candidate was also asked such questions as the following:[4]

What method or methods would you adopt in order to inculcate the principles of morality, justice, truth, humanity, industry, and temperance?

What significance do you attach to each of the above terms?

How would you deal with a child who was (1) obstinately disobedient? (2) physically and mentally indolent? (3) addicted to falsehood? (4) impulsive?

It was expected that the answers to questions of this type would reveal the character of the candidate and to no inconsiderable extent his temper and disposition.

In addition to an investigation of those qualities which are commonly implied in the term "good moral character," there were occasionally included, in the candidate's examination, questions designed to bring out his attitude toward religion and politics. The following suggestions to school committees with respect to inquiring about these more intangible beliefs and atti-

---

[3] *New Jersey School Report, 1851*, p. 112.
[4] Adapted from *Maine School Report, 1848*, p. 57.

tudes appeared in the *Annual Report* of the Rhode Island state superintendent of schools for 1851: [5]

While a committee should not endeavor to inquire into the peculiar religious or sectarian opinions of a teacher, and should not entertain any preference or prejudices founded on any such grounds, they ought, without hesitation, to reject every person who is in the habit of ridiculing, deriding or scoffing at religion.

And while the examination should in no case be extended to the *political* opinions of the candidate, yet it may with propriety extend "to their manner in expressing such belief or maintaining it. If that manner is in itself boisterous and disorderly, intemperate and offensive, it may well be supposed to indicate ungoverned passions, or want of sound principles of conduct, which would render its possessor obnoxious to the inhabitants of the district, and unfit for the sacred duties of a teacher of youth, who should instruct by example as well as by precept."

The candidate's capacity to govern the school was also a matter of great concern to school committees. Letters of recommendation from previous employing boards frequently included a statement on the schoolmaster's discipline. But, in the case of new teachers, much reliance had to be placed upon the size, appearance, and age of the applicant. The crudeness of these early examinations is illustrated by an actual New England situation described by Philbrick as follows: [6]

A young man had been engaged to teach his first school and had already taught two weeks of the term when he was summoned before the Committee for examination in compliance with the requirements of the law. At the time and place designated, he presented himself. It was a cold winter evening at a respectable farmer's house. On arriving he was soon conducted away from the family, including some of his pupils, gathered around the blazing hearth, to a fireless upper room dimly lighted with a tallow candle. Being seated at a table opposite the chairman of the committee, the interrogatories and answers proceeded as follows:

Chairman: How old are you?
Candidate: I was eighteen years old the 27th day of last May.

[5] *Rhode Island School Report, 1851*, p. 32.
[6] Philbrick, John D., "Examining and Certificating Teachers," in *American Institute of Instruction Lectures* (Boston, 1869), p. 113.

Chairman: Where did you last attend school?
Candidate: At the Academy of S.

Chairman: Do you think you can make our big youngsters mind?
Candidate: Yes, I think I can.

Chairman: Well, I am satisfied. I guess you will do for our school.
I will send over the certificate by the children tomorrow.

In many rural districts, the examination of candidates was carried on in much the same fashion as the case just described. Among the more intelligent committees, the examination with respect to the ability of the candidate to govern the school was amplified beyond merely securing information as to his weight and height. It was not uncommon to seek his views upon the subject of discipline, to inquire under what circumstances and to what extent he deemed it proper or necessary to resort to force, and what species or mode of punishment he would adopt in certain hypothetical cases.

ACADEMIC REQUIREMENTS

The standard of academic attainments varied considerably with the cultural levels of communities and improved gradually during the two decades prior to the Civil War. Competency in reading, writing, and arithmetic was a universal requirement and some knowledge of orthography, English grammar, and geography was expected of teachers in the more populous districts.[7] As other subjects, such as American history and algebra, crept into the course of study, teachers were expected to show some mastery of these. Before the establishment of state school systems and prior to the emergence of professional school officers, there is little evidence of improvement in the academic qualifications required of teachers. Those school committees which took their legal and social responsibilities seriously gave oral examinations. These were in no way standardized but consisted chiefly of demonstrations by the applicant of handwriting specimens, readings of selected passages, and the solution of simple

---

[7] The subjects enumerated in the Wisconsin School Code of 1849 were orthography, reading, writing, English grammar, geography, and arithmetic. The district boards were given authority, however, to include such "other branches of education" as they might deem necessary and advisable.

problems in arithmetic. The fact that ignorant committee members were sometimes unable to answer their own questions did not apparently deter them from assuming the examining responsibility nonchalantly. In Indiana, the original law dealing with examinations provided that the circuit judge should appoint three examiners for each county. One applicant appearing for an examination soon after the law was enacted was asked this question: "What is the product of 25 cents by 25 cents?" His response was: "I don't know." The examiner appeared a bit perplexed and said he thought the answer was six and one fourth cents but he wasn't sure.[8]

Most teaching certificates were valid for only one year and the examinations had to be repeated annually. The absurdity of this procedure, coupled with the farcical performance of school committees attempting to examine teachers was pointed out by John Swett with reference to San Francisco in 1863. According to this author, "the 'old schoolmasters' of San Francisco were examined every year by doctors, lawyers, dentists, contractors, and business men, to 'see if they were fit to teach the common school' they had been teaching years in succession."[9] As might well be expected, teachers objected strenuously to this procedure. In Cincinnati when a reexamination of all teachers was ordered by the Board of Examiners in 1846, there was apparently a general disturbance of teacher morale, for in 1847 the president of the Board of Trustees and Visitors reported that "the repugnance with which the requirement was at first met has yielded to a general acknowledgement of beneficial results."[10]

There were many educators who favored the annual examination plan on the ground that it enabled the examiners to sift out those possessed of doubtful or deficient qualifications and those who had become grossly immoral. They held that examinations excited the teacher's mind and stimulated him to renewed efforts; that it furnished a good opportunity to make or

[8] Hobbs, Barnabas C., *Education in Indiana*, p. 35. (From "Early School Days" in one of Hobbs's State Reports.)
[9] Swett, John, *History of the Public School System in California* (San Francisco, 1876), p. 53.
[10] *Eighteenth Annual Report of the Trustees and Visitors of Common Schools to the City Council of Cincinnati* (1847), p. 6.

elicit suggestions for the improvement of teaching; that it afforded occasion for informing teachers about new laws passed or proposed; and, finally, that a public examination—and many examinations were open to the public—was a good medium for arousing the interest of taxpayers and citizens. One examiner in New Jersey, in arguing the advantages of annual public examinations, concluded his remarks with this statement: [11]

Indeed, why should there not be a county competition, to exhibit the best teachers, the best schools, and the best-educated scholars, with far more propriety than which county can produce the fattest hog or the largest turnip.

An equally inefficient and wasteful practice was to grant certificates whose validity was limited to the town, township, or county in which they were granted. Reciprocity seldom existed even in theory and committees, superintendents, and examining boards everywhere were swamped with applicants waiting to be examined.

The assumption by the states of the responsibility for public education and the provisions made for carrying it out eventually had a marked influence on procedures in examining and certifying teachers. In view of the fact that educational administration as represented by laws and practices was at various stages of development in the colonies at the time of the Revolution, it is not surprising to find wide differences in school policy persisting in the states years after the Constitution was drafted. A full discussion of the legislation and subsequent action bearing on the licensing of teachers in individual states could easily constitute a separate volume. Such a document would reveal a series of laws, many of which were relatively ineffective but nevertheless pointed in the direction of a wider control over the qualifications of teachers.

IMPROVEMENTS IN CERTIFICATION PROCEDURES

The machinery for certification was almost identical with that of supervision. At first it was handled entirely by local school committees, with suggestions emanating from the state school

[11] *New Jersey School Report, 1850,* p. 56.

officer (wherever this officer had been created) in regard to qualifications. With the advent of town and county superintendents,
the function of certification was usually transferred to these officials, where, for the most part, it rested until well after the Civil
War. In a few states [12] the state superintendent exercised some
authority directly and in some states examining boards were
appointed to assist in the matter of certification. The centralization of licensing in the hands of the state department did not
take place until the present century and a few states still share
this important responsibility with local school officers.

As a result of the concentration of the functions of examining
teachers in the hands of professional educators, two important
changes occurred in the appointment of teachers to public-
school posts. The first was the modification of the examination
procedure used in selecting teachers, including a tendency to
substitute written for oral examinations in determining the
academic fitness of candidates.[13] The second change involved an
extension of the original certification plans to include a greater
variety of certificates and a wider validity to those granted.

Neither of the above improvements was universal. In fact,
as late as the Civil War and even beyond this date one can find
antiquated and outworn practices paralleling progressive methods in the certification of teachers in nearly if not every state
in the Union.

The Nature of Teachers' Examinations

State superintendents were able, through their suggestions to
local examining officers, to improve the quality of examinations.
That the procedure remained inadequate and highly unreliable

---

[12] In New York from 1843 the state superintendent, county superintendent (1843–
1847), and town superintendent were all authorized to certificate teachers.

[13] The State Superintendent of Schools in Vermont recommended the adoption
of the written mode of examining teachers as early as 1848. (*Vermont School Report,
1848*, pp. 32–33.) Maine was using written examinations about the same time
(1848). The secretary of the Maine board of education in his annual report of 1848
says, "I believe that the examination [teachers' examination] can be made most
thoroughly by written questions and answers. This mode has already been adopted
in many towns in our state and prevails extensively in some of the New England
states." (*Maine School Report, 1848*, p. 55.) Examination by printed questions was
adopted in Boston in 1846. (*Common School Journal*, Horace Mann [ed.], Vol. IX
[1847], p. 104.)

throughout this period in spite of the combined efforts of state and local officials cannot be questioned. On the other hand, the substitution of written for oral questions furnished tangible evidence in the results obtained, which had been entirely lacking under the more primitive system. These data served as a protection against disappointed candidates who heretofore could spread their biased versions of the examination far and wide. Furthermore, the new procedure provided a basis for standardization. Future county officials and examining boards could now review the results of the past and could profit by the experience of their predecessors in preparing questions.

Where there had been no comparability in knowledge required to teach in the common schools, there gradually developed a certain likeness. It is true that the information required to answer the questions asked on the examinations would be considered unimportant to even the most conservative of our present-day educators, since it was quite unrelated to the business of everyday life. Unfortunately, the author was not able to unearth questions which might be considered as truly representative of practice in the United States.[14] Perhaps the concept of the knowledge which a qualified teacher should possess is best portrayed in a book of examination questions prepared by Isaac Stone, principal of the Kenosha High School, entitled *Complete Examiner*.[15] As a result of twenty years of experience as a teacher and a superintendent of schools, Mr. Stone assembled more than twenty-five hundred questions which he apparently deemed typical of the better examinations given. In his "Hints to Candidates" he says: "When you can give positively correct answers to all questions in the Complete Examiner, you need not hesitate to present yourself for examination before *any Board of Examiners*." [16]

In all probability, many of our modern teachers would not have succeeded in passing these tests, judging from the nature

---

[14] Readers interested in examinations given to city-school teachers might well consult the Reports of the Committee on Qualifications of Teachers in Philadelphia, 1858, 1859, 1860, 1861.

[15] Stone, Isaac, *The Elementary and Complete Examiner* (New York, A. S. Barnes and Company, 1864).

[16] *Ibid.*, p. 12.

of the questions asked. The following are a few sample questions from Mr. Stone's *Examiner:*

Orthography: What is an Improper Triphthong?
           Name the Semi-vowels.

Reading: What are Cognates? How would you teach them?
        What is the Antepenultimate? the Pre-Antepenultimate?
        Define Pitch. How many general distinctions of Pitch?

Geography: Bound Norway and tell how many square miles it has.
          Inhabitants. Climate. Soil. Products. Government.
          Religion. Education. Principal towns. Mines.
          Name the seas, bays and gulfs on the map of the Eastern
          Hemisphere.

Grammar: Define Proximate Analysis. Ultimate Analysis. What
        is a mixed sentence?

Arithmetic: Give the proof by counting out the nines (in multiplication).
           If the difference of time between London and Oregon
           City is 8 hours, what is the difference of longitude?

One might well be disposed to question whether or not achievement on examinations of this character bore any significant relation to successful teaching. In terms of our present-day theory of education, the tests were certainly irrelevant. On the other hand, at a time when normal schools were equipped to prepare considerably less than five per cent of the teaching personnel, it was absolutely essential that machinery for examining and certificating teachers be developed and that a degree of uniformity and objectivity be obtained. The written examinations and the lengthening of the tests to include a wide range of subject matter contributed to this end. As the examinations became more comprehensive, there was provided the assurance to the public that the successful candidates were at least literate and reasonably familiar with the content of the school program. In a few states where normal schools had already introduced courses on the theory and practice of teaching, questions of a pedagogical nature were included in the examinations. In a California examination reported by the state superintendent (1864–1865), twenty questions on teaching theory and practice were asked. These concerned such matters as "the principal objects of a recitation," "the method of regulating whispering in school," the attitude of the candidate toward "giving prizes," "the object of the study of arithmetic," "the uses and abuses of school exhibitions," "who was Horace Mann," and the "particular advantages of oral spelling and written spelling." [17]

The larger towns and the cities ordinarily responded more readily to modifications in examining procedure than the state at large. As early as 1847 there was apparently some attention given to educational theory, as is evidenced by a list of printed questions used in teachers' examinations in Columbus, Ohio. The fifty questions which made up the examination included five general, five government, five grammar, five reading, five orthography, five penmanship, five arithmetic, five geography, five definitions, and five theory of teaching.[18]

While still occupying a relatively unimportant place in the minds of school committees and examining officials, some knowledge of pedagogy was gradually coming to be accepted as an essential part of a teacher's equipment. The old idea that mastery of subject matter should constitute the sole criterion for evaluating a teacher's qualifications was giving way to a more enlightened point of view. That examining officials became conscious during this period of the importance of professional alertness on the part of teachers is apparent from the resolutions unanimously adopted by school examiners at a state convention in Ohio in 1856. It was voted at this meeting:[19]

That the following questions should be answered in writing by each and every applicant, to wit:—

What school if any have you attended with direct reference to fitting yourself for teaching?

What books on the subject of teaching have you read?
To what educational papers are you a subscriber?

[17] California Department of Education, *First Biennial Report of Superintendent* (1864–1865), pp. 103–4.
[18] *Common School Journal*, Vol. IX (1847), pp. 364–66.
[19] Coggeshall, W. T., "System of Common Schools in Ohio," in *American Journal of Education*, Henry Barnard (ed.), Vol. VI (1859), p. 537.

THE DURATION AND VALIDITY OF CERTIFICATES

Not only was a perceptible change made in the type of examinations given to candidates for teaching positions, but an equally significant modification began to appear in the certification procedure as well. In the early history of state school systems it was general practice to limit the life of teaching certificates to a single year's duration and the area in which they were valid to the local unit of supervision. In most instances no limitation was placed upon the specific subjects which the holder of a certificate might teach. The form presented by the state of Wisconsin in 1852 illustrates the nature and scope of the typical teaching certificate.[20]

I do hereby certify that I have examined . . . and do believe that he she is qualified in regard to moral character, learning and ability to teach a common school, in this town, for one year from the date hereof.

Given under my hand this . . . day of . . . A.D., 18 . . .

(Signed)

Town Superintendent of Schools
for the town of . . .

The inadequacy of a certification plan which gave to all teachers, regardless of their qualifications, equal privileges was pointed out by many county and state superintendents rather early in their experience with certification. An illustration of a rather crude attempt at differentiation in the matter of validity is furnished by an Iowa county where the duration of the certificate issued was related to the success of the candidate in the examination. The procedure was as follows: "Those answering fifty per cent of the questions were permitted to teach for four months, sixty per cent for six months, seventy per cent for eight months, eighty per cent for ten months, and ninety per cent for one year." [21]

In reality, this represented four grades of certificates. Cities and school districts employing principals and a large number of teachers quite commonly made a distinction between cer-

[20] Patzer, C. E., *Public Education in Wisconsin* (Madison, 1924), p. 126.
[21] Aurner, Clarence R., *History of Education in Iowa* (Iowa City, State Historical Society of Iowa, 1914), Vol. I, p. 82.

tificates, although the duration of the licenses tended to remain the same. In Cincinnati, as early as 1845, three classes of certificates were granted based on "the qualifications which the applicants, on examination, shall seem to possess." [22] Since in Cincinnati teachers were classified as first, second, and third assistants, it is presumed that the certificates granted conformed to this nomenclature. Principals' certificates apparently existed, for in this same year (1845) the Board of Examiners reported that "in order to obtain a Superior Principal's certificate, the candidate must be well versed in the whole" (referring to the "leading branches of a good business education"). [23]

California was one of the first states to provide a graded plan of certification and, according to Philbrick, [24] it represented a model which might well be emulated. In this state (California), three district boards existed for the examination of teachers. The first, the State Board of Examinations, had power to grant certificates of the first grade, valid for four years; certificates of the second grade, valid for two years; certificates of the third grade, valid for one year; and life certificates, which could be revoked only for immoral or unprofessional conduct or want of qualifications to teach. The second examining authority was the County Board of Examiners, which granted three grades of certificates, the validity of which extended from three years for the first grade to one year for the third grade. The remaining legal agency in the matter of certification was the City Board of Examiners, to which special laws applied. These boards had power to grant certificates of the same grades and for the same duration as the state board, but the validity was restricted to the city in which they were issued. Considerable reciprocity existed between cities, counties, and between the state and the city.

Another feature of the California law of 1864–1865 which was fairly unique was the recognition of state-normal-school diplomas as licenses to teach. Graduates of teacher-training institutions generally were subjected to the same examinations as those without any professional training whatsoever.

---

[22] *Sixteenth Annual Report of the Trustees and Visitors of Common Schools in Cincinnati, Ohio* (1845), p. 20.

[23] *Ibid.*, p. 20.   [24] Philbrick, John D., *op. cit.*, pp. 123 ff.

Most of the states still had a long way to go in reorganizing their certification machinery at the time of the Civil War. It is significant, however, to note that the pattern was already constructed and the general direction indicated.

To recapitulate, certification was first administered by lay school committees, then by town and county superintendents or by special examining boards, and eventually, although not during the period under discussion, by state authorities. It was a slow, evolutionary movement in the direction of professionalizing the process. While town and county superintendents were in many instances almost as inefficient and incompetent as the lay committees in performing the task of examining and certificating teachers, the general impression of educators of the time was that the procedure was vastly improved as a result of this change.

Even though marked advances in the qualifications of teachers did not always follow the substitution of professional machinery for the antiquated methods employed by laymen, the structure promised much by way of future progress. For the first time, the state was really able to exercise some control over teacher certification through its apportionment of school funds and could jack up those communities or districts which persisted in employing unqualified teachers. The factor which counted most heavily in bringing recalcitrant school committees to their senses was money; and even though the amounts derived from the permanent school funds constituted a relatively small proportion of local costs, they were still a potent weapon in maintaining standards.

SUGGESTED READINGS

COOK, KATHERINE, *State Laws and Regulations Governing Teachers' Certificates*, pp. 6–12, U. S. Bureau of Education, Bulletin 1921, No. 22 (Washington, Government Printing Office, 1921).

CUBBERLEY, ELWOOD P., *State School Administration* (Boston, Houghton Mifflin Company, 1927), pp. 622–23.

DUTTON, S. T., and SNEDDEN, D. S., *Examination and Certification of Teachers in Their Administration of Public Education in the United States* (New York, The Macmillan Company, 1908), pp. 245–49.

PHILBRICK, JOHN D., "Examining and Certificating Teachers," in *American Institute of Instruction Lectures* (Boston, 1869), pp. 105–48.

XVI

The Graded School and Its Influence on the Teaching Profession

IT is difficult for those of us who live in the twentieth century to fully comprehend the serious obstacles which surrounded the public-school teachers of early America. The total absence of training facilities, the dearth of suitable textbooks and teaching materials, the primitive condition of schoolhouses and the crude supervision provided for education generally, made the task of the teacher an unenviable one and for the most part relatively ineffective.

To the above limiting factors, there must be added still another which greatly complicated the teaching process—the ungraded school. With the exception of cities, children of all ages, sizes, and degrees of educational achievement were thrown into the same schoolroom to be instructed by one master. The common schools included children from six years of age and below to sixteen and above, and the teaching was a matter of individualized instruction. The number of pupils per teacher ranged from below forty to over one hundred. Individual desks had not commonly been introduced and children were crowded together on long seats and benches. Much discomfort resulted from this practice and distractions of all sorts were unavoidable. Not only did this condition add to the general confusion and increase disciplinary problems markedly, but it also proved a serious handicap to the learning process. To what extent the severity of early schoolmasters was due to the physical conditions under which they worked is a matter of speculation. That it was almost impossible to remain sweet-tempered under such circumstances no one could deny. A few of these educational prisons are still to be found in some of our backward rural areas but for the most part they have given way to more efficient arrangements.

Early Efforts toward Specialization

The first attempt toward ameliorating the unhappy conditions confronting both teachers and pupils in the rural districts was the separation of the older children from the younger ones by establishing summer schools for the latter and barring them from school during the winter months.[1] A woman teacher frequently taught the summer school and gave primary instruction to those who were too young to assist on the farm. This alleviated the task of the schoolmaster during the winter term, by reducing the range in the ages and achievements of pupils, and constituted a rough plan of gradation. The next step in the evolution of the elementary school was the employment of a female teacher for the younger and primary children and a male teacher for older and more advanced scholars.

The school laws enacted by the states usually designated the subjects to be taught in the common school. Reading, writing, and arithmetic were fairly universal requirements from the beginning and other subjects were added as the state school system developed. This general core of common-school subjects was taught to all pupils and increased in difficulty with the advancing ages of children. To this degree, there always existed a measure of gradation even in the district schools.

A somewhat better classification of pupils prevailed in the cities than in the rural areas. Cubberley points out the fact that as early as 1800 Providence, Rhode Island, had begun to classify pupils on the basis of the difficulty of subjects and was definitely moving in the direction of a graded system.[2] By 1828 [3] the course of study in Providence had been expanded considerably and a clear differentiation made between primary schools designed for children of ages four to seven, where reading and spelling were taught, and writing schools established for children of age seven and above, in which the subjects writing, arithmetic, grammar, geography, bookkeeping, and epistolary composition were offered in addition to reading and spelling. In 1838 the high

---

[1] Barnard, Henry, *Proceedings of the American Education Conventions*, 1849–1852.
[2] Cubberley, Elwood P., *Public Education in the United States* (Boston, Houghton Mifflin Company, 1934), p. 301.
[3] *Ibid.*, pp. 306–7.

school was introduced in Providence for those who were qualified to undertake "the branches of a good English education" and the nomenclature of the middle school modified from "writing school" to "grammar or writing school." In 1840 the age range of the grammar schools was stipulated as seven to fourteen and that of the high school as fourteen to seventeen. Additional subjects were included in the course of study. In 1848 a somewhat different classification was announced. The primary schools, designed for children of ages five to seven and one half, added arithmetic and music to their programs; intermediate schools were provided for the age group seven and one half to ten; grammar schools began with children of ten and retained them until they reached fourteen; and the high school carried on from this point, remaining the same as in 1840.

Comparable changes were made in other cities, during this same period of time, as new buildings were erected to care for increased enrollments. There was little uniformity among these cities, however, in the time required to complete the work of any particular division. Cubberley lists twenty-eight important cities scattered throughout the United States that introduced some form of graded schools between 1820 and 1860.[4] It was common practice in these school systems to base promotion from a lower to a higher division—for example, primary to intermediate—upon formal examinations. The educational ladder remained divided into three or four separate and distinct segments for a considerable number of years, and was only united into one complete unit as general supervision was introduced.

As was true of several other important improvements of this period, the cities led the way in establishing patterns of organization and influenced significantly the practices of rural districts. Considerable emphasis was placed upon the consolidation of schools wherever travel distances of pupils made this possible and, despite the fact that parents in rural areas clung tenaciously to the one-room school (an observation not peculiar to this period), there were forces under way which promised revolutionary changes in organization during the ensuing decades.

[4] *Ibid.*, pp. 307–8.

Pupil Classification within Buildings

Paralleling this broad separation of schools into units related to the ages and achievements of pupils, there gradually emerged a more uniform classification of pupils within the various divisions. This began first by grouping children into classes and assigning assistant teachers to help the master or principal with the recitations. Early in the century there were communities in which the school building was so arranged that assistant teachers could hear recitations in small rooms adjoining the main classroom while the principal held forth in the large assembly. Individual instruction thus gave way to simultaneous instruction. This constituted an important step in bringing about grading.

As new buildings were constructed or old ones revamped, there was a tendency to provide smaller rooms and more of them. Four-room schoolhouses were quite commonly built in cities during the late thirties and early forties and, with the rapid increase in enrollment, some division of labor was imperative. During this same period textbooks were increasing in numbers and the grading of subject matter was taking place, so that a finer classification of pupils could more easily be achieved than it had been in the past.

Successful experience with class grouping soon led to a more refined division of the elementary school, which culminated in our present system of grades. The particular pattern which was evolved was undoubtedly borrowed from Germany, where a graded plan of school organization had been developed essentially like the one finally adopted in America.

American educators, including Henry Barnard, Horace Mann, Calvin E. Stowe, Dr. Stephen Olin, and Charles Brooks were favorably impressed by the German plan and spoke and wrote extensively about it. These individuals wielded tremendous influence on educational policy in the United States and their studies abroad led them to a consensus of opinion with respect to the graded plan so efficiently operating in Germany. To give it currency throughout American cities, it was only necessary for a disciple like John D. Philbrick of Boston to demonstrate the feasibility of the idea. Philbrick, in 1847, as principal of the

Quincy Grammar School, organized after the German model what was probably the first city graded school in America. A new building was erected composed of twelve separate school-rooms, one for each teacher. Individual desks and chairs were provided for pupils and an assembly hall, large enough to accommodate at least six hundred and sixty pupils, was built on the top floor. This building served as a model which was destined to be copied by school systems for the next fifty years.

By 1860 nearly every city and town had a fairly unified system of schools, organized on a grade basis, with definite time limits established for each grade and a course of study designed for pupils of varying ages. While some differences existed in the length of the elementary-school period, the disparity was not great. The course was seven, eight, or nine years in length, with a strong preference emerging early in favor of eight. The entrance age was commonly six, so that pupils were expected to complete their work at fourteen.

Strangely enough, the period scheduled for the elementary education of children was determined originally by the church. Fourteen was the age of confirmation in the evangelical churches and of the first communion in the Catholic churches in Germany. Since this marked the advent of puberty, it was considered by church leaders to be an appropriate time for the discharge of pupils from school.

Practices in the American high school, an institution which was well under way by 1860, never presented problems in the matter of grading comparable to those abounding in the elementary schools. In the first place, the number of pupils involved was relatively small because of the high mortality and, secondly, grouping by subjects had long been the accepted procedure in the Latin grammar schools, so that the arrangement of annual programs to suit the abilities and achievements of pupils was largely a problem of adaptation.

The full significance of the graded plan of organization for teachers can scarcely be comprehended, since it was paralleled by so many other changes in the development of our educational system. Without doubt, it increased the number of teachers considerably, because of smaller classes. This change was partly due to the modification in school architecture in the direction of small classrooms in contrast to the assembly-hall type of buildings which prevailed before, and partly to the demands of parents and educators for greater individual attention to pupils. Not only were more teachers required, but more women teachers were demanded to partially offset the higher costs incident to smaller classes. These were commonly assigned to the lower grades because of the misapprehension under which the public labored, that discipline was a man's strong forte. The division into grades created specialists. Teachers experienced in handling classes of small children concentrated on the problems peculiar to this group, and there gradually developed a methodology of teaching for the various age and achievement levels of pupils. This was significant for the normal schools, since it provided them with a body of important knowledge to be passed on to prospective teachers. A less fortunate result was the policy established of paying women teachers smaller salaries than men and especially a differentiation in favor of those employed in the higher branches of the school system. While numerous illustrations of this policy can be found during the colonial period, the number of women engaged in teaching prior to the Revolutionary War was at no time large enough to have established a clear precedent. It took nearly a hundred years—until women achieved suffrage—before any serious questioning arose with respect to the desirability of this discrimination.

Perhaps the greatest contribution of the graded system from the viewpoint of the classroom teacher was the freedom which it granted her to devote her efforts to the education of a fairly homogeneous group of pupils without the confusion and disruption which the old system entailed. Whereas she frequently had been a mere "recitation hearer," she now became a full-fledged teacher, and the line of demarcation between principal-teacher and assistant-teacher gradually disappeared. Teachers were responsible for the success of their own classes and their ingenuity was taxed to the utmost. Such independence led teachers to study and to become alert to new procedures and methods and was a major factor in professional growth.

SUGGESTED READINGS

BUNKER, FRANK F., *Reorganization of the Public School System*, Chap. II, "The Rise of the Graded School," U. S. Bureau of Education, Bulletin 1916, No. 8 (Washington, Government Printing Office, 1916).

CUBBERLEY, ELWOOD P., *Public Education in the United States* (Boston, Houghton Mifflin Company, 1934), pp. 300 ff.

EBY, FREDERICK, and ARROWOOD, C. F., *The Development of Modern Education* (New York, Prentice-Hall, Inc., 1934), pp. 721 ff.

GILMAN, D. C., "The Idea of a Graded School," in *Connecticut School Report, 1859*, pp. 100–8.

REISNER, EDWARD H., *The Evolution of the Common School* (New York, The Macmillan Company, 1930), pp. 365–88.

XVII

The Influx of Women Teachers in American Public Schools

PRIOR to 1830 the teaching profession was made up almost entirely of men. During the colonial period and for five or six decades after the Revolutionary War, women had played a very minor role in the work of the public schools. In the few instances in which they were employed, female teachers were assigned to the smaller children, and taught during the summer months when male help was at a premium. By tradition, teaching had been a masculine task which, coupled with the fact that women were uneducated as a class, tended to bar them from serious consideration whenever teaching vacancies occurred. The public, during this earlier period, would have looked with disfavor upon any marked invasion of women into the teaching profession. The prevailing attitude toward the position of women was well portrayed by Horace Mann in his efforts as secretary of the Massachusetts Department of Education to modify public opinion. He said: "Four fifths of all the women who have ever lived, have been the slaves of man,—the menials in his household, the drudges in his field, the instruments of his pleasure; or at best, the gilded toys of his leisure days in court or palace." [1]

The factors which led to a changed point of view with respect to this historic tradition were numerous and complex. In 1776 Jefferson had declared that "all men are created equal" and his ideas of democracy had stirred the imagination of the thinking citizens of his time. While men continued for years to scoff at equal rights, they nevertheless gradually began to modify their attitude toward the place of women in society. One of the first evidences of this appeared in their willingness to provide them with a measure of educational opportunity. A larger

[1] *Eighth Annual Report of the Massachusetts Department of Education* (1845), p. 61.

proportion of women than ever before were admitted to the academy which was a flourishing institution between 1800 and 1860.[2] When they had availed themselves of schooling comparable in amount and quality to that possessed by many of the schoolmasters, women constituted a perpetual threat to the province heretofore reserved for men.

The spread of infant schools and the evolution of the primary school as an integral part of the educational system increased the demand for teachers and opened the door a bit wider for women. With the introduction of the graded system, the argument commonly advanced that disciplinary problems made women unacceptable as teachers lost much of its potency. Since pupils under the new plan of grouping were to be classified on an age-attainment basis, the older and more obstreperous children could, for the most part, be segregated under the instruction of male teachers, thus removing the bête noire which had previously barred women from teaching.

The Attitude of Educational Leaders

Educational leaders in the third and fourth decades of the nineteenth century enthusiastically advocated the appointment of females to positions in the lower rungs of the school ladder. In 1840 Henry Barnard, in his *Second Annual Report*, after deprecating "the disproportionate and altogether inadequate compensation paid to female teachers" goes on to state: [3]

I am aware that there are many unqualified teachers among the females who have been employed as such in the common schools; but as a class, they manifest a livelier interest, more contentment in the work, have altogether superior success in managing and instructing young children, and I know of instances, where by the silken cord of affection, have led many a stubborn will, and wild, ungoverned impulse, into habits of obedience and study even in the large winter schools. But this last is not their sphere of usefulness. And it is necessary to modify the practice, and the arrangements of school districts, so as to constitute a class of primary schools for small children, and then to employ the same

[2] Several women's colleges were also established during this period, including Troy Seminary, Mount Holyoke, Rockford College, Elmira College, Vassar, and Georgia Wesleyan.

[3] *Connecticut School Report, 1840*, pp. 27–28.

teacher, if found qualified, through the year, before the superior efficiency of woman, in the holy ministry of education, can be exerted and felt.

The board of education in Boston in 1841 was favorably disposed toward the admission of women to teaching, as is shown by its comments: [4]

It is gratifying to observe that a change is rapidly taking place, both in public sentiment and action, in regard to the employment of female teachers. The number of male teachers, in all the summer and winter schools, for the last year, was thirty-three less than for the year preceding, while the number of females was one hundred and three more. That females are incomparably better teachers for young children than males, cannot admit of a doubt. Their manners are more mild and gentle, and hence more in consonance with the tenderness of childhood. They are endowed by nature with stronger parental impulses, and this makes the society of children delightful, and turns duty into pleasure. Their minds are less withdrawn from their employment, by the active scenes of life; and they are less intent and scheming for future honors or emoluments. As a class, they never look forward, as young men almost invariably do, to a period of legal emancipation from parental control, when they are to break away from the domestic circle and go abroad into the world, to build up a fortune for themselves; and hence, the sphere of hope and of effort is narrower, and the whole forces of the mind are more readily concentrated upon present duties. They are also of purer morals. In the most common and notorious vices of the age, profanity, intemperance, fraud, &c., there are twenty men to one woman; and although as life advances, the comparison grows more and more unfavorable to the male sex, yet the beginnings of vice are early, even when their developments are late;—on this account, therefore, females are infinitely more fit than males to be the guides and exemplars of young children.

Horace Mann voiced similar sentiments in the *Common School Journal* in 1846, pointing out that: [5]

Reason and experience have long since demonstrated that children under ten or twelve years of age can be more genially taught and more successfully governed by a female than by a male teacher. Six or eight

---

[4] *Fourth Annual Report of the Board of Education*, Boston (1841), pp. 45–46.
[5] *Common School Journal*, Horace Mann (ed.), Vol. VIII (1846), p. 117.

years ago when the employment of female teachers was recommended to school committees, not a little was said against the adoption of the suggestion. But one committee after another was induced to try the experiment and the success has been so great that the voice of opposition is now silenced.

State superintendents generally endorsed the point of view expressed by Barnard and Mann and, despite the reluctance of many school committees to depart from tradition, the number of female teachers increased phenomenally. In 1846 the proportion of females to the total teaching personnel in Connecticut was 56 per cent (including summer-school teachers) and by 1857 it had reached approximately 71 per cent.[6] A similar trend occurred in other states. The report of the state superintendent in New Jersey for 1862 refers to the changed policy in the employment of teachers as follows:[7]

It is somewhat remarkable that the number of female teachers has been gradually increasing from year to year, until it now exceeds the number of male teachers. Ten years ago, the number of male teachers was more than double that of female teachers; now the whole number of males is 1104 and the whole number of females is 1108.

In Vermont, the proportion of female teachers had reached approximately 70 per cent by 1850 and the state superintendent, in his annual report that year, remarked that he "believes there *is* a limit beyond which it is not desirable that females should be employed as teachers in our common schools; but he cannot believe that this limit has yet been fully reached."[8]

Maine, Rhode Island, New Hampshire—in fact, all the states—moved in the direction of supplanting men with women teachers in the lower grades of the school system. Some states were slower in accepting this innovation than others. Pennsylvania, for example, while responding to the trend so markedly apparent in New England, increased the proportion of female teachers only from 28 per cent in 1834 to 36 per cent in 1856.

[6] The females exceeded males in both winter and summer schools. In 1839 there were 1292 teachers in Connecticut in the winter schools. Of this number 996, or 77 per cent, were males.

[7] *Annual Report of Superintendent of Public Schools in New Jersey, 1862*, p. 7.

[8] *Fifth Annual Report of the Common Schools of Vermont* (1850), p. 20.

WOMEN TAKE OVER THE FERULE

Similarly in Ohio, the change was a gradual one, the proportion of females remaining fairly constant at approximately 40 per cent until 1850 and reaching only 46 per cent by 1855.[9] Differences in local conditions and attitudes undoubtedly influenced the rapidity with which females gained ascendancy over males in the teaching profession.

The influx of women in the profession was also reflected in the attendance at normal schools. In New York and Massachusetts in 1858, about two thirds of the pupils in teacher-training institutions were females. Comparable conditions prevailed elsewhere. The handwriting on the wall was now unmistakable—for better or for worse, the domain formerly dominated by man was rapidly passing into the hands of the "fairer sex."

Educators were not alone in their efforts to change public opinion and secure equal opportunities for women in public-school teaching. Legislators, prominent laymen, and ministers joined hands with educational leaders in bringing about this revolutionary policy. Assemblyman Hulburd of St. Lawrence County, New York, in 1844 submitted an elaborate report to the legislature in which he spoke of the value of competent and well-qualified female teachers in the great work of education: [10]

It is not the result of gallantry or of that complaisant homage which is the accorded due of the female sex, that has given to that sex an unequivocal preference in teaching and controlling the young. It is not superior science, but superior skill in the use of science—it is the manner and very weakness of the teacher that constitutes her strength and assures her success. For this occupation she is endowed with peculiar faculties. In childhood the intellectual faculties are but partially developed—the affections much more fully. At that early age the affections are the key of the whole being. The female teacher readily possesses herself of that key, and thus having access to the heart, the mind is soon reached and operated upon.

Town and county superintendents occasionally lamented the tendency of women to replace men in the classroom and upon occasion the public voiced opposition. Their protests were usu-

---

[9] *American Journal of Education*, Henry Barnard (ed.), Vol. VI (1859), p. 548.
[10] *New York State Educational Exhibit* (Chicago, World's Columbian Exposition, 1893), pp. 45–46.

ally based upon the failure of some female to maintain discipline or upon some deep-rooted conviction that older pupils should be instructed by men. A town superintendent in New Jersey reported in 1849 that "although, in point of erudition" he found females "in every instance fully equal (if not superior) to the male teachers, still they oftentimes evinced that want of sturdy determination of purpose which is requisite to carry out their authority, and keep the best order in the school." [11]   In Pennsylvania, another superintendent, after mentioning the success of many women teachers in his county, expressed the hope that the men who enlisted in the army would return to their posts, saying: "It must be acknowledged that in a few cases the 'big boys' are a little unruly." [12]   A similar argument was advanced by a superintendent in Rhode Island, who bemoaned the necessity of restraining the activities of scholars, pointing out that in many schools a female teacher, however well qualified, could not be employed "for the same reason that she cannot so well manage a vicious horse or other animal, as a man may do." [13]

Most of the objections raised after the establishment of primary schools were directed toward the employment of women in the intermediate, grammar, and high-school divisions of the school system. The superintendent of the San Francisco (city and county) schools argued as follows: [14]

It must be admitted that thoroughly competent men are capable of enduring much more of the fatigue and toil of the school room than women. [He also, like other Californians of a later period, seemed to have attributed unusual effects to the climate, for he goes on to say:] Again, we find in California a degree of maturity in our youth at the ages of ten to twelve years, that elsewhere is not common at a much later period. The boys and girls (masters and misses I should say, perhaps) of our lower grades of schools, are generally such as should have the firm, persistent and more potent guidance and discipline of men.

It was thought by some that large classes could be better taught by men and a questionnaire study on the relative efficiency of

[11] *New Jersey School Report, 1849*, p. 67.
[12] *Pennsylvania School Report, 1865*, p. 121.
[13] *Rhode Island School Report, 1855*, p. 209.
[14] *San Francisco School Report [City and County], 1857*, p. 19.

male and female teachers in Maine led the superintendent to conclude that there seemed to be a tendency to prefer male schoolteachers for schools having more than twenty scholars and that the matter of discipline was the chief consideration.[15] These opinions were held by a small minority of the supervisory officers.[16] For the most part, school executives enthusiastically advocated the employment of women, and the annual reports of state school superintendents from 1840 to the Civil War are replete with discussions of the advantages to be derived from the appointment of females to teaching posts. It would be difficult to list these claims in the order of their importance. They consisted of eloquent statements of the peculiar qualifications of women for teaching, their superior character, their greater permanence in the profession, and, finally, the economy resulting from their employment. The last, in the author's judgment, weighed more heavily with boards of education and school committees than all the other claims put together. Without discounting the sincerity of Horace Mann, Henry Barnard, and other educational leaders of this period, in their efforts to advance the status of public education by opening the doors of the teaching profession to females, it should be pointed out that it was the only expedient move to make. The phenomenal growth of schools, due to the rapid increase in population, made almost impossible demands upon society to provide teachers. Since business oppor-

[15] *Maine School Report, 1864,* p. 52.

[16] Several state superintendents sent out questionnaires to local school officers inquiring about the relative merits of male and female teachers. In 1861 the results of such a study were discussed in the *New Jersey State School Report.* To the question, How do your female teachers compare with your male teachers as instructors? the following responses were made by 180 town superintendents: 107 answered that their female teachers compared favorably with their male teachers as instructors; 18 said they were equally as good; 21 said they were in comparison "very good," or "as good," or that they did "very well," or that there was "no difference"; 5 said they taught "reasonably well," or "moderately well," or "as well" as the average; 9 said they were "superior" or "excelled"; 11 said they were "inferior" or "not as good"; 9 could not, for various reasons, make a judgment. To the second question, How do they compare as disciplinarians? the replies were not so uniformly favorable. One hundred and seventy-two superintendents answered the question as follows: 62 said "favorable"; 31 said "equally good"; 19 said "but little difference" or "quite as well"; 12 said they were "better" than the males; 25 indicated they were "inferior"; 17 said they did "moderately well" or "poorly" or "indifferently well"; 6 could not form a judgment. The superintendent of common schools in Maine reported similar findings in his *Annual Report of 1864* (pp. 52–54).

tunities and skilled trades tended to draft the abler masculine spirits of the time, the residuum fell far short of realizing the hopes and ambitions of our educational leaders for the instruction of youth. To rely alone upon men was certain to spell failure. The cost of attracting and retaining in the profession the proportion of males that formerly held sway in the classrooms of America would have met with a storm of opposition from taxpayers. New schoolhouses, normal schools, institutes, and educational supplies had made heavy inroads on local and state budgets and some measure of relief seemed almost imperative. Since it was possible to secure the services of equally qualified women teachers for as little as one third to one half the salaries required by men, the solution finally resolved seemed inevitable. While educators were frequently apologetic for the wide disparity in wages paid to members of the opposite sexes, they nevertheless were quick to use it as an argument in securing adequate teaching service for the schools.

INFLUENCE OF THE CIVIL WAR ON THE EMPLOYMENT OF WOMEN TEACHERS

The last and perhaps hardest blow dealt to male teachers during this eventful period was the outbreak of the Civil War. Responding to the call of their states to join the army, hosts of men left their classrooms never to return. While many of them lost their lives on the battlefield, more of them came back to enter occupations which promised larger financial returns than teaching. In Indiana, the proportion of men teachers dropped from 80 per cent in 1859 to 58 per cent in 1864. Ohio decreased the percentage of men teachers from 52 in 1862 to 41 in 1864, and New York is reported to have lost 1119 male teachers between 1862 and 1863.

Women teachers exceeded men in number for the first time in Iowa in 1862, and one observer in this state commented that "the loss of men from the ranks of teachers began when they were needed to fill up the ranks of Iowa regiments." [17] The state superintendent of schools in Pennsylvania remarked in 1864 that "a very large proportion of our male teachers have voluntarily en-

[17] Aurner, Clarence R., *op. cit.*, p. 76,

tered the army, or have been drafted," and indicated that it was an established fact that "there are more teachers from Pennsylvania in the Union army than there are from any other class composed of the same number of individuals." [18]

While the war accounted for the withdrawal of thousands of men from the ranks of teaching, it was not primarily responsible for the changed policy in employing teachers which was rapidly taking place in the United States. The movement began, as was pointed out in an earlier discussion, in the late thirties and made steady progress during the ensuing years. The fundamental reasons were economic in character and it remained only a matter of time before women established themselves as supreme in this vocational field.

In appraising the significance of this policy, there are many factors to be considered. Opportunities for women were enhanced manyfold. Where previously they had been barred from participating in the education of youth, they were now given preference over men. This radical departure from tradition had its impact upon other vocations heretofore reserved for males and tended to widen the sphere in which women could work. It removed the barriers which had restricted the education of females to the common branches of learning and increased their strength in the competition for jobs in nearly every walk of life. Public respect for the civic contribution of women improved steadily. On the other hand, the removal of men from the profession had its unfortunate results. The wages of females were uniformly lower and salary policies tended more and more to be established in terms of the going rates for women, accounting, in part, for the relatively low rate of compensation which has been accorded members of the public-school teaching profession.

Women teachers were a transient group, withdrawing after a few years of service to be married. This reduced their political effectiveness, slowed up educational reforms, and impeded the improvement of professional welfare. Men were more active in the work of teachers' associations and their more intimate knowledge of civic affairs made them better strategists in dealing with state legislatures and boards of education. It is perhaps too early

[18] *Pennsylvania School Report, 1864,* pp. 42–43.

to predict the ultimate effects of this revolutionary change of entrusting public education largely to women. That the pendulum swung too far as a result of the enthusiasm of Henry Barnard, Horace Mann, and their contemporaries is the opinion of many modern educators. Efforts to arrive at a golden mean whereby both men and women will share equally have, however, thus far met with little success.

Suggested Readings

Knight, Edgar W., *Education in the United States* (New York, Ginn and Company, 1934), pp. 364–65.

Maine School Report, 1864, pp. 52–54.

New Jersey School Report, 1861, pp. 16–19.

Reisner, Edward H., *The Evolution of the Common School* (New York, The Macmillan Company, 1930), pp. 384–88.

"The Schoolmistress," in *Harper's Magazine*, June–November, 1878 (Vol. LVII), pp. 607–11.

XVIII

Schoolteaching—A Part-time Job

THE public has always looked upon schoolteaching as a part-time job and, in considering the salaries to be awarded, it has attached undue weight to the proportion of the year in which teachers were not formally engaged in the classroom. Even today, when schools are commonly in session for ten full months, there is an inclination for school boards and lay citizens to view the teacher's task as a relatively easy one, consisting, as it does, of a five-day week with generous vacations scattered throughout the year. The fact that teachers are heavily burdened with homework and their summers frequently spent in professional study is more often overlooked than recognized by those outside of the profession itself.

The situation at the beginning of the nineteenth century was quite unlike that which confronts the profession today. Statistics as to the actual number of days schools were in session are so scarce as to make generalizations unreliable for particular states. Historians are rather unanimous, however, in their conclusions that most teachers were employed in "keeping school" only a few months during the year and that some outside occupation was necessary to enable them to eke out an existence. Two sessions—a winter term and a summer term—were commonly held but were usually taught by different individuals. The latter session was designed for young children whose efforts could not be exploited on the farm, and constituted a relief to the already overcrowded winter schools which were more usually organized to care for the older pupils. Women frequently taught the summer and men the winter schools. There was a great variation in the length of the winter term even within the same commonwealth, depending upon public support and the general economic and cultural level of the taxpayers. The larger towns were usually favored with longer sessions than the rural districts. It is certain that the average length of the winter terms was considerably less than four months when all schools are grouped together. Johnson, in his book *Old-Time Schools and School-Books*, describes the prevailing practice in Massachusetts as follows: [1]

In the larger towns, school kept almost continuously, but as a rule the towns were content with a master's winter school of ten or twelve weeks attended by the older children, and a summer term of equal length taught by a woman, chiefly for the benefit of the little ones. The poorer communities had to get along with a single term of two or three months, or possibly of only a few weeks.

The winter schools opened immediately after Thanksgiving, when the harvesting was completed, and closed early in the spring, in time for plowing and planting. Schoolmasters were often occupied during the summer on the farms and Samuel Goodrich, the textbook writer, refers in his autobiography to one of his teachers, Lewis Olmstead, as "a man who made a business of ploughing, mowing, carting manure, etc., during the summer months." The reader will observe that the general nature of the schoolmaster's outside employment had not changed greatly from that of colonial days.

No important advances were made in extending the school year until after 1840, when state school organizations got under way and began to examine educational conditions with a view to improvement. State aid helped in many districts and the leadership exercised by state superintendents of schools influenced many local communities to press for longer school terms. The extension of the school year was a very gradual one and is well illustrated by the experience of Wisconsin. In 1849 the average number of days schools were taught in this state was 71; in 1855 it had increased to 84; the following year it was extended to 99; in 1858 it had reached 122; and by 1860 it had arrived at its highest point, 136 days. [2]

[1] Johnson, Clifton, *Old-Time Schools and School-Books* (New York, The Macmillan Company, 1917), p. 118.
[2] *Wisconsin School Report, 1865*, p. 5.

The general situation by 1865 was vastly improved, as the following statistics will show.[3]

State	*Average Number of Months during Which School Was Maintained, 1864–1865*
Massachusetts	7.8
Nevada	7.4
California	7.36
New York	7.36
Illinois	6.5
Ohio	6.28
Vermont	6.0
Pennsylvania	5.8
New Hampshire	5.7
Maine	5.7
Wisconsin	5.5
Indiana	4.3
Kentucky	4.3
Kansas	4.0

City teachers universally fared better than those in the less populous areas. There was no farm work there to interrupt school attendance and the length of school year in many of the larger towns corresponded closely to our present practice. The Cincinnati schools in 1839–1840 ran from July 22 to June 19. If the vacation periods were the same in length as they were the previous year, the number of days' schooling surpassed that commonly provided today. Schoolteachers in these more favorable districts, therefore, devoted their major energies to their school duties and were looked upon by their fellow citizens as professional workers. Where farming and salesmanship consumed the larger proportion of the teacher's time, it was quite natural for him to be publicly regarded as a jack-of-all-trades. In spite of the marked extension of the school year which took place generally throughout the United States during the fifteen years preceding the Civil War, the rural teachers remained part-time employees of school committees. This fact accounts largely for the indifference of many of these teachers toward professional improvement and educational reforms.

The industrial movement and the growth of cities were powerful factors in improving the teacher's economic and social status, and in advancing the cause of public education generally. As

[3] California Department of Education, *First Biennial Report of Superintendent* (1864–1865), p. 41.

long as the majority of the people had to make their living by tilling the soil, it was obvious that teachers and teaching conditions would be sadly neglected, and that no great amount of education would be demanded for those who were destined to return to the farms. The very complexity of industrial life, however, focused attention upon education and constituted a real challenge to teachers. City children were not drafted for seasonal work and were available throughout the year for instruction. Furthermore, they needed to know more than reading, writing, and arithmetic in order to assume the responsibilities of municipal life and the whole thought and energy of teachers were required if the demands of the situation were to be effectively met.

Despite the unfortunate conditions which still surrounded the rural schoolteacher at the end of this epoch-making period in American education, the progress represented in the extension of the school year was nothing short of phenomenal. That it still left much to be desired for both pupils and teachers is obvious; that it was a long step forward in the direction of professionalizing the teaching personnel is equally certain.

SUGGESTED READING

JOHNSON, CLIFTON, *Old-Time Schools and School-Books* (New York, The Macmillan Company, 1917), pp. 100–50.

XIX

The Extension and Improvement of Textbooks, Courses of Study, and Teaching Materials

THE modern classroom teacher is deluged with such a wealth of textbooks, supplementary readers, instructional devices, courses of study, and professional literature that she is at a considerable loss as how best to utilize both her own time and that of her pupils. Within the period of her memory, a constant avalanche of printed school material has been flowing from the presses. Yet the extensive publication and use of textbooks is of relatively recent origin. One has but to canvass the situation at the beginning of the nineteenth century to discover that this great business 'of writing, printing, and marketing schoolbooks is largely a phenomenon of the last one hundred and twenty-five years and that other instructional aids have an even shorter history than textbooks.

An early picture of the conditions which existed between the years 1790 and 1800 is graphically drawn by the Reverend Herman Humphrey, one-time president of Amherst, in a letter to Henry Barnard, in which he wrote as follows: [1]

Our school books were the Bible, Webster's Spelling Book (third part mainly), one or two others were found in some schools for the reading classes—grammar was hardly taught at all in any of them, and that little was confined almost entirely to committing and reciting the rules. Parsing was one of the occult sciences in my day; we had some few lessons in geography by questions and answers, but no maps, no globes, and as for blackboards, such a thing was not thought of till long after. Children's reading and picture books we had none, the fables in Webster's Spelling Book came nearest to it. Arithmetic was hardly taught at all in the day schools; as a substitute, there were some evening schools

[1] In Peck, Ellen Brainerd, "Early Textbooks in Connecticut," in *Connecticut Quarterly*, January–March, 1898, p. 63.

in most of the districts. Spelling was one of the daily exercises in all of the classes.

While the above description applied specifically to Connecticut, it was fairly typical of schools in general. It is true that there were other books on the market, such as Dilworth's *Schoolmaster's Assistant* (an arithmetic by an English author); Pike's *Arithmetic; The New England Primer;* Lily's *Latin Grammar;* Caleb Bingham's *Young Ladies Accidence* and his *American Preceptor* (a book used in teaching reading); Morse's *American Universal Geography;* and a few antiquated texts of pre-Revolutionary War vintage.

Even when an exhaustive list of texts is reviewed,[2] however, one is struck by the paucity and inadequacy of materials available to both teachers and school children at the beginning of the nineteenth century. Many of the books written before 1800 were by Old World authors and savored of English form and custom. Dilworth's arithmetic made no allusion to decimal currency and his spelling book contained long lists of the abbreviations of honorary English titles. The Revolutionary War stimulated the production of American textbooks, partly because the English supply had been cut off during the hostilities and partly, as Cubberley points out, because of a desire to create books peculiarly adapted to American schools.

The phenomenal success of Noah Webster's "Blue Backed" Speller (a combined speller and reader published in 1783) led educators and writers to attempt similar accomplishments in other areas of instruction, and by 1830 textbooks had been written and were available for use in practically every subject which commonly appeared in the curriculum of the elementary school. Samuel Goodrich had published a history of the United States in 1822 which met with such popular favor that he was destined to live on easy street as a result of the royalties earned from this and other later books.[3] Warren Colburn, about the same time (1821), wrote a more elementary arithmetic than

---

[2] See Cubberley, Elwood P., *Public Education in the United States*, pp. 289 ff., for a good discussion of schoolbooks after the Revolutionary War.

[3] Davenport's *History of the United States* preceded Goodrich's ("Peter Parley") text but was not very popular.

had yet been published, entitled *First Lessons in Arithmetic on the Plan of Pestalozzi*. This book simplified the task of teaching arithmetic and was more extensively used than any other text in this field for several years. Similarly Jesse Olney's *Geography and Atlas* (1828) was based on the principles of Pestalozzi and was less formidable than other geography texts. Olney introduced the idea of home geography and suggested that beginners start the subject by studying the town in which they lived. Prior to the appearance of the first famous McGuffey books in 1836, Lindley Murray's *English Reader* and Caleb Bingham's *American Preceptor* and *Columbian Orator*, all of which appeared around 1800, were quite commonly used in teaching reading.

Despite the improvements made, textbooks during the early decades of the nineteenth century still remained encyclopedic in nature and were ill adapted to the interests and capacities of children. Teachers expected pupils to memorize the facts and such absurd practices as singing out the names of states and their capitals and the reciting of rhymes made up almost wholly of geographical facts were common techniques used in educating the young.

Reading and spelling books were often employed to impress upon children certain principles of morality and piety. Selected passages from the Bible and stories illustrating love, obedience, and other virtues were included in most of the readers prior to 1860. The subject matter in arithmetic was in no way related to life outside the classroom, and the problems presented for solution were often beyond the comprehension of the schoolmaster, not to mention the poor scholars. Even when the disciples of Pestalozzi attempted to introduce a more rational approach to learning, their textbook efforts were sadly short of their philosophy and left much to be desired.

By 1860 the number of textbooks had reached such proportions that superintendents, principals, and teachers were crying for uniformity. The state superintendent of schools in Wisconsin depicted the situation in his annual report for 1856 as follows: [4]

There is one evil incident to the great market for school books in the United States, which is in some respects, as perplexing as it is important.

[4] *Wisconsin School Report, 1856*, pp. 101–2.

It has engaged the attention of some of our ablest men, who have endeavored to remove the difficulties, and to organize some plan which shall be worthy the confidence of the people and the friends of education in the whole country. The evil to which reference is had, is the rapid and constant increase of books designed for use in schools. It is to be expected that men of cultivated and active minds will find employment to a greater or less extent in the department of education; yet while our presses are throwing off, almost every day, some new school book, the majority of them can hardly be said to possess any sterling value, and certainly no claims to favor . . . it must be confessed that there is too great a diversity in our text-books to harmonize with that uniformity which should characterize a homogeneous system.

Two years earlier (1854) this same state officer had made an estimate of texts used in the schools of Wisconsin, in which he indicated fifteen different spelling books, eighteen readers, ten geographies, fifteen arithmetics, and twenty grammars.[5] Several years prior to this (1839) there were one hundred and forty-one different schoolbooks in use in the Connecticut schools in the five subjects mentioned above.

Since teachers adhered closely to the textbooks in these days, it is no wonder that educators were confused and perplexed by the problem. However troublesome the multiplication of texts proved to be, there were one or two distinct advantages which resulted from the competition among authors for favor. Perhaps the most important one was the improvements made in the quality of the books written and in their adaptability to the changing modes of instruction. While it is true that many of the newer texts were poor adaptations of older models, still some advances were made. The establishment of normal schools and the introduction of pedagogy into teacher-training classes gradually led authors to take account of newer and improved methods in writing textbooks. Of almost equal importance was the influence which textbook production had on the introduction of new subjects in the curriculum. With these new aids to instruction, it was no longer necessary to devote from one half to three quarters of the school day to arithmetic. Such subjects as history and civics, geography, vocal music, drawing, and physical edu-

[5] *Wisconsin School Report, 1854*, p. 26.

cation could be, and were at least superficially, covered in the more progressive districts.

The evil effects of uniformity which have since been deprecated were not apparent before the Civil War; and in an era when schools were badly organized and teachers untrained, some unifying measure was necessary. The textbook represented the curriculum, and children, in passing from one district to another, suffered undue hardships whenever widely differents texts were used.

With the development of the textbook industry, book agents arrived on the scene to demonstrate their wares and show the superiority of their goods over those marketed by rival firms. Apparently this added somewhat to the existing confusion, for as early as 1854 a report of the school committee of Springfield, Massachusetts, included some suggestions for teachers in dealing with these salesmen. The report states: [6]

School Committees and Teachers are exposed to much annoyance from Book Agents. Their importunities for patronage are so urgent and persevering that it is difficult to get rid of them except by yielding to their wishes. And in furtherance of their mission, they sometimes intrude themselves into the schools without the knowledge or consent of the Committee, to the no small interruption of the exercises and even make use of means to get their books introduced without the action of the Committee, especially in remote districts, where the schools are not so directly under the eye of the Committee. The only safe rule on this subject is that no agent shall even enter a school room without being accompanied by someone of the Committee, or having their consent in writing, and that no book shall be used in any school that is not placed on the list of books adopted, *by an express and recorded vote of the Committee.*

High-pressure salesmanship developed quite naturally with the increase in the number of textbooks, and book agents constituted something of a nuisance both to teachers and board members. In situations where the state board of education was responsible for the adoption of books, tremendous influence was brought to bear upon individual members by the more successful publishers. Those whose books were already used in the schools

[6] *Report of the School Committee of the City of Springfield, Massachusetts, 1854*, pp. 9–10.

fought vigorously against change and carried on an active campaign to retain their publications in the classrooms of the state. In Vermont, the state law provided that textbooks should be adopted by the state board of education every five years. The board was required to get the opinions of prominent teachers as to the relative merits of the books under consideration and was compelled to publish both the comments of teachers and the reasons why the particular books adopted were chosen. In 1867 a difference of opinion apparently arose between the secretary of the board (state superintendent of schools) and the board of education over the adoption of certain texts. The book companies concerned entered into this fight with great enthusiasm and, if the comments of the secretary can be relied upon, they "struck below the belt" in their efforts to achieve their ends. In presenting his position to the public, the secretary of the board remarked as follows: [7]

I am aware that my public and hearty denunciation of the evil effects upon our common schools of the unauthorized use of Greenleaf's *Higher Arithmetic*, and my equally public commendation of Guyat's Geographies and Wilson's Readers, have aroused the hostility of certain publishers and that reports derogatory to my official and personal character have, in an under-hand way, been circulated. I have been informed that—to use the language of a certain circular that will be alluded to presently—"certain educational gentlemen, and those high in authority," have not only accused me of corruption, but have stated the precise sum which I am reported to have received for my corrupt services.

The evils growing out of state-wide adoptions of textbooks appeared very shortly after the uniformity craze became general, and charges of corruption and dishonesty were numerous even in the early sixties. In spite of the inexcusable practices of some publishing companies, however, book agents were extremely helpful to many school boards and textbook committees in raising the general standards of the books adopted for school use. They focused attention on illustrations, organization of material, and the philosophy underlying the author's method of presentation—

[7] *Vermont School Report, 1867*, pp. 168–69.

matters which had been commonly overlooked in earlier years. As a result, teachers and school committees became textbook-conscious and their appraisals were more intelligent and logical than they had been in the days before competition among book companies was so keen.

Succeeding generations have been equally perplexed by the textbook problem. The multiplicity of published materials, the varying philosophies regarding methods of teaching, the adaptability of content to the interests and abilities of pupils, and the cost incident to supplying free textbooks are still puzzling matters to teachers and administrators.

Courses of Study

Prior to the organization of the graded system of schools, the course of study consisted of whatever textbook material the pupil could absorb in the course of a school year, together with the additional information, if any, which the schoolmaster provided. Each succeeding year the course of study was resumed at the point in the textbook where it had left off the preceding term. As the graded system was introduced, this rather crude procedure was modified and more exact prescriptions were designated by school committees (particularly in the towns and cities) with respect to the amount of work to be covered in the various grades. This sometimes consisted in stipulating the number of pages or sections to be covered in the different textbooks and, in a general way, the degree of competency to be acquired.

The use of attainment goals as a basis of promotion to higher levels of the school system is well illustrated in the following rules of the Dorchester, Massachusetts, committee for 1847: [8]

No child shall be admitted to the grammar schools under ten years of age unless the said child shall be able to read and spell correctly in the reading books prescribed for the primary schools, be well acquainted with the first eleven sections of Colburn's *First Lessons in Arithmetic*, with so much of Fowle and Fitz's *Geography* as relates to New England and Massachusetts—and the whole of Mitchell's *Primary Geography*.

[8] *Regulations of the School Committee of the Town of Dorchester, June, 1847*, Section IV, Rule 2, p. 9.

The course of study used in the common schools of Cincinnati in 1848 is representative of the more progressive practice and shows the degree of prescription which was exacted: [9]

CLASSIFICATION AND COURSE OF STUDY
for the
COMMON SCHOOLS OF CINCINNATI

Sections

First
Bible, Rhetorical Reading, (Fifth Reader, 170 pages,) Written Arithmetic completed and reviewed, Tower's Mental Algebra finished, Algebra through Equations of the first degree, Grammar through Syntax, U. S. History completed, Geography reviewed with the use of Terrestrial Globes, Declamation, Composition, Music, * Penmanship, Drawing—Shades and Shadows.

Second
Bible, Rhetorical Reading, (Fourth Reader finished,) Mental Arithmetic reviewed, Written Arithmetic to Involution, U. S. History continued, Tower's Mental Algebra through 21 sections, Analysis of Words and Sentences, Grammar through Etymology, Penmanship, Drawing, (perspective).

Third
Bible, Spelling, Reading, (Fourth Reader, 150 pages,) Defining, Mental Arithmetic completed and reviewed, Written Arithmetic through Fractions, Wilson's U. S. History, Geography finished, Grammar commenced, Music, Penmanship, Drawing, (linear).

Fourth
Bible, Spelling, Reading, (Third Reader finished,) Defining, Colburn's Mental Arithmetic through 11th section, Written Arithmetic through compound rules, Geography of the Western Continent finished, Penmanship, Elements of Drawing.

Fifth
Bible, Spelling, Reading, (Third Reader, 100 pages,) Oral Defining, Colburn's Mental Arithmetic through 4th section, Written Arithmetic through simple rules, Local Geography of Western Continent, Elements of Drawing.

Sixth
Bible, Spelling, Reading, (Second Reader finished,) Oral Defining, Colburn's Mental Arithmetic through 2nd section, Outline Geography continued, Elements of Drawing.

[9] *Nineteenth Annual Report of the Trustees and Visitors of Common Schools in Cincinnati, Ohio* (1848), p. 61.

Seventh
Bible, Spelling, Reading, First Reader finished and 80 pages of Second Reader completed, Outline Geography of Western Continent, Mental Arithmetic through Ray's First Part, Elements of Drawing.

Eighth
Bible, Spelling, Reading, Sanders' Primer finished, and 20 pages of the Eclectic First Reader completed, Oral Arithmetic continued.

Ninth
Bible, Alphabet on Cards or Black-board, Spelling as far as words of one and two syllables, Sanders' Primer commenced, and 20 pages completed, Oral Arithmetic commenced.

N.B. The pupils are required to pass from one Section to another, on examination, so soon as qualified in the Studies of the Section, satisfactory to the respective Teachers to whom the pupils are to be transferred, with the approbation of the local Trustees. The general transfer to take place at the end of each year.

* The Scholars under the Principal and the First Assistant of each department, (male and female) or as many as can be seated in one room, shall compose a class in Music.

Besides these written prescriptions which represented the official course of study in a few communities, the nature of the subject matter in the curriculum was influenced by the system of public examinations which were held annually in many American communities. In these exhibitions the examining committee, composed of the most learned men on the board of education or other specially designated individuals, asked scores of questions in all fields of study in an effort to test out the success of both teacher and pupils in the year's work just completed.[10] The character of the examination gave the teacher a clue as to the subject matter which required greatest emphasis if further exhibitions were to prove beneficial to him, and constituted a rough indication of the program to be followed. Many local reports of examining committees (included in the annual reports of boards of education) pointed out specific weaknesses in the work reviewed and made, by implication at least, specific recommendations for improvement.

[10] In Cincinnati this group was designated as the "Board of Examiners and Inspectors of Common Schools,"

The high-school outlines were similar in nature to those in the common schools and not infrequently one finds such words as "commenced," "continued," or "completed" after the name of the subject and textbook, no precise specifications being designated.[11] The arrangement of courses of study on a topical basis superseded the textbook-designation procedure, but this advanced step was not generally taken in American schools until after 1860.

From the viewpoint of the teacher, the two most significant features of course-of-study development during this period were (1) the increase in the number of subjects in the curriculum, and (2) the gradation of materials in the various subjects according to the ages and achievements of pupils. The latter made teaching easier, whereas the former called for a broader knowledge of subject matter and increased the difficulty of qualifying for teaching positions. Curriculum-revision programs were uncommon and teachers had relatively little committee work to do. They sometimes gave suggestions as to the relative merits of textbooks; but once the school committee had adopted them, their share in the making of the course of study was completed.

The Development of Classroom Apparatus and Equipment

Classroom equipment and instructional devices were almost unknown to American schoolmasters in 1800. There were no maps, no pictures, no globes, no blackboards, no slates, no pencils, no steel pens, and no commercial-school apparatus. Ingenious teachers here and there unquestionably employed the method of "object teaching" on occasion and devised their own crude illustrations; but it remained for the coming generation, stimulated by an unprecedented industrial and commercial development, to create supplies and equipment to instrument the Mark Hopkins method of imparting knowledge.

As simple a device as the blackboard was unknown until about 1809 and did not come into common use until after 1820. Slates appeared in classrooms shortly after this latter date and since paper was expensive in these early days it had to be used sparingly, thus adding to the schoolmaster's difficulty in teaching

[11] *Report* of the Principal of the Central High School, Philadelphia, 1840.

writing. In the absence of pencils, teachers and older pupils spent an inordinate amount of time making and mending quill pens and compounding ink of an extremely poor quality.[12] Steel pens did not replace the old "quills" until about 1850. The first copy slips on the market appear to have been Caleb Bingham's, published in 1796. Prior to this date, and for several years after the turn of the century, schoolmasters devoted a great deal of attention to setting copies and an important qualification for entrance into the profession was the ability to write a good hand.

Conditions in 1860 were vastly superior to those just described and, while many district schools were exceedingly barren and devoid of pictorial aids and improved equipment, the majority of teachers and pupils enjoyed the advantages of the more modern supplies and teaching devices which had been created during the preceding half century.

As early as 1839 Henry Barnard reported for Connecticut that maps were provided in all the city districts which were empowered with taxation, that globes were less popular but were gradually being introduced, that blackboards were not uncommon but were little resorted to by the teacher, and that six school libraries had been established in the state. He bemoaned the fact in his reports of 1840 and 1841 that diagrams, models, and specimens of real objects were almost entirely omitted from the equipment of public schools and suggested that: [13]

Little children who are now required to sit still, on seats without any backing to lean against . . . and without any occupation for the hands, the eye or the mind, might be usefully employed with a slate and pencil, in printing the alphabet, combining letters, syllables, words, and whole sentences, *and in copying the outlines of angles, circles, solids, maps, diagrams or real objects.*

In New England during this period, the most important agency for stimulating the use and improvement of instructional supplies was the Holbrook School Apparatus Manufacturing

---

[12] In Indiana, ink was made from maple bark, sumac, and oak balls in vinegar. In its season, pokeberry juice was sometimes used, although its tendency to sour made it less desirable than the compound mentioned above.

[13] *Connecticut School Report, 1841*, p. 29.

Company of Hartford, Connecticut. Josiah Holbrook, as early as 1826, had established an educational exchange in Boston for the sale of school apparatus. The pioneer work which he began in this field led to the development of an industry which was destined to vie with the textbook business for prestige.

By 1850 the Holbrook Company was well established and had agencies in several parts of the United States. A complete set of their equipment consisted of a numerical frame, for the instruction of beginners in arithmetic; geometrical solids, for the

American Journal, 1866

APPARATUS FOR A PRIMARY OR DISTRICT SCHOOL

pupils more advanced in arithmetic and mensuration—to give them a clear mental picture of spheres, cubes, pyramids, prisms, and the like; the sectional block, for the illustration of cube root; a globe; a hemisphere globe, which opened through the center; the tellurian, to illustrate the various phenomena resulting from the relations of the sun, moon, and earth to each other; and a planetarium, to illustrate the entire solar system,

The above set, together with a teacher's manual, cost twenty dollars in 1856. In Connecticut, the state assembly appropriated sufficient funds to enable local districts to purchase the complete equipment for as little as three dollars. By 1860 the use of this apparatus and instructional supplies of a similar nature was widespread, not only in New England but also in other parts of the country.

State teachers'-association journals and the annual reports of state superintendents were effective instruments in extending the use of classroom materials and equipment. Considerable space was devoted in these educational periodicals to the discussion of apparatus and its possible use in improving instruction, and by the end of this period (1860) a degree of standardization had been arrived at in the minds of progressive educators, if not in the practices of local districts. In an issue of Barnard's *Journal* in 1866 a list appeared of the "indispensable articles in schools of every grade." In addition to a table with a level top for the teacher to place apparatus on, and some real objects in nature and art, the suggested equipment was as follows: (1) a clock; (2) the cardinal points of the heavens painted on the ceiling or on the teacher's platform, or the floor of the recitation room; (3) blackboards, fixed and movable; (4) a terrestrial globe properly mounted or suspended by wire; (5) map of the district, town, county, and state; (6) the measure of an inch, foot, yard, and rod marked off on the edge of the blackboard or wall; (7) real measure of all kinds of lineage, superficial, solid, and liquid, as a footrule, a yardstick, quarts, bushels, an ounce, pound, for the exercise of the eye and hand; and (8) vases for flowers and natural grasses.[14]

The significance of this development for teachers and teaching is too obvious to warrant a lengthy discussion. One has but to imagine the difficulty of explaining verbally to children the relative geographical positions of Europe and America contrasted with the ease of pointing this out on a globe, in order to appreciate the worth of this single contribution. When to this is added the amount of time saved and the increased accuracy of the knowledge acquired by pupils in substituting a tellurian for

[14] *American Journal of Education*, Vol. XVI (1866), pp. 570 ff.

any verbal efforts at explaining the phenomena of the sun's declination and the processes of the equinoxes, the work of Mr. Holbrook and his associates takes on new meaning.

Mention has been made of the extension of school libraries. This movement made rapid gains during the period under discussion and schools were able to supply both teachers and pupils with books to which otherwise they would never have been exposed. It was a step in the direction of enriching the leisure hours of teachers, children, and parents and of making the school a genuine educational institution.

The Increase in Educational Literature and Its Significance for the Teaching Profession

Books on education were not available to schoolmasters in the early part of the nineteenth century. Preparation for teaching consisted of a knowledge of subject matter in the various areas included in the school curriculum. Many teachers, particularly in New England, came directly out of the colleges with only a classical education as their stock in trade and looked upon teaching merely as a steppingstone to some other more respectable vocation. A larger number had completed only the work offered in the common schools or academies and, with a superficial mastery of a few subjects, saw in teaching the least undesirable of the occupations available to them. There were no peculiar skills or points of view which were considered essential for success in "keeping" school.

Despite this general attitude toward teaching on the part of both the public and those engaged in the business itself, there were individuals here and there who were conscious of serious weaknesses in the status of the profession, and directed their efforts toward reform. Among these was the author of the first important American book on pedagogy, Samuel R. Hall, who in 1829 published his *Lectures on School Keeping*. Hall had previously established a private normal school at Concord, Vermont, in 1823 and had gleaned from his experiences many ideas about teaching which heretofore had not been publicly expressed. His little book was directed to teachers and marked the beginning of a series of educational treatises which were designed to aid the classroom teacher in her work in the primitive district schools of that time. The content of Hall's work on schoolkeeping is of especial interest because it reflects the problems and conditions confronting teachers and reveals the philosophy of the more advanced educators during the early decades of the nineteenth century. The book consisted of thirteen lectures, ten of which were entitled "Practical Directions to Teachers," the last chapter being devoted exclusively to female teachers. The range in the subject matter covered was wide, including such topics as the following: responsibility of the teacher—importance of realizing and understanding it; importance of gaining the confidence of the school—means of gaining it; manner of treating scholars— uniformity in government—firmness; mode of teaching spelling, reading, arithmetic, geography, English grammar, writing, history, composition, and general subjects not particularly studied; and means of exciting the attention of pupils.

Considering the current popular notion of education, Hall's advice to teachers was unusually progressive. He emphasized the need of knowing the subject matter thoroughly, but pointed out that teachers "should make every study as pleasant as possible" and not adhere strictly to the textbooks. He stressed the idea that the information imparted should have real value, pointing out: "That which gives to any branch of study its greatest value, is its practical utility." He warned against depending upon rote memorization of rules without checking the child's understanding of the meaning of the words learned. Hall also proposed other subjects for study not included in the typical school program, of which he deemed composition preeminent. Without question, he was well in advance of his contemporaries in his notions.

Other pioneer authors followed Hall's example in opening up this new field of pedagogy and by 1848 there were at least eight professional books on the market dealing with teaching, in addition to Hall's *Lectures on School Keeping* and a collection of quotations from *Locke and Milton on Education*.[15]

---

[15] These eight were *The School and Schoolmaster* by Alonzo Potter and George B. Emerson; *The Teacher's Manual* by Thomas H. Palmer; *The Teacher Taught* by Emerson Davis; *Slate and Blackboard Exercises* by William A. Alcott; *Theory and Practice*

The nature of these contributions was not significantly different from the one just discussed. Considerable attention was given to the qualifications of a good teacher and the best methods of governing a school, with a tendency to discourage corporal punishment except in extreme cases and to substitute an appeal to the heart. While not radical in a modern sense, the suggestions of these authors with respect to teaching methods deviated markedly from the prevailing practice. They leaned noticeably toward the rational as opposed to the mechanical procedures, and away from the artificial in the direction of the natural. These authors modified the educational philosophy of many teachers; but since the "pouring in" process of instruction had been so universally employed prior to the advent of normal schools, the transition to what Page termed "the waking up mind" process was by no means rapidly achieved.[16]

Teachers generally did not read these books and as late as 1863 John D. Philbrick, in addressing the National Teachers Association, pointed out that of the one hundred thousand teachers in this country, but a small proportion ever saw an educational periodical and only a few of those receiving higher salaries could boast of a respectable educational library.[17] Indirectly, however, through institutes, association conventions, state reports, and the educational journals, the new gospel was spread and classroom practices were gradually modified.

The increase in the number of educational periodicals was phenomenal between 1829 and the Civil War. Up to the former year four magazines with an educational emphasis are reported by Davis as having been established. By 1860 the number had reached approximately one hundred and twenty.[18] Many of these periodicals [19] enjoyed only a brief existence and were either

---

of Teaching by David P. Page; *The District School as It Was* by Warren Burton; *Confessions of a Schoolmaster* by William A. Alcott; *The Teacher* by Jacob Abbott. A few other books having a more remote relation to teaching, such as H. L. Smith's *History of Education, Ancient and Modern,* also existed at this time.

[16] Page, David P., *Theory and Practice of Teaching* (New York, A. S. Barnes and Company, 1893), p. 97.

[17] National Teachers Association, *Journal of Proceedings,* 1863, p. 57.

[18] Davis, Sheldon Emmor, *Educational Periodicals during the Nineteenth Century,* U. S. Bureau of Education, Bulletin 1919, No. 28 (Washington, Government Printing Office, 1919), pp. 92 ff.

[19] Most of the journals were published monthly.

supplanted by others or abandoned entirely for lack of support. Their influence, however, in keeping the school cause alive was tremendous and many alert teachers were led to appraise and improve their practices as a result of the suggestions emanating from editors and contributors.

A discussion of the educational literature of this period would not be complete without mention of the works of the two greatest educators of this generation. The annual reports of Horace Mann as Secretary of the Massachusetts Board (1837–1849) and his *Lectures on Education* (published in 1845) together with the reports of Henry Barnard in Connecticut (1838–1842) were enlightening contributions which helped to elevate the profession and to promote the general interests of the public schools.

The Influence of Pestalozzi on Teaching Methods in America

From the standpoint of child welfare, the greatest contribution of the period under discussion was the modification made in teaching methods. While the full fruits of the Pestalozzian philosophy were not enjoyed in the United States until after the Civil War, sufficient experimentation had been done in Massachusetts and a few isolated cities elsewhere to pave the way for a great revolution in classroom procedure. As the reader will have already gathered from previous chapters, schoolteaching up to 1850 consisted almost entirely of hearing recitations. Before the days of class organization, individual pupils were called up to the teacher's desk and asked to recite what they had learned from the textbook. Grouping children into classes according to achievement did not alter the procedure significantly, as the teacher continued to hear the various pupils in the class repeat whatever they had been able to memorize from the textbook. For pupils it was "Theirs not to reason why, theirs but to do and die." The fact that memorization gave no assurance of understanding aroused but little concern from teachers.

As the state superintendent of schools in Wisconsin so aptly put it in his annual report in 1856: [20]

---

[20] *Wisconsin School Report, 1856*, p. 95.

One would almost imagine they were aiming to do, with their pupils, as the angel did with Habbakkuk, when he took him by the hair of his head, and transported him, in an instant, from Judea to Babylon. But, when the astonished pupil is thus transported, though it be from addition to cube root, or from etymology to the last line of the immortal *Essay on Man* he knows little of the process by which he might reach these points again without some angel's help.

The only explanation for the persistence of these unintelligent procedures seems to be that it was a deeply rooted tradition to "pour in" facts and blindly assume that such knowledge would be effective. This, coupled with the fact that teachers were ignorant and untrained, accounts for the unquestioning attitude which most schoolmasters assumed toward current methods of teaching.

No one American educator can be credited with the reforms which were finally instituted. American travelers in Switzerland and Germany had been much impressed early in the nineteenth century with the success of the Pestalozzian instruction in the elementary schools of these two countries, and in 1821 Warren Colburn's *First Lessons in Arithmetic on the Plan of Pestalozzi* was published in the United States. A school based on the principles of this great philosopher had been in operation in Philadelphia between 1809 and 1813 and, while it enjoyed considerable local prestige, its influence was not widely felt. This was due, perhaps, to the fact that the teacher (Neef) resigned after four years of service to accept a post in the West, leaving no one to carry on the experiment. In 1839, and again in 1847 and 1849, Henry Barnard distributed to the teachers of Connecticut pamphlets on Pestalozzi and his method of instruction. Horace Mann was also convinced of the superiority of the newer mode of teaching and in his seventh report (1843) he discussed at considerable length the Prussian schools and the teaching procedures common to them. Mann's influence in promoting the philosophy of Pestalozzi was directly observable in the Westfield State Normal School in Massachusetts, which introduced "object teaching" in 1848. A further benign influence toward the transplantation of this revolutionary point of view to American soil was the appearance of several Swiss educators in America during the decade 1848–1858. These gentlemen, among whom were Louis Agassiz, the great naturalist, Arnold Guyot and Hermann Krusi, Jr., lecturers and teachers, gave firsthand testimony to the success of the system abroad, and brought many a doubting Thomas into the Pestalozzian fold. The man who was most responsible for the general acceptance of this new methodology in America was Edward A. Sheldon of Oswego, New York. Mr. Sheldon, as Superintendent of Schools in Oswego, was a close student of the Swiss and German ideas and in 1859 had seen in a museum in Toronto, Canada, the models and instructional materials of the English and Colonial Infant Society. This latter organization had adopted for its schools the formalized English type of Pestalozzian work and the ideas which Sheldon gleaned from his visit to Toronto led him in 1860 to revise the curriculum and classroom procedure of the Oswego schools in conformity with the English pattern.[21] A year later a public normal school was established in Oswego for the purpose of training teachers in the new methods for work in the city schools. The program of Sheldon and his associates in the normal school was referred to in American periodicals as the "Oswego Plan" or the "Oswego Movement" and the school system became a sort of mecca for curious and interested educators. Needless to say, it won enthusiastic support in every section of the country and, while the results of applying the new techniques were fraught with disaster in many communities because of the ignorance of teachers, the ultimate outcomes were definitely favorable.

To those who are unacquainted with Pestalozzi's ideas, a brief discussion of essential principles may be welcomed. In essence, his idea was that the child was a natural organism whose inner life unfolds according to definite laws, like that of a plant rooted in the soil. He recognized three separate aspects of this organism: the intellectual, the physical, and the moral and religious—often popularly referred to as "the head," "the hand," and "the heart." He evolved several general principles to be observed in the training of this organism, which may be sum-

[21] Oswego had a population of about twenty-three thousand in 1864 and the schools were classified into four grades: primary, junior, senior, and high. The object system was first introduced into the primary grades and later extended into the junior.

marized as follows: (1) Development must be harmonious. (2) General education must precede the vocational. (3) The increase of power and not knowledge is most essential. (4) The child's powers burgeon from within. (5) Grading is a most essential principle. (6) In method, follow the order of nature.[22]

Since the last-mentioned principle is the one with which we are most directly concerned, it can properly be amplified for the sake of clarity. Pestalozzi held that instruction is merely the scientific art of helping nature to unfold and the teacher, therefore, should eliminate any obstacles that may hinder this process and should provide whatever assistance he can by way of encouraging the unfolding of these natural powers. He recognized *sense impression as the absolute foundation of all knowledge.* It was his observation, as it had been that of other philosophers before him, that children learn from hearing, feeling, seeing, smelling, and tasting and that all these senses should be utilized in the process of teaching. He emphasized the importance, therefore, of sharpening and quickening these sense perceptions by urging children to use them—by looking carefully at objects and noting their form and size and weight. From such experiences they could proceed to reason about them and make individual judgments. The acceptance of this theory implied the substitution of real objects for textbook descriptions and thoughtful preparation of lessons by the teacher in advance of class for the old worn-out questions and answers contained in books. It demanded a degree of ingenuity and alertness on the part of teachers in supplying the needed objects, information, and questions which were quite unnecessary under the old type of instruction.

Among the observable outcomes of the acceptance in America of the theories of Pestalozzi were several which were related to the curriculum. The most important of these were the introduction of mental arithmetic, oral language work, elementary science, nature study, and home geography, and some modifications in the work in writing, drawing, and music. The attempt to reduce the teaching of the latter subjects to a logical, analytical method resulted in a deadly mechanical and ineffective procedure.

[22] Eby, Frederick, and Arrowood, C. F., *The Development of Modern Education* (New York, Prentice-Hall, Inc., 1934), pp. 638–45.

Speakers and writers on educational method during the two decades just preceding the Civil War discussed the pros and cons of several procedures which were frequently designated as follows: the Catechetical Method (questions and answers); the Explanatory Method; the Synthetical Method (first presenting parts of things and the relations of the parts, then the whole made up of these parts); and the Analytical Method (presenting objects and subjects as wholes, then the parts and the relations). The last-mentioned method was essentially the Pestalozzian idea and usually, after disposing of the other procedures by showing up their imperfections, the speaker or author arrived at the Analytical Method as the only true and scientific way of instructing children.

Other discussions of methodology dwelt upon the relative merits of the concert as opposed to the individual method of reciting lessons. The former was considered useful in learning rules and definitions and helpful in verbal recollection, but not so applicable to other forms of learning. The individual method was deemed advantageous in that the teacher could test out the knowledge or ignorance of each pupil through cross-examination, but limited because it was time-consuming and wasteful.

In the high school, the method of instruction by lectures was exceedingly popular (at least with the teachers) and included, in addition to the informal oral instructions which accompanied recitations upon textbooks, formal lectures prepared expressly for the class, many of them fully written out. Of thirty lectures given in a single week at the Central High School in Philadelphia in 1846, more than half were written out in advance and presumably read by the instructor. The high schools of this period apparently followed the teaching procedures which commonly prevailed in the colleges and were less susceptible to the newer modes of instruction which were so vigorously recommended to teachers in the lower grades of the school system.

The struggle to introduce a more progressive and natural technique of teaching into the American public schools had a leavening effect upon the whole teaching profession. Attention was focused upon the philosophy of method, and out of the

study and discussions there developed a more scientific and scholarly attitude toward education and teaching as a vocation. It put
the capstone on the recently arrived at notion that teaching should
be a profession and that particular knowledge and skill were required as a prerequisite for success in this field of endeavor.

School Discipline and Government

The heated discussions of teaching methods which took place
at institutes and conventions, and in the educational journals of
the time, were commonly accompanied by debates on the proper
mode of disciplining pupils. To some it seemed that the very
foundations of our public schools were being threatened by a
group of radical educators whose idealism and naïveté had
stripped them of all common sense and judgment. The suggestion
that the rod should be dispensed with and that appeal should be
made to the heart of the child was a revolutionary idea to many
teachers and to the public generally. At the beginning of the
century it was taken for granted that schoolmasters would maintain order and decorum by the application of the ferule, and
school committees looked carefully to the size and strength of
applicants in making appointments. The history of the district
school is replete with accounts of flogging and the taming of
unruly scholars. The ancient aphorism "Spare the rod and spoil
the child" was accepted literally by most of these early masters
as sound pedagogy and those who questioned it were dubbed
queer by their contemporaries. The fact that some strong per-
sonalities among the teaching force found it desirable to use it
sparingly did not subtract from the generally accepted principle
that it was a prerogative of the teacher to administer corporal
punishment whenever he deemed it expedient.

With the advent of graded schools and the influx of female
teachers, the question of the efficacy of corporal punishment became more and more controversial. The situation is well illustrated by Page in his discussion of the issue, in 1847, in *Theory and
Practice of Teaching*. The author, realizing that his readers would
be greatly divided on the subject, treated the topic most diplo-
matically and began as follows: [23]

[23] Page, David P., *op. cit.*, pp. 197–98.

I am aware that when I enter this field I am treading on ground every inch of which has been disputed. . . . There are strong men and I believe honest men, who run to the opposite extremes in their doctrine and practice, and who defend the one course or the other as if the existence of the world depended upon the issue. There are those who not only claim the right to chastise, but who insist that whipping should be the *first resort* of the teacher in establishing his authority; and to show that this is not a dormant article of faith, they daily and almost hourly demonstrate their efficiency in the use of the rod, so that their pupils may be living witnesses that they act in accordance with their creed. Again there are others who as earnestly deny the right of the teacher to resort to the rod at all, and who urge with all their power the efficacy of moral suasion to subdue and control the vicious and the stubborn in our schools, and who are ready to assert unequivocally that no man is fit to be employed to teach the young who has not the ability to govern all the various dispositions he may meet in any school, without the use of corporal punishment.

Page himself, as the reader will infer from the foregoing quotation, took a middle-of-the-road position, discouraging whipping except when absolutely necessary to maintain discipline. His point of view was shared by Horace Mann and most of the progressive educators of his generation. It was based on a principle which was as old as teaching itself, that the authority of the teacher must not be questioned within the realm of the schoolroom and, in order to establish and maintain respect for this authority, the teacher could mete out such punishments as were in his judgment reasonable and proper.

There is plenty of evidence in support of the conclusion that corporal punishment lost favor during this era, and as early as 1845 the school committee of Roxbury, Massachusetts, in their annual report, pointed out to the citizens that "some of our teachers have already determined to inflict no more corporal punishment; others have virtually discontinued it, and are approaching a final decision to that effect; and all, we believe, are looking to that result as exceedingly desirable, and will spare · no endeavors to reach it." [24]

The approval by the school committee of this forward-looking

[24] *Roxbury, Massachusetts, School Report, 1845*, p. 13.

point of view and their pronounced intention of dismissing "any teacher who shall manifest an appetite for the rod, hereafter, and shall entertain such views of boy-nature" are indicative of a changed psychology with respect to teacher-pupil relationships. Not only were those engaged in the business of education beginning to look with disfavor upon corporal punishment as a means of maintaining discipline but intelligent laymen and members of other professions were seriously questioning the

Harper's, 1879

LAYING DOWN THE LAW

justification for its use. As early as 1853, an Indiana judge, in rendering an opinion on a case, expressed a philosophy far in advance of those commonly held by teachers. He pointed out that "the public seem to cling to a despotism in the government of schools which has been discarded everywhere else," and added: "One thing seems obvious, the very act of resorting to the rod demonstrates the incapacity of the teacher for one of the most important parts of his vocation, namely, school government. For such a teacher the nurseries of the republic are not the proper element. They are above him. His true position will readily adjust itself." This judge was not only a philosopher but also something of a prophet, as the following statement shows: "It can hardly be doubted but the public opinion will, in time, strike the ferule from the hands of the teacher, leaving him as the true basis of government, only the resources of his intellect and heart." [25] While this judge in all probability did not represent the prevailing opinion of his bar associates, he was an intelligent observer of trends and voiced the sentiments of the more liberal citizens of his generation.

City school systems responded more quickly to the newer point of view than did the rural districts. In 1867 the use of corporal

Harper's, 1879

THE SCHOOL RULED BY LOVE

punishment in the Syracuse schools was prohibited and, while this action caused some consternation among the teachers, the general discipline of the schools was reported later to have improved and "the atmosphere of almost every room became brighter." [26] On the other hand, the country districts clung more tenaciously to the old order of things and the Vermont superintendent, protesting the prevailing practice in that state, raised the question in 1860: "Can it be possible that it has really been

[25] Cooper *v.* McJunkin (1853), 4 Ind., 290, in Weltzin, J. F., *The Legal Authority of the American Public School* (Grand Forks, N. D., The Mid-West Book Concern, 1931), pp. 240–41.

[26] Smith, Edward M., *History of the Schools of Syracuse* (Syracuse, N. Y., 1893), p. 131.

necessary to inflict bodily punishment upon one child out of every seven that have even entered the doors of our schoolhouses?"

While whipping probably represented the most extreme form of physical punishment, there were other measures employed which, from both a physical and a mental-hygiene point of view, were equally as harmful to children. One of these was to insist that the offender hold a heavy Bible at arm's length until his muscles were so fatigued that he literally writhed in pain. Still another form of punishment was to require the rebellious pupil to place his back against a wall of the room and his feet approximately a foot from its base, then to slide his body down till the knees were bent at right angles. He was then in the awkward situation of being in a sitting position without any seat. A third substitute for flogging was what was commonly known as "holding a nail into the floor." This consisted of having the pupil bend forward and, placing the end of a single finger upon the head of a nail, remain in that position until his body was thoroughly agonized. Just how prevalent these absurd practices were cannot be reliably deduced from the records, but the fact that they were tolerated at all seems almost incredible. Educational writers gave no quarter to schoolteachers who resorted to these extreme punishments and their gradual disappearance from the classroom was unquestionably achieved in large part by the changed attitude toward child nature, voiced by these early educational statesmen.

A variety of lesser evils was perpetrated on children in the name of education. Pupil offenders were subjected to ridicule, to humiliation, to confinement, and to the imposition of tasks as a means of reform. The prevailing opinion among early teachers was that children were by nature inclined to be bad and that the only way of driving the devil out of them was through punishment. It was in part a reflection of the religious doctrine of original sin with which they were all imbued and was in general harmony with public opinion.

Pestalozzi's influence did much to overthrow this philosophy and to substitute for it a more constructive program of school management. As early as 1865 the superintendent of schools in

Providence expressed an enlightened point of view on pupil-teacher relationships pointing out that: [27]

The besetting sin of many teachers is their proneness to ridicule their pupils; to make invidious comparisons, and to provoke them to wrath by bitter sarcasms and vulgar epithets. To succeed, a teacher must gain the confidence and affection of his pupils. He may have the most splendid talents, the most profound and exact knowledge, and may be earnestly devoted to his work; but without this, the most vital element to success is wanting. And this can be secured only by a kind, urbane and courteous manner in the schoolroom.

The discussion thus far has dealt exclusively with punishment and said nothing of rewards. While lacking the emotional quality of the former controversy, the subject of school prizes came in for much criticism after 1845. It had been the custom of teachers rather generally to offer some award as an incentive to exertion in school. In some instances the school committee or some philanthropically inclined citizen provided the prizes which consisted usually of books, medals, or money. Since only a small proportion of the pupils could hope to win an award, there were many educators who arrived at the conclusion that the disappointments which resulted from failure more than offset the happiness derived by the few who were successful. They further questioned the good growing out of the spirit of rivalry which prize giving engendered among the pupils. It was obvious that no matter how hard some pupils might try they lacked the ability to achieve heights easily accessible to others. Similar objections were raised to the practice of moving pupils to the head and the foot of the class in accordance with their achievements. The humiliation suffered by many youngsters in their futile efforts to compete with the more gifted can scarcely be fully comprehended.

While the questioning of such procedures did not eliminate prize giving, it did reduce it significantly and, what is perhaps of even greater importance, it started a chain of thought about time-honored practices which led teachers to become less gullible and to think for themselves.

[27] *Rhode Island State Report, 1865*, p. 39.

SUGGESTED READINGS

CUBBERLEY, ELWOOD P., *Public Education in the United States* (Boston, Houghton Mifflin Company, 1934), pp. 288–315.

EBY, FREDERICK, and ARROWOOD, C. F., *The Development of Modern Education* (New York, Prentice-Hall, Inc., 1934), pp. 633–56.

JOHNSON, CLIFTON, *Old-Time Schools and School-Books* (New York, The Macmillan Company, 1917), Chaps. IV–XIV.

KNIGHT, EDGAR W., *Education in the United States* (New York, Ginn and Company, 1934), pp. 423–57.

REISNER, EDWARD H., *The Evolution of the Common School* (New York, The Macmillan Company, 1930), pp. 404–13.

XX

The Organization and Work of Teachers' Associations

FROM the standpoint of educational reform and the elevation of the teaching profession, the contribution of teachers' associations during the period 1836 to 1860 was second only to the establishment of normal schools. Not only did state legislatures give ear to the memorials presented by these recently organized teaching groups, but the rank-and-file members of the profession themselves were lifted out of their apathetic mood by the spirited activities of their own leaders.

The formulation of teachers' associations did not occur at any one time nor were their antecedents always of the same stock. The period following the turn of the nineteenth century was an era of propaganda, and associations of all types sprang up with the avowed purpose of preserving and advancing the democratic ideal. Many of these associations focused their attention upon free public schools, believing that only an educated citizenry could nourish and promote the interests of a democratic state. One of the earliest of these organizations was the Pennsylvania Society for the Promotion of Public Economy, formed in 1817. It split up in 1827 and one of its branches became the Pennsylvania Society for the Promotion of Public Schools. This latter group was active in developing a favorable public opinion toward schools and paved the way for many of the reforms which came later.

In 1826 Josiah Holbrook originated the Lyceum movement at Millbrook, Massachusetts, and in 1831 a national meeting of the American Lyceum was organized and a constitution adopted. The object of this association was "the advancement of education, especially the common schools, and the general diffusion of knowledge." The movement spread rapidly in New York,

Massachusetts, Rhode Island, Pennsylvania, Virginia, and Illinois and in the convention of 1838 this society recommended the formation of associations of schoolteachers throughout the country. While teachers responded in many communities to this invitation, they were decidedly overshadowed by prominent laymen and educational statesmen. The Lyceum program at first was an ambitious one, including propaganda and agitation for normal schools, taxation for schools, the establishment of libraries, and lecture courses for adults. By 1845 it had lost much of its youthful vigor and thereafter consisted largely of lecture courses.

An association with similar purposes was the Western Academic Institute and Board of Education, organized in 1829 at Cincinnati and later transformed into the Western Literary Institute and College of Professional Teachers. This organization was a powerful influence in the West and South in the improvement of education and constituted a bulwark of strength against the foes of free public schools. As was the case with the American Lyceum, it cut across state lines and included in its membership both teachers and laymen. In addition to the formation of numerous county associations and the holding of conventions where educational issues were freely discussed, this society employed an agent to visit the schools and study conditions, memorialized the legislature in behalf of public education, and issued a journal (*The Western Academician and Journal of Education and Science*) devoted to the cause which they were sponsoring. One of their unique contributions was sending Professor Calvin E. Stowe to Europe to study education there. Upon his return, several state legislatures were persuaded to publish his *Report on Elementary Education in Europe*, which aroused a great deal of discussion and influenced future educational policies in many parts of the country.

Less ambitious efforts were made in states not included in the Western Academic Institute. In New Jersey the Society of Teachers and Friends of Education was organized to achieve objectives similar to those held by the Lyceum and Institute. North Carolina and Florida formed school societies and held conventions to promote the interests of the public schools. In fact, there was scarcely an area in the whole United States that remained unaffected by the propaganda and enthusiasm of these early organizations.

Another group which laid their claims clearly before the people were the representatives of organized labor. The activities of the Philadelphia workingmen were among the first to attract attention. They pressed office seekers for statements of their position on free public schools, investigated educational conditions in Pennsylvania, and made reports condemning the lack of school opportunities. Local associations of mechanics and manufacturers in other states were equally aroused about school problems and petitioned governmental bodies for increased support.

Public-school teachers, though active, did not play the leading roles in most of these propaganda societies, nor was their economic, social, or professional welfare a major consideration in the work of the associations. The provision of free schooling for all children through public taxation was the basic plank in the platforms of school and education societies generally in the United States, and the welfare of the teacher was a secondary consideration. It is true that normal schools were frequently advocated and that public attention was sometimes directed to the need for well-qualified teachers. This was incidental, however, to the broader demands of these groups that the needs of the democracy required equal educational opportunities for rich and poor alike.

The high point in the efforts of these state and sectional societies occurred in 1849, when a national convention of the Friends of Common Schools and of Universal Education was called at Philadelphia. As a result of this convention, the American Association for the Advancement of Education was formed and Horace Mann was elected the first president. The purposes of the new association, as stated in its constitution, were "to promote intercourse among those who are actively engaged in promoting education throughout the United States; to secure the cooperation of individuals, associations and legislatures in measures calculated to improve education and to give to such measures a more systematic direction and a more powerful impulse." This convention was an effort to revive the waning interests formerly fostered by the American Lyceum and the Western Literary Institute. Neither of these organizations had been functioning for several years and while the battle for free public education had been won, in principle at least, new educational problems were developing so rapidly that some concerted effort seemed imperative. A new feature of this society was the composition of the membership and, as Cubberley suggests, "this convention formed a transition from the earlier type of organization, composed largely of college men and publicists interested in education, to the more modern type of educational organization composed primarily of teachers and supervisory officers of the schools." [1]

Representatives from fifteen states attended this convention, many of whom were teachers and school administrators. The life of the association was slightly less than a decade (1849–1858), its reason for existence passing with the formation of the National Teachers Association in 1857.

During the period in which education societies flourished (1826–1845), there were several local teachers' associations in existence which were engaged in promoting educational reforms and the welfare of their own professional groups. The nature of these societies and the activities sponsored by them will be discussed later in this chapter. The great lesson which teachers learned from the American Lyceum, the Western Literary Institute, and state and county educational associations was the effectiveness of organized effort and the best methods and procedures to use in securing action by legislative bodies. Teachers had, for the most part, been extremely individualistic, naïve in their political techniques, and unrealistic in their approach to the solution of professional problems. Contact with spirited laymen and educational statesmen in the great work of public-school societies improved the strategy of teachers and made them more sophisticated. They were now ready to embark upon state and national associations of their own.

Before discussing the origin and work of the purely local, state, and national associations of teachers, it is important to mention one organized group of educators whose history and activities influenced American education significantly. This was

[1] Cubberley, Elwood P., *Public Education in the United States*, p. 706.

the American Institute of Instruction, organized in Boston in 1830. It was a select organization of scholars and educators (the elite in the profession) whose membership, in its early life, was restricted to males and confined chiefly to New England. The grammar-school masters and public-school teachers took no part in its proceedings for several years after its founding. Its professed purpose was "combined and concentrated action" for an improved condition of American education. Until 1836 the public was excluded from attendance at meetings. Despite the early limitations of the society as regards membership, it proved to be a most stimulating agency in improving educational conditions. Practical school problems were ably discussed at annual conventions and resolutions were drafted favoring needed reforms of the day. Among the achievements claimed by spokesmen of the institute as a result of memorials to legislative bodies was the appointment of a state superintendent of schools in Massachusetts and the establishment of normal schools. Institute members also believed that their efforts had contributed to the improvement of school architecture and to the provision of more generous salaries for teachers.[2] While it is difficult to separate the unique contributions of this association from those of other professional agencies, their claims seem reasonably modest and are probably justified.[3]

The American Institute remained a New England organization for fifteen years and then became a Rhode Island association in 1845.[4] Because of its selective features, it was not representative of the teaching personnel of New England; and while a forerunner of the National Society of Teachers, it had few of the characteristics of the latter organization. It was a "high-brow" society and something of a hybrid, having certain features of the educational societies and some of the qualities of the emerging teachers' associations.

Local Teachers' Associations

As a result of the rapid growth in population and the multiplication of schools in cities, teachers began to realize the op-

---

[2] American Institute of Instruction, *Journal of Proceedings*, 1869, pp. 7–8.
[3] It was supported in part by the school fund of Massachusetts.
[4] It was revived as a New England association about 1885.

portunities afforded to exchange ideas and to share experiences with fellow schoolmasters. It seems logical, therefore, that the teachers in New York City and Boston should have been among the first to form teachers' associations for mutual welfare and improvement. As early as 1798 a teachers' association was in existence in New York City and its meetings were held every Saturday evening at Federal Hall. Since the Free School Society was not founded until 1805, the members of this early teachers' organization were undoubtedly private-school masters. The earliest association of semipublic-school teachers seems to have been formed in 1811 and was incorporated as The Society of Teachers of the City of New York for Benevolent and Literary Purposes. The relief aim of the association was the dominant one, the needs of aged schoolmasters and of widows and children of members having apparently been forcefully called to the attention of the founders.

The activities of this first association are not reported in any published journal and one can only speculate as to the degree of influence which it exerted on its members or the educational system. It does not appear to have been very successful in achieving its goals, for the constitution apparently expired by nonuser and was revived by act of the legislature in 1818.

The officers of the new society announced, to the public, altruistic purposes and a highly ambitious program. They intended to collect information of a professional nature from foreign countries and from sister states, to assist in the creation of a graded-school system and especially a high school, and finally to improve the prestige and station of the members of the society.

By 1828 the New York Society of Teachers was no longer functioning and the Mathematical Club, under the leadership of Dr. Adrian of Columbia College, replaced it. From the title it would appear that only those teachers with mathematical proclivities would be happy in such an organization. While undoubtedly this club provided intellectual stimulation to its members, it did not meet the needs for which earlier associations had been formed.

The next step in the direction of a general teachers' association was the organization of the Ward School Teachers Association in 1845. This group, which devoted their meetings chiefly to debates, essays, and lectures, was replaced in 1848 by the Teachers Association of the City and County of New York. Only sixty individuals were enrolled and female teachers were still excluded from membership. In fact, no serious proposal to invite them to join the society appears to have been entertained until 1856; and apparently the response was not enthusiastic even then, for in 1860 the executive committee reported that women "were as yet almost unknown in the association." It is interesting to note, however, that the Negro teachers were permitted to join the club in 1857 and one of them, a Mr. Peterson, was elected librarian.

Current issues received attention in the society's debates and in one of the meetings in 1853 the topic "Ought Female Teachers to Be Placed on the Same Footing with Male Teachers in the Matter of Compensation Where the Services Are the Same?" was vigorously discussed. The answer in terms of majority opinion appears to have been, "Absolute Right says: Yes, and Relative Fact says: No."

Interest in the organization apparently waned in the late fifties and, as one author describes it, "there was a gradual slumber extending itself like a leaden cobweb over the existence of the association." [5] Membership declined and a general lack of interest prevailed. One early writer attributed the general apathy of New York teachers toward the association to the academic character of the meetings and the general procedure followed. His comments were: [6]

The languor, that leads to an untimely suicide of Associations, is caused by the incessant discussion of futile questions. The great bore that pervades our American meetings is the cry of "Mr. President, I rise to a point of order!" "The gentleman may state his point of order," replies the President. That usually brings all kinds of disorder into the meetings.

[5] *American Journal of Education*, Vol. XV (1865), p. 498.
[6] *Ibid.*, p. 496. (From George Bachelor, "History of All the Teachers' Associations Ever Established in New York," address, November, 1861.)

Despite the weakness of these early New York societies and the frequency with which they changed their name in an effort to expand and strengthen their organization, they never completely disintegrated. The need for group action and expression was always apparent to the more energetic and intelligent schoolmasters of this early period, and the defeats and discouragement which they experienced did not completely hide the possibilities of developing a strong association which someday would prove to be a powerful influence in stimulating professional growth.

The Boston Association

The Boston teachers were only a year behind New York in organizing a similar society, known as the Associated Instructors of Youth in the Town of Boston and Its Vicinity. Like the New York association, it was restricted to male teachers and was both a benevolent and a literary society. The constitution stated that financial assistance would be provided to a member who was "reduced in his circumstances by misfortune" and that a substitute would be paid out of the society's funds in case of illness. In the event that a member died, the association was empowered to "superintend the funeral" and pay all the bills and make such provision for the widow as the directors deemed appropriate and feasible. The Boston club bore also some resemblance to a modern teachers' credit union, for they were authorized to lend money, preferably to members, the duration of the loan not to exceed one year.

Although this organization was active for several years, there appears to be no trace of their proceedings from 1817 to 1835. In 1813 they advocated education for girls and deplored the small salaries paid schoolmasters. The latter was evidently a matter of real concern and the dismal picture of the teacher's lot was dramatically expressed by one of the members as follows:[7]

I need not swell the catalogue with his poverty and the necessity of his *observance* of the virtue of economy until its practice borders on parsimony—these are known too well to require formal mention in this place.

[7] "Association of Teachers in Boston," in *ibid.*, p. 533.

I will only add that with all his savings and "short commons" he must look forward, with frequent *chills* to the tedious days of weary old age, when he must work however feeble, or become dependent on casual bounty, and die with the miserable consolation of leaving a destitute family to the mercy and charity of the world. Alas! beneficence among her numerous and splendid establishments in the metropolis has not yet even looked about for a spot to found an asylum for the decayed schoolmaster.

In 1835 the Boston association was revived and the name changed to Association of the Masters of the Grammar Schools. No printed reports of the proceedings of this society have been uncovered and the next trace of their activities appeared in 1844, when they entered into a controversy with Horace Mann over a report[8] which he, as Secretary of the Massachusetts Board of Education, had made on European school systems. In a pamphlet of one hundred and forty-four pages the Boston masters accused Mr. Mann of ignorance of education in general and of the Boston schools in particular, of depicting the Massachusetts schools as ineffective in order to magnify his own importance, and of arriving at hasty conclusions. The discussion, carried on in a series of pamphlets, waxed so warm that Mann lost his temper and compared the thirty-one Boston schoolmasters who had attacked him to "thirty-one vulgar fractions multiplied into themselves producing an insignificant product."

The schoolmasters were definitely on the defensive because of their reactionary practices and resented the suggestions of change which Mr. Mann had incorporated in his report. Despite the rightness of his position, the controversy lost Mann many supporters; and when a call was extended to the teachers of Massachusetts to assemble for the purpose of organizing a state teachers' association, it was issued to "practical teachers" intended, thereby, to exclude Mann.

The activities of the local association were apparently overshadowed by the larger projects undertaken by the Massachusetts State Teachers Association formed in 1845, and the only achievement of any interest recorded was the opening of a

[8] *Seventh Annual Report of the Secretary of the Massachusetts Board of Education, 1843.*

room for teachers' headquarters in Boston in 1857. The club-room was equipped with library facilities and provided a meeting place for teachers and educational committees. This enterprise was supported originally by principals and teachers in Boston and in neighboring communities. It later became the head-quarters of the *Massachusetts Teacher* and the American Institute of Instruction and was financed chiefly by these larger asso-ciations.

OTHER LOCAL ASSOCIATIONS

In nearly every large city, teachers formed associations during this period and experienced many of the same problems as the New York and Boston societies.[9] County teachers' organiza-tions were fairly common by 1850 and there is some indication that the movement was stimulated by the experience of European teachers, though the extent of this influence is not known. A brief article appearing in the *Connecticut Common School Journal* in 1838–1839, entitled "Teachers' Association," shows that American educators were at least aware of the for-mation of teachers' societies abroad. The editorial ran as follows: [10]

The formation of these associations has been very generally recom-mended and we are glad to know that they are coming into existence in many towns in this state. . . . They are coming into existence all over France, under the encouragement and recommendation of the minis-try. They have been and still are found important aids in the promo-tion of education in Holland. "These societies or associations are numerous," says a traveller in Holland. "They are generally of a local character. Eight, ten, or more schoolmasters residing near each other, form an association for the discussion of subjects connected with edu-cation, and report through their secretary to the editor of the *Contribu-*

---

[9] One who taught in Philadelphia during the early part of the nineteenth cen-tury reported the existence of a teachers' association there as early as 1812 and re-marked that "its objects were more for convivial and financial purposes—the fixing of rates of tuition and the enjoyment of a supper—than for professional im-provement, although many of its members were sadly in need of such improvement, having, as it were, fallen into the position of schoolmasters from inability to start in any other respectable occupation." (*American Journal of Education*, Vol. XIII [1863], p. 748.)

[10] *The Connecticut Common School Journal*, Vol. I (1838–1839), p. 48.

tions (a periodical devoted to Common School education) who publishes what he thinks is likely to be of general benefit. There are at present upwards of two hundred of these societies, and above two thousand schoolmasters are thus associated."

A complete history of local teachers' societies during this period would be difficult to write, since the proceedings of the individual associations are, in many instances, not available. Their purposes and patterns, however, seem to have been pretty much identical. The improvement of the teacher's economic welfare was clearly one of the major objectives; this and the more altruistic purposes of increasing teaching efficiency and promoting school reforms constituted the chief professed aims of local teachers' associations.

Probably the opportunity which the meetings provided for friendly intercourse and enjoyment was a powerful factor in keeping the societies alive. The achievements of these local associations cannot adequately be appraised. It is certain that some societies were pressure groups and presented their claims for higher salaries and better working conditions with some degree of success.[11] Current educational issues were often clarified in the meetings of the associations and a consensus of opinion was arrived at leading to a more direct attack upon school problems. Some of these issues were trivial and the positions taken by teachers indefensible; others were crucial and experience later demonstrated the soundness of the resolutions passed.

A few illustrations of both types of resolutions are included below, because they indicate the controversial subjects upon which teachers were focusing their attentions:

Resolved that corporeal [*sic*] punishment should be inflicted in common schools.[12]
That the separation of the sexes in our school is detrimental to the interests of society.[13]

[11] The public-school teachers' association of Baltimore reported in 1866: "The association has twice secured an increase of salary for the public school teachers of Baltimore and its influence has been favorably felt wherever it has been directed." (*American Journal of Education*, Vol. XVI [1866].)

[12] *Armstrong County Teachers Association*, Pennsylvania, October 28, 1857.

[13] *Jefferson County Teachers Association*, New York, February 13, 1855.

That we will not engage in any school from which the Bible is excluded.[14]

That prizes should be given to pupils in our common schools for excellence in scholarship.[15]

STATE TEACHERS' ASSOCIATIONS

The signal success of state education associations, the American Lyceum, the Western Institute, and the American Institute of Instruction in securing school reforms convinced the leaders in the teaching profession that organization on a large scale was the surest way of improving the status of teachers and of advancing the educational interests of the state. The existence of other professional and vocational societies also stimulated teachers to follow the precedent, which had been rather universally established, of uniting themselves into associations for mutual improvement. As Daniel Read expressed it in his address at the national teachers' convention in 1858: [16]

If mechanics and farmers have their fairs, artists their art unions and academies, merchants their chambers of commerce, surely not less important, nay, essential to high progress, are the various societies of teachers which create among themselves a bond of union, a fellowship of interest, a participation of professional improvement and professional rank.

A similar line of argument was pursued by the State Superintendent of Schools in Rhode Island, who stated in his annual report in 1853: [17]

Other professions and trades have long ago realized the importance of such meetings. Our clergy of the different denominations have their regular associations for inter-communication. The men of science in Europe and America have for many years held their annual meetings for the advancement of science. Our medical men hold their regular meetings in the several states, and have lately formed a national association. The mechanical trades have also their periodical gatherings;

[14] *Warren County Teachers Association*, New Jersey, 1855.

[15] *Bradford County Teachers Association*, December 13, 1857.

[16] *Journal of Proceedings of the National Teachers Association, Cincinnati, 1858.* (From an address by Daniel Read.)

[17] *Rhode Island School Report, 1853*, p. 6.

indeed association and incorporation were among the first causes of the elevation of the trades in the social scale.

Local teachers' societies, while not universally successful, had also discovered many advantages in association. Not only were the lectures and debates on current educational problems enlightening, but group petitions got a readier response from school boards than did the individual requests of teachers in days prior to the formation of associations. Since many of the troublesome school issues extended beyond the confines of the local districts, the need for state-wide organizations was clearly observable.

Rhode Island, New York, and Massachusetts established state teachers' associations in the year 1845, the first meetings being held in Providence, Syracuse, and Boston, respectively. The Rhode Island and Massachusetts societies were, in many respects, divisions of the American Institute of Instruction, broken down into state groups for the convenience of members with regard to attendance. The unique feature of these associations was the dominant role played by teachers. The Massachusetts association was limited to teachers only (this was partly by way of a rebuke to Horace Mann, resulting from his controversy with the thirty-one Boston schoolmasters); and the membership in other associations was restricted to those engaged in the profession of education, with classroom teachers constituting a large majority. A number of states organized similar societies in quick succession, and by 1856 seventeen state teachers' associations had been formed.[18]

THE OBJECTIVES OF STATE TEACHERS' ASSOCIATIONS

The objectives of these organizations were almost identical in nature (the later associations having imitated the earlier ones), as expressed in their constitutions. The Wisconsin and Pennsylvania statements listed below are fairly typical.[19]

---

[18] Rhode Island, New York, Massachusetts, Ohio, Connecticut, Vermont, Michigan, Pennsylvania, Wisconsin, Illinois, New Jersey, Iowa, New Hampshire, Indiana, Missouri, North Carolina, and Alabama. (See Cubberley, Elwood P., *Public Education in the United States*, p. 708, for date of organization and place of meeting.)

[19] Wisconsin State Teachers Association, *Constitution* (1853), Article I.

This Association shall be called the Wisconsin Teachers Association, and shall have for its object the mutual improvement of its members, and the advancement of public education throughout the state.

The Pennsylvania association expressed its purpose in this fashion: "as a means of elevating the profession of teaching and of promoting the interests of education in Pennsylvania." [20] The Vermont organization used quite a different phraseology, although the two aims of teacher improvement and advancement of the educational interests of the state are both present. The purposes were expressed as follows: [21]

To rouse from its slumbers the public mind, to interest and encourage the heart of the common school teacher, and to impress upon superintendents, teachers of academies and higher seminaries, their great responsibilities as exponents of the public school interests.

The Place of Women in Teachers' Associations

Women were admitted to membership in most states but, in keeping with the public opinion of the time, they were not allowed to lecture or read papers at conventions.[22] The nearest approach to the recognition of females as equals was the permission extended to them to prepare addresses to be read by some male officer of the association. While the constitution granted them this privilege, there were few women included in the programs of state teachers' associations prior to 1860. Wisconsin is rather typical of general practice. The first woman to appear on the program in that state was Mrs. Walter Racine who had prepared a paper for the 1857 convention on "Methods of Teaching." This was four years after the association was formed. Despite the numerical gains, therefore, which women had made as members of the teaching profession, they were still barred from exercising any real leadership.

During the early history of state teachers' associations the officers were universally men. One wonders at the patience and

---

[20] "Pennsylvania State Teachers Association," in *American Journal of Education*, Vol. XV (1865), p. 654.

[21] "Vermont State Teachers Association," in *ibid.*, pp. 620–21.

[22] The California Education Society, when it was organized in 1863, limited membership to males only.

loyalty of womankind as he notes the discriminations which were so generally imposed and continued in many respects throughout the twentieth century.

THE NATURE OF STATE ASSOCIATION MEETINGS

The addresses at state conventions were not unlike those common to our present-day association meetings. Table 2 is fairly representative of the topics discussed.

Table 2. Representative Addresses Given at State Teachers' Associations 1845–1860

General	Methods and Discipline	Administration and School Organization
Education of Females	Phonetics	School Government
Who Should Be Teachers?	Reading	State School Law
Responsibilities of Citizenship	Oral Instruction	Compensation of Teachers
Truancy, Its Causes and Cure	Methods in Study	Graded Schools
Courtesies of the Schoolroom	Object Teaching	Compulsory Attendance
National Welfare as Dependent upon Universal Education	Blunders in Spelling	Examination of Teachers
Education for the Times	Analytic and Synthetic Modes of Teaching	On Town and County Superintendents
Use of Bible in Schools	Textbooks	Coeducation
Teachers' Institutes	Primary Instruction	Duty of State to School
Normal Schools	Popular Fallacies in Teaching	Reform Schools
Material Value of Education	Mental Arithmetic	School Supervision
The Effect of General Intellectual Culture on Manual Labor	Discipline	
Military Drill in Our Schools	Corporal Punishment	

Departmental meetings did not develop until after the Civil War, the number of teachers in attendance in many states scarcely warranting any division of the audience into smaller groups.[23] Social issues received but little attention in the conventions of state teachers' associations and the reforms advocated by speakers were directed almost solely toward administrative reorganization, methodology of teaching, and the general

[23] The number in attendance at the Wisconsin convention in 1855 was approximately 150; and 100 at the New Jersey convention the same year.

improvement of teacher education. Capital and labor, the practices of big business, politics, the courts, the press, and similar
topics were seldom brought to the attention of teachers. Religion,
while presumably a settled issue as far as the schools were concerned, received consideration because of the controversy on
Bible reading in the schools.

The convention addresses were scholarly and, because of the
recency of professional subject matter, were undoubtedly of interest to the members of the associations. Modern platform artists
would have found it exceedingly difficult to compete with those
eloquent gentlemen of the eighteen-fifties who were drafted for
the program of state teachers' associations and county institutes.

RESOLUTIONS

Perhaps the most significant feature of teachers' conventions
was the resolutions which they adopted, for in these appear the
real planks of their platforms and the reforms and changes which
they helped to achieve. A summary of the chief resolutions of
teachers' associations for the years 1846–1860 throws considerable
light on both the issues confronting the profession and the attitude of teachers toward them.

In 1846 the New York State association recommended "the
use of the Bible as a means of moral instruction without note
or comment." The New Hampshire teachers passed a similar resolution in 1854. By 1857 the Vermont association had
become concerned about this and went on record favoring
"daily reading of the Bible in the schools and the introduction of
vocal music." Two years later (1859) the Illinois teachers recommended "the reading of the Bible, without note or comment, in
all our schools." It is quite apparent from the frequent discussions of Bible readings and such resolutions as those just reported
that the leaders in the associations were desirous of maintaining
a united front before the public with respect to Scripture reading
without sectarian interpretation.

A second point of view which took form in the resolutions of
the associations was the rights of female teachers to compensation
more nearly comparable to that of males. In 1850 the Massachusetts teachers and in 1853 the New York State association

urged a material increase in the salaries of female teachers. The Illinois, Wisconsin, and Vermont associations each took a long step in advance of this position in the late fifties by advocating equal pay, the Vermont resolution reading "that male and female teachers of equal qualifications and performing equal services should receive equal compensation."

The establishment of normal schools constituted another plank in the platform of several of the associations and appeared in the resolutions of the New York State organization in 1852, the Wisconsin association in 1854, and the Iowa society in 1858. It is to the credit of these public-school teachers that they were alert to the needs of their own profession and saw in training schools the opportunity to raise the general level of teacher qualifications. A similar stand was taken on the establishment of institutes.

In light of the recent controversy over federal support for private and parochial schools, it is interesting to observe that the New York State Teachers Association settled the issue in their own minds negatively as early as 1853, resolving "that parochial schools are not adapted to the circumstances of our population and ought not to receive governmental support."

Other miscellaneous resolutions and recommendations which indicate the variety and scope of teacher interests concerned such matters as the following:

Discouragement of the use of tobacco on the part of both teachers and pupils.
Longer tenure for school committees.
Higher salaries for state superintendents of schools.
The use of single desks in schools.
Compulsory school attendance.
Establishment of a reform school for juvenile offenders.
Abolition of the "rate bill" system in common schools.
Coeducation through all grades of the schools.
Support of schools by a direct ad valorem tax.
Uniformity of textbooks.
System of graded certificates for teachers.

The above is by no means an exhaustive list of resolutions but will serve to show the multifarious questions about which teachers concerned themselves.

While this discussion of teachers' associations is intended to portray their activities up to the Civil War only, a few of their resolutions pertaining to the "Great Rebellion" seem pertinent at this point. While attendance at conventions was markedly reduced by the war, the work in most associations was not entirely halted. Nearly all the Northern associations proposed resolutions in support of the government's cause. The Massachusetts teachers in 1862 passed a series of resolutions in relation to the questions at issue in the existing rebellion, the results to be sought and expected, the duties of teachers, and their confidence in the President and his advisers. The Illinois association in 1861 also adopted a number of patriotic resolutions. The general type of action taken during these troubled days is illustrated by the following resolution passed by the Kansas society in 1864:

Resolved that as philanthropists and Christians we deprecate war; but finding ourselves involved therein through the madness and infatuation of the advocates of slavery, we will fight it through till our Union is restored and firmly established on the broad foundations of universal freedom, equal laws, and even-handed justice.

The Pennsylvania Association in 1861 went so far as to appropriate money for the purchase of a cannon to be presented to the Northern army. The resolution at this convention called for a gift of three hundred dollars from the association's treasury, together with as much more as could be raised by voluntary contributions from teachers, for the purchase of a cannon and equipment on which would be inscribed: "Presented to the Government of the United States by the Pennsylvania State Teachers Association for the Purpose of Putting Down the Rebellion." A Dr. Burrowes was delegated to collect the additional money and carry out the wishes of the teachers as expressed in the resolution. At the annual meeting in 1863 he reported that seven hundred and twenty dollars had been collected, and the association instructed him to make the purchase. Either the doctor was slow in fulfilling his mission or the red tape of securing the acceptance of the gift impeded action, for in 1864 a letter from Dr. Burrowes was read at the convention stating that "arrangements had been made to purchase the Teachers' Cannon but it was found that the government ammunition would not fit it and hence it was not yet in position." In all probability, the war ended before the gun was properly equipped for action, and the "rebels" suffered no serious losses from this patriotic gesture.

The Civil War aroused considerable agitation for indoctrinating pupils with patriotic zeal. A resolution was proposed and passed by the Vermont association in 1862 "that the study of the constitution should be introduced into schools and more specific attention given to the geography and history of the state." New Jersey teachers were similarly concerned and, at their convention in 1862, they resolved:

That the study of the Constitution of the United States and the leading features of our system of government should be introduced into all our schools, both public and private, and that we, as teachers, will use every means in our power to diffuse a better knowledge of the laws under which we live, and to inspire our pupils with that love of liberty and of country so indispensable to the perpetuation and preservation of the glorious institutions bequeathed to us by the patriots and sages of the Revolution.

The untimely death of Abraham Lincoln also focused the attention of Northern educators upon the importance of teaching the basic elements of good citizenship and thereby averting another national disaster. The following resolution of the Wisconsin association in 1865 represented the point of view which was expressed at several of the state conventions:

Resolved, that in common with all classes of our fellow citizens, we deeply mourn the death of our late beloved President, Abraham Lincoln; that we recognize in his assassination the crowning perfidy and guilt of a rebellion the most wanton, wicked and causeless the world ever saw; and that we will labor with renewed zeal and energy to so extend schools that we shall secure the universal education of our people, and thus prevent the recurrence of so disastrous a revolt against good government, liberty and law.

Journals of State Teachers' Associations

One of the first steps following the inauguration of state teachers' associations was the establishment of official "organs" through which members and other interested individuals could be informed of the work of their respective associations and the current educational thought of the time. The financing of these journals proved to be a most difficult task, particularly during the early life of the associations. Despite the indifference of most teachers toward this important enterprise, however, a surprisingly large proportion of these journals weathered the storm. By 1860, seventeen official state organs had been founded by the associations and several others had come under their control.[24]

Teachers did not generally subscribe to the association journals if the experience of New England is in any way indicative. According to the *Connecticut Common School Journal*,[25] not one fourth of all the teachers in New England either took or read any of the periodicals devoted to the work in which they were engaged. This failure on the part of teachers to subscribe to their own state organs led associations to seek other means of support. Direct financial aid from the state was one of the most important means of supporting teachers' journals.[26]

With the multiplication of educational periodicals, however, states became more and more reluctant to grant direct aid to specific organs, and associations were gradually forced to find some other way of financing their journalistic ventures.

---

[24] The journals actually founded by state teachers' associations were as follows: *Illinois Common School Advocate*, 1841; *Journal of Rhode Island Institute of Instruction*, 1845; *New York Teachers Advocate*, 1845; *Massachusetts Teacher*, 1848; *Ohio School Journal*, 1852; *New York Teacher*, 1853; *Michigan Journal of Education*, 1854; *Illinois Teacher*, 1855; *Indiana School Journal*, 1856; *Wisconsin Journal of Education*, 1856; *Missouri Journal of Education*, 1857; *Missouri Educator*, 1858; *North Carolina Journal of Education*, 1858; *Alabama Educational Journal*, 1858; *Vermont School Journal*, 1859; *Educational Monthly* (Kentucky), 1859; *Iowa Instructor*, 1859. (Davis, Sheldon Emmor, *op. cit.*, p. 37.) Other organs, such as the *Pennsylvania School Journal*, 1852, and the *New Hampshire Journal of Education*, 1857, were not originally created by the state teachers' associations but were taken over later by these organizations.

[25] Vol. XII (1857), p. 121.

[26] Ohio, Michigan, Connecticut, New York, Massachusetts, Pennsylvania, and North Carolina all received some financial aid from the state for the state teachers' association journals.

Another avenue of support was provided through legislation authorizing local boards or school officers to subscribe, making payments from local funds. A less effective means was through the official and semiofficial "designations" circulars of state superintendents urging teachers and officers to take subscriptions for the journal. This usually consisted of a brief statement over the superintendent's signature to the effect that the journal was his official organ and teachers and officers were implored to to support it. When mere exhortation failed, it was possible to bring pressure to bear upon teachers through the control which the state and county superintendents and examiners exercised over certification. In Indiana, for example, in 1862 a convention of examiners voted to add five per cent to the grades of all candidates who subscribed to a school journal, preference being given to the *Indiana School Journal*. Pressure of this sort, however iniquitous, brought results.

The pronounced objectives of the journals, as represented by the editors,[27] were frequently rather broad, as is illustrated by the following excerpts taken from the Michigan and Alabama organs respectively:

To promote the correct and thorough and general education of the sons and daughters of the State of Michigan.

The object of this journal [Alabama Educational Journal] is to record the educational movements going on among us and about us, both for the sake of diffusing information in respect of them and that they may be preserved as matters of future history.

These aims are fairly representative of the pioneer efforts of school journalists. Promoting education, disseminating more liberal views, and securing intelligent legislation were hoped-for outcomes of teachers' journals.

The content of early educational periodicals was equally as general and diffused as the objectives sought. A few carried

[27] Editorial boards usually consisted of a resident editor and from three to seventeen associate editors, the number of the latter ranging commonly from six to fifteen. Quite frequently one of the associate editors was designated "mathematics editor" and his job consisted in proposing and solving difficult problems in mathematics. The other associate editors were assigned responsibilities for preparing or securing articles for the journal.

articles bearing directly upon classroom procedure but such discussions were in the minority. An analysis of several volumes of school journals by Davis [28] shows that from 13 to 40 per cent of the space during the years 1840–1860 was devoted to discussions of school administration; 8 to 13 per cent, to grade method; 5 to 7 per cent, to school management; 4 to 24 per cent, to current educational news and notes. Considerable space was also given to miscellaneous and nonprofessional items, moral and religious instruction, and unclassified educational material.

Editorial boards were confused as to both the needs of the readers whom they were serving and the functions which their journals were designed to meet. The most noticeable trend in content was in the direction of reducing the attention given to administration and increasing the space devoted to current educational news and notes. In spite of the absence of any clearly conceived philosophy on the part of the editors, these journals rendered a unique service to the profession. It must be remembered that educational literature was relatively scarce during this period and that few teachers were able to maintain individual libraries. The only way of keeping them informed was through some inexpensive avenue such as the educational journal. While it must be acknowledged that many teachers did not avail themselves of even this meager bit of school literature, there were scores of them whose practices were modified and whose vision was expanded because of its existence. Indirectly the journals exercised considerable effect on school practices through their influence on school officers. The latter were great imitators and the educational journals occasionally contained reports on modern practices and experiments in various city and county school systems. Such features as the Oswego plan of "object teaching" discussed elsewhere in this treatise received a great deal of attention and space in the official organs of teachers' associations, and unquestionably led to many modifications in school programs. Perhaps of equal significance was the unifying influence which journals exerted on the profession through the clarification of educational issues and policies. In an era of untrained teachers, these journals provided direction and

[28] Davis, Sheldon Emmor, *op. cit.*, p. 65.

aroused sentiment in favor of, and against, many practices which formerly had not received any considerable attention and which were directly related to the teaching process.

Association Secretaries

Some associations in their infancy initiated a policy which in a later period was adopted by practically all state teachers' associations, namely, the employment of an agent to promote the interests and welfare of the organization. The Connecticut teachers in 1854 and the Indiana association in 1855 appointed such agents to devote full time to the work of the association. It was their task to visit school systems, encourage membership in the association, secure subscriptions to and manage the business affairs of the state journal, and keep the officers of the society alert to the educational and professional needs of the state. While these early attempts to promote the associations' interests through employed agents were only partially successful, because of the financial difficulties encountered, they demonstrated the need for such an officer and portrayed the type of activities in which he might engage with great profit to the profession. The duties and work of our present secretaries of state teachers' associations were envisaged by educational statesmen prior to the Civil War. It took time and much effort to convince the teaching profession of the advantages to be derived from a permanent paid officer of this character.

Any attempt to state objectively the achievements of state teachers' associations would probably lead one into the statistical error of deducing causation from a high degree of correlation. Practically every important reform, during the period 1845–1860, in administration, teacher training, professional growth in service, and the general realm of professional welfare was sponsored or supported by state teachers' associations. That these organizations contributed significantly to the achievement of most of the improvements listed above can scarcely be questioned, but the extent of their aid cannot be expressed in numerical terms. Educational leaders believed that the associations were primarily responsible in many states for the outstanding accomplishments of the period. One educator in 1859, speaking of the Ohio association, stated his views as follows: "Recommendations of the Ohio Teachers Association have been embodied in laws for teachers' institutes, for school libraries, for high schools, for township boards of education, for a state instead of a county tax, and for a state commission." [29]

Similar claims were made for the Pennsylvania association in 1865, as the following statement reveals: [30]

By discussion and agitation, and by memorials addressed to the Legislature, the law itself was thoroughly revised and its powers greatly enlarged—a County Superintendency was given—a costly school architecture was prepared and issued to every district—the School Journal was made the organ of the School Department and sent at the expense of the State to each school board—a separate School Department was erected—a complete and well-conceived Normal School organization was engrafted upon the law . . . That these results were mainly due to the enlightened and well-directed efforts of the Association can not be doubted. Its work in securing the improvement of the organic law has been well done, and is well nigh complete.

Equally as extravagant claims were made for other associations. Bateman in reminiscing about the activities of the Illinois association says: "Through its influence came the State Superintendency, the County Superintendency, the Normal Schools, the State University, and even the school system itself." [31]

THE NATIONAL TEACHERS ASSOCIATION

The crowning event of this period so prolific of organization was the establishment of the National Teachers Association at a convention held in Philadelphia in 1857. The need for such an organization had been expressed in several state gatherings of teachers but the leading spirit behind the movement was T. W. Valentine, President of the New York State Teachers Association. This gentleman proposed the convention and secured the cooperation of several of the other associations in launching the

[29] *American Journal of Education*, Vol. VI (1859), p. 552.
[30] *Ibid.*, Vol. XV (1865), p. 669.
[31] Bateman, N., "Our Pilgrim Fathers," in Illinois State Teachers Association, *Proceedings, 1897.*

new enterprise. The call for the meeting was signed by the presidents of ten state associations,[32] and was issued to "all practical teachers in the North, the South, the East, and the West." The distinctive feature of this new society was the limitation placed upon membership. Former national organizations, such as the National Association of the Friends of Education, had been open to both educators and laymen, and was not in any real sense of the term a professional society. The National Teachers Association, on the other hand, proposed to confine its membership to those engaged in the business of education as teachers, superintendents, or editors and was modeled more after the state teachers' associations than the education societies which preceded them. Forty-three charter members [33] (forty-one men and two women) signed the constitution, which stated that the object of the association was "to elevate the character and advance the interests of the profession of teaching, and to promote the cause of popular education in the United States."

The presiding officer at the Philadelphia convention emphasized two outcomes which might properly be expected from a national association: (1) "wider and juster views of education and corresponding methods of instruction" and (2) "a large amount of professional benefit to its members." An address prepared by William Russell and read by Mr. Valentine of New York emphasized the need for gathering and interpreting the statistics of our country so that public-school conditions would be known. In spite of the small attendance, enthusiasm ran high and there was no lack of faith on the part of the founders in the ultimate success of the venture. The first president was Z. Richards, Principal of Union Academy, Washington, D. C.

Women were not admitted to full membership until 1866, the original regulation in the constitution stating that: [34]

Any *gentleman* who is regularly occupied in teaching in a public or private elementary, common school, high school, academy, scientific

---

[32] New York, Massachusetts, Vermont, New Hampshire, Pennsylvania, Indiana, Wisconsin, Illinois, Iowa, and Missouri.

[33] Of these forty-three original members of the association, twenty-one were from Pennsylvania. The expense of traveling limited the attendance at national meetings for several years to come.

[34] National Teachers Association, *Constitution*, Article 2.

school, college or university, or who is regularly employed as a private tutor, as the editor of an educational journal or as superintendent of schools shall be eligible for membership.

It was provided, however, that:

Ladies engaged in teaching may, on the recommendation of the Board of Directors, become honorary members, and shall thereby possess the right of presenting in the form of written essays (to be read by the Secretary or any other member whom they may select) their views upon the subject assigned for discussion.

All applications for membership (male or female) were referred to the Board of Directors (composed of the officers of the association), where a majority vote was required for election. It was then necessary for the applicant to sign the constitution of the association and pay a two-dollar fee. The annual dues were to be one dollar and a life membership could be purchased for ten dollars. The membership continued small for several years, seventy-three teachers being elected at the Cincinnati meeting in 1858 (sixty-seven men and six women) and twenty-five new members, all men, joining at the Buffalo convention in 1859.

The times were not propitious for developing national associations because of the great political and sectional strife which was rampant throughout the country. The repeal of the Missouri Compromise, the excitement of the Frémont and Buchanan Campaign, and the memorable Lincoln and Douglas debate in Illinois served to produce discordant views among teachers as well as the masses of the population and tended to distract attention from purely educational problems.

The vision of early leaders in the association doubtless preserved its life and won the support of public-spirited citizens. The program advocated by President Richards at Cincinnati in 1858 was no narrowly conceived platform of a selfish professional group. Among the reforms which he urged were "the creation of a teaching profession by professional methods," "the examination of teachers by competent examining boards," "the establishment of departments of pedagogy in connection with all schools who send out teachers," "a national bureau of education," and "a national journal of education." Such worthy objectives were wholly compatible with the views of prominent lay leaders and educational statesmen of the day and commanded the respect of friends of education everywhere.

RESOLUTIONS OF THE NATIONAL TEACHERS ASSOCIATION, 1857–1863

Since the National Teachers Association was organized near the close of the period under discussion, the resolutions acted upon by the society prior to the Civil War furnish a rather inadequate picture of the nature and scope of its activities. The Philadelphia convention in 1857 was held for the purpose of organizing the association and no important resolutions were proposed at that meeting. The following year, in Cincinnati, a vigorous discussion took place on "Parochial Schools,—Are They in Harmony with the Spirit of American Institutions?" and led to the adoption of the following two resolutions:

1. That in endeavoring to promote the great cause of general education, this association will not recognize any distinctions on account of locality, position, or particular departments of labor, but that all teachers, whether in colleges, academies, public, private or parochial schools, in every part of our land shall be regarded by us as brethren and fellow laborers in one common cause.

2. That while we regard schools established by private enterprise, not only as necessary in the present condition of things, but as most valuable and indispensable aids in public education, we nevertheless hold that it is the great duty of the state to provide the means for the full and free education of all the youth within its borders.

These resolutions were rather innocuous and much milder than the one passed by the New York State Teachers Association several years before (1853).[35] The national group were somewhat divided in their views about the issue of parochial schools. Horace Mann said he was "opposed to them and to all sectarianism," adding that "the sectarian interpreted the Scriptures for others in a spirit of narrowness, not according to the largeness of the Almighty." He concluded his remarks with the

[35] See page 257.

statement that "sectarianism was pernicious in the extreme, and he would always oppose it in this country." A contrary point of view, however, was expressed by several members, one man from Indiana indicating that "he was warmly in favor of Parochial Schools and he thought those now in existence a blessing rather than a curse." The resolutions finally adopted represented a middle-of-the-road position and left out of consideration entirely the question of financial support.

The only other resolutions adopted at the 1858 meeting were one commending to teachers Barnard's *American Journal of Education* as a work of great value and a resolution calling for the appointment of a committee to report "a basis for keeping 'School Registers' and making 'Annual Reports' adapted to the wants of teachers and school officers throughout the country."

In 1859 the convention was held in Washington, D. C., and at one session the association was honored by the attendance of the President of the United States. The program apparently did not provoke much controversy and the resolutions were not particularly significant. It was proposed to inaugurate a journal, the name of which was to be *The National Teacher;* [36] appropriate resolutions were made upon the death of Horace Mann; and the association congratulated itself upon the wide representation of members attending the convention. Perhaps the most significant recommendation of the association from an educational standpoint was one embodied in the resolution:

That the inculcation of the Christian religion is necessary to the happiness of the people and the perpetuity of our institutions, and we should be pleased to see every teacher in our broad land imbued with its spirit; *yet we would not shut the doors of our schoolhouses upon well-qualified and apt teachers because they do not hold membership in any religious denomination.*

This early recognition by the association of the importance of a tolerant attitude toward the religious life and affiliations of teachers unquestionably had its influence on the policies of school boards in the matter of teacher selection.

The Buffalo meeting in 1860 was devoted to a wide variety of subjects, as is revealed by the resolutions adopted. The associa-

[36] This was referred to the Board of Directors for consideration.

tion favored adult education and adult classes, physical education and schoolroom gymnastics, and a national system of statistics. The latter need had been recognized by Henry Barnard for several years and was one of the major considerations in establishing later a Bureau of Education in Washington.

Since the association suspended its conventional activities in 1861 and 1862 because of the Civil War, there were no further official public pronouncements until August, 1863, the date of the Chicago meeting. Despite the dissension which the war had produced, this convention was well attended. Several interesting topics were discussed and resolutions drafted in harmony with the dominant point of view expressed by the members. There was considerable agitation for emphasizing in the schools instruction in citizenship and the principles of good government as a basis for developing unity and advancing the cause of democracy. Most of the resolutions included below need no interpretation to be fully appreciated. The intent is clear and the emotional tone produced by the war is in some instances apparent.

1. Resolved, That a committee of five be appointed to consider and report what the times and the condition of the country demand of educators, in the way of teaching the principles of our government; also the rights and duties of the citizen under the same.

2. Resolved, That the publication of a suitable collection for teachers, containing songs of a professional, social, *patriotic*, and religious character, would supply an acknowledged want and be likely to meet favor.

3. Resolved, That it is imperative that the History, Polity and Constitution of our government be taught in all our schools wherein the maturity of the pupils is equal to the subjects.

4. Resolved, That this teaching should never be prostituted to the inculcation of merely partizan sentiments and principles.

5. Resolved, That while we deprecate the discussion of merely party or sectional topics by teachers' associations, we yet deem no person worthy to hold the honorable position of teacher or officer in any educational institution who is not fearlessly outspoken and true, at all times, both by voice and vote, to the great questions of loyalty, patriotism, and the unconditional support of the National Government, in this crisis of our country's fate.

6. Resolved, That the loyalty of this convention needs no re-assertion—
that we are with our country and for our country, now and forever,
one and inseparable.

Resolutions of a very general character pertaining to teacher
welfare and improvement were also adopted at this meeting.

The next two conventions were relatively free from discussions
of patriotism and governmental loyalty and were devoted
largely to educational projects which had been initiated in
earlier meetings.

The great contributions of this newly formed national association came after the close of this remarkable period of educational
development. This society was the climax of an evolutionary
process in organization which began around 1800, and its foundation constituted one of the greatest achievements of the
profession before the Civil War. A medium for threshing out
controversial issues, for expounding progressive ideas, and for
molding public opinion on educational and professional matters was now an established fact and one could rightfully antic-
ipate a long and useful life for a house built upon so firm a
foundation.

SUGGESTED READINGS

American Journal of Education, Henry Barnard (ed.) (new series, No. 9),
No. XXXIV (March, 1864), pp. 3–60; (new series, No. 11),
No. XXXVI (September, 1864), pp. 535 ff.; (new series, No. 15),
No. XL (September, 1865), pp. 477–537; (new series, No. 18),
No. XLIII (June, 1866), pp. 745 ff.

CUBBERLEY, ELWOOD P., *Public Education in the United States* (Boston,
Houghton Mifflin Company, 1934), pp. 704–12.

DAVIS, SHELDON EMMOR, *Educational Periodicals during the Nineteenth Century*, U. S. Bureau of Education, Bulletin 1919, No. 28 (Washington, Government Printing Office, 1919).

HAYES, CECIL B., *The American Lyceum, Its History and Contribution to
Education*, U. S. Office of Education, Bulletin 1932, No. 12 (Washington, Government Printing Office, 1932).

XXI

The Economic and Social Position of Schoolteachers

THE economic and social status of teachers immediately after the Revolutionary War did not differ in any perceptible way from conditions prevailing during the latter part of the colonial period. Schoolmasters continued to be poorly paid for the few months during which they were engaged to teach and were forced to supplement their meager wages by employment outside of their chosen fields. Education, in spite of the vocal support given to it by statesmen of the early republic, was considered secondary in importance to the business of political reorganization, the expansion of American trade, and the improvement of agriculture. Immediate utility was the criterion by which citizens rated the value of one's occupation and, with so many imminent practical problems requiring solution, schoolteaching fell rather low in the scale. Since public esteem has always been a vital factor in determining the attractiveness of a vocation, it could scarcely be expected that talented individuals would look toward education as their life career. Instead, the queer, the lazy, and the incompetent took to teaching for want of something better to do and, in spite of numerous exceptions, the schoolmasters of the early eighteen-hundreds were not so greatly respected as their colonial predecessors—and hence were not generously treated.

This situation had not changed greatly by 1840, although there were a number of hopeful signs pointing in the direction of an improved professional status. The many educational reforms already discussed, which either began or were well under way during the second quarter of the nineteenth century, tended to elevate the position of the public-school teacher and directed the attention of lay citizens to the importance of the task.   Normal schools, teachers' institutes, state and county supervision, improved certification, the extension of the school program, and the establishment of educational journals—all these innovations had been matters of great public interest and discussion, and the achievement of each one of these improvements strengthened the position of the teacher both socially and financially.

If the reader finds the teacher's living and working conditions as described in the following pages a bit squalid, he should remember that the situation generally was greatly superior to that which prevailed in the earlier history of the profession and that progress was made at a tremendous sacrifice of time and effort on the part of our educational leaders.

SALARIES

The American people have always attached great significance to the financial standing of citizens, and the respect accorded the various vocations with few exceptions has been directly related to the monetary awards provided.   In this regard teachers have labored at a serious disadvantage.   The situation in San Francisco in the early history of California was humorously depicted by John Swett in one of his "Random Rhymes for School Teachers" in which the futility of their seeking generous rewards is described as follows: [1]

> As well suppose that a game of euchre
> Will fill your pockets with filthy lucre,
> As think that teaching the city's scholars
> Will line your pockets with silver dollars
> Mum is the word and nothing to say;
> Live on faith and expect no pay.

Whether the class of individuals who composed the great body of American public-school teachers—untrained and incompetent in many instances as they were—was responsible for the niggardly attitude of the public toward their pay, or whether the small rewards account for the mediocre qualifications of

[1] Ferrier, W. W., *Ninety Years of Education in California, 1846–1936* (Berkeley, Calif., Sather Gate Book Shop, 1937), p. 67.

schoolteachers is a moot question. In the minds of educational leaders it was the latter, and state superintendents were continuously pointing out the hopelessness of improving the teacher personnel of the schools without raising wages. J. T. Clark, in his *Essay on Common School Education in New Jersey*, written in 1855, expressed the point of view held by most of the school administrators of his day, as follows: [2]

The want of adequate remuneration is of itself a sufficient reason why the teachers are generally so miserably qualified for their duties. They are even better prepared than they can afford to be. Ask a man of ability and promise to spend time, money and labor in fitting himself properly to teach school for two hundred and eighty-four dollars a year and board himself! The idea is absurd. The majority of teachers are exactly what one would expect them to be. The reason is obvious why the very name of teacher has been, and is yet to some extent, a term of reproach. . . . Many a farmer will much more willingly pay a liberal price to a competent man for shoeing his horse well—he would even go farther to secure the services of a smith of experience and reputation—than to obtain a suitable individual to mould and form the character of his child.

While it is true that salaries in the smaller school districts were ridiculously low, amounting to as little as a dollar a week with board, teachers in the larger towns and cities fared much better. The situation after 1840 has been carefully analyzed by Burgess and the following averages, in Table 3, taken from his computations show salary trends for both rural and urban teachers between 1841 and 1864 inclusive.

Three facts stand out in Table 3. First, that salaries of all teachers rose rather steadily from 1845 to about 1858; second, that city teachers received anywhere from two to three times as much salary as that paid to rural teachers; and, third, that women fared badly in comparison with men, the disparity between the salaries of city men and women teachers being noticeably greater than that prevailing in rural districts.

Since these averages represent wage conditions for the whole country, they do not show the differences which existed among the various states nor the practices which prevailed in the wealthier and perhaps more socially minded communities. Unfortunately, reliable wage data for this period were not readily available for all sections of the country.

Table 3. Average Weekly Salaries of Teachers, 1841 to 1864 [1]

Year	Rural		City	
	Men	Women	Men	Women
1841	$4.15	$2.51	$11.93	$4.44
1842	4.07	2.43	11.97	4.49
1843	3.99	2.45	12.04	4.36
1844	3.87	2.48	12.21	4.27
1845	3.87	2.51	11.88	4.09
1846	4.03	2.53	11.53	4.18
1847	4.09	2.61	11.81	4.27
1848	4.22	2.69	12.33	4.40
1849	4.23	2.72	13.11	4.54
1850	4.25	2.89	13.37	4.71
1851	4.43	2.95	14.10	4.87
1852	4.53	2.96	14.55	4.94
1853	4.73	3.13	15.55	5.23
1854	5.12	3.28	15.75	5.42
1855	5.77	3.65	16.80	5.79
1856	6.07	3.85	16.76	6.10
1857	6.48	4.03	17.61	6.59
1858	6.64	4.19	18.61	6.93
1859	6.42	4.27	18.30	7.16
1860	6.28	4.12	18.56	6.99
1861	6.30	4.05	18.07	6.91
1862	6.00	3.82	17.81	6.80
1863	6.31	4.01	18.19	6.95
1864	7.86	4.92	20.78	7.67

[1] Burgess, Warren R., *Trends of School Costs* (New York, Russell Sage Foundation, Education Monograph, 1920), p. 32.

One can get some impression of the situation for a given year from Table 4, which shows the average *monthly* wages paid to both male and female teachers in seven of the states in 1853, together with the length of school year in weeks or months. Table 4 shows a much wider variation in the salaries of female teachers than in those paid to men. The reasons for the differences in the average salaries among the several states are not always discernible at first glance. Rural states like Vermont tended to pay teachers less generously than its more densely populated neighbors. Beyond this, there seems to be no logical explanations for the differences except custom and chance.

Table 4. Average Monthly Salary of Public-school Teachers in 1853 According to States [1]

State	Average Monthly Salary		Length of School Term
	Male Teachers	Female Teachers	
Vermont..................	$13.55	$ 5.54	24 weeks
Massachusetts............	37.25 [2]	16.36 [2]	7½ months
Connecticut..............	18.50	8.20	——
Pennsylvania.............	18.75	11.46	5 months
Illinois..................	17.63	10.32	6 mos. 23 days
New Hampshire...........	15.68	6.96	——
Wisconsin................	18.17	9.64	——

[1] *Michigan Journal of Education*, Vol. I (1854), pp. 133–37.
[2] Teacher's board accounted for in wage.

The practice of "boarding 'round," discussed later at some length, makes the salaries received a bit difficult to interpret, since the value of board was a variable and wage quotations did not always stipulate whether or not it was included in the rate. However, even when generous allowance is made for "keep" the wages will seem exceedingly low to present-day teachers. Steady improvement in salaries occurred in most states after 1845. The situation in Wisconsin, for which facts have been compiled as given in Table 5, is fairly typical of the trend in the various states and shows the general rise in wages between 1849 and 1865.

The salaries of women teachers continued to be lower than those paid to men, although, as Table 5 shows, the position of female wages in relation to those of males improved somewhat in Wisconsin during the sixteen years for which facts are presented. This trend is also observable in Table 3, showing the average salaries of teachers for the country at large. The disparity in salaries between men and women teachers provoked considerable discussion and agitation and appeared several times in the resolutions of teachers' associations and institutes. Despite the theoretical justifications for equal pay, which were more usually conceded than not, practice was not significantly influenced by them and women continued to suffer discriminations because of their sex, in all states, until the equal-pay laws of the present century were passed.

*Table 5. Monthly Wages and Ratio of Wages of
Female to Male Teachers* [1]

Year	Male Teachers	Female Teachers	Ratio Per Cent
1849	$15.22	$ 6.92	45
1850	17.14	8.97	52
1851	17.15	8.35	43
1852	15.83	8.64	54
1853	18.17	9.94	50
1854	18.75	11.00	60
1855	23.10	12.08	52
1856	25.38	13.80	54
1857	24.60	15.16	62
1858	27.02	14.92	55
1859	22.93	14.29	63
1860	24.20	15.30	63
1861	23.01	14.62	63
1862	25.82	15.82	61
1863	27.11	16.81	62
1864	32.39	19.43	60
1865	36.45	22.24	61

[1] *Wisconsin School Report, 1865*, Part 2, No. 9, p. 8.

The scale of payment in cities was higher than the averages reported for states, although when proper account is taken of the increased cost of living the differences are not so great as they appear to be from the bare facts. In Cincinnati, the monthly salary of first-class male assistants was $28.33 ($340 for twelve months) in 1839; $30 in 1847; $35 in 1848; $45 in 1850; $65 in 1853; and $66.66 in 1858. Women teachers in this city were advanced much less rapidly than men during the earlier years under consideration and the increase was scarcely perceptible for those holding lower licenses. The salary of a female first assistant was $20 a month in 1839; $30 in 1853; and $37.50 in 1858. The vast majority of women received only sixteen and eighteen dollars a month from 1837 to 1853.

The salary schedule in Cincinnati was based on the type of certificate held and years of experience in teaching. A teacher holding a principal's certificate received a differential because of the higher qualifications which she possessed. The scale as announced in the *Common School Report* of 1853 was: [3]

Principals of male department, with Principal's certificate and two years of experience in teaching, per month	$85.00
Principals of female department, with the same qualifications as male principals	42.00
Male assistants with Principal's certificate, and one year's experience in teaching	65.00
Male assistants, with assistant's certificate	46.00
Female assistants, without experience in teaching or with assistant's certificate less than No. 1	20.00
Female assistants, with No. 1 certificate and six months' experience in teaching	24.00
Female assistants, with Principal's certificate and one year's experience in teaching	30.00
Principal of night school	25.00
Assistant of night school	20.00

High-school principals in Cincinnati, while not included in the salary schedule, received much higher salaries than those awarded principals of the common schools. When high schools were first organized in 1848, the principal was paid $83.33 a month; by 1851 his salary had been increased to $125. Modifications were made in salary arrangements whenever circumstances dictated it. An increase in the examination requirements for assistant teachers called for a corresponding increase in salaries in 1854.[4] Apparently the readjustment in wages did not offset, at least in the minds of those teachers affected, the higher certification requirements, since the president of the board of education mentioned in his report that "it was not expected that a measure so reasonable and easy, so indispensable to the due elevation and progress of our standard, would be received with reluctance or opposition." [5]

---

[3] *Twenty-fourth Annual Report of the Common Schools of Cincinnati* (1853), p. 62.

[4] *Cincinnati Common School Report, 1855.* Prior to February, 1854, assistant female teachers were required to possess no other attainments than spelling, definitions, reading, grammar, geography, arithmetic, and American history. The board added, on the above date, that female assistants should by the close of the year pass an examination in penmanship, algebra, logic, and the theory and practice of teaching.

[5] *Ibid.*, p. 19.

Comparable improvements in salaries occurred in other cities. Primary-school teachers (first assistants) in Philadelphia were paid $150 a year in 1843; $200 in 1849; and $240 in 1858. The salaries of first-assistant teachers in the boys' grammar school increased from $275 to $350, and principals enjoyed similar increases during this same period.

The salary arrangements prevailing in several large cities at the beginning of the Civil War are shown in Table 6.

Table 6. Rates of Teachers' Salaries in Eight Different Cities, 1861–1862 [1]

Names of Cities	High Schools			Grammar and District Schools				
	Principal	Male Assistants	Female Assistants	Male Principals	Male Assistants	Female Principals	Female First Assistants	Other Female Assistants
St. Louis, 1862..	$1600	$ 800 1000	$ 500 700	$ 800 1000	—	$ 400 550	— $ 400	$325 375
Chicago, 1862...	1600	500 1000	500	700 1200	—	—	400 500	250 400
Cincinnati, 1862.	1500	1080 1188	630 900	1068 1152	$ 717 807	—	—	240 540
Boston, 1859....	2400 2800	1200 2000	500 600	1600 2000	800 1600	—	500	300 450
New York, 1860.	3000	1000 2500	—	—	—	—	—	—
Philadelphia, 1858.........	2000	1200 1500	—	800 1200	—	300 600	—	200 300
New Orleans, 1856.........	1800	1500	1000	1200	1000	1000	800	600
San Francisco, 1860.........	2500	1000 2400	1250	2000	—	800 1000	900 1000	850

Remark: Where two rates are given in the above table, the minimum and maximum sometimes refer to different persons and distinct grades; but for the most part they refer to the same individual and the same position—the minimum being the salary of a new teacher the first year, and the maximum the increased and permanent salary after two or three years' service.

[1] *St. Louis School Report, 1861–1862*, p. 55.

The classroom teachers in New Orleans and San Francisco were apparently more generously treated than those in the other cities listed. While there seems to be relatively little uniformity in the actual wages paid to the instructional groups in all the cities studied, males were constantly favored over females and high-school teachers received larger salaries than their colleagues in the grammar and district schools.

The Boston teachers were better paid in 1858 than those in either Cincinnati or Philadelphia, and the scale in operation provided for annual increments for the majority of the personnel. Eight separate classifications were included in the schedule, ranging from primary-school teachers and assistants in the grammar school to the principal or, what was termed in Boston, the "master." [6]

One of the most significant developments of this period, which is best illustrated by the Boston schedule, was the policy of providing financial incentives in the form of stipulated annual increments to be given with each year of experience in the school system up to the established maximum. While the practice was not generally followed in cities before 1860, the principle adopted by the Boston school committee was destined to become the model for many school systems in a later period.

The significance of the wages paid to schoolteachers can be appreciated only when measured in terms of the scale of pay which prevailed in other walks of life and in relationship to the cost of living. While considerable statistical data exist on the former topic, they are so fragmentary, except as they apply to laborers and artisans, as to render final conclusions and judgments unreliable. Beyond a comparison furnished by Burgess,[7] the opinions and statements of observers during this period are probably the best sources of information from which to draw any general picture of the relative economic position of teachers.

Horace Mann, in 1843, apparently made a careful survey of wages in one Massachusetts community, for in the *Common School Journal* of that year he commented as follows: [8]

Not long since in one of the most cultivated towns in the Commonwealth I took great pains to ascertain the wages of journeymen, shoemakers, carpenters, blacksmiths, painters, carriage-makers, wheel-

---

[6] *Report of the Boston School Committee, 1858*, p. 124.

[7] Burgess, Warren R., *op. cit.*, p. 71. According to compilations by Burgess, the weekly wages of laborers advanced from $4.86 in 1841 to $7.98 in 1864 and the wages of artisans rose from $8.28 to $12.66 during the same period of time.

[8] *Common School Journal*, Vol. V (1843), p. 355.

wrights, harness-makers, cabinet and piano-forte makers and some others. The result . . . showed that while every class of these received more, some . . . received 50 [per cent] and a few 100 per cent more than was paid to any of the teachers of the district schools in the same town.

He also stated in this same report that "the price paid to the great majority of female teachers is less than is paid to the better class of female operatives in factories." [9] In 1847 the battle for higher wages for teachers was still raging in Massachusetts and Horace Mann, in his typical style, pointed out: "We pay best,—1st, those who destroy us,—generals; 2nd, those who cheat us,—politicians and quacks; 3rd, those who amuse us,—singers and dancers; and last of all those who instruct us,—teachers." [10]

Connecticut apparently did not treat its pedagogues any more generously than Massachusetts, for in 1847 the school visitors of Vernon complained that: [11]

A young man busy in the summer, looks around in the fall to determine how he shall spend the winter months. He thinks of turning peddler, or of working at shoemaking. But the one will expose him to storms, the other he fears will injure his chest. He therefore concludes that although he can make more money in these or some similar employment, he will nevertheless teach school for a meagre compensation.

Then, directing their attention to female teachers, the visitors argued:

The question with them is whether they shall go into the factory, do housework or teach. At the first they can clear four dollars per week, perhaps five; at the second, one dollar fifty cents; at the third one dollar, or one dollar twenty five cents, if in a large school perhaps a little more. The contest is between the factory and the school.

In this same county (Vernon), four years later the highest salary of a male teacher was $450 a year with board, and the lowest

[9] *Ibid.*, p. 203. Factory workers in New England commonly worked from twelve to fourteen hours a day, a fact which was overlooked by most educators in making comparisons. The ten-hour day demanded by labor in its platform did not become a reality in most states until after 1860.

[10] *Ibid.*, Vol. IX (1847), p. 367.   [11] *Connecticut Board of Education, 1847*, p. 48.

was $12 a month and "board 'round." In New Hampshire, a similar situation existed and it was reported by Secretary Patterson of the state board of education in 1858 that "the salary of a common foot soldier in the United States Army is greater than the salary of the best female teacher in the public schools of New Hampshire and we pay a bookkeeper more than the president of a college." [12]

Females in Vermont could earn two or three dollars a week as seamstresses and one dollar and a quarter to one dollar and seventy-five cents as domestics, whereas schoolteaching paid only from one dollar to a dollar and a half "with board picked up at a distance of a mile or two by traveling here and there like a mendicant from door to door." [13] The state superintendent in Maine in 1855 remarked that the mechanic and clerk often receive double the salary paid to the teacher. [14]

In Philadelphia, as late as 1864, the women teachers were also deemed poorly paid, the controllers arguing somewhat satirically in their annual report for that year that "there are upwards of one thousand teachers upon each of whom is lavished per diem a sum scarcely equal to the amount paid to the washerwoman and about 800 of these obtain only two thirds of a washerwoman's wages. A large proportion of the teachers receive each less than the janitress who sweeps the School-House." [15]

The low evaluation placed upon teaching was by no means limited to the East if the statements of superintendents are to be believed. The state superintendent in California in 1863 discussed the average salary of $357 (including both male and female teachers) in this manner: [16]

Out of this annual average salary, Teachers must board and clothe themselves, and pay their income tax! An average servant girl receives three hundred dollars ($300) a year, *and her board;* an average farm hand gets the same; and even an able bodied Chinaman gets three hundred dollars ($300) a year, boarding himself. The lowest

[12] *Report of the Commissioner of Education, 1897–1898,* Vol. I, p. 422.
[13] *Ibid.,* p. 414.   [14] *Maine School Report, 1855,* p. 12.
[15] *Forty-sixth Annual Report* (Philadelphia, 1864), p. 31.
[16] California Department of Education, *Thirteenth Annual Report of the Superintendent of Public Instruction* (1863), p. 11.

monthly wages paid to any male Teacher was twenty-nine dollars ($29), the Teacher boarding himself. A missionary ought to be sent to that district at once by the State Educational Society.

It is apparent from the reports of county and state school officers that taxpayers during the early history of public education in the United States were no more sensitive to the economic needs of teachers than they have been in recent years, and that women teachers, especially, were paid ridiculously low wages for the responsibilities which they were asked to assume. In spite of this shortsighted policy, which prevailed rather generally, the supply of technically qualified women who were willing to accept teaching positions at existing rates was in most instances equal to the demand. It is true that domestics and mill hands were paid as much or more than teachers, but the former were not white-collared workers and the positions did not offer the same degree of independence nor the same amount of leisure time as teaching. The doors to other respectable vocations had not yet been opened wide to women and, acting upon the law of supply and demand, the public was slow in responding to the appeals of the profession for more adequate remuneration.

Cost-of-living data are not available for the cities and states for which salary facts have been cited and the true economic position of teachers can only be inferred from Burgess's index and from isolated reports of superintendents and other educators. We are fortunate in having for the years subsequent to 1840 a rather accurate estimate of the weekly cost of food, shelter, clothing, and incidentals for a small family, assuming that they lived on the same scale as a typical workingman's family in 1901. Since the annual fluctuations were not particularly striking except during Civil War days, the cost-of-living facts in Table 7 are presented for each five-year interval only and for 1864.

From Table 7 it is apparent that the cost of living did not change significantly during the twenty years immediately preceding the Civil War. The first substantial rise (not shown in the table) occurred in 1863, and prices continued inordinately high until 1870. When the figures on cost of living are compared

Table 7. *Cost of Living per Week from 1841 to 1864 Inclusive* [1] (*for a small family using the same commodities over the entire period*)

Year	Cost per Week
1841	$ 7.00
1846	7.39
1851	6.63
1856	8.00
1861	7.66
1864	13.10

[1] Burgess, Warren, R., *op. cit.*, p. 54.

with the weekly salaries of teachers shown in Table 3, several possible generalizations can be made. On the basis of the raw data, one might properly conclude that only men teachers in city schools at any time during the twenty-three-year period received the equivalent of the cost of subsistence. Since most of the other teachers were single, the discrepancy between the wage figures and the cost of living for a small family does not imply a starvation wage but it certainly indicates that the standard of living was low.

A second observation leads to the conclusion that teachers of all types were better off economically in 1860 than they were in 1841 but that their gains were almost completely, if not totally, absorbed during the Civil War by the increased cost of living.

There were some who believed that the only "true . . . standard of compensation should be the *value* of the service rendered" and argued that "if compensation is to be measured by home demands, or by the extent of a man's family, we must adopt a sliding scale" and that a teacher's salary by this reasoning which they deemed fallacious "must be increased for every addition to his family and diminished for every death." [17] This "family allowance" idea was rejected as unsound and impracticable, but the advocates of "merit" never demonstrated just how salaries could be reliably related to the quality and amount of the service rendered. The Indiana state superintendent proposed in 1866 that: [18]

So far as practicable, the teacher's pay should grade according to ability, not of necessity, according to the grade of examiner's certificate.

[17] *Philadelphia School Report, 1864*, p. 29.   [18] *Indiana School Report, 1866*, p. 80.

Certificates are issued chiefly upon scholarship; but scholarship is not all that enters into the account in estimating the *ability* of a teacher. Ability to *instruct*, to discipline, to inspire with a love of learning; in short, all that goes to make a successful educator should enter into the account, hence so far as practicable, the pay should grade accordingly.

This principle, so loudly acclaimed by several of these early schoolmen, has constituted a controversial issue in compensating teachers down to the present time.

Since the salaries of teachers were dependent upon the generosity of local school boards and committees, the variation in the wages paid was tremendous. This resulted in wide differences in the qualifications of the teachers employed and in the actual service rendered. In order to protect both children and teachers against the policies enacted by niggardly and ignorant school committees, the legislatures in several states during recent years have enacted minimum salary laws, stipulating the salary levels below which no local school district can go with impunity. This idea was by no means a product of the twentieth century. John Waughop, Superintendent of Schools in Cook County, Illinois, advanced a similar proposal as early as 1855, as the following statement taken from his biennial report shows: "I am of the opinion that the price of teachers should be established by law, or at least there should be a price less than which no town should employ a teacher, but pay as much more as they can afford for better teachers." [19]

Similarly, the single-salary-schedule idea [20] was advocated in a few quarters but was not followed to any considerable extent until later in our history. Tradition had led laymen and most members of the teaching profession to believe that the older the pupil the more difficult the task of instructing him, hence the justification for higher salaries for teachers in the upper grades of the school system regardless of their training.

Occasionally an intelligent observer would see the fallacy in this arrangement, even though he lacked the courage to openly attack it. The chairman of the school committee in Manchester,

[19] *New York Teacher*, Vol. I, p. 93.
[20] A schedule in which teachers are paid according to their training and experience qualifications regardless of teaching position held.

New Hampshire, in 1858 was clearly aware of the importance and difficulty of the primary teacher's task, for, in his discussion of salaries in the annual school report (1858), he argued as follows: [21]

While I believe a faithful Primary school teacher is required to do the most work in her school room, and should really be the best teacher, she will not naturally expect so large a salary as one who is engaged in a Grammar or High School. While $250, except in the case of especial merit, should be the highest salary for instruction in Primary or Middle Schools, an additional sum of $25 or $50 will be demanded for good Grammar School assistants and a corresponding increase for assistants in the High School.

Teachers in the lower grades apparently accepted their humble position in this hierarchy without complaint. It is true that the training of high-school teachers was in most instances more advanced than that required of, or possessed by, teachers in the primary and intermediate grades and, therefore, the salary policies did not produce the serious injustices which occurred later when a larger proportion of elementary teachers began to extend their training.

The most significant contribution of this period in salary scheduling from the standpoint of future developments was not the establishment of precedents in the nature of the scales adopted, but rather the questioning of old practices and procedures by some of the more intelligent educators of the time. The superintendent of schools in Cincinnati in 1854 recognized the weaknesses in the traditional practice and stated the case for primary teachers most effectively in the school report for that year. After decrying the promotion policy in Cincinnati which robbed the primary children of their best teachers, this administrator called the attention of the board of education and the public to this indefensible procedure and argued as follows: [22]

The flowering shrub and the fruit tree, while tender plants, we commit to the care of the professional horticulturalist, and he alone can give them the precise cultivation which their several natures respec-

---

[21] *Manchester [New Hampshire] School Committee Report, 1858*, pp. 46–47.
[22] *Cincinnati School Report, 1854*, p. 33.

tively demand; but, nothing in the vegetable, nothing in the whole physical world, can afford even a faint symbol of the susceptibilities of culture and training possessed by the human soul in its infancy. Surely, then, we should employ at this period only the most delicate hand, the most consummate skill in its education. Again; in the great conflict of the educational corps with the almost overwhelming forces of vice and ignorance, ought we to place the rawest troops where the fate of the battle must turn? The character of the man depends more upon the training of the child, between four and eight years of age, than upon all the subsequent efforts of the educator. Early childhood is the vulnerable point; that carried for virtue and intelligence, and humanity is safe.

The soundness of this point of view has since been repeatedly substantiated by psychologists and educators, but even today the public is still laboring under the old notion that younger pupils know less and therefore require the services of less accomplished teachers than do older children.

The economic status of teachers was unquestionably improved during the eighty-four-year span immediately preceding the Civil War. City teachers and male instructors in particular were enjoying a standard of living in 1860 which was markedly superior to that provided for teachers during any preceding period. Rural districts were slower in responding to the insistent demands of the profession for a living wage, and the salaries of female teachers generally lagged behind those awarded men. Similarly, primary- and grammar-school teachers were treated less generously than those employed in the high schools. The War of 1812 and the panics of 1837 and 1857 temporarily impeded progress and threw out of balance the relationship between the prices of necessities (food, clothing, and shelter) and wages paid by public bodies. These recessions, while inconvenient and embarrassing to teachers, were not of long duration and did not seriously affect the upward trend of salaries. Some communities were forced to reduce the length of the school year because of the financial depressions until the industrial world was restored to normalcy, and teachers were sometimes compelled to wait for their pay until taxes could be collected. With few exceptions, these financial difficulties were of relatively short duration and it is to the credit of teachers that they did not desert their ill-paid positions during the trying times.

The principles underlying the compensation of the teaching personnel were not clearly defined or understood. City systems began to establish uniform scales of payment during the forties and fifties, and in a few instances recognition was provided for increased training and experience. Equal pay for men and women still remained a controversial issue in 1860, although sentiment was gradually being created in favor of less discrimination between the sexes, if the resolution of teachers' associations and the discussions of state superintendents are accurate indices upon which to base conclusions.

The responsibility for securing wage improvement can scarcely be credited to any single group in the profession or in society at large. It was due in part to general prosperity and in part to a greater appreciation of the value of education by the public. Perhaps of equal significance was the pressure brought by teachers' organizations and school administrators on school boards to raise the economic position of teachers to higher levels. While individual bargaining remained the customary practice of establishing wages, teachers profited by the propaganda spread through educational literature and the addresses of public-school statesmen. Considerable strength was given to the demands of teachers for higher salaries by the improved training status resulting from the establishment of normal schools, institutes, and other professional training agencies.

"Boarding 'Round"

While amount of salary probably constitutes the best single measure of occupational status, there are other factors inherent in a vocation which make the position occupied more or less attractive to those in the process of choosing a career. In this respect, teaching presented one disadvantage which was peculiar to this profession. This was the arrangement commonly provided whereby teachers lived with the patrons of their respective schools. It was the custom in nearly all the states, outside of the cities and towns, for the teacher to "board 'round" in the families which had children in his school and this "keep" reduced the cash wage provided in many instances to a miserable pittance. While practice varied somewhat, it was not unusual for the teacher to spend a week in the home of each family— or the proportion of the year that the number of school children in the family was to the total number of children in the district—and enjoy whatever standard of living the particular school patron maintained. While such a policy gave the teacher an insight into the home life and background of his pupils which modern teachers can scarcely possess, the discomforts suffered as a result of this practice made the vocation distasteful to teachers and drove many independent spirits into other walks of life.

The extent of boarding around was large. In 1862 the number of teachers in Vermont who were subjected to this mode of life was 3354, or 68 per cent of all those employed. Connecticut reported a similar situation earlier, the proportion of winter teachers boarding around in 1846 constituting 84 per cent of those reporting (911 out of 1085 teachers). Since there were only 1413 winter teachers in the whole state at this time, it is apparent that the prevailing practice was to board around. Reliable statistics are not available for other states, but the policy appears to have been a common one before the Civil War. The evil effects resulting from it were mentioned frequently by county and state superintendents of schools, although a number of educators claimed that the advantages outweighed the disadvantages. That it meant longer school terms because of the lower assessments necessary to finance the schools seems evident. This argument was a powerful one with laymen and accounted for the persistence of the practice in many states. A county superintendent in Pennsylvania stated the basic argument in his report for 1862 as follows: [23]

By this mode the burden of boarding the teacher is never felt; whereas, if the teacher were boarded in one place, and money paid therefor, the cash cost of supporting our schools would be nearly double. Board such as our teachers receive, is worth from $1.50 to $2.00 per week.

The other values claimed for boarding around were largely imaginary and certainly detrimental to professional study. It

[23] *Pennsylvania School Report, 1862*, p. 120. (M'Kean County.)

was claimed by some that the practice was good because it brought the teacher more immediately in contact with the people, thus enabling her to become better acquainted with their habits, feelings, wishes, and prejudices; that she learned the character of the pupils better and was thus able to manage them more wisely in the school.

Those who opposed it—and by 1860 the number of educators who deemed it a "relic of olden times" seemed to have been in the majority—argued that it was bad for the health of the teacher, particularly females, who must trudge a mile or two in stormy weather to and from school; that the frequent change in diet and lodging was detrimental to health; that the necessity of keeping up a spirited conversation around the fireside, discussing politics, theology, the rebellion, and a thousand other topics, left the poor teacher weary and worn out for the preparation of his next day's assignments; and, finally, that it deprived teachers of privacy and independence. The patrons of the school were less hospitable on the whole to females than to males and many homes were not open to the former. In all probability, this was due to the feeling that they required more attention and were generally more trouble to the housewives. Just how much influence the increase in the number of women teachers had on the abolition of this practice is not known but, from the early discussions, it seems likely that it was a primary factor.

The experiences of teachers boarding around, if assembled and written up, would provide readers with a fascinating tale of early American home life. Unfortunately, only a few descriptions are recorded for public perusal. One of the most interesting accounts is a diary excerpt of a Vermont schoolmaster reported by Mason S. Stone. The record runs as follows: [24]

Monday. Went to board at Mr. B's; had baked gander for dinner; suppose from its size, the thickness of the skin and other venerable appearances it must have been one of the first settlers of Vermont; made a slight impression on the patriarch's breast. Supper—cold gander and potatoes. Family consists of the man, good wife, daughter Peggy, four boys, Pompey the dog, and a brace of cats. Fire built in the square

[24] Stone, Mason S., *History of Education, State of Vermont* (Montpelier, Vt., Capital City Press, 1936), pp. 92–93.

room about nine o'clock, and a pile of wood lay by the fireplace; saw Peggy scratch her fingers, and couldn't take the hint; felt squeamish about the stomach, and talked of going to bed; Peggy looked sullen, and put out the fire in the square room; went to bed and dreamed of having eaten a quantity of stone wall.

Tuesday. Cold gander for breakfast, swamp tea and nut cake—the latter some consolation. Dinner—the legs, &c. of the gander, done up warm—one nearly despatched. Supper—the other leg, &c. cold; went to bed as Peggy was carrying in the fire to the square room; dreamed I was a mud turtle, and got on my back and could not get over again.

Wednesday. Cold gander for breakfast; complained of sickness, and could eat nothing. Dinner—wings, &c., of the gander warmed up; did my best to destroy them for fear they would be left for supper; did not succeed; dreaded supper all the afternoon. Supper—hot Johnny cake; felt greatly revived; thought I had got clear of the gander, and went to bed for a good night's rest; disappointed, very cool night, and couldn't keep warm; got up and stopped the broken window with my coat and vest; no use; froze the tip of my nose and one ear before morning.

Thursday. Cold gander again; much discouraged to see the gander not half gone; went visiting for dinner and supper; slept abroad and had pleasant dreams.

Friday. Breakfast abroad. Dinner at Mr. B's; cold gander and potatoes—the latter very good; ate them and went to school quite contented. Supper—cold gander and no potatoes, bread heavy and dry; had the headache and couldn't eat; Peggy much concerned; had a fire built in the square room, and thought she and I better sit there out of the noise; went to bed early; Peggy thought too much sleep bad for the headache.

Saturday. Cold gander and hot Indian Johnny cake; did very well. Dinner—cold gander again; didn't keep school this afternoon; weighed and found I had lost six pounds the last week; grew alarmed; had a talk with Mr. B. and concluded I had boarded out his share.

This amusing record is perhaps slightly exaggerated, but it is quite believable that many teachers were subjected to similar impositions. As a guest, the schoolmaster was in no position to protest against cold bedrooms, poor food, or noisy children. If he enjoyed any privacy whatsoever, it was due to the thought-

BOARDING 'ROUND

291

fulness of his host or hostess; and the accommodations and entertainment provided must be accepted no matter how inadequate they might be.

Suggested Readings

Burgess, Warren R., *Trends of School Costs* (New York, 1920. Russell Sage Foundation, Education Monograph, 1920).

History of Wages in the United States from Colonial Times to 1928, U. S. Department of Labor, Bureau of Labor Statistics, October, 1929 (Washington, Government Printing Office).

XXII

Professional Status of Teachers

THE social and economic status of teachers was directly related to the professional character of the one hundred thousand individuals who were employed in this capacity in 1860. To many disinterested observers, the prestige and rewards which members of the teaching profession enjoyed were fully commensurate with their contribution. It was pointed out by state and county school officers and substantiated in many areas by statistical data that the majority of teachers were immature, inexperienced, untrained, and lacking in professional interest.

The evidence clearly corroborates the criticism of juvenility. The average age of teachers in Maine in 1866 was twenty-one and three quarter years; in Pennsylvania it was under twenty-four years in 1856. In this latter state, of 7428 teachers in thirty-eight counties, 2328 or nearly one third of the total were under twenty-one years of age. Similar facts were reported for Vermont,[1] and in other states the repeated complaints of school officers of the immaturity of teachers points to the conclusion that American schools were manned, even in the later years of this period, by youthful pedagogues whose inexperience constituted a serious handicap to the development of a highly efficient educational program.

To make matters worse, particularly in the country districts, teachers often remained in one position but a single year. Of 1896 teachers in the winter schools of Connecticut in 1857, the number who taught the same school for two successive years was only 348. While this number was increased the following year to 672, it still left two thirds of the schools with the prob-

[1] In 1847 the average age of teachers was reported as 22.4 years.

lem of breaking in new teachers. The amount of experience of the Pennsylvania personnel in 1856 is probably representative of prevailing conditions throughout the country. The number of teachers in thirty-four counties, together with amount of experience, is reported as follows: [2]

Those who have taught less than one year	1,793
Those who have taught between 1 and 3 years	2,035
Those who have taught between 3 and 6 years	1,058
Those who have taught over 6 years	1,124
TOTAL	6,010

In this same study of experience the state superintendent in Pennsylvania inquired as to the number of teachers who intended to make teaching a permanent business. Interestingly enough less than half planned to follow teaching as a career (2735 out of 5784 reporting) and were using it either as a stopgap to matrimony or a steppingstone to some other vocation. New York State had approximately 20,000 teachers in 1853. It was the state superintendent's estimate in 1855 that one third of the teachers would leave their positions within a year and that their places would be filled almost entirely by novitiates. In commenting on the situation in Rhode Island, the chief executive of the state school system pointed out that the average amount of time spent by teachers in that state was not more than two years and this was distributed among at least three separate schools. He stressed the waste resulting from such a condition and emphasized the effects upon pupils, saying: [3]

The children must lose all the wisdom he [the teacher] had acquired by his experience and work among them, and the hallowed associations of teacher, friend and honored guide must be dissolved, as the gorgeous promises of coolness and moisture made by a summer morning are dissipated by the fiery eye of the sun.

Many states did not collect facts from local districts relating to teaching experience and an accurate portrayal of conditions

[2] *Pennsylvania School Report, 1856*, pp. 8–10.
[3] *Rhode Island School Report, 1856*, p. 25.

in the country generally cannot be given in statistical terms. The great amount of attention directed by school committees and administrators everywhere to the peripatetic nature of teachers is indicative of the chaotic state of the public-school teaching profession. Not only were teachers youthful, inexperienced, and untrained, but the quality of their work was severely criticized both inside and outside of educational circles. The criticism was voiced in Pennsylvania by one educator that the services of 25 per cent of the teachers in forty-three counties (2005 out of 8035) in 1856 could better be dispensed with and that another 45 per cent was of average quality only.[4]

Such an indictment may not have been wholly justified but it suggests the inefficiency which was apparently extant in the teaching personnel. In view of the fact that training institutions had not yet been able to make a dent upon the professional qualifications of teachers, the situation in Pennsylvania was in all likelihood rather typical of conditions in other states.

Occasionally one hears the remark even today that "you can tell a schoolteacher as far as you can see one," implying that teachers bear some distinguishing marks in their form of dress, speech, deportment, facial expression, or carriage. While such generalizations are not based upon scientific evidence, there can be no denying the fact that teachers are usually characterized in the movies and on the stage as a rather odd and eccentric lot. This attitude is not of recent origin. Literary artists like Dickens and Washington Irving left indelible impressions of their schoolteacher characters upon the public mind. To indiscriminating persons every schoolmaster appeared as a Squeers or an Ichabod Crane.

A contributor in 1855 to the *New York Teacher*, the official organ of the state teachers' association, in discussing the distinctive attributes of teachers, remarked that: [5]

There is something in the personal appearance of teachers which plainly indicates their profession—a certain nervousness, in the motions—a precision . . . and more than all else, a sad deficiency in the adipose

---

[4] *Pennsylvania School Report, 1856*, p. 10. [5] *New York Teacher* (1855).

matter, by which the figure and face are narrowed and lengthened. In their mouths the figurative language of Isaiah's lamentation would bear its liberal meaning, "My leanness, my leanness—Woe is me." Shakespeare in his play, *Julius Caesar*, recognizes this prejudice. In Caesar's address to Anthony, he says:

> Let me have men about me that are fat
> Sleek-headed men—and such as sleep o' nights;
> Yond Cassius has a lean and hungry look.
> He thinks too much—such men are dangerous.

Whether or not this commentator's rather facetious description was an accurate one is a matter of speculation. It is significant, however, that the matter had been called to his attention and shows that teachers were considered, in some quarters at least, to be a rather drab group of individuals.

RESTRICTIONS AND RULES PERTAINING TO TEACHERS

The teacher's private life has always been open to public scrutiny like a goldfish in a glass bowl. Tradition has given teachers a place in society comparable to that accorded to ministers and the restrictions placed upon their conduct have been many and varied. Unlike members of the medical and legal professions and even government employees, they have been denied the privileges of leading their lives according to the dictates of their own consciences. The explanation for this lies in the nature of the business in which they are engaged. Entrusted with the responsibility of instructing the young, they stand *in loco parentis* before the law and the public and are expected to keep themselves above reproach and to be subservient to the wishes of the most pious patrons in the community. Only as the mores and standards of conduct have changed with succeeding generations have teachers been released from their chains and shackles and been permitted the breath of freedom enjoyed by their brethren and sisters in other walks of life. During the generations covered between 1776 and 1860, the public was especially critical of the conduct of teachers and invoked the most rigid moral and religious standards upon them.

The prevailing attitude toward teachers was well summarized

in the *Fourth Annual Report of the Boston Board of Education* in 1841 as follows: [6]

. . . If, then, the manners of the teacher are to be imitated by the pupils,—if he is the glass, at which they "do dress themselves," how strong is the necessity, that he should understand those nameless and innumerable practices, in regard to deportment, dress, conversation, and all personal habits, that constitute the difference between a gentleman and a clown. We can bear some oddity, or eccentricity in a friend whom we admire for his talents, or revere for his virtues; but it becomes quite a different thing, when the oddity, or the eccentricity, is to be a pattern or model, from which fifty or a hundred children are to form their manners. It was well remarked, by the ablest British traveller who has ever visited this country, that amongst us "every male above twenty-one years of age, claims to be a sovereign. He is, therefore, *bound to be a gentleman*."

In a previous chapter dealing with the certification and examination of teachers, the emphasis placed upon moral and character qualities was treated at some length. One of the issues which provoked considerable discussion among prominent laymen and educators was the use of tobacco by teachers and the responsibility of the profession for discouraging its consumption among pupils. Whereas in recent years attention has been focused upon cigarette smoking by women teachers, in early days the propriety of men indulging in the use of tobacco in any form was a matter of dispute. Judging by the number of times the topic was discussed in state and local teachers' association meetings and the amount of space given to it in superintendents' reports and educational magazines, the matter was deemed of considerable importance. Ministers preached vigorously against the use of tobacco and warned their parishioners of its evil consequences. Statesmen were enlisted in support of the cause and their testimony used to convert others to abstinence. John Quincy Adams's opinion was sought and quoted in the *Common School Journal* in 1846. Adams's attitude is interesting, since a pronouncement by a man so prominent in public affairs carried greater influence than an expression of opinion by an ordinary

[6] Page 57.

citizen and was heralded by the moralist educators as indisputable evidence of the deleterious effects of tobacco. Adams based his objections to the "weed" on the ground that it impaired one's health. His letter to Horace Mann is reproduced below:[7]

Quincy, Mass.,
Aug. 19, 1845

Dear Sir;—I have received your letter of the 13th instant, and shall deem myself honored by the inscription to me of your introduction to the proposed publication of the Reverend B. I. Lane's work on Tobacco and its Mysteries. In my early youth, I was addicted to the use of tobacco in two of its mysteries, smoking and chewing. I was warned by a medical friend of the pernicious operation of this habit upon the stomach and the nerves; and the advice of the physician was fortified by the results of my own experience. More than thirty years have passed away since I deliberately renounced the use of tobacco in all its forms; and although the resolution was not carried into execution without a struggle of vitiated nature, I never yielded to its impulses; and in the space of three or four months of self-denial, they lost their stimulating power, and I have never since felt it as a privation.

I have often wished that every individual of the human race afflicted with this artificial passion, could prevail upon himself to try but for three months, the experiment which I have made; sure that it would turn every acre of tobacco-land into a wheat-field, and add five years of longevity to the average of human life.

I am with great respect, dear Sir,

Your friend and Christian brother,

JOHN QUINCY ADAMS.

Mann, one of the acknowledged liberals of his generation, was apparently convinced of the evil effects of tobacco and was decidedly opposed to teachers using it, for in the state teachers' association convention in Columbus, Ohio, in 1856 he reported the following resolution drawn up by a committee of which he was a member: "Examiners ought not to give certificates to teachers who chew tobacco or use profane language."[8]

The New York state association had passed a similar resolu-

[7] *The Common School Journal*, Vol. VIII, No. 6 (1846), p. 95.
[8] Coggeshall, W. T., *op. cit.*, p. 539.

tion at an earlier date, declaring "that any man who habitually uses tobacco is disqualified for being a school teacher." [9] Not only did state associations bring pressure upon teachers to abstain from the use of narcotics, but local associations, as well, expressed their opinions in no uncertain words. In Pennsylvania, the Crawford County society voiced a point of view which was expressed in many other local association resolutions: "that no teacher should use or countenance the use of tobacco in any form." [10]

Town and county superintendents were equally as positive in their denunciations, one New Jersey administrator contending that "some regulation should be made in our school law with regard to the use of tobacco by teachers and pupils." According to this superintendent, [11]

No teacher should receive any public money who uses tobacco in any form. They should be excluded, as well as those who use intoxicating drinks, and this by law. . . . The use of the weed is morally wrong, and physically a great evil. . . . How little parents know, when their child comes home with its head ready to burst, and the stomach rejecting food, how much of it is attributable to the contaminated breath of the teacher.

Such an exaggerated position seems almost unbelievable in view of the present tolerance of the public toward tobacco users. The antinarcotic crusade resembled the temperance movement in the emotional outbursts which it stimulated. The proportion of male teachers who were addicted to the habit is not known. In all probability the number was small, since public opinion was so overwhelmingly opposed to their using it. On the other hand, the attention given to the topic warrants the assumption that some teachers indulged in spite of the insistence of reformers that disastrous results would follow. Perhaps most of these miscreants confined their smoking and chewing to quiet places apart from the multitude in order to retain their positions as teachers.

[9] *Common School Journal*, Vol. VIII, No. 17 (1846), p. 258.
[10] *Pennsylvania School Journal*, Vol. I (1853), p. 424.
[11] *New Jersey School Report, 1852*, p. 136.

As might well be anticipated from the attitude of the public toward teachers using tobacco, there was no quarter given to those who drank intoxicating liquors, particularly after 1830 when the influence of the temperance movement began to be felt. There are only a few cases of intemperance among teachers reported during this period and the general situation is well characterized by the State Superintendent of Schools in Pennsylvania who wrote in his annual report in 1838: [12]

The profession of teaching is much elevated. Instances of bad moral character and intemperate habits, are hardly to be met with; though formerly School Masters, who above all others should be perfectly exemplary as a class, were not remarkable in this respect.

Along with tobacco and liquor, teachers were denied the privilege of gambling or using profane language. These vices were specifically mentioned as grounds for dismissal in California in 1852.[13] Then as now, communities varied in their ideas about what constitutes exemplary conduct, and one needs to be cautious in drawing conclusions about the standards imposed by the public at large and the country as a whole. The restrictions just discussed, however, were certainly fairly general and represented the point of view held by the great majority of American school boards.

In the smaller communities, where the schoolteacher's life was more closely scrutinized than in the towns and cities, there was scarcely an activity in which he engaged which escaped their observation. One schoolmaster who suffered under this yoke of constant public surveillance apparently rebelled when his interest in one of his assistant teachers had aroused criticism from some of his patrons. His letter to the editor of the *New York Teacher* shows both the nature of his difficulty and the bitterness which his critics had engendered: [14]

L——, Dec. 9, 1852

Mr. Editor: I am a young teacher, and have fallen into an unexpected difficulty. You must know I am a bachelor, and have a female assistant,

---

[12] *Pennsylvania School Report, 1838*, p. 33.
[13] *First Annual Report of Superintendent of Public Instruction, California* (1852), pp. 26–27.
[14] Excerpt from the *New York Teacher*, Vol. I (1853), pp. 126–27.

and influenced, I suppose, by some evil spirit, we have had the presumption, as we both board at the same place, to walk to and from school together occasionally. We have done more; we have a few times called upon some of our friends together, for I *did* deem that politeness required that I should extend to her the common civilities of society. But I was mistaken; it seems there is a "code especial" for teachers, to which the Normal six o'clock law is intended as a precursor. When I was engaged my trustees did not inform me that I must treat my assistant in such a way as to disgrace my manhood, and I therefore, in my *innocent simplicity*, supposed that I was at liberty to demean myself as a gentleman toward her. But, alas! The good people of the village have decided that this is beyond all precedence, and can not be allowed. The careful old ladies and prudish old gentlemen of the vicinity, after having thoroughly canvassed the matter, have decided that we "must not do so no more," and consequently the trustees have administered discipline. However, being a stubborn youth, I am not yet conquered; but my assistant, poor girl! so like a drooping flower beneath the scorching rays of a summer's sun, I am afraid that she will by and by tell them to mind their own business.

What I wish to ask, Mr. Editor, is—and I ask of you, because you have the reputation of being a universal genius, and I believe you to be devoted to the interests of teachers generally—why is it that the teacher, who is expected to devote his whole time and energies for a less remuneration than they would secure to him in any other profession, who is expected to know more than most folks, and to be proportionally better, and who is required to know every body, to be with every body, and to be every body's particular friend? Why is it, I ask, that he must give up every right with which, as a citizen and a man, he is endowed? Suppose that I *am* paying attentions to the lady in question, what business have my *patrons* and the trustees to wag *their* tongues about it? And I wish to say to those same patrons and trustees, through the columns of your journal, that I consider they are meddling when they have no business; and as they have already flung the glove to me, I shall undoubtedly pick it up, and keep the company of my assistant just as much as she and I please.

This is another evil incident to teaching, that ought to be remedied. Our patrons—and wonderfully *patronizing* they are sometimes truly!— have generally altogether too much to say about our private affairs. Our business is every body's business; and a lawyer or a gentleman of any other calling, subjected to such treatment as we often receive, would wring the proboscis of the offender, and perhaps administer a dose of the *cat*. I know this is a difficulty peculiar to country districts and small villages; but the mass of teachers are in just such situations, and consequently they as a body are interested in this question. Teachers should be men of refined feelings; and no person who has more appreciation of decent treatment than a human donkey, can tamely submit to all that we are sometimes obliged to bear. Teachers, while they faithfully and sedulously perform their duties, should boldly maintain their rights, and resist every attempt to encroach upon them.

I do not intend, for $35.00 per month, to resign all the privileges guaranteed to me by the social compact. I am a citizen, and I shall exercise the immunities of citizenship as I deem proper, the whole town of L—— notwithstanding.

Hoping to hear your opinion and the opinions of some of your correspondents upon this subject of being nose-led by our *patrons* continually.

I subscribe myself your humble servant,

ABEL SAMSON.

T. W. Valentine, Esq.

P.S. I like the bold tone of your journal, and shall do all in my power to secure its hearty support. A.S.

The editor apparently appreciated the young man's attitude and replied in a rather humorous vein as follows:

Well, Mr. Samson, since you ask our advice, you shall have it in few words. "Go ahead," say we; you are on the right track, and we will defend you "to the death"—though, for that matter, you seem abundantly *able* to defend yourself. You have just as good a right to have your Delilah as your namesake of old—only beware lest she betray you into the hands of the Philistines. Once shorn of your strength, you may have to "go it blind," as he did. But the best way to shut the mouths of gainsayers, is just to take one more walk with your assistant— *down to the minister's*—and secure her services for life by making a Mrs. Samson of her. *We* tried that once, and have never seen cause to regret it.—Res. Ed.

It would be interesting to know what happened to Mr. Samson as a result of his outburst. Since school committees were not regular subscribers to the *New York Teacher* he probably did not lose his position because of the letter. On the other hand, if he persisted in ignoring the counsel of his school patrons, he was in all likelihood hunting another post the following year.

There is but little written about teachers joining the church and participating in religious affairs. Perhaps, for most teachers, this was so universally accepted as a part of their responsibilities that it did not constitute an issue. One rather unusual case occurred in a New Jersey county, however, which suggests that some teachers did not conform in this respect. A county superintendent had examined a candidate and found him thoroughly proficient in scholarship and accepted the applicant's statement that he was in the habit of attending church on the Sabbath. The appointment was then made; and when the first term was nearly expired, the superintendent learned that the teacher had not been within any church or worshiping assembly since his arrival in town. Armed with this evidence, the superintendent sent a message to the offender to the effect that his conduct was not according to his representations. This drew from the teacher the following vigorous reply: [15]

Without advancing an apology, or deeming any requisite, I must confess I am astonished that you threw out such absurd insinuations, or made an attempt at such fallacious logic; by so doing you aimed a deadly blow at the foundation of genuine religion, and charged me with a lack of moral duty for not performing a mere ceremony of church attendance which is not a criterion of morality. It may not be amiss to mention, at this time, one inconsistency of many bigoted attendants at church; for instance, they may pray for "thy kingdom come, thy will be done," and the very next day vote that the devil's will be done (unconsciously) by supporting men who would tear innocent persons from their families and bind them to eternal bondage.

This independent and outspoken teacher was an exception and if he were living today he would unquestionably be fighting for academic freedom and the right of teachers to organize. His case was taken under advisement by the superintendent and trustees and no record seems to have been uncovered showing the final disposition of it.

During the Civil War days, when the country was torn by

[15] *New Jersey School Report, 1851*, pp. 112–13.

strife and divided in its loyalties, there were many patriotic zealots who wished to rid the schools of all teachers who were not one hundred per cent for the Union. A Maine school committee in 1863 proposed that "any teacher, male or female, who use their influence in favor of Jeff. Davis or his emissaries, should be stricken from the list of teachers as unfit to have the charge of a school with one *live* scholar." [16]

During this same year the State Superintendent of Instruction in Kansas proposed that teachers be required to give an oath of allegiance to the United States and to the state government, saying, "We do not wish our children instructed by persons of doubtful loyalty." [17]

Whether or not there was any basis for doubting the good faith of teachers and their disposition toward their government was never demonstrated. Since teachers themselves in their respective associations passed resolutions upholding the government's cause and pledging their wholehearted support, it appears likely that the fears of the oath advocates constituted "much ado about nothing." In Kentucky, where loyalties were definitely divided, attempts to enforce oaths of allegiance upon trustees and teachers met with stubborn opposition. The effects of such efforts were anything but wholesome.

One can only speculate about the significance of these restrictions on the welfare of the teaching profession. To many individuals engaged in educational work, these taboos were certainly not objectionable, since their early home training and philosophy of life would have tended to draw them naturally into the reformers' camp. To others, the higher standard of conduct imposed was most irritating and they inwardly rebelled against the "fences" which kept them from enjoying the freedom accorded the average citizen. The social and economic historians of this period point out that private and public manners had not been greatly altered as late as 1850 by the reform movement, that "the masculine habit of chewing tobacco and the attendant spitting of tobacco juice" was almost universal in America, that drinking was indulged in at dancing parties and at other social occasions by both men and women of high station, and that

[16] *Maine School Report, 1863*, p. 49.   [17] *Kansas School Report, 1863*, p. 20.

gambling in various forms went on everywhere. Most of the people belonged to a church and while they did not always attend regularly, they endorsed it as an institution and subscribed to the principles of the Christian religion.

Relations between the sexes were somewhat formal, and women were denied many of the privileges commonly granted to men. Sexual immorality was not generally countenanced and, when publicly known, reacted unfavorably upon the social position of the offenders. Where the general code differed from that established for teachers, there was often a feeling of injustice and dissatisfaction on the part of the more independent and romantic spirits in the teaching profession. Just how many of these abandoned teaching for the less restrictive vocations cannot be accurately predicted, nor can one reliably forecast the effect of the taboos on the decisions of those about to choose a career.

PART III

The Emergence of the Professional Teacher

PART III

INTRODUCTION

THE HISTORY of the United States since the Civil War is so familiar to most readers that it is unnecessary to sketch here in any detail those events of the last seventy-five years which have left their imprint upon the professions as well as upon other workers in society. Many social and political changes occurred during the above period that were reflected in the public schools and in the status of the teaching profession. Students are familiar with the fact that the South was so impoverished by the Civil War and Reconstruction that education was markedly impaired, that teachers generally suffered losses in salary during the panic and depression years of this period, that the extension of suffrage to women enhanced the position of female teachers and led to the passage of equal-pay laws, that the World War temporarily diverted the interest of men away from teaching and created serious shortages in the supply of trained teachers, that technological improvements and inventions released the time and energy of children from field and factory work and produced significant increases in school enrollments, that the rapid growth in population and the extension of compulsory education to include many children between fourteen and eighteen years of age made heavy demands upon teacher-training institutions, and that the struggle for economic power and for material gain tended at times to submerge the important task of public education.

Other important trends and events also had their influence upon teachers during this great epoch. The disappearance of the frontier set a premium upon education, gave impetus to the growth of the American high school, and indirectly affected the demands on the teaching profession; urbanization freed children from household and farm duties and led to the development of extracurricular programs, thus adding to the responsibilities of teachers and the schools; and, finally, the new immigration from European countries, representing as it did a wide variety of races and cultures, produced perplexing educational problems and constituted a challenge to American teachers.

It is apparent from the foregoing discussion that the history of the teaching profession is so closely interwoven with developments in the social and economic structure generally that it is difficult to portray the experiences of this important group without at the same time repeating the history of American society. In the following pages the author has attempted to bring out into relief the story of the public-school teacher in the United States since 1865. It will be necessary at times for the reader to make his own associations with the outside world of events and to recall related trends which had their influence upon American teachers.

XXIII

The Preparation of Teachers for Work in the Public Schools

THE establishment of state normal schools for the preparation of teachers was acknowledged generally by educators to be one of the most urgent needs of the country immediately following the Civil War. In 1860 there were only eleven such institutions in existence and these were confined to Massachusetts, New York, Connecticut, Rhode Island, New Jersey, Illinois, Michigan, and Minnesota. The number of normal-school graduates at this time was still too small to make any observable impression upon the teaching profession as a whole, and only isolated evidences of the worth of this type of specialized training could be assembled in its defense. The Southern states, in particular, had made no provision for the training of teachers apart from institutes and it was necessary to carry on vigorous campaigns there before public moneys were appropriated for so obvious a necessity as normal schools. Even in those states whose neighbors showed unbounded faith in the usefulness of such institutions, the legislatures were obstinate and resisted strenuously the efforts of educational statesmen to create this new school venture at public expense.

The history of these campaigns for normal schools was described by one author (referring specifically to New Hampshire) as follows: [1]

. . . an early and promising attack, a victory, long in doubt; ignorance and prejudice behind the intrenchments; indifference, perhaps treachery within the lines; a deficient commissariat, skirmishes without results, compromises without advantage, indomitable pluck on one side, invincible obstinacy on the other—triumph at last.

[1] Newell, M. A., "Contributions to the History of Normal Schools in the United States," in *Report of the Commissioner of Education, 1898–1899.* (Washington, Government Printing Office, 1900), Vol. II, p. 2295.

With the possible exception of an "early and promising attack," the foregoing historical description would have applied equally well to nearly all the states when normal schools were first proposed. New Hampshire did not establish a normal school until 1871 and then only with the expressed provision that it should be without cost to the state except for a maximum annual allowance of three hundred dollars to defray the necessary expenses of the trustees. Vermont, located in the center of the normal-school belt, first authorized the creation of such a school in 1866. Maine preceded Vermont by three years, having made an unsuccessful attempt to substitute normal departments in the eighteen academies of the state.

For a period of twenty-five years after the Civil War, the struggle to weld normal schools into the structure of the state school system continued. The protracted nature of this movement is revealed by an examination of the dates when normal schools were first introduced into several of the states. California established a normal school in 1862; Kansas, in 1864; Indiana, in 1865; Wisconsin, in 1866; Nebraska, in 1867; Missouri, in 1870; Alabama, in 1873; Tennessee, in 1875; South Dakota and Oregon, in 1883; Virginia and Louisiana, in 1884; South Carolina, in 1886;[2] Arizona (Territory) and Florida, in 1887; North Carolina, in 1889; and Georgia, in 1890.[3]

By 1900 the normal-school idea was sufficiently widespread to leave no doubts as to its ultimate success. The battle to make this institution an integral part of the state school system had been won. The teacher-training problems confronting educators during the next quarter century had to do with higher standards of admission, the nature of the curriculum offerings, extension of facilities to meet the increased demands for teachers, and matters of general improvement. By 1898 there were one hundred and sixty-seven public normal schools in the United States, of which twelve were located in New York, thirteen in Pennsylvania, and nine in Massachusetts. Private normal schools

[2] South Carolina had experimented with a state high school and normal school for girls as early as 1860 and later with a normal school at Columbia (1874). These were temporary in character.

[3] For a more detailed report of the establishment of normal schools in the various states see Newell, M. A., *op. cit.*, pp. 2263–470.

were slightly more numerous than public institutions, although the faculty and equipment of the latter were regarded as superior.

Harper's, 1878

NORMAL-COLLEGE TYPES

Despite this great increase in the number of normal schools, the demand for trained teachers was far in excess of the supply. The inadequacy of teacher-training facilities to meet the needs of the profession around 1900 can be appreciated when the annual number of both public- and private-normal-school graduates is compared with the total number of teachers employed in the public schools. In 1896–1897 there were 403,333 teachers in the United States, most of whom were teaching in the elementary schools. The following year the United States Commissioner of Education reported the number of graduates of public normal schools to be 8188 and that of private training schools 3067.[4] A conservative estimate of the number of new teachers required annually to care for turnover and expansion would be 50,000, or four and a half times the number of normal-school graduates.

It is obvious from these facts either that other agencies were carrying the responsibility for preparing teachers for the public schools or that a vast army of teachers entered the profession without adequate training for their work. The latter is the correct explanation. Statistics are not available to show the proportion of teachers who had attended normal schools or were graduates of them during these years. Massachusetts, however, which would have ranked with the best of the states in this respect, reported in 1897–1898 that only 38.5 per cent of her teachers in public schools had received normal-school instruction and only 33.5 per cent were normal-school graduates. Of the remaining two thirds of the teaching personnel, a few had attended college, some had received a little preliminary training in high school, but the majority were appointed without reference to their fitness for their work.

Admission Requirements to Normal Schools

Admission requirements to normal schools were by no means uniform throughout the country nor even within a given state. A great deal of discretionary power was left with the training-school principal and the number of applicants unquestionably influenced his admission standards. In the earlier history (1850–1870) of these schools, it was a common procedure to take pupils directly from the elementary school, with or without a certificate of achievement, examine them formally or informally upon their knowledge of the common-school subjects, and, if they could demonstrate reasonable competency in these, to admit them.

Even as late as 1900 high-school graduation was seldom required as a prerequisite for entrance into the normal school.

---

[4] Butler, Nicholas M., *Education in the United States* (New York, American Book Company, 1910), pp. 376–77.

The common standard was two years of high-school work or the equivalent.[5]

Courses of Study

Not only did admission requirements vary widely but the length of the normal-school course was by no means a constant. Some states provided a four-year course, others a three-year, and still others a two-year program of studies. In general, the higher the entrance requirements the shorter the course of training. Students who came well grounded in both the common- and high-school subjects could easily assimilate the pedagogical and academic instruction of the normal school in two years' time.

The four-year courses, of which there were only a few, were designed to meet the needs of high-school teachers and those aspiring to principalships. A large amount of time was spent during the first year of training in mastering the content of the common-school subjects. During the second and sometimes the third year, students were introduced to methods of teaching, psychology, philosophy, history of education, observation and practice teaching, and some of the higher branches of the academic subjects.

The Rhode Island course of study was outlined according to the number of lessons in each subject. The full course (seven half years) included in 1890: 100 lessons in composition and grammar, 300 in arithmetic, 100 in chemistry, 150 in drawing, 100 in the English language, 100 in geography, 100 in physiology and hygiene, 50 in bookkeeping (single-entry), 100 in general history, 100 in geometry, 100 in reading, 200 in Latin, 100 in rhetoric, 100 in algebra, 100 in botany, 100 in physics, 100 in English literature, 50 in physical geography, 50 in geology, 50 in psychology, 50 in logic, 50 in ethics, 50 in zoology, 50 in pedagogy, 50 in primary methods, 50 in methods in geography, 50 in methods in grammar, 50 in mineralogy.[6]

---

[5] Massachusetts was one of the exceptions to this rule. In this state, candidates for admission to normal schools had to be graduates of approved high schools or must have received an equivalent education.

[6] "Catalogue and Circular of Rhode Island State Normal School, 1890," in *ibid.*, p. 2295.

Of the above total of 2550 lessons, only 350 were in any way related to pedagogy, the balance consisting of straight subject matter.

While no two courses of study appear to have been alike, the following concrete illustration will serve to give the reader some impression at least of what a normal-school program looked like in 1890.

Course of Study in Castine Normal School,[7] Maine, 1890

FIRST YEAR

F Class	E Class	D Class
Arithmetic, from percentage.	Arithmetic, methods.	Algebra.
Grammar.	Grammar.	Geometry.
Geography.	Geography.	Physics.
School economy.	Algebra.	Physical geography.
Reading.	Physiology.	Drawing.
Writing, one-half term.		
Elementary music, one-half term.		

SECOND YEAR

C Class	B Class	A Class
Geometry.	Psychology.	Didactics and history of education.
General history.	Chemistry.	Practice teaching.
Physics.	United States history.	English literature.
Rhetoric.	Civil government.	Astronomy.
Botany.	Moral philosophy.	Geology, one-half term.
Bookkeeping, one-half term.	Practice teaching.	

Practically all the normal schools included observation and practice teaching, either in a model school under their immediate control or in a public school to which they had access, as a

7 "Catalogue and Circular of the State Normal School at Castine, Maine, 1890," in *Report of the Commissioner of Education, 1898–1899*, Vol. II, p. 2301.

regular part of their curricular program. In this way advanced students were provided with opportunities to observe and teach in these schools under the supervision of experienced teachers.

Harper's, 1878

CALISTHENICS AT THE NEW YORK NORMAL COLLEGE

Pangburn summarizes the professional work of normal schools in 1890 as follows: " . . . thirteen weeks in the History of Education, twenty-seven weeks in the Science of Education, thirty-one weeks in Methods in the Elementary Branches, and twenty weeks in Mental Science, a week being defined as forty-five minutes a day for five days." To this must be added fifty periods in observation and one hundred and thirty-one periods in practice teaching.[8]

During the years 1860–1890 the Oswego Normal School in New York State exercised greater influence over teacher training than did any other single institution. Hundreds of graduates of this school secured positions as directors or heads of the practice schools of newly established teacher-training institutions and carried with them the instructional techniques for which Oswego was famous. Between 1861 and 1886 a total of 896 out of 1373 graduates of this normal school accepted positions outside of the State of New York, whereas but 175 students came to the normal school from outside.

Another notable normal school, but of less significance nationally, was the one at Worcester, Massachusetts. This institution emphasized two features in its program of work which were not present in the procedures employed in other normal schools. They were the system of apprenticeship and the method of encouraging pupils to make a firsthand study of children.

The apprenticeship plan has been employed so frequently in recent years that it scarcely needs amplification. It consisted of having the advanced student serve in one of the public schools of Worcester as an assistant to a teacher. The assistant's work involved taking part in the instruction, management, and general work of teaching under the direction of the teacher and occasionally substituting for the teacher at the discretion of the latter. In order that the student might understand better the problems of pupils of different age and achievement levels, he was attached to at least three grades during his six months' term of service. Four days each week were devoted directly to assisting in the public schools and one day was spent at the normal school in consultation with faculty members about the apprenticeship work, or in reading in the library, or in informal discussions with other normal-school students. The apprentice was required

[8] Pangburn, Jessie M., *The Evolution of the American Teachers College* (New York, Bureau of Publications, Teachers College, Columbia University, 1932), p. 14.

to keep a diary of his activities and experiences, which was inspected periodically by his instructors at the normal school.

The Worcester plan had merit both because it brought the student in contact with real-life situations and provided him with practical experience, and because it kept the normal-school staff in close touch with actual schoolroom problems. Faculty members were responsible for visiting the apprentice while he was engaged in his work and for offering suggestions and advice when needed.

The second feature of this school was the method used in teaching psychology—a suggestion of G. Stanley Hall. Instead of relying upon textbooks for their sole information about the human mind, students were asked to record their own observations of children's reactions, and to test the observations of others. This was a marked departure from the procedure commonly used in normal schools, in which the textbook constituted practically the only source of information. At Worcester no single textbook was assigned in psychology; it was expected, rather, that the student would become familiar with several sources and in addition, where feasible, that he would test out the thesis or generalization learned by actual observation or introspection.

There were other progressive normal schools prior to 1900 but their influence was mostly confined to the immediate area in which they were located. Oswego surpassed all others in its effect upon teaching practice; and Worcester, because it represented in some measure the ideas of G. Stanley Hall, attracted considerable attention, particularly in the East.

Teacher Training at the Turn of the Century

The status of teacher training at the close of the nineteenth century was vastly superior to conditions prevailing in 1860. The normal school had become a recognized and accepted part of the public-school system and supplied from ten to forty per cent of the public-school teachers in the various states. The vast majority of normal-school graduates taught in the elementary schools, although the demand for high-school teachers was beginning to have its effect upon the nature of the normal-school offering in a few of the states. One of the most notable instances of this was the New York State Normal College at Albany. This institution announced, in 1890, its intention of granting pedagogical degrees and made a bid for the patronage of prospective secondary-school teachers. Colleges and universities, during the two decades immediately preceding 1900, had evinced some interest in the needs of high-school teachers and administrators by offering instruction in didactics and establishing chairs of pedagogy, although the movement was by no means free of opposition. The need had been clearly demonstrated by the large number of college and university students who went into high-school teaching and by the demands of principals and superintendents for teachers with some knowledge of method in addition to mastery of the academic subjects. By 1890 there were 114 colleges and universities out of a total of 400 that enrolled students in teachers' courses. The number of such students amounted to 3414, or approximately 8 per cent of all the students enrolled in the 400 collegiate institutions. Thirty-one universities had chairs of didactics by 1892,[9] and several others had combined chairs of pedagogy with one other subject, such as philosophy or mental science. A few others provided lectureships in education.

These newly organized departments of education were not always considered academically respectable, and the professors in charge were looked upon somewhat disdainfully by their traditionally minded associates. President Eliot of Harvard represented the point of view held by many conservative educators of his time and voiced the sentiments of his institution as follows: "The faculty [of Harvard] in common with most teachers in England and the United States, feel but slight interest or confidence in what is ordinarily called pedagogy." [10]

Despite such opposition and skepticism, college and university presidents gave way reluctantly to the trend of the times. The topic was debated at meetings of the New England Colleges

---

[9] The first permanent chair of didactics was established at Iowa University in 1873, and was followed by professorships at the University of Michigan in 1879 and the University of Wisconsin in 1881.

[10] *Report of the Commissioner of Education, 1890–1891* (Washington, Government Printing Office, 1894), Vol. II, p. 1076.

and Preparatory Schools, and Charles Kendall Adams of Williams College urged the association strongly to support the teaching of pedagogics in colleges and universities as the surest means of improving secondary education in the United States. Graduate study in pedagogy was provided in New York University in 1887–1888 and the results were so salutary that a School of Pedagogy was established in 1890. This was the first purely professional school for teachers on the graduate level. About the same time (1889) the New York College for the Training of Teachers was chartered with Nicholas Murray Butler as its first president. This institution purposed to devote its efforts solely to the training of teachers and proposed to equip them to instruct not alone in the traditional subjects of the curriculum but in manual training as well. It was hoped that this institution would be to the teaching profession what the better law and medical schools were to their respective professions. A model school, the Horace Mann School, was taken over for practice teaching and observation purposes, and postgraduate courses were added for the benefit of those who had already acquired the Bachelor's degree or possessed similar attainments. The name of this school was changed in 1892 to Teachers College and shortly afterwards an arrangement was made with Columbia University whereby courses were accepted for degrees in that institution. The national and even international character of this new professional school was manifest early in its history, and under the leadership of James E. Russell it was destined to influence educational theory and practice beyond the wildest dreams of its founders. One of the peculiar contributions of this institution was the preparation of educational leaders and normal-school instructors.

By 1900, then, the agencies for the preparation of teachers had expanded widely and a new era in professional training had definitely begun. The normal schools, while largely, as President Butler characterized them, "academies or high schools with a slight infusion of pedagogic instruction," had weathered the storm for a full half century and were now in a favorable position to modify their offerings in keeping with changed demands and new conditions; the colleges and universities had begun to make provision for the professional preparation of secondary-school teachers by introducing chairs and professorships in education, and a few of the larger universities had gone so far as to establish professional schools devoted exclusively to the preparation of teachers. While all the resources of these institutions combined could not begin to supply the country with trained pedagogues—because of the neglect of the past and the rapid increase in school population, calling for unprecedented numbers of new teachers—still the need was recognized and the agencies for meeting it were commonly acknowledged.

THE TRAINING OF TEACHERS SINCE 1900

There was no sudden or sharp break in the evolution of teacher-training institutions in the United States to warrant a separate discussion of the progress in normal-school development since 1900. It is necessary, however, to summarize achievements at various intervals in our history in order to take stock of the gains made and of the forces which seem to be shaping the direction in which institutions are moving. The turn of the twentieth century has been arbitrarily selected as a breaking point in the discussion in order to accomplish the purposes indicated above.

There were several weaknesses in the teacher-training program in 1900 which required attention. The admission requirements to normal schools were obviously too low and high-school graduation was clearly indicated as the next step in raising standards. Furthermore, the period of training needed lengthening. Teachers with only two years of professional study, a good part of which was a review of old academic subject matter, were still poorly equipped to meet the everyday problems of the classroom. The expansion of pedagogy threatened to destroy scholarship unless more time could be added to the course of study. It was evident to many of the leading educators that teachers, armed with the best pedagogical methods known to man, would be ineffective unless they possessed a thorough knowledge of subject matter. To further complicate the situation, it was becoming increasingly apparent that the colleges and universities were not going to provide enough secondary-school teachers to meet the demand and that the state could not continue to delegate this responsibility entirely to privately controlled institutions.

The reform measures, then, which appeared most imminent were (1) to raise the requirements for admission to normal schools to high-school graduation, (2) to extend the length of the normal-school course to give more time for cultural subjects and the mastery of subject matter, and (3) to widen the scope of the offerings to care for the preparation of secondary-school teachers.

In addition to the above needs, there were some educators who believed that a division of labor among the normal schools in those states having several training institutions would be a move in the right direction and that such a reorganization would remove competition among the normal schools and would result in an improved course of study.

Progress in achieving these goals was rather rapid, considering the cost and effort involved. Between 1895 and 1905 Ruediger reported in a study of fifty-one normal schools that the percentage of such schools requiring high-school graduation for entrance increased from fourteen to twenty-two per cent. In 1908 the Department of Normal Schools of the National Education Association included among its resolutions a recommendation to the effect that "the state normal schools make high-school graduation, or equivalent, a basis for admission to the standard normal course." [11]

The pressure thus brought to bear, coupled with the tremendous increase in the number of four-year high schools, led gradually to the acceptance of the foregoing standard of admission, and by 1930 the goal had been practically achieved.

For a considerable period of time, during which efforts were being made to increase entrance standards, the normal schools commonly provided a two-year course of study, with an additional year or two for those whose academic background was obviously limited. As four-year high schools multiplied in number and graduation became more and more the basis upon which students were admitted to teacher-training schools, the normal schools saw an opportunity to extend the professional preparation of teachers to higher levels. Experimental work and research in education, beginning in the late nineties and increasing by leaps and bounds during the first two decades of the twentieth century, had added a tremendous fund of scientific knowledge to the impoverished pedagogical curriculum of earlier days. To transmit this new wealth of information, in addition to the cultural and academic subjects essential to a well-rounded education, required an extension of the normal-school-training period.

Perhaps of greater weight than the desire of normal-school faculties and presidents to improve the training qualifications of teachers was the stimulus provided by students and graduates of normal schools who were dissatisfied with the low standards which prevailed. This discontent did not result from their un-quenched thirst for knowledge but, rather, from a desire to extend their schooling in order to secure more attractive and responsible positions. Since the normal school had never been an integral part of the higher education system evolved in the United States, it was not possible for students to transfer, either at normal-school graduation or before, to a recognized college without serious loss of credit. Summer schools in colleges and universities were offering unusual opportunities for those inter-ested in securing degrees, and to be graduated from, or affiliated with, a normal school whose work was less than standard was by no means flattering. Unpleasant controversies and disagree-ments between normal schools and colleges were numerous and hastened the efforts toward standardization. The demands of students were, therefore, responsible in part for the improve-ment in standards and for the extension of the period of study.

While many states were slow in responding to these pressures for change and continued to muddle along with their outworn curricula, there were others who saw the handwriting on the wall. Some of the latter changed from a two-year to a three-year curriculum and some went so far as to shift to the four-year program. This led eventually to a change in the nomen-clature of many schools, the term "normal school" giving way to "teachers' college." The transition has by no means been completed and another decade or so will be required before the state normal school becomes an institution of mere historic interest. The trend since 1920 is unmistakably in the direction of replacing two- and three-year normal schools with four-year teachers' colleges. During the above year (1920) there were 46 teachers' colleges and 137 state normal schools in the United States. In 1928 the former had increased to 137 and the normal schools had been reduced to 69.[12] By 1933 the number of state teachers' colleges had reached 146 and state normal schools had shrunk to 50.[13] A similar loss occurred in the case of city normal schools, the number decreasing from 33 in 1920 to 16 in 1933.

The results of these shifts were not immediately salutary in many institutions. There was much confusion over what should be included in the new curriculum, and most of the normal-school faculties were poorly prepared to meet the higher standards implied in the change. One of the characteristic features of the metamorphosis has been the assumption of the degree-granting power of teachers' colleges. Bachelor's degrees are now commonly given in these institutions and in a few instances graduate degrees are also granted. At first the accrediting agencies were reluctant to recognize the conferments of these teacher-training institutions, because of the meager scholastic preparation which they offered; and even today transfer of credits sometimes constitutes an embarrassment to the student whose Alma Mater has not fully met the requirements of the accrediting associations. Recent improvements in both faculty and curricular offerings have removed many of the former obstacles, and it is reasonable to suppose that the gap between teachers' colleges and liberal-arts institutions is gradually being bridged.

The extension of the normal-school-training period to include four years of collegiate work was accompanied by a multiplication of curricula to meet the varying needs of the field. The general course designed for teachers of all types was no longer deemed sufficient in an era of specialization. Therefore, provi-

[12] Frazier, B. W., *Teacher Training*, U. S. Bureau of Education, Bulletin 1929, No. 17 (Washington, Government Printing Office, 1929), p. 6.

[13] *National Survey of the Education of Teachers*, U. S. Office of Education, Bulletin 1933, No. 10 (Washington, Government Printing Office, 1935), Vol. III, p. 2.

sions were made for kindergarten and primary teachers, for teachers in the intermediate grades, for rural teachers, for teachers of vocational subjects, and for secondary-school teachers.[14] At the present time a prospective teacher in most states can select a field of specialization from a rather wide choice of curricula and expect to be qualified to teach this subject or grade at the completion of her college work.

One might be led to expect from this great transformation of normal schools into teachers' colleges that the number of inadequately trained teachers would fast disappear. Unfortunately, state certification requirements have not changed rapidly enough as yet to achieve this desirable end. As late as 1930 the official statistics of the United States Office of Education showed that of 60,300 graduates of teachers' colleges and normal schools combined, in 1930, approximately 19 per cent were from one-year curricula, 48 per cent from two-year, 15 per cent from three-year, and only 18 per cent from four-year. Ambitious, therefore, as the teachers' colleges have been, in their catalogue offerings, to induce students to take the full four-year course of instruction, they have fallen far short of their goal. This is not surprising in view of the phenomenal growth in the teaching personnel and the physical impossibility of providing a trained teacher for every classroom. Up until 1929 the demand for teachers was greater than the supply, even with certification requirements admittedly low. The degree to which the gap between supply and demand of trained teachers has been closing is indicated by the fact that whereas there were 5.6 positions for every teacher in training in 1894, there were only two positions available for her in 1926 and, judging from recent estimates, the number of positions now is scarcely greater than the number of teachers in training.[15]

It would have been suicidal, therefore, for the newly established state teachers' colleges to have insisted upon a four-year course of study for all students. All the facts point to the conclu-

[14] In 1930–1931 publicly supported teachers' colleges prepared twenty-one per cent of the junior-high-school teachers and seventeen per cent of the senior-high-school teachers.

[15] *Biennial Survey of Education, 1924–1926*, U. S. Bureau of Education, Bulletin 1928, No. 25 (Washington, Government Printing Office, 1928), p. 972.

sion that a gradual modification in training standards was the only feasible solution to the problem of preparing teachers for the public schools.

PROVISIONS FOR THE TRAINING OF RURAL TEACHERS

Since the administration of public schools in the United States has been left largely in the hands of local school boards and committees, the quality of education provided has varied directly with the wealth of the taxing unit and the vision of school-board members. While in recent years some of the state governments have granted considerable financial support to the poorer school districts within their jurisdictions, in an effort to equalize educational opportunities, the disparity between rural and city schools is still marked.

The reasons for this are numerous. Rural teaching has been relatively unattractive to well-qualified candidates because of bad living accommodations (unheated rooms and antiquated sanitary arrangements), and the absence of social and cultural opportunities. To these handicaps must be added the niggardly salaries which have been provided rural teachers since colonial days. As a result, the better-prepared teachers have moved as rapidly as possible into the urban centers, leaving the rural schools to their less competent sisters.

This situation, described above, has been accepted as inevitable by both educators and the public. It appears to be inherent in the conditions of country life, and until transportation and housing have improved to the point where the advantages of urban life no longer outweigh those in the wide, open spaces, there is no reason to expect any significant change in practice. In the meantime efforts are being directed toward ways of improving the training of teachers for the rural schools.

Prior to 1908 there were less than half a dozen normal schools which attempted to provide special courses for rural school-teachers and in only six states had legislation been passed authorizing the operation of teacher-training high schools. The latter institution was the only immediate hope of the rural areas for securing teachers with any professional training whatsoever. The teacher-training high school was most popular in the

United States between 1910 and 1925, twenty-four states employing this agency during these years as a means of supplying the rural schools with teachers. While requirements varied somewhat among the states and at different times, it was general practice by 1925 to extend the four-year high-school program one year to include certain professional studies. Five states (New York, Michigan, Minnesota, Vermont, and Ohio) had developed a fully departmentalized program by 1924, under the direction of a qualified normal-school instructor, and provided special quarters, library, and equipment for students in this division. The State Department of Education supplied professional supervision over the work in the teacher-training departments and insisted upon a rather high quality of instruction. In the other states [16] the standards were lower. Frequently, full-time special teachers were not employed to direct the professional program of studies and the teacher-training students were not segregated from regular pupils.

The curriculum can scarcely be described, for there was little uniformity except within individual states. In Kansas, where the organization of teacher-training classes was of the worst type, the state course of study in 1919 included civics, physiology, psychology, methods and management (including observation), and review of arithmetic and the other common branches. Beyond these specific studies the student must have had work in American history, physics, and agriculture. No practice teaching was required or expected.

While this curriculum was not representative of the better high-school teacher-training programs in other states, there were many situations where the offerings were not noticeably superior. The most significant difference between the Kansas arrangement and the one in Minnesota (acknowledged to be one of the best) was in the provision of practice-teaching opportunities in the latter state and the inclusion of certain courses peculiarly adapted to rural-school teaching. In Minnesota, for example, students were required to spend from one hundred

---

[16] Florida, Iowa, Maine, Missouri, Montana, Nebraska, Oklahoma, Tennessee, Wisconsin, Wyoming, Arkansas, Georgia, Kansas, North Dakota, South Dakota, West Virginia, North Carolina, Oregon, and Nevada.

and twenty to one hundred and eighty clock hours in observation and practice teaching, most of which was spent in actual teaching. New York, which did not require practice-teaching opportunities, introduced into the curriculum some studies commonly omitted from the typical training program, such as rural sociology, rural-school management, and industrial arts. This program compared favorably with those provided in state normal schools that professed to offer special courses of study for rural teachers.

The high-school training class grew out of the inability of normal schools to provide sufficient teachers for the rural schools and was a makeshift institution designed to serve the needs of an emergency. As soon as the state normal schools and teachers' colleges caught up with the demands of the field in supplying teachers for the city and town schools, they turned their attention to the preparation of rural teachers. Since 1925 states have gradually abandoned high-school training classes and by 1933 there were only seven states which relied upon this agency, in any way, for preparing teachers.[17] Like the institute, the teacher-training high school fulfilled its purpose well at a time when the facilities of better-equipped agencies were overtaxed. That it was a temporary expedient in no way denies the genuine contribution which it made to the welfare of children in rural districts. But that it has gone for good no one now seriously questions.

Special-type Normal Schools

The story of teacher training in the United States would not be complete without brief mention, at least, of the part played by city, private, and denominational normal schools.

Following the Civil War, many of the large cities established their own training schools, which consisted usually of departments tacked to the public high school. The amount of professional preparation provided in these institutions ranged from one to three years, the two-year curriculum becoming gradually the most common pattern. By 1914 every city, save one, of three hundred thousand inhabitants or more, and four fifths of those having a population of one hundred thousand or over,

[17] Iowa, Kansas, Michigan, Minnesota, Montana, Nebraska, and Wyoming.

maintained normal schools or training classes in connection with their public-school system.

The growth of these schools was stimulated by the rapid increase in school population and the inability of state normal schools to supply the municipalities with trained teachers. Like the teacher-training high schools, they were created to meet an existing emergency and, like the former institution, they have largely disappeared with the expansion of other better-equipped training schools. By 1930–1931 only about one fifth of the ninety-four cities of the United States having a population of one hundred thousand or more retained their municipally supported training schools. With a few possible exceptions, there appears to be no apparent justification or need for the continuance of these institutions and in all likelihood, as city budgetary problems become more acute, even these remaining few will be taken over by the state or abandoned altogether.

The city normal schools, while serving a useful function generally, have been responsible for the high degree of "inbreeding" which is characteristic of the teaching personnel in American cities. They have trained local girls almost exclusively, a policy which has been conducive to provincialism and the establishment of barriers to the introduction of new ideas and methods.

Private and denominational training schools were also prosperous between 1865 and 1880. In the latter year the Bureau of Education listed 114 private normal schools. Because of the changes in classification it is difficult to determine the exact date when they reached their flood tide. It is certain that they began to decline gradually when the states really accepted responsibility for teacher training, and in 1934 all that remained of these once-popular agencies were 9 teachers' colleges and 28 private normal schools.

Both the municipal and the private teacher-preparatory schools were inferior in staff and equipment to the more generously supported state institutions. Competition and lack of funds have hastened their downfall and, if one is safe in forecasting the future on the basis of recent trends, the date of their extinction is not far off.

The Growth of Teacher Training in Colleges and Universities since 1900

As the previous discussion reveals, before 1900, the preparation of secondary-school teachers was confined chiefly to the colleges and universities and while these institutions were slow in introducing pedagogy into their program of studies, the trend in this direction was unmistakable by 1910. As early as 1900 the number of departments of education in colleges and universities had reached 24, and within a decade the Educational Directory listed 156 heads of education departments or professors of pedagogy.

Since 1910 the number of "education" positions in colleges and universities has multiplied severalfold, and the actual number of deans of schools of education and heads of education departments listed in the Educational Directory in 1932 had mounted to the astounding figure of 593.

The problems involved in the development of this new division in colleges and universities were not unlike those which confronted the normal schools in their early history. There were few individuals qualified to offer methods courses for secondary-school teachers and there was a tendency to append this work to some of the older subject-matter departments and to assign staff members who were ill equipped for their mission to handle these courses. Some of the universities commandeered public-school officials who had achieved a professional reputation in the field. In a great many instances the work was of an inferior quality and aroused considerable opposition and criticism.

During the first decade of the century there were relatively few opportunities provided college and university students for practice teaching. Frank McMurry in 1893–1894 had experimented with a primary model school at the University of Illinois; but his efforts were apparently not crowned with success, for the school was soon discontinued. A canvass, in 1908, of fifty selected universities showed that only sixteen of those institutions required practice teaching and twenty did not offer students any opportunity for classroom experience under supervision. Since 1910, practice-teaching facilities have been greatly improved, and today practically every college that attempts to prepare teachers for the secondary schools either operates a model school of its own or has a working arrangement with the public schools in the immediate environs.

The course offerings in education have increased in number and variety to the point where special advisers and interpreters are required to assist the student in planning a program that bears some relation to the position for which he desires to prepare. This problem has been accentuated by the wide range in the requirements of state certification bureaus and the total lack of uniformity in the titles and descriptions of equivalent course offerings in the colleges themselves.

No attempt will be made here to describe the curriculum of a modern school of education. The reader is referred to the annual announcement of any large university for an appreciation of the nature and scope of the work offered. After skimming one of these catalogues, he may be interested, by way of contrast, to examine the course announcements in pedagogy of the University of Michigan for the year 1889–1890, which were fairly typical of the educational offerings in colleges and universities prior to 1900. The Michigan schedule was as follows: [18]

First semester

1. Practical: The arts of teaching and governing; methods of instruction and general schoolroom practice; school hygiene; school law. Recitations and lectures. Textbook: Compayre's Lectures on Pedagogy. (4) * * * *

3. History of Education: Ancient and mediaeval. Recitations and lectures. Textbook: Compayre's History of Pedagogy. (3) * * *

5. School Supervision: Embracing general school management, the art of grading and arranging courses of study, the conduct of institutes, etc. Recitations and lectures. Textbook: Payne's Chapters on School Supervision. (3) * * * *

Second semester

2. Theoretical and critical: The principles underlying the arts of teaching and governing. Lectures. (3) * * *

[18] *University of Michigan, Ann Arbor, Calendar, 1889–1890, p. 56.* (In *National Survey of the Education of Teachers,* U. S. Office of Education, Bulletin 1933, No. 10 [Washington, Government Printing Office, 1935], Vol. V, pp. 34–35.)

4. History of education: Modern. Recitations and lectures. Textbook: Compayre's History of Pedagogy. (3) * * *

6. The comparative study of educational systems, domestic and foreign. Lectures. (2)

7. Seminary: Study and discussion of special topics in the history and philosophy of education. (2) * * *

The functions of departments of education in colleges and universities have been extended beyond the mere preparation of secondary-school teachers. The training of school superintendents, principals, research directors, normal-school and college instructors, and a host of other educational workers is now considered to be an essential function of schools of education. The graduate schools, particularly, have engaged in extensive research programs and are contributing significantly to the solution of educational problems. New procedures have been originated and tested, principles formulated and organized, and educational literature expanded. The contribution of colleges and university departments of education to the development of the profession has been one of the great achievements of the twentieth century.

Graduate schools of education have exercised a marked influence on the work in state teachers' colleges and normal schools, through the training of staff members for these institutions and the publication of textbooks and materials of instruction. Divisions of field studies, such as the one at Teachers College, Columbia University, under the direction of Professor George D. Strayer, have made numerous surveys of public-school systems and have been influential in improving educational conditions in various parts of the United States. The period under discussion witnessed the development of experts and specialists, whose intensive study and knowledge have led to innumerable reforms with respect to educational organization and administration, the curriculum, and methods of teaching.

The future of departments of education in colleges and universities will depend to a considerable extent upon the economic status of the profession and the prosperity of the country generally. Barring any nation-wide catastrophes, the favorable position which these schools of education now hold would seem to presage a long and successful life.

As one reviews the history of teacher training in the United States, he can scarcely avoid the conclusion that in our efforts to supply enough teachers for the public schools we have sacrificed quality for quantity. No other alternative seemed consistent with a democratic school system. If every pupil were entitled to be educated at public expense, then teachers must be trained in sufficient numbers to make public education a reality. Training standards could be raised only as the supply of teachers approached or exceeded the demand. The American policy of attempting to educate everybody has, until recently, thrown a terrific burden upon teacher-preparatory institutions, with the result that, on the average, teachers in the United States have not attained a high academic status. Educators are prone to classify teaching with the professions of medicine and law when, in reality, the latter groups have advanced their training standards at least three years beyond those commonly required of teachers.

A second observation, which is not altogether unrelated to the previous discussion, is that the training of teachers is a relatively young movement in America. In fact, it is only one hundred years old, which is a brief period of time in institutional history. It has been a century of exploration, experimentation, and change in teacher training. Institutes came and went; the reading circle flourished and died; the normal school was transformed into the teachers' college; and schools and departments of education in colleges and universities enjoyed unprecedented prosperity and growth, and threatened to overshadow the academic divisions of higher institutions. In fact, the whole period was one of change. No clearly conceived pattern of teacher training has yet evolved in America. We have not had long enough experience with any single institution to get a true measure of its worth. Whether or not the teachers' college, our latest innovation, will give way to some other training agency is a matter of speculation. That it will undergo radical modification seems almost certain.

SUGGESTED READINGS

CARNEY, MABEL, *Preparation of Rural Teachers in High Schools*, U. S. Bureau of Education, Rural School Leaflet, No. 33 (Washington, Government Printing Office, 1924).

DEARBORN, NED, *The Oswego Movement in American Education* (New York, Bureau of Publications, Teachers College, Columbia University, 1925).

GORDY, J. P., *Rise and Growth of the Normal School Idea in the United States*, U. S. Bureau of Education, Circular of Information, No. 8, 1891 (Washington, Government Printing Office, 1891).

JUDD, C. H., and PARKER, S. C., *Problems Involved in Standardizing State Normal Schools*, U. S. Bureau of Education, Bulletin 1916, No. 12 (Washington, Government Printing Office, 1916).

LUCKEY, GEORGE W. A., *The Professional Training of Secondary Teachers in the United States* (New York, The Macmillan Company, 1903).

"Major Issues in Teacher Education," in *American Council on Education Studies* (1st series), Vol. II, No. 4 (February, 1938).

National Survey of the Education of Teachers, U. S. Office of Education, Bulletin 1933, Nos. 1–6 (Washington, Government Printing Office).

NEWELL, M. A., "Contributions to the History of Normal Schools in the United States," in *Report of the Commissioner of Education, 1898–1899* (Washington, Government Printing Office, 1900), Vol. II, pp. 2263–470.

XXIV

The Certification of Teachers

THE development of normal schools, teachers' colleges, and education departments in colleges and universities has been closely related to policies of teacher certification. The establishment of state normal schools tended to raise the requirements for first-class teaching certificates and, despite a protracted lag, led gradually to higher standards for all classes of licenses. Whereas public teacher-training institutions were usually in advance of certification standards, private schools and colleges required prodding by state departments.

Just so long as prospective secondary-school teachers were not required to present credits in "education" courses for a teaching certificate, most of the higher institutions of learning were quite satisfied to look disdainfully upon the subject of pedagogy. But as soon as courses in education became a common requirement for certification, the colleges and universities hastily reorganized their programs and staffs to care for the large number of students who planned to teach upon completion of their college work. Normal-school graduation, at one time, did not exempt the candidate for a teaching certificate from taking the elementary examinations, which were designed primarily to exclude illiterates and those whose schooling had not extended beyond the sixth grade. The absurdity of this procedure was forcefully pointed out by early educators, and by 1898 twenty-eight states recognized graduation from normal schools and universities as evidence of qualification for certification. At the present time all states grant certificates to the graduates of their own teacher-training institutions without further examination.

To describe adequately teacher-certification policies and regulations in the United States one would have to treat the subject for each state separately. There is no uniformity in the amount of training required for a teaching certificate, in the number of grades of certificates granted, in the conditions for the renewal of licenses, nor in the extent to which they are valid. The history of certification is equally as confusing, consisting as it does of innumerable changes in state legislation and in the regulations of state departments of education. Two states side by side may have had widely different systems of certification for a period of seventy-five years, each modifying their requirements several times and only occasionally in the same direction.

Despite the heterogeneity which is the characteristic feature of teacher certification in the United States, there are a few central trends, appearing mostly within the past fifty years, which promise eventually to bring order out of chaos. Among these are the following:

1. The centralization of the licensing function in the state department of education.
2. The substitution of approved training for teachers' examinations.
3. The differentiation of certificates according to the nature of the student's preparation, and the abandonment of blanket licenses.
4. The gradual abolition of life certificates.
5. The raising of training levels for all types of teaching certificates, with some inclination to make four years of training above high-school graduation the minimum for teaching in the elementary school and five years the minimum for teaching in the secondary school.
6. The requirement of a certain number of specialized courses in education in the candidate's program of studies.

CENTRALIZATION OF LICENSING

The trend toward centralizing the licensing function in the state department of education was not especially observable until late in the nineteenth century. In a few states, like New York, the State Superintendent exercised some authority over the granting of certificates even before the Civil War. But notwithstanding such an early start, centralization in the Empire State was not fully achieved until 1894, and in the interim certificates were granted by town commissioners, town superintendents, and county school commissioners without much regard for the rules of the State Department of Education.

In most states, local school officers, such as town and county superintendents, continued to exercise the licensing function throughout the nineteenth century and well into the twentieth. The first signs of centralization usually appeared when the state superintendent was authorized to grant teachers' licenses that were state-wide in validity and to supervise and coordinate the certification procedure for the whole state. The latter responsibility consisted in preparing regulations covering examinations and licenses and the formulation of the examination questions. The county or local school superintendent usually corrected the test papers and issued the certificates. From this intermediate stage, it seemed only a step to complete centralization and the abolition of local licensing agencies. Because of political barriers and the indifference of both teachers and citizens toward the problem, however, the final transition to complete centralization was deferred for years and in a few states it has yet to be accomplished.

Table 8 shows the degree to which local control has been replaced by centralized authority in the certification of teachers and the period of time required in making the shift. The trend indicated in this table would lead one to conclude that by 1940, or soon thereafter, state departments of education or state boards will issue all teaching certificates and will exercise complete control over the licensing function. This will constitute a significant milestone in the elevation of the teaching profession. Politics, inefficiency, and waste have frequently accompanied the examination and certification of teachers by local agencies. The varying standards of local officers have been brought to light many times in the grading of papers, even when the examinations themselves were prepared by the state department. Not only are the results unreliable when examinations are left to local administrators, but competition is likely to be restricted to local candidates, thereby encouraging a high degree of

Table 8. *Tendency toward Centralization of Certificating Authority in State Departments of Education   1   2   3* [1]

	Number of States 4					
	5 1898	6 1903	7 1911	1921	1926	1933
1	2	3	4	5	6	7
State systems (State issues all certificates)................	3	5	15	26	36	39
State-controlled systems (State prescribes rules, gives questions, and examines papers; county authorities issue some certificates)................	1	(8)	2	7	4	3
Semi-state systems (State makes regulations and gives questions; county authorities issue certificates and correct papers)	17	(8)	18	10	5	3
State-county systems (both issue certificates; county retains full control over examination for one or more certificates)	18	(8)	7	3	2	2
State-local systems..........	—	—	—	2	1	1
County system (County grants all certificates)............	4	4	1	—	—	—

[1] *National Survey of the Education of Teachers*, U. S. Office of Education, Bulletin 1933, No. 10 (Washington, Government Printing Office, 1935), Vol. V, p. 44.

1. Cook, Katherine M. State Laws and Regulations Governing Teachers' Certificates. U. S. Government Printing Office, 1928. p. 19. (Bureau of Education, Bulletin, 1927, no. 19.)
2. —— —— U. S. Government Printing Office, 1921. p. 9. (Bureau of Education, Bulletin, 1921, no. 22.)
3. State departments of education. Rules and Regulations, governing certification, 1933.
4. Temporary and emergency certificates and permits not included.
5. See also Blodgett, James H. Legal Provisions of the Various States Relating to Teachers' Examinations and Certificates. In U. S. Bureau of Education. Report of Commissioner of Education, 1897–98. vol. 2, pp. 1662–91. U. S. Government Printing Office, 1899.
6. See also Jackson, William R. The Present Status of the Certification of Teachers. In U. S. Bureau of Education. Report of Commissioner of Education, 1903. vol. 1, pp. 463–519. U. S. Government Printing Office, 1905.
7. See also Updegraff, Harlan. Teachers' Certificates Issued Under General State Laws and Regulations. U. S. Government Printing Office, 1911. pp. 12–135. (Bureau of Education, Bulletin, 1911, no. 18.)
8. No data.

inbreeding. Along with these unfavorable concomitants of local certification, there usually went low standards and low wages.

Centralization has resulted, however, not so much from the unfortunate conditions just discussed as from changes in the relationship between supply and demand and from improvements in transportation resulting in a more mobile population and a better-informed public. So long as normal schools were unable to graduate enough teachers to replace the annual withdrawals from the profession and to meet the needs of expansion, local agencies were necessary to supplement the state's crop of normal-school graduates. Since the rural schools were seldom able to attract trained teachers, the job of examining and licensing village and rural teachers was left to the county school officers or local examining boards as the easiest way out of the dilemma. With the expansion and improvement of normal schools and education departments in colleges and universities, the argument for the untrained teacher and the old examination system of granting licenses lost most of its weight. Normal schools introduced special courses for rural teachers and by 1925 it would have been possible to fill most of the vacant teaching positions in the United States with trained teachers if local boards of education had been disposed to do so. Since the depression of 1929 there has been no need for local recruiting stations, and the centralization of teacher-training policies and certification procedures can now logically be consummated.

Improved transportation facilities have also been an important factor in the improvement of teacher training. Privately owned automobiles and commercial bus lines have brought the normal schools (now teachers' colleges) within easy reach of the country boy or girl interested in teaching as a profession. Those physical and economic barriers which formerly deterred students from entering standardized teacher-preparatory schools no longer exist.

The Decline in the Use of Teachers' Examinations

Closely related to the centralization of certification in the state department of education is the tendency to abandon the method of granting licenses by examination and to substitute for this outmoded procedure a specified training requirement.[1] The adoption of this policy came as a direct result of state control of certification and the expansion of teacher-training facilities. While examinations had been the traditional basis for licensing teachers in the United States before the advent of normal schools, the procedure had never proved entirely satisfactory, in spite of its universal acceptance. California, as early as 1863, recognized state-normal-school diplomas as licenses to teach, and gradually in all the states a policy was established exempting the graduates of publicly supported teacher-training institutions from examinations.[2] This was the first step in the direction of reform. The next move was to allow for equivalent training so that the thousands of students in colleges and universities who aspired to teaching positions might submit credentials rather than be subjected to an expensive and unreliable examination process. The South Carolina law in 1898 provided for special licensing arrangements with higher institutions by stipulating that: [3]

Universities and colleges are authorized to provide a course of study, to be approved by the State Board of Education on completion of which the degree of Licentiate of Instruction is to be given the student, and the presentation of the diploma for this degree to a county board of education will entitle the holder to a first grade teacher's certificate to teach in the public schools of the county.

A more common provision was one similar to that found in the Texas law in 1897 to the effect that "diplomas conferred by the Regents of the University of Texas on students completing some degree course, and also the degree course of the school of Pedagogy, have the force of permanent state certificates." [4]

From the recognition of work in specific colleges and universities, the tendency in recent years has been to broaden the

[1] For example, 64 semester hours' normal-school credit, including a minimum of 24 semester hours' professional work or completion of 2 years'; 64 semester hours' college work, including 6 semester hours in education.

[2] By 1900 fully half of the states exempted normal-school graduates from taking teachers' examinations. See *Report of the Commissioner of Education, 1897–1898*, Chap. XXXV, pp. 1659–91.

[3] "Teachers Examinations and Certificates," South Carolina Education Law, 1898, in *Report of Commissioner of Education, 1897–1898* (Washington, Government Printing Office, 1899), Vol. II, p. 1684.

[4] *Ibid.*, p. 1685.

provision to include studies pursued in accredited institutions regardless of location.

Despite the rapid expansion in teacher-training facilities, the policy of granting certificates upon examination has persisted in many states and even today has not been entirely abandoned. The trend, however, is definitely away from certification by examination. In 1911 all the states granted some certificates on this basis. By 1926–1927 twelve states had practically abolished examinations as a condition for issuing certificates and, according to Bachman's findings,[5] there were only twenty-five states in 1933 that still issued elementary-school certificates on the basis of examination.

The giving of examinations in recent years does not imply that the applicant for a teacher's license has no scholastic preparation. In the majority of states where certificates are still issued upon the results of tests, high-school graduation is the lowest academic prerequisite. Just how much longer low-grade certificates and the old examination system will persist no one can foretell with exactitude. Legislatures are slow in subtracting from the powers of local officials, and county politicians can be counted upon to oppose any transfer of authority to the state department. The output of teacher-training institutions, however, will soon be so numerous as to remove all necessity for the appointment of untrained teachers and there will be no excuse for the continuance of the old selective agencies. The records provided by state teachers' colleges and universities will furnish sufficient evidence of the candidate's academic and professional qualifications.

The Trend toward Differentiation

Before 1900 not more than six states differentiated in their certification requirements between high-school and elementary teachers, and even as late as 1906 Cubberley reported that "in almost all of our states a teacher's certificate of any grade is good to teach in any part of the school system in which the teacher

---

[5] Bachman, Frank P., *Education and Certification of Elementary Teachers*, Field Study No. 5 (Division of Surveys and Field Studies, George Peabody College, Nashville, Tenn., 1933), p. 17.

may be able to secure employment." [6] A license to teach in these early days then carried with it the freedom to practice one's art at any grade level or in any subject from the kindergarten to the university. In a few instances as in Montana, special certificates for penmanship, music, drawing, and a modern language were issued on the request of district boards, and occasionally a special certificate was issued to kindergarten teachers. In general, however, specialization is a product of the twentieth century, the last two decades witnessing a rapid transformation in the licensing procedure from "blanket" to special certificates.

Differentiation by subjects or fields of work was established to some extent in the certification provisions of several states by 1920. It was fairly common practice at this date to issue special licenses to principals and supervisors, and practically all states had special certificates for teachers of music, drawing, home economics, manual training, and physical education. These latter certificates were granted on the basis of either training or examination in the special subject. Several states were also beginning to issue separate licenses to primary-, elementary-, and high-school teachers, so that the principle of specialization was firmly embedded in state certification regulations by the close of the World War.

By 1930 practically all states issued certificates specifically for elementary grades, twenty-six states issued certificates designated for junior-high-school teachers, and thirty-one states issued special certificates for high-school teachers. In addition to the foregoing restrictions, junior- and senior-high-school certificates have been broken down in some states into licenses to teach science, mathematics, English, etc. No one seems to know just where the point of diminishing returns is in the matter of specialization, but it is the judgment of many educators that we have already reached it. However true this may be, it appears unlikely that the states will retrace their steps and return to blanket certificates. Specialization has unquestionably improved teaching and a certain amount of it is highly essential if progress

---

[6] Cubberley, Elwood P., "The Certification of Teachers," in National Society for the Scientific Study of Education, *Fifth Yearbook* (Chicago, The University of Chicago Press, 1906), p. 59.

is to continue. What is most needed at the present time is a greater degree of uniformity in certification regulations, in the nomenclature used, and in the requirements established. Until this is achieved, it will be extremely difficult to make a scientific study of certification problems.

LIFE CERTIFICATES

The certificates awarded by the state to candidates for teaching licenses have, in most instances, carried a wider validity and been more permanent in character than those issued by local authorities. The latter have consisted in recent years of emergency and low-grade licenses whose validity has been restricted to the county or district in which the recipient proposed to teach. In many states, however, a certification ladder exists, whereby a teacher, by improving her educational status and through the accumulation of teaching experience, can ascend rung by rung until she reaches the top and acquires that envied possession—the life diploma.

Life certificates originated early in the history of state school systems. The State Superintendent of Public Instruction in New York was authorized in 1843 to issue certificates, valid till revoked, to candidates who could present satisfactory evidence of being qualified to teach in the common schools of the state. While the word "life" does not appear in connection with this certificate, there was no time limit placed upon its validity.

County superintendents in Pennsylvania issued permanent licenses to teachers as early as 1854 and the qualifications required were apparently low, since the State Teachers Association, in its meetings in 1855 and 1856, protested vigorously against the practice of awarding permanent certificates to candidates who were inadequately prepared to teach. Illinois authorized the State Superintendent in 1861 to issue certificates of eminent qualifications upon examination "to be of perpetual validity in every school district in the State." Similarly West Virginia, by a law of 1863, provided for the conversion of county certificates of the highest order into state life certificates revocable only "for immorality or disloyalty, clearly proven." California made provision for life diplomas in 1873, one prerequisite being ten years of experience or an aggregate of seventy months, twenty-one months of which must have been in the public schools of California.[7]

It is apparent from the cases just cited that several of the states during these earlier years recognized the importance of granting professional certificates to qualified individuals who planned to make teaching their lifework. The effect of this policy on the profession generally was salutary. Ambitious young men and women bent their efforts to acquire these permanent licenses, and in several instances the requirements necessitated professional study and presupposed successful experience. Unfortunately, however, the qualifications in many states for eligibility to this honored circle of life-certificate holders have been neither uniform nor high, and the gradual accumulation of these permanent diplomas has made it increasingly difficult to promote continuous professional growth.[8] The number of states which were issuing life certificates in 1897 and the trend since that date are shown in Table 9, following.

It is interesting to note therein that eight states have discontinued the practice of issuing life certificates since 1927,[9] and that several others have already announced future dates for the termination of this licensing procedure. This tendency reflects the point of view of many educators toward the granting of permanent licenses. It is their contention that teacher-training standards change rapidly and long-term certificates tend to stifle professional growth. They maintain further that the state

---

[7] "Digest of Public School Laws," in *Report of the Commissioner of Education, 1893–1894* (Washington, Government Printing Office, 1896), Vol. II, p. 1292.

[8] The following quotation is taken from Herbst's analysis of life certificates in 1938: "In fifteen states experience varying from one year to fifteen years only is required. In the case of the latter, however, these five-year certificates requiring additional training for each five-year renewal have been issued previous to granting the life certificate. In seventeen states experience plus additional training above that required for the certificate then held by the teacher is needed. This experience varies from two to five years and the amount of additional training from nine quarter hours to one full year. In five states no experience seems to be required, although the amount of training necessary is more than that needed for the regular teaching certificate." (Herbst, R. L., *Teacher Certification Practices in 48 States with Special Reference to the Issuing of Life Certificates* [State Department of Public Instruction, Dover, Del., April, 1938], mimeographed report.)

[9] These eight states are North Carolina (1930), Arkansas (1931), Maine (1932), South Carolina (1932), Louisiana (1934), Vermont (1934), Utah (1935), and New York (1936). Reported by Herbst, R. L., *op. cit.*

Table 9. *Showing States Issuing Life Certificates, 1897–1938* [1]

States	1897	1911	1921	1927	1938
Alabama	x	x	x [2]	x [2]	
Arkansas	x	x	x	x	
Arizona	x	x	x	x	
California	x	x	x	x	x
Colorado	x	x	x	x	x
Connecticut				x	x
Delaware [3]					
Florida	x	x	x	x	x
Georgia	x	x		x	x
Idaho	x	x	x	x	x
Illinois	x	x	x		x
Indiana	x	x	x		x
Iowa	x	x	x	x	x
Kansas	x	x	x	x	x
Kentucky	x	x	x	x	x
Louisiana				x	
Maine	x	x	x	x	
Maryland	x	x			
Massachusetts			x		x
Michigan	x	x	x	x	x
Minnesota	x	x	x	x	x
Mississippi	x	x	x	x	x
Missouri	x	x	x	x	x
Montana	x	x	x	x	x
Nebraska	x	x	x	x	x
Nevada	x	x	x	x	x
New Hampshire	x	x	x	x	x
New Jersey	x	x	x	x	x
New Mexico		x	x	x	x
New York	x	x	x	x	
North Carolina	x		x	x	
North Dakota	x	x	x	x	x
Ohio	x	x	x	x	x
Oklahoma		x	x	x	x
Oregon	x	x	x	x	x
Pennsylvania	x	x	x	x	x
Rhode Island	x	x	x	x	x
South Carolina			x	x	
South Dakota	x	x	x	x	x
Tennessee	x	x	x	x	x
Texas	x	x	x	x	x
Utah	x	x	x	x	
Vermont			x	x	
Virginia	x				
Washington	x	x	x	x	x [4]
West Virginia			x		x
Wisconsin	x	x	x	x	x
Wyoming	x	x	x	x	x

[1] Adapted from *Reports of the Commissioner of Education* for 1897, 1911, 1921, and 1927. For 1938, taken from Herbst, R. L., *op. cit.*

[2] Conditional life certificate valid for period of six years and subject to continuance on conditions stated on its face.

[3] Permanent certificate before 1919 with following restrictions: valid for five to ten years and candidate must pass an examination for renewal.

[4] Discontinued issuance September 1, 1938.

should always retain control over the training qualifications of its personnel. The significance of these arguments has been realized, in recent years, when current requirements for certification have been compared with the qualifications of present holders of life diplomas. The latter group includes many teachers with but one and two years of training above high-school graduation who would be unable to qualify now in many states for the lowest-grade certificate issued. A similar argument has been advanced against awarding life certificates to graduates of our modern teacher-training institutions. What is deemed a high standard today may easily become a low one within a decade.

Some of the evil effects of granting life diplomas have been partially corrected by curtailing the number issued and by increasing the training requirements for eligibility. State departments have also become exceedingly cautious in the matter of granting these permanent licenses, although authorized to grant them, and a sizable reduction in the number of active certificates is therefore gradually being effected. The injurious consequences of life certification will persist long after the practice has been abolished—until, indeed, the last holder of a life certificate has retired. To preserve the state's integrity there appears to be no alternative but to honor the outstanding permanent diplomas and trust that the professional enthusiasm of the holders will overcome any feelings of complacency which life certificates may engender.

IMPROVEMENTS IN TRAINING REQUIREMENTS

State certification requirements are a rough measure of the educational status of a commonwealth. Where a high degree of centralization exists and the state issues all certificates, and where normal-school graduation is the minimum training requirement for teaching in the public schools, the index of educational efficiency will be high. On the other hand, in those states where several agencies are authorized to issue licenses and where examinations are still the chief basis upon which certificates are granted, the educational index will, in all probability, be low.

Certificates are really significant to the degree that they represent scholarship and training. In the early history of state school systems and extending throughout the nineteenth century, the amount of education required of teachers, both academic and professional, was pitifully small. The American high school was something of a luxury in 1870 and even by 1890 the number of secondary-school graduates was still unimpressive. Elementary teachers—and most teachers were in the elementary schools—were seldom high-school graduates, their education consisting of from six to eight grades in the common schools. Only a small proportion of teachers received any normal-school training before 1880.

The qualification most commonly insisted upon for certification was the ability to pass an examination set by the county superintendent of schools or a local examining board. The Virginia requirements in 1892 are typical of those which prevailed in most of the states prior to 1900 and show the almost total dependence placed upon examinations in recruiting teachers. The Virginia law provided that: [10]

The county superintendent shall examine persons applying for license to teach in the free public schools, and, if satisfied as to their capacity, acquirements, morals, and general fitness, he shall grant them certificates of limited duration subject to revocation, all under the supervision of the State Superintendent. He shall also hold examinations for those desiring to teach in his county for the school year at such time and place as may be required by a district board. Examinations will be held in orthography, reading, writing, arithmetic, grammar, geography, physiology and hygiene, and for a first or second grade certificate, in the theory and practice of teaching. Applicants to teach schools in which the higher branches have been introduced must be examined upon those branches also.

Virginia had four normal schools in 1894 (two for whites and two for colored) but they were unequal to the task of supplying enough teachers to man the schools. The number of years of schooling of the candidates who entered by the examination door is not recorded anywhere, but the average was certainly low. It was fairly common practice to base the grade of certificate

[10] "Digest of Public School Laws," in *Report of the Commissioner of Education, 1893–1894*, Vol. II, p. 1127.

on the marks earned in the examinations. The Kansas plan as it existed in 1897 is an illustration of this principle.[11]

> Certificates of three grades are issued: First, age required, eighteen years; experience, twelve school months; examination, common English branches, Constitution of the United States, bookkeeping, theory and practice of teaching, elements of natural philosophy, temperance; general average, 90 per cent; minimum, 70 in any one branch; valid three years and, by indorsement of local superintendent, in any county. Second, age, 17 years; experience, three school months; examination as above, less bookkeeping and elements of natural philosophy; general average, 80 per cent; minimum, 60 per cent; valid two years. Third, valid one year.

It is also interesting to note, in the Kansas regulations, the inclusion of a minimum age requirement, varying with the grade of certificate. In the absence of training qualifications or a specified number of years' schooling, some protection against immaturity was deemed essential. In a few states, the minimum age for men was higher than that of women, the Maryland law making nineteen years the lowest limit for men and seventeen years for women.[12]

Certification procedures remained fairly static for the three decades following the Civil War. The most significant change was the increase in the number of normal-school graduates given licenses without examination, which gradually reduced the proportion of individuals teaching on low-grade certificates. Improvement, however, was extremely slow and the professional status of teachers in 1900 was only slightly better than in 1860.

Since 1900 there has been a steady increase in the educational equipment of public-school teachers. Certification requirements have been altered to suit the conditions of supply and demand; and the trend has been almost universally upward, due to the rapid increase in high-school attendance and in the enrollments of colleges, universities, and teacher-training institutions. By 1910 states were beginning to consider the desirability of requir-

---

[11] "Teachers' Examinations and Certificates," in *Report of Commissioner of Education, 1897–1898* (Washington Government Printing Office, 1899), Vol. II, pp. 1670–71.

[12] In Illinois it was eighteen years for men and seventeen years for women.

ing high-school graduation as a minimum basis for all licenses. Indiana actually took this step in 1907, Utah in 1911; and several other states passed laws gradually increasing the requirement of high-school attendance from one to four years for the lower-grade certificates.[13]

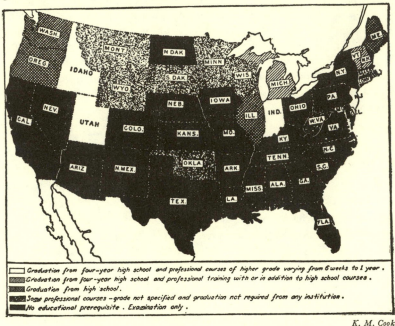

K. M. Cook

FIGURE I. STATE LAWS AND REGULATIONS GOVERNING
TEACHERS' CERTIFICATES, SHOWN BY STATES

By 1921 substantial progress had been made in spite of the interruption caused by the World War. The situation for the above year is well illustrated by Cook in Figure I, showing the academic and professional prerequisites for the lowest-grade certificates in the forty-eight states.

In spite of the gains made over the preceding decade, the picture is anything but complimentary to the teaching profession. In more than half of the states in 1921, the certificating agencies were authorized to issue licenses to applicants who had no

[13] Updegraff, Harlan, *Teacher Certificates Issued under General State Laws and Regulations*, U. S. Bureau of Education, Bulletin 1911, No. 18 (Washington, Government Printing Office, 1911), p. 186.

training qualifications whatsoever. While presumably teachers' examinations are one measure of educational status, their unreliability and lack of validity make them a very inadequate substitute for training.

Perhaps educators got satisfaction in 1921 in the realization that the picture was still worse in 1911. The reader may recall that Indiana was the first state in 1907 to make high-school graduation a prerequisite for any certificate. By 1921 fifteen states had either achieved this requirement or had passed legislation demanding it within a given period of years. California led in the quality of the standards which it established. In this state, normal-school training equivalent to two years above high-school graduation was made the requirement for elementary certificates, and college graduation, including one year of graduate work, was required for high-school teachers. Here, at

Table 10. Scholarship Prerequisites for Certificating Teachers without Experience, Temporary and Emergency Certificates Not Considered [1]

Minimum Scholarship Prerequisites	Number of States		
	1921	1926	1937
1	2	3	4
High-school graduation and 4 years' training of higher grade..	0	0	5
High-school graduation and 3 years' training of higher grade..	0	0	8
High-school graduation and 2 years' training of higher grade..	0	4	11
High-school graduation and professional training, 1 year of higher grade...............................	0	9	8
High-school graduation and some professional training, but less than 1 year...........................	4	14	2
Four years' secondary school (may or may not include professional courses)...........................	14	6	6
No definite scholarship requirement stipulated........	30	15	8 [2]

[1] Adapted from Frazier, Benjamin W., *Development of State Programs for the Certification of Teachers*, U. S. Office of Education, Bulletin 1938, No. 12 (Washington, Government Printing Office, 1938), p. 73.

[2] 1937 classification includes Massachusetts, in which the minimum scholastic requirement for teacher employment is usually three or four college years; and Oklahoma, in which completion of two to four years of high-school work is prescribed for a limited elementary certificate.

least, was one example for states to emulate in reorganizing their certification programs.

The progress made during the next sixteen years was really astounding when compared with preceding achievements. Table 10 shows the improvements made in scholarship prerequisites between 1921 and 1937.

The marked decline in the number of states in which no definite scholarship requirement was stipulated for certification (from thirty to eight) together with the big increase in the number of states which had established from one to four years of training above high-school graduation (from none to thirty-two) made this period a noteworthy one for the teaching profession.

The trend since 1937 has been in the direction of raising the training requirements for certificates still higher. If the states come to accept the idea that public-school teaching should be a profession comparable in its requirements and its services to law and medicine, then certification standards will have to be lifted to unprecedented heights and our training institutions reorganized to meet the increased demands.

SPECIAL REQUIREMENTS IN PEDAGOGY

When the study of pedagogy became an integral part of the training program of prospective teachers, state certification regulations were modified in conformity with the new emphasis on education, as opposed to the stress formerly laid on the strictly academic subjects. This was reflected both in the college credentials required for certification and in the examinations given as a basis for licensing. One of the earliest of these requirements was the passing of an examination in "the science and art of teaching." The titles used to designate the specialized areas of educational knowledge, such as psychology and the theory and art of teaching, were not uniform throughout the country, although the nomenclature before 1900 was less confusing than it has been in recent years.

In 1906 approximately three fourths of the states required one pedagogical subject for one or more certificates, and the subject most frequently mentioned was the theory and art of teaching. Occasionally some other subject, such as school law, psychology, or the history of education, was required for certification but seldom before the turn of the century.

Since practice varied widely among the states with respect to subject prescriptions, it is difficult to describe the situation without recording the data for each state. The trend since 1900 has been definitely in the direction of extending the requirement of pedagogical subject matter. As examinations have gradually given way to training credentials, it has become fairly common practice to designate the number of hours' credit which are required in specific educational courses.

In order that the reader may have some appreciation of this twentieth-century phenomenon, the professional requirements for licenses in Indiana and Alabama are outlined, in Tables 11 and 12, for the four separate years in which the United States Bureau of Education issued bulletins bearing on certification laws and regulations.

Table 11. Professional Requirements for Licenses in Indiana, 1895–1927 [1]

Pedagogical Subjects Prescribed			
1895	*1911*	*1921*	*1927*
Science of Education	Science of Education	Science of Education	Principles of Teaching
	School Laws of Indiana	School Laws of Indiana	Psychology and Its Application to Education
	Educational Psychology	Educational Psychology	Secondary Education
	Experimental Psychology and Child Study	Experimental Psychology and Child Study	Principles of Teaching and Supervised Teaching
	History of Education	History of Education	Junior High School
	School Systems of Europe and America	School Systems of Europe and America	
	Principles of Teaching	Principles of Teaching	

[1] This table does not include subjects required for superintendents', principals', or supervisors' licenses.

While the number of courses mentioned in the Indiana illustration just cited (Table 11) is actually one less in 1927 than in 1911, the scope of the work apparently was extended. The most noticeable change occurred in both state programs between 1897 and 1911.

Table 12. *Professional Requirements for Licenses in Alabama, 1895–1927* [1]

Pedagogical Subjects Prescribed			
1895	*1911*	*1921*	*1927*
Theory and Practice of Teaching	Theory and Practice of Teaching History of Education School Law	Theory and Practice of Teaching History of Education School Law School Management Elementary Psychology	Theory and Practice of Teaching History of Education School Laws of Alabama Class Management General Psychology Educational Psychology High School Methods

[1] This table shows the total number of subjects mentioned specifically as a basis for certification in Alabama for the years indicated.

THE INFLUENCE OF "REFORMERS" ON CERTIFICATION PROCEDURES

Certification requirements in recent years have been comparatively uninfluenced by reformers, religious fanatics, and faddists. Some of the prescriptions incorporated in licensing laws may be unwarranted in terms of the value of the subject matter represented, and in all probability much that is now deemed essential will be replaced by the demands of another generation of educators. But present certification requirements represent, for the most part, an educational philosophy based upon the experience of practical schoolworkers. The religious belief of the candidate, his theory of government, and his point of view regarding the mores of the people are not considered a part of his qualifications for a certificate. If his educational training measures up to the standard and his character references are not especially damaging, he will be issued a license notwithstanding his unorthodox views or his liberal affiliations. In some states, particularly in recent years, no matter how excellent one's qualifications may be, a certificate will be withheld until the applicant has an appointment to a teaching position. This is merely to protect the state against an oversupply of licensed teachers and is in no way intended to be discriminatory.

The requirements for certification have not always been limited to strictly professional matters. In Arkansas, for example, in 1893, certificates were not granted to atheists, the examiners being charged in the law "not to license any person to teach who is given to profanity, drunkenness, gambling, licentiousness, or other demoralizing vices, or *who does not believe in the existence of a Supreme Being*." [14]

It was during this same period in our history that the temperance societies were exerting great pressure on the schools in an effort to instill in the minds of children the evil effects of alcoholic beverages. To insure the spread of their propaganda these reformers had laws enacted requiring every candidate for a teacher's certificate to pass what was commonly termed a temperance examination. In most states where such examinations were held, the test was designated Physiology and Hygiene, and included a question or two on the effects of alcohol upon the human body. Such wording as the following will illustrate the implications behind the questions: What effect has alcohol upon the circulation? If the candidate failed to respond that arteriosclerosis set in almost immediately after imbibing, he was in danger of being denied a certificate.

Another approach which was sure to reveal the applicant's attitude toward temperance was to ask him to describe the effects of the use of alcohol (1) upon the brain, (2) upon the lungs, and (3) upon the digestive organs. Failure on the part of the candidate to sound the death knell for the habitué of strong drink, with an opportunity such as this question provided, made the examiner feel fully justified in refusing him a license.

The reformers in Tennessee and Texas were not willing to confine their propaganda to the injurious effects of alcohol. They extended it to include tobacco and modified certification procedures so as to bar all candidates who displayed ignorance of the deleterious results of cigarette smoking. The Tennessee requirement stated that "the temperance examination, includ-

---

[14] "Digest of Public School Laws," in *Report of the Commissioner of Education, 1893–1894*, Vol. II, p. 1166.

ing the effect of cigarette smoking on the human system, is obligatory." [15] The Texas regulation was somewhat broader, the term "narcotics" being substituted for "cigarette smoking."

Not only were individuals rejected for failure to pass a satisfactory examination on the harmful effects of alcohol and tobacco, but those who passed could have their certificates revoked for failure to teach the temperance lessons. Teachers apparently observed this mandate without complaint. In all probability, they accepted the temperance propaganda at face value and believed everything the textbooks said about cigarettes and alcohol. In any event, they showed no disposition to rebel against teaching temperance according to the instructions given.

Certification laws in many states specified the causes for which licenses could be revoked, and it seems probable that modern tenure statutes have imitated these earlier laws in selecting causes for the dismissal of teachers. Immoral conduct is one of the oldest causes for revoking certificates. Alabama, in 1895, provided that licenses would be canceled whenever it appears "that the holders have been guilty of intemperance or unworthy or disgraceful conduct." Several states specified "unfitness for teaching" as a basis for canceling licenses. Georgia mentioned "cruelty to pupils" in the list of causes for revocation.

In a number of states, the law provided that teachers' certificates could be revoked for cause without listing the specific reason as in the cases just cited. A few regulations combined a general cancellation provision with a specifically mentioned one. Thus the Washington state law stipulated that "all certificates are revokable for cause, including neglect to attend the annual county institute." [16]

Legislation in some of the states explicitly provided that teachers were entitled to "a fair hearing" before their certificates could be canceled, and in a few states the procedure to be followed was defined in considerable detail. A practice which originated rather early in some states and which has become common

---

[15] "Teachers' Examinations and Certificates," in *Report of the Commissioner of Education, 1897–1898*, Vol. II, p. 1685.

[16] *Ibid.*, p. 1688. Failure to attend institutes unless excused by law was given as a cause for revocation of certificates in Washington, West Virginia, and South Dakota in 1897–1898.

within the last half century is the voiding of certificates where the holder allows a space of as much as three to five years to elapse without following some educational pursuit. This policy has discouraged many teachers from returning to the profession after extended absence and has tended to lift standards and increase the stability of the teaching group generally.

CURRENT CRITICISMS

Perhaps the most serious criticism launched against licensing plans is the failure to work out reciprocity relationships between the states. This is partially accounted for by the diverse nature of the credentials granted and the lack of uniformity in the terminology applied to licenses. Even in neighboring common-wealths where training standards are fairly uniform and comparable, there is no assurance that a certificate to teach in one state will be honored in the other. Legal barriers restricting the movement of qualified teachers are varied and numerous in the United States. They include unwarranted requirements such as a course in the school laws of the state, the state constitution, or state history.[17] To meet some of these prescriptions, the candidate would have to attend one of the higher institutions of a particular state. Still another barrier is the practice-teaching clause, found in some regulations, which requires that the candidate for a certificate shall have had a certain specified number of hours of practice teaching, regardless of the fact that he may have been employed as a public-school teacher in some other state for several years.

Rigid requirements pertaining to the number of clock hours in designated courses also act as barriers to free interstate movement of teachers. Some states insist that candidates shall have taken courses, the titles of which shall not vary one iota from those mentioned in certification regulations, no matter how closely the content may be related to the prescribed title. Such interpretations are obviously made to protect the interests of local teachers and are not designed to elevate professional standards.

The licensing problem is accentuated by the fact that, legally, education is a state function rather than a federal one. It would

---

[17] For example, Idaho School Law, The Provisions and Principles of the Constitution of Arizona, and Montana Government and History.

be a relatively simple procedure to substitute a federal certification plan for the forty-eight separate and distinct state arrangements which are now in force, were it not contrary to the fundamental principles upon which our government was established.   Improvements and reorganization can come only through leadership and cooperation.   The chaotic conditions which prevail in the whole licensing procedure at the present time are so obvious to even the casual student of the problem that no further study of practices is required to convince certification officials of the need of reform.   It seems probable that some educational foundation or some national association interested in the professional status of teachers will provide the leadership necessary to bring order out of the present confusion.

Suggested Readings

BACHMAN, FRANK P., *Education and Certification of Elementary Teachers* (Division of Surveys and Field Studies, George Peabody College, Nashville, Tenn., 1933).

CAMPBELL, D. S., and SMITH, C. C., *The Education of Secondary School Teachers* (Division of Surveys and Field Studies, George Peabody College, Nashville, Tenn., 1936).

COOK, KATHERINE M., *State Laws and Regulations Governing Teachers' Certificates*, U. S. Bureau of Education, Bulletin 1921, No. 22 (Washington, Government Printing Office, 1921).

———— *State Laws and Regulations Governing Teachers' Certificates*, U. S. Bureau of Education, Bulletin 1927, No. 19 (Washington, Government Printing Office, 1927).

"Digest of Public School Laws," in *Report of the Commissioner of Education, 1893–1894*, Vol. II, pp. 1063–1300 (Washington, Government Printing Office, 1896).

FRAZIER, BENJAMIN W., *Development of State Programs for the Certification of Teachers*, U. S. Office of Education, Bulletin 1938, No. 12 (Washington, Government Printing Office, 1938).

HERBST, R. L., *Teacher Certification Practices in 48 States and the District of Columbia with Special Reference to the Issuing of Life Certificates* (State Department of Public Instruction, Dover, Del., April, 1938), mimeographed report.

National Survey of the Education of Teachers, U. S. Office of Education, Bulletin 1935, No. 10 (Washington, Government Printing Office, 1935).

HERBST, R. L., "Statutory Status of Six Professions," in National Educational Association, *Research Bulletin*, Vol. XVI, No. 4 (September, 1938).

STRATFORD, WILLIAM D., "Restrictions to the Free Interstate Movement of Teachers," unpublished manuscript.

"Teachers' Examinations and Certificates," in *Report of the Commissioner of Education, 1897–1898*, Vol. II, pp. 1659–91 (Washington, Government Printing Office, 1899).

UPDEGRAFF, HARLAN, *Teachers' Certificates Issued under General State Laws and Regulations*, U. S. Bureau of Education, Bulletin 1911, No. 18 (Washington, Government Printing Office, 1911).

XXV

Teachers' Institutes

THE matter of providing the public schools with a staff of well-trained teachers has always been one of great concern to those genuinely interested in the welfare of children. In the United States the problem has been especially perplexing because of both the rapid growth in population, calling for phenomenal increases in the supply of qualified teachers, and the manifold opportunities open to ambitious young men and women to acquire prestige and wealth in vocations that are less restrictive than teaching.

If all children between seven and fourteen years of age in the United States were to be provided with public-school opportunities, it was obvious to thoughtful educators in the eighteen-forties that one of two alternative procedures must be followed. Either the gates to the profession must be kept open, as they had been prior to 1839, to graduates of the common schools, or special agencies and institutions must be created to prepare prospective teachers for the responsibilities which they were expected to assume. The weaknesses of the first alternative had already been clearly demonstrated and only the ignorant and the lazy believed that the old order of things could continue. Despite the penetrating logic of the advocates of normal schools and training classes, it was evident to intelligent citizens that progress was bound to be painfully slow and that thousands of individuals already engaged in the business of teaching would be only slightly influenced, if touched at all, by any of the contemplated changes in teacher training. Normal schools, if adequately supported, could in the course of time provide the initial training of all new entrants into the profession. In the interim, some other agency would have to be relied upon to lift the educational status of teachers from its present level of mediocrity to a position of respectability.

The first medium hit upon for achieving this transformation was the teachers' institute. By 1860 this agency was a going concern and many states were appropriating public funds for its support. As has been pointed out in a previous discussion, the general opinion among educators and laymen was that the institute was a powerful factor in the improvement of teachers in service, and that it had rendered a unique contribution to the cause of public education, fully justifying the claims and prophecies of its founders.

The wave of institute development continued for several decades after the Civil War and the number of teachers attending in the various states increased severalfold. The situation in Michigan is fairly typical. Eight institutes were held in this state in 1860, with 1251 individuals enrolled. A decade later the number of institutes had jumped to 16 and the attendance increased to 2005. During the next decade the growth was even more rapid, the number of institutes advancing from 16 to 65 and the attendance totaling 4482. Even when account is taken of the increase in the number of teachers in the state, the proportion who were subjected to institute experiences in 1880 was decidedly larger than in 1860. Similar conditions prevailed in other states [1] and the United States Commissioner reported 2003 institutes with an enrolled attendance of 138,946 for the year 1886–1887. It appeared to educators and critical observers that the institute had come to stay.

The nature of the programs undertaken in most states was not significantly different from that attempted before the Civil War. County superintendents, normal-school principals and instructors, and state superintendents of schools conducted the institutes and arranged the programs. [2] Then, as now, popular teachers and speakers were kept busy during the institute season and, as one author expressed it in 1900, "if the annals of the

[1] Ohio reported attendance at institutes to be 1294 in 1860 and 10,972 in 1880. In Illinois, the number of teachers attending institutes in 1869 was 4651 and in 1877 it was 8010.

[2] New York State developed an institute faculty, and in Massachusetts the agents of the State Board of Education devoted considerable time to institute programs.

institute were written in full, they would contain the names of many of the most eminent scholars and teachers, men of letters and men of science, of the last sixty years." [3]

Probably the greatest stimulus to the growth of institute work was the financial support provided in the various states and the penalties imposed in many counties and cities for nonattendance. By 1890 the institute was firmly embedded in school laws and most of the commonwealths gave it both legal recognition and financial aid. Tuition was usually free, although voluntary contributions by teachers were sometimes accepted in order to extend the length of the institute session and to provide better programs of instruction. Seven states out of eighteen in which county institutes were held in 1882–1883 made attendance compulsory; and in the case of city institutes, the prevailing practice was to require teachers to attend.

The value of the lectures and discussions depended in no small degree upon the wisdom and insight of the conductor and those associated with him in managing the program. Methods of teaching reading, arithmetic, geography, language, and the other subjects in the common-school curriculum constituted the chief subject matter of the typical institute session. These were supplemented by a few evening lectures of an inspirational character and by discussions of current state educational problems and issues. Because of the small amount of time set aside for institute instruction,[4] the work was exceedingly superficial and could not, by the widest stretch of the imagination, be considered an adequate substitute for normal-school training.

The programs of two Massachusetts institutes are shown on pages 363 and 364. The first one was a county program held in 1882, and the second one was presented in 1909 at an institute held in South Framingham. They show the time and attention devoted to various subjects and topics and indicate to some degree the modifications which were made in institute programs during the twenty-seven-year period 1882–1909.

[3] Hinsdale, B. A., "The Training of Teachers," in Butler, Nicholas M. (ed.), op. cit., p. 27.

[4] The time devoted to institutes varied materially. In most states, an annual session of from three to six days was held. In a few states, the institutes extended over a period of two to three weeks.

County Institute Program for October 5 and 6, 1882 [5]

Prepared by the Honorable J. W. Dickinson, Secretary of
Massachusetts State Board of Education

Wednesday evening			Thursday evening		
7.30	Lecture by Rev. Washington Gladden		7.00	General discussions	
			7.30	Lecture	
Thursday morning			***Friday morning***		
		Minutes			*Minutes*
10.00 to 10.10	Opening exercises..........	10	9.30 to 9.40	Opening exercises..........	10
10.10 to 11.00	Arithmetic analysis, fractions and percentage (Mr. George A. Walton)	50	9.40 to 10.30	Geography, plan of topical teaching.......... (Mr. Martin)	50
11.00 to 11.10	Recess........	10	10.30 to 10.40	Recess........	10
11.10 to 12.00	Drawing...... (Mr. Charles M. Carter)	50	10.40 to 11.30	Language and grammar...... (Mr. Dickinson)	50
			11.30 to 11.40	Recess........	10
Thursday afternoon			11.40 to 12.30	Mineralogy.... (Mr. Martin)	50
1.30 to 1.40	Questions proposed by members of the Institute..........	10	***Friday afternoon***		
1.40 to 2.30	Method of assigning lessons and hearing recitations....... (Mr. Dickinson)	50	2.00 to 2.10	Questions by members......	10
			2.10 to 3.00	Reading, elementary and advanced........ (Mr. Walton)	50
2.30 to 2.40	Recess........	10	3.00 to 3.10	Recess........	10
2.40 to 3.30	Botany, elementary course.... (Mr. George H. Martin)	50	3.10 to 4.00	School government and moral instruction..... (Mr. E. A. Hubbard)	50
3.30 to 3.40	Recess........	10			
3.40 to 4.30	Lessons in teaching color....... (Mr. Dickinson)	50			

The graded program provided in the South Framingham
schedule was a decided improvement over the one used in 1882,
where all teachers attending were compelled to listen to discussions whether or not they pertained directly to their own subject
or grade of instruction. In the brief time devoted to these lec-

[5] Smart, J. H., *Teachers' Institutes*, U. S. Bureau of Education, Circular of Information 1885, No. 2 (Washington, Government Printing Office, 1885), p. 205.

Program of Teachers' Institute under the Direction of the State Board
of Education, High School Building, South Framingham.
Wednesday, April 28, 1909 [6]

. . . .

9.10 A.M.: Opening exercises
9.20 A.M. to 10.10 A.M.:

Drawing, grades 1–3	Frederick L. Burnham, Agent of the Board
Geography, grades 4–6	Charles P. Sinnott, Bridgewater
History, grades 7–9	Arthur C. Boyden, Bridgewater
Uses of the recitation, high school	James W. MacDonald, Agent of the Board

10.20 A.M. to 11.10 A.M.:

Arithmetic, grades 1–3	John C. Gray, Chicopee
Language, grades 5–6	Miss Flora Kendall, Fitchburg
Arithmetic, grades 7–9	J. H. Carfrey, Wakefield
Mathematics, high school	Wallace E. Mason, N. Andover

11.20 A.M. to 12.10 P.M.:

Story telling, grades 1–3	Caroline G. Hagar, Fitchburg
Reading, grades 4–6	Mr. MacDonald
Geography, grades 7–9	Mr. Sinnott
History, high school	Mr. Boyden

Intermission

1.40 P.M. to 2.30 P.M.:

Language, grades 1–4	Miss Kendall
Drawing, grades 5–9	Mr. Burnham

2.45 P.M.
General address, "Hygiene," Dr. Thomas F. Harrington, Boston

tures, however, the instructors could scarcely do more than acquaint the listener with a point of view, and one wonders just how effective a program of this sort was in improving teaching in the public schools. The extravagant claims of those who

---

[6] Ruediger, William C., *Agencies for the Improvement of Teachers in Service*, U. S. Bureau of Education, Bulletin 1911, No. 3 (Washington, Government Printing Office, 1911), pp. 25–26.

sponsored the programs or participated in them seem quite unjustified when tested by reason or subjected to critical analysis.

Tradition and lack of imagination on the part of educators accounted for the persistence of the typical county and city institute after 1890. While full-time public normal schools were still unable to supply the rural districts with trained teachers, there was nothing to prevent the establishment of an agency which would lay greater emphasis on professional training than the institute could possibly hope to do. In fact, as a later discussion will reveal, summer schools were actually introduced before 1890. This in no way altered institute programs, however, which continued to emphasize their old training-school features and attempted to compete with the newly created summer schools.

The question of whether or not the institute had outlived its usefulness was not generally raised until after 1900. In fact, a survey of the status of Teachers' Institutes made by Ruediger in 1911 for the Federal Bureau of Education [7] indicated that they were in a most prosperous condition, if judged by the number of teachers enrolled and the amount of financial support provided by governmental agencies. With few exceptions, attendance was compulsory and the amount of money provided ranged from twenty-five dollars per county in Georgia to fifty thousand dollars for work in the State of New York. Great emphasis was placed in institute programs upon the needs of rural-school teachers and those engaged in the work of the elementary schools. County institutes were more popular and usually of longer duration than those in the cities. It was becoming increasingly apparent, with the development of expert supervision, summer schools, and municipal normal schools, that the old type of institute was no longer needed to advance the professional status of city teachers. This group was, therefore, among the first to be relieved of the compulsory-attendance requirement although, in some states, the institute "craze" was so widespread that no amount of logic could remove the legislation which imposed this agency upon districts regardless of need.

Beginning about 1910, a few of the states with the more adequate normal-school facilities and opportunities for summer-

[7] *Ibid.*

school study began to place less and less dependence upon institutes for the in-service preparation of teachers. In spite of the acknowledged superiority of other available agencies, however, institute supporters continued to resist the efforts of critical educators and laymen to abolish this outmoded medium for training teachers. In 1922 forty-four states were using the institute in one form or another, and in thirty of these states it was maintained by law.[8] A more recent discussion indicates some loss in status, but as late as 1933 twenty-six of the forty-eight states were still holding institutes on schooltime.[9]

That they ultimately are doomed to extinction seems certain, since the needs they were originally created to serve have largely disappeared. Whether or not they will reappear in some other form, such as refresher courses, conferences, or teachers' meetings, is a matter of conjecture.

SUGGESTED READINGS

DE LONG, LEO R., *City School Institutes in Pennsylvania* (Camp Hill, Pa., Ell Ess Dee, Educational Publishers, 1930).

LONMEN, GEORGINA, "The Teachers' Institute as an Agency for Training Teachers in Service," in National Education Association, *Addresses and Proceedings* (1922), Vol. LX, pp. 1141–49.

MILNE, JAMES M., *Teachers' Institutes; Their Past and Their Future* (Syracuse, N. Y., C. W. Bardeen, 1894).

RAY, E. E., "The Present Status of Teachers' Institutes," in *Ohio Schools*, Vol. VIII, No. 1 (July, 1930), pp. 14–15.

ROSS, CARMON, *The Status of County Teachers' Institutes in Pennsylvania* (University of Pennsylvania, Philadelphia, 1922), Ph.D. thesis.

RUEDIGER, WILLIAM C., *Agencies for the Improvement of Teachers in Service*, U. S. Bureau of Education, Bulletin 1911, No. 3 (Washington, Government Printing Office, 1911).

SMART, J. H., *Teachers' Institutes*, U. S. Bureau of Education, Circular of Information, 1885, No. 2 (Washington, Government Printing Office, 1885).

[8] National Education Association, *Addresses and Proceedings* (1922), Vol. LX, p. 1142.

[9] Jensen, Frank, "The Teacher Institute No Longer Serves a Major Purpose," in *The Nation's Schools*, Vol. XII, No. 3 (September, 1933), p. 50.

XXVI

Summer Schools

AN agency which gave promise from the beginning of supplementing normal schools and replacing institutes was the American summer school. This institution has some of the features of the normal school and some of the characteristics of the institute. With communities maintaining relatively short school years and long summer vacations, a golden opportunity existed to supply teachers with at least a part of the much-needed professional and academic training which educators and laymen had been so earnestly urging.

Strangely enough, the idea was not first projected by an administrator nor by a professor of pedagogics. Rather it was born in the mind of a Harvard scientist, Professor N. S. Shaler, who suggested to his colleague, Louis Agassiz, the establishment of a seaside laboratory at Nantucket for the benefit of university students and teachers of science in the secondary schools. Agassiz, acting upon this suggestion, issued a prospectus in 1872 of the first summer school in the United States. Because of its historic interest and its value as showing the general nature of the program to be undertaken, it is presented here in full: [1]

Museum of Comparative Zoology
Cambridge, Mass., December 14, 1872.

Programme of a course of instruction in natural history to be delivered by the seaside in Nantucket during the summer months, chiefly designed for teachers who propose to introduce the study into their schools, and for students preparing to become teachers.

"Zoology in general and embryology of the vertebrates," by L. Agassiz, director of the Museum.

---

[1] Willoughby, W. W., "The History of Summer Schools in the United States,"

"The extinct animals of past ages compared with those now living and the methods of identifying them," by N. S. Shaler, professor of paleontology in the Lawrence Scientific School.

"Comparative anatomy and physiology of the vertebrates," by Dr. B. G. Wilder, professor of anatomy and physiology in Cornell University, Ithaca, N. Y.

"The animals and plants living in deep waters, and the peculiar conditions of their existence," by L. F. de Pourtales, assistant in the U. S. Coast Survey.

"Embryology of the radiates," by A. Agassiz, assistant in the Museum of Comparative Zoology.

"Natural history and embryology of the mollusks," by . . . .

"How to make biological collections to illustrate the history of insects injurious to vegetation," by Dr. H. A. Hagen, professor of entomology in Harvard University.

"Natural history and embryology of the articulates," by Dr. A. S. Packard, professor of entomology in the Massachusetts Agricultural College.

"Natural history of the fishes and reptiles," by F. W. Putnam, general secretary of the American Association for the Advancement of Science.

"Natural history of birds and mammals," by J. A. Allen, assistant in the Museum of Comparative Zoology.

"On breeding, and nests and eggs of birds," by . . . .

"Practical exercises in the use of the microscope," by . . . .

"Instructions in drawing and painting of animals," by Paulus Roetter, artist in the Museum of Comparative Zoology.

"On fisheries and their management," by Prof. Spencer F. Baird, assistant secretary of the Smithsonian Institution.

"On fish breeding," by Theodore Lyman, assistant in the Museum of Comparative Zoology.

"The fauna of the North Atlantic, compared with one another, and with those of other parts of the world," by . . . .

"The plants of the sea," by . . . .

"The physics of the sea," by . . . .

"Physical hydrography," by Prof. W. Mitchell, assistant in the U. S. Coast Survey.

"Chemistry of feeding and breathing," by Prof. W. Gibbs, Rumford professor of physics in Harvard University.

---

in *Report of the Commissioner of Education, 1891–1892* (Washington, Government Printing Office, 1894), Vol. II, p. 899.

"Chemistry of the sea and air," by Prof. James Crafts, professor of chemistry in the Technological Institute, in Boston.

The terms of admission and the day of opening will be advertised as soon as all necessary arrangements in Nantucket can be made, including information concerning board, etc. A number of aquariums and the necessary apparatus to dredge in deep water will be provided. The superintendent of the U. S. Coast Survey and the U. S. Commissioner of Fisheries have promised their cooperation to the extent of their ability without interfering with the regular service of their departments. Profs. Shaler, Wilder, Packard, and Putnam, and perhaps others, may spend the whole, or nearly the whole, season in Nantucket, with a view to superintend the laboratory work, while the other gentlemen will stay there only part of the time, or as long as required by the share they are able to take in the course of instruction.

In behalf of the faculty of the Museum of Comparative Zoology in Cambridge, Mass.

L. Agassiz.

While the course was designed for teachers, the response was by no means overwhelming and only a few students enrolled.

Harper's, 1877

The First Summer School in America

The idea, however, was a fascinating one and a New York manufacturer, John Anderson, either through faith in Agassiz or in the possibilities of this new venture, offered to contribute the Island of Penikese, in Buzzards Bay, and fifty thousand dollars for the establishment and operation of a summer school of zoology to be directed by Agassiz. This school opened in 1873 with forty-three students. Unfortunately, Louis Agassiz died shortly after acquiring the island and the following year the school was directed by his son, Professor Alexander Agassiz. The project proved to be so expensive that it was abandoned after the second summer. Several other similar experiments were tried in New England and the Middle West, and a rather notable one at Johns Hopkins.[2] All these were on a small scale and enrolled only a few students each session. They are significant for our discussion only in that they were attended by teachers and that they stimulated other enterprising educators to attempt larger and more practical experiments.

CHAUTAUQUA

Probably the real genesis of the modern summer school was the Lake Chautauqua Institute established in 1874. This was originally a camp-meeting institute with a religious purpose, which was soon transformed into a Sunday-school assembly with considerable emphasis placed upon methods of teaching the Bible. Here normal-school procedures were introduced and the early programs of the assembly were devoted to Sunday-school work, Bible study, and conferences on methods of teaching. The attractive surroundings at Lake Chautauqua drew students and teachers from all over the United States. The sponsors of the Chautauqua movement were men of vision and, instead of confining the program to strictly religious topics, they saw an opportunity to present, in addition, a rich educational and cultural offering, thereby expanding the scope of the summer school to meet the needs of social, educational, and religious workers. The school became even more popular than the founders had anticipated, and by 1890 it embraced the following six separate and distinct departments:

---

[2] In 1876 a summer school of biology was established at Salem, Massachusetts; Harvard organized a summer school of botany in 1874; Bowdoin College conducted a summer session for students interested in botany, chemistry, and mineralogy in 1876; Syracuse, Cornell, Butler University, Concord School of Philosophy and Literature, and a few other isolated institutions began work in specialized areas about the same time. The North Carolina University conducted a summer normal school for teachers as early as 1877.

1. The Chautauqua Assembly, composed of summer meetings at Chautauqua, Sunday-school normal department, the school of language, and the Chautauqua Teachers' Retreat.
2. The Chautauqua Library and Scientific Circles.
3. The Chautauqua College of Liberal Arts, formerly known as Chautauqua University.
4. The Chautauqua School of Theology.
5. The Chautauqua Press.
6. The Chautauqua Extension and Summer Assemblies.

From the standpoint of the teaching profession, the Teachers' Retreat, opened in 1879, was the most significant segment of this great institution. Francis W. Parker was principal of this school, and the nature of the program is clearly indicated in the following description which appeared in the Chautauqua announcement in 1891: [3]

The faculty of the teachers' retreat will present and illustrate the system of teaching and training now in operation in the professional training class of the Cook County normal school, by talks on psychology, pedagogics, and methods, and lessons upon the principles and methods of teaching the natural sciences, geography, history, elocution, literature and number.

The distinctive feature of the professional training may be designated by the word concentration. All the teaching and training is concentrated upon the central subject of life and the laws of life, physical, mental, and moral.

All the talks and lessons of every teacher will be in the closest relation and under one common principle. The director will explain the principles of psychology and pedagogics, and each teacher in his or her department will illustrate and apply to practical schoolroom work the theory presented by the director.

Chautauqua also maintained a School of Physical Culture and a School of Music, both of which were well attended by teachers. Because of its association with Chautauqua, the Teachers' Retreat was probably unrivaled during the last two decades of the nineteenth century.

[3] Willoughby, W. W., *op. cit.*, p. 926.

MARTHA'S VINEYARD SUMMER INSTITUTE AND OTHER
EARLY EXPERIMENTS

A New England experiment, however, soon challenged
Chautauqua's supremacy. In 1878, four years after the Chautauqua venture was launched, Colonel Homer B. Sprague, Ph.D.,
at that time head of the Girls' High School in Boston, established
"The Martha's Vineyard Summer Institute." This school was
designed, especially, for the improvement of teachers in service.
It was to be five weeks in length, and the professors in each
department, men of universal talents in near-by colleges and
universities, were to receive whatever tuition was forthcoming,
the fee consisting of fifteen dollars per pupil for work in each
department. As many as two or more courses per student were
permitted but not encouraged. The schedule provided for class
lectures in the forenoons and for public lectures and entertainments in the afternoons and evenings. Friday evenings were
reserved for receptions and Saturdays for excursions and recreation.

The original plan called for courses in botany, French, geology
and numerology, natural history, German, industrial drawing,
Latin and Greek, zoology, elocution and English literature, and
pedagogics. Despite the apparent recognition of the importance
of offering pedagogy in a school of this nature, the subject was
not given the first year "owing," as one account says, "to the
modesty of Mr. Greenough," the instructor chosen to teach
Didactics, in not advertising the course as much as the rest.
Eighty students enrolled for the first session and the professors in
charge, at the end of the summer, voted unanimously to continue the project. Didactics was included in the offerings for
the first time in 1880. Despite some financial reverses suffered
during its infant years, this institution weathered the storm successfully and by 1890 it was in a flourishing condition. The department of education, which at first had been unable to attract
enough students to support a professor, became by 1890 "the
tail which wagged the dog." In 1888 a "school of methods"
was organized as a part of the Institute under the supervision of
Mr. A. W. Edson, agent of the Massachusetts Board of Educa-

tion. This department held a session of three weeks and was staffed by a dozen or more instructors, who gave courses in methods of instruction in the ordinary branches of the common schools. In 1889 there were three hundred and fifty students enrolled in the education department alone. The success of this innovation was so phenomenal that in 1890 a department of high-school methods was begun. For several years to come, the attendance at the Martha's Vineyard Institute was large and the school enjoyed an excellent reputation.

Somewhat comparable in scope and emphasis was the program of the National Summer School of Methods. This institution was organized in the early eighties and attracted large numbers of students from various parts of the United States. It was first conducted in Saratoga, New York, and was later transferred to Glens Falls. Other summer schools appeared at about this same time. The University of Wisconsin, under the auspices of the Wisconsin Teachers' Association, began a summer school in 1887. Indiana started summer instruction in 1889; Cornell, in 1892. The University of Chicago adopted the four-quarter-session plan in 1891. Several of the smaller colleges and schools were also open to students in the summertime and offered opportunities to teachers to advance their training.

One of the most successful of the pioneer summer schools was "The Summer School of the South" at Knoxville, under the auspices of the University of Tennessee. As early as 1902, two thousand students were enrolled in this great university summer school to study under the guidance of such eminent men as G. Stanley Hall, Walter H. Page, President Thompkins of the Chicago Normal College, and President Alderman of Tulane. The course of study included a wide variety of subjects with considerable emphasis on industrial and mechanical arts.[4] The school remained popular for several years and was a powerful influence in stimulating educational reforms in the South and in heightening the enthusiasm and interest of teachers.

By the turn of the century, many educators were looking to the summer school as the agency which promised most by way

[4] "The Summer School of the South," in *The Outlook*, August, 1902 (Vol. LXXI), pp. 894–96.

of improving the masses of poorly trained teachers in the profession.

CRITICISMS OF THE SUMMER-SCHOOL MOVEMENT

The summer-school movement was not entirely free of criticism. There were those who believed that teachers should keep away from pedagogues and pedagogics during the vacation months and give their souls a chance to expand. One educator, Dr. W. B. Harlow, writing in *The Academy* as early as 1886, opposed summer schools, saying, "During these times of recreation, the companionship of others of our own profession may be agreeable; but if this results in so narrowing our lives that no other topic but school can awaken our enthusiasm, let us for two months at least flee from one another as if we were in danger of catching the plague." He then asks the question: Are the majority of "true teachers, after ten months of faithful labor in crowded rooms" in a "fit condition to spend their vacation in brain work?" [5]

There were others who objected to the spreading of summer-school propaganda on the ground that the real students seek the university rather than the university seeking the students. No arguments of this character could stop a movement so fundamental to the improvement of American public-school teachers as the summer school. It is true that there were teachers who could profit more by vacations than by study, but they constituted but a small minority of the teaching personnel. The vast majority of classroom teachers had never graced the halls of a normal school and their only claim to professional skill was the modicum of learning they had received at the hands of institute instructors.

An analysis of summer-school statistics for the year 1895 shows that six weeks was the most frequent period of instruction provided, although the range extended from two weeks to four months. Apparently six-week sessions have always been popular, allowing, as they do, for brief vacation opportunities both before and after the period of intensive study.

[5] Harlow, W. B., "Summer Schools," in *The Academy: A Journal of Secondary Education* (Syracuse, N. Y., George A. Bacon, 1886), Vol. I, No. 4, p. 152.

Recognition of Summer-school Study by Certification Authorities

Prior to 1900 many of the summer schools had no well-established system of evaluating the work done by students and no clear-cut procedure for certificating or crediting the courses successfully passed. It was not uncommon for ambitious male teachers in those districts where the school terms were short to acquire a college education by attendance during the vacation months. Frequently these foresighted individuals were looking for a way of escape from the school business and were using teaching as a steppingstone to vocations which promised larger financial rewards. Generally speaking, however, teachers attended summer schools without aspiring to degrees, or without acquiring any academic or professional credits in the modern sense of the term. In some cases, when summer normal schools were substituted for institutes, teachers were required to attend in order to hold their jobs; in others, it was an asset in securing a better position.

As soon as the summer-school movement got well under way, state departments and other licensing agencies began to recognize summer-school attendance in their regulations for granting higher licenses or for extending old ones. A report by Ruediger, in 1911, shows that several states followed such a procedure. In Louisiana, for example, first-, second-, and third-grade certificates could be extended one year by attending a state summer normal school for nine weeks. Similarly, South Carolina renewed first- and second-grade certificates if the holder showed evidence of having attended an institute or summer school. Missouri and Texas both recognized summer-school study in their certification regulations, and Wisconsin stipulated six weeks' attendance at a professional school, with credit in two subjects, as a basis for renewal of second-grade certificates.

Even as late as 1910, however, there seemed to be no uniform policy pursued by public normal schools in the matter of granting credit toward diplomas for summer-school study. In several of the states, academic credit was allowed. In others, the advantages were chiefly related to certification and promotion.

Nebraska was rather unique in that it provided a well-developed system of junior normal schools, consisting of a course of study, progressive from summer to summer, which led to graduation and the elementary certificate.

Judging from the estimate made by Ruediger, the summer-school students in colleges and universities were a fairly heterogeneous group. He reported that fifty per cent of those enrolled in these schools were teachers and that approximately fifty-seven per cent of the total number of students were working for degrees.[6]

While the trend toward degree requirements and diplomas seems quite evident to one looking back over the history of professional education, it was by no means apparent in 1910. A great deal of confusion was caused by the wide variety of practices which prevailed, and some of our present-day teachers whose training antedates this transitional period from certificates by examination to those awarded on the basis of academic credit have suffered loss in status as a result. Colleges and universities now insist on records of credits earned and of the time spent in the pursuit of specific studies. This situation constitutes an embarrassment to some teachers whose aim in these earlier years was to acquire a particular teaching certificate for which frequently no prescribed course of study existed.

Growth in Summer-school Enrollment

Statistics as to the exact number of teachers attending summer schools in 1910 are not available—probably not more than 20,000 in universities and colleges. The enrollment in the summer normal schools was much larger than this. Texas alone reported an attendance of 12,965 in 1910; Wisconsin, 4000; Virginia, 5000; Tennessee, 2500 or more; and Nebraska, 1414. When the enrollments in other states, for which facts are not available, are added to the above figures, it is certain that the attendance of teachers at summer normal schools was far in excess of that reported for colleges and universities.[7]

In 1911 the United States Bureau of Education began to collect and report facts on summer schools. Unfortunately, teachers are not separated from total enrollments in the figures presented,

[6] Ruediger, W. C., *op. cit.*, pp. 51–52.　　　　[7] *Ibid.*

so that an accurate portrayal of trends for this group is not possible. Table 13 shows the number of men and women students enrolled in summer schools for the period 1911–1918.

Table 13. Students Enrolled in American Summer Schools, 1911–1918 [1]

Year	Men	Women	Total
1911	38,140	80,167	118,307
1912	46,657	95,560	142,217
1913	62,625	118,663	181,288
1914	77,455	141,339	218,794
1915	86,581	155,230	241,811
1916	68,347	134,023	202,370
1918	33,445	126,977	160,422
AVERAGE	59,036	121,704	180,744

[1] Adapted from "Summer Schools in 1918," in *Biennial Survey of Education, 1916–1918*, U. S. Bureau of Education, Bulletin 1919, No. 91 (Washington, Government Printing Office, 1921), p. 513.

Table 13 shows a marked increase in enrollment for both men and women from 1911 to 1915, after which the effects of the war are strikingly observable. The steady increase from 1911 to 1915 is largely due to the higher training requirements established for teachers by state departments of education. The summer-school movement had met with universal approval by 1915 and had, to a large extent, supplanted teachers' institutes as a means of improving the training qualifications of teachers.

Since the World War the enrollments in summer sessions of colleges, universities, and teacher-training institutions have increased significantly. In 1917 the number of students in the above schools was 132,683. By 1921 this number had jumped to 267,971 (an increase of 49.1 per cent), and in 1927 it had reached 383,855. The increase in summer-school enrollment in colleges and universities far exceeded that of teacher-training schools, the former rising from 54,624 in 1917 to 239,570 in 1927 (an increase of 228 per cent), and the latter increasing from 78,059 to 144,285 (or 87.4 per cent) during the ten-year period.[8]

[8] *Biennial Survey of Education, 1926–1928*, U. S. Office of Education, Bulletin 1930, No. 16, p. 434. These figures are not comparable to those presented in the previous table because the method of reporting was modified. The former included a number of Y. M. C. A. schools and other institutions not properly classified as teacher-training institutions or colleges and universities.

There are several possible explanations for the unusual increase in college and university enrollment and for the less rapid gain in attendance at teacher-training summer schools. One might assume at first glance that other vocations and professions were more attractive during this period than education and that students were less enthusiastic about courses in education. Adequate statistics on enrollment in education courses are not available for the earlier years of this period [9] but the upward changes in certification requirements which took place during this decade, coupled with the trend in recent years, make such a conclusion unfounded. A more rational interpretation is that students shifted from teacher-training institutions to colleges and universities because of the wider offerings and superior faculties available in the latter. This was the period when advanced degrees first became popular and higher institutions were transformed to meet the demand. Education departments in colleges and universities made great strides after the World War in improving and expanding faculty personnel, course offerings, and library facilities. While some teacher-training schools are now equipped to prepare students for Master's and Doctor's degrees, the number is still relatively small.

The peak in summer-school enrollment was reached in 1931, the total for the 555 colleges, universities, and teacher-training institutions reporting amounting in that year to 422,754.[10] Of this number, 271,095 (or 64.1 per cent) were enrolled in courses in education. The effect of the depression was reflected in the enrollments in 1932, and by 1933 the total number of summer-school students had shrunk from an all-time high point reached in 1931 to 303,754 (a loss of nearly 30 per cent). During the past few years a slight upward trend has been indicated, and the future depends almost entirely upon the economic status of the profession and the degree to which confidence in the financial stability of the country is restored.

The summer-school trek, which, to foreign observers, has been an interesting phenomenon in American education, has

[9] Published data for the years 1926 to 1931 show a decided increase during this period in the proportion of students taking summer courses in education.

[10] *Journal of the National Education Association*, November, 1932 (Vol. XXI), p. 258. The total number of summer schools in 1932 was 565.

been stimulated by several administrative measures. Perhaps the most powerful influence has been the state certification regulations which have been undergoing almost constant revision since the inception of the summer school. The prescription of degrees and the requirement of specific courses in education are now almost universal and new members of the profession, especially, are compelled to meet these advanced requirements in order to receive licenses. Some states have laid out programs of study which must be met within a specified period of time by all teachers whose educational qualifications are inferior. These impositions have aroused considerable opposition on the part of the older teachers whose training antedates the present generation and for whom college or university study holds no appeal. Public sentiment, however, seems favorably disposed toward the upward movement and the trend seems definitely to be in the direction of lifting the masses of teachers to new academic and professional heights.

A second administrative device which has encouraged summer-school attendance has been salary recognition by local boards of education for increased training. Some communities give bonuses to teachers for summer-school attendance; others have adopted what is commonly known as the "single-salary" schedule, by which teachers are paid in accordance with the amount of training and experience they have, regardless of the position they hold in the school system. The incentives provided in this type of schedule have been effective in raising the general training levels of teachers.

Still a third factor has been supervisory and administrative suggestion which, in some instances, has amounted to coercion. The indifferent and lazy teachers have been aroused from their intellectual slumbers by personal conferences with supervisory officers, who have stressed the need of teachers' keeping abreast of modern educational theory and have pointed out the vulnerable points in their training. While this is perhaps the last measure to be employed and the least desirable procedure to be followed, it has been found useful in certain stubborn cases that failed to respond voluntarily.

The summer activities of teachers have become an important

element in programs of supervision. There is a noticeable tendency to provide teachers with guidance in the selection of courses and to outline programs of study which have a direct bearing upon the grade and type of work in which teachers are engaged. This has been increasingly necessary with the wide extension in summer-school offerings and the tendency on the part of some teachers to select "snap" courses for credit.

Colleges, universities, and teacher-training institutions have broadened the scope of their programs in an attempt to care for the needs of every type of teacher in the modern school system. The work is not always restricted to the campus but includes travel courses, field trips, summer camps, and specially arranged conferences as well. While methods courses and the traditional educational offerings in psychology, philosophy, and subject matter are still the *pièce de résistance* of the summer-school curriculum, there are numerous other items on the educational menu which are of great interest and worth to teachers. Considerable efforts in recent years have been made to broaden the teacher's horizon, to stimulate her to study and reflect about the relation of her work to society, and to deepen her understanding of political science, economics, and sociology. While the proponents of these more recently added courses have been accused of introducing irrelevant subject matter into the already diffused program of studies, the popularity of the courses, together with the enthusiastic testimonials of students, have removed any initial doubts which college administrators may have had with respect to their efficacy. No one acquainted with the complex problems of public education in the United States can doubt the contribution of the American summer school to the improvement of teaching and the welfare of children. That it has failed to achieve all that educators have expected or even claimed must be admitted, and that its critics have not been at a loss to find vulnerable points upon which to launch their attacks is also granted. But when the advantages and achievements of the summer school are compared with the acknowledged weaknesses of this institution, the balance is clearly on the credit side.

Whether or not the American summer school will be replaced, like the institute, by some other agency is a matter of conjecture.

At the present time there is no indication of a waning interest. It seems more probable that the summer school will undergo modification to keep pace with the changing needs of educational workers, that the standard of scholarship will be raised for those working for advanced degrees, that laboratory provisions will be expanded, that model and demonstration schools will be more generally provided, and that supplementary travel and field courses will be added to enrich the experience of students. In spite of the remarkable progress which has been made since 1918 in improving the professional training of teachers, the task is only half completed. Thousands of rural teachers have less than two years of training above high-school graduation, and even in the cities there is still plenty of room for improvement. Beyond this pressing necessity of raising present training levels to greater heights, there will remain in education a demand on the part of even the best-educated teachers for summer-school opportunities, in order that they may keep abreast of the rapid changes in social life and their implications for public education.

SUGGESTED READINGS

AVENT, JOSEPH E., *Summer Session in State Teachers Colleges as a Factor in the Professional Education of Teachers* (Richmond, Va., The William Byrd Press, 1925).

JUDD, C. D., *The Summer School as an Agency for the Training of Teachers in the United States*, Contributions to Education (Nashville, Tenn., George Peabody College, No. 3, 1921).

Report of the Commissioner of Education, 1894–1895, Vol. II, pp. 1483–1503. (A check list of American summer schools.)

RUEDIGER, WILLIAM C., *Agencies for the Improvement of Teachers in Service*, U. S. Bureau of Education, Bulletin 1911, No. 3 (Washington, Government Printing Office, 1911), pp. 51–52.

"Summer Sessions for Teachers," in *National Survey of the Education of Teachers*, Vol. III, U. S. Office of Education, Bulletin 1933, No. 10 (Washington, Government Printing Office, 1935), pp. 403–41.

WILLOUGHBY, W. W., "History of Summer Schools in the United States," in *Report of the Commissioner of Education, 1891–1892* (Washington, Government Printing Office, 1894), Vol. II, pp. 893–959.

XXVII

University Extension

CREDIT for the first extension course in America goes to Professor Benjamin Silliman of Yale College, who, in 1808, gave a series of popular lectures in chemistry for the benefit of a class of "ladies" and "gentlemen" in New Haven. The class met in the college laboratory and the lectures were accompanied by experiments. Silliman extended his work in 1834 to Hartford, where he gave a course in geology. His lectures there were well attended, the enrollment numbering three or four hundred of the most intelligent citizens of the town. The success of the enterprise is evidenced by the fact that during the following year Professor Silliman offered courses in Salem, Lowell, and Boston. The Boston course, sponsored by the Society for the Promotion of Useful Knowledge, brought both prestige and money to the Yale professor. The subscriptions amounted to two thousand dollars, and the enthusiasm with which his lectures were received is well expressed in Mr. Abbott Lawrence's comment that "no man had ever drawn together in Boston such audiences, both for number and character."

Silliman continued his extension activities until 1859 and was most influential in developing a favorable mind-set toward adult education. In spite of his phenomenal success, however, the university extension movement did not spring from his activities. Paralleling the work of this Yale scientist was the educational program of the American Lyceum,[1] the real forerunner of university extension. This medium for disseminating learning flourished in the Northern and Eastern states before

[1] The word "lyceum" comes from the Greek *Lykeion*. It was a grove in the suburbs of Athens originally devoted to military exercises, but in the time of Aristotle it was employed by him for the delivery of lectures.

the Civil War and was conspicuous as an institution in the West and the South between 1865 and 1890. The Redpath Lyceum Bureau of Chicago was probably more influential than any other single agency in promoting the lecture movement. This bureau, through efficient administration, reduced the cost of lyceum lectures so that they were within the reach of the average man's pocketbook. But these ten-day schools were destined soon to give way to more systematic programs of instruction. Two agencies, the summer school and university extension, both closely affiliated with colleges and universities, gradually supplanted the lyceum as an institution of serious study.

Strange as it may seem in light of Yale's acknowledged success with extension activities, neither college administrators nor professors were primarily responsible for the spread of this new movement. Instead, the idea was first presented publicly to the American Library Association, in 1887, by Professor Herbert B. Adams of Johns Hopkins University. Professor Adams, in his address before this group, dwelt at length upon the English scheme of university extension and suggested its introduction into America through the avenue of public libraries. His remarks were not wasted upon an unappreciative audience. The public librarian at Buffalo, New York, adopted the idea almost immediately and instituted a series of twelve lectures dealing with important economic questions of the day. Librarians in several other cities, of which St. Louis was perhaps the most conspicuous, were also favorably impressed by Professor Adams's suggestions and proceeded to inaugurate university extension in their respective communities.

The Chautauqua Summer School, a thriving institution by 1888, also contributed to the development of this new movement. The professed objects of Chautauqua were in harmony with the purposes of university extension and many of the leaders in the former movement, with which Dr. W. R. Harper was actively affiliated, were later engaged in introducing and directing university-extension programs.

The Brooklyn teachers in 1888, under the guidance of Mr. S. T. Steward, were aroused to action and outlined a proposal which combined certain features of the English extension program with the Chautauqua reading courses. Some of the leading professors of Harvard, Yale, Princeton, and Columbia participated in the preparation of syllabi for this work and in the general direction of the program.

The event which weighed more heavily than all others in giving sanction to the movement was the appropriation by the New York State legislature, in 1891, of ten thousand dollars for organizing university extension under the University of the State of New York. Melvil Dewey, at one time (1888) chief librarian at Columbia University and later secretary of the University of the State of New York and director of the State Library, was largely responsible for the leadership which New York State was to assume in the advancement of university-extension programs. Dewey had been president of the American Library Association and was a close student of library problems. He addressed the University Convocation on the subject of university extension in Albany in 1888 and again in 1889. On the latter occasion a committee was appointed to report on a program for carrying out the work, "including a plan for lending to communities, for use during university extension courses, suitable libraries, collections, apparatus and illustrations."

The following year, 1890, a committee of college presidents was appointed to confer with the regents and this group brought in a favorable report on university extension in February, 1891, suggesting that it be supervised by the state and that high standards of work be maintained.

The traveling library, an English creation, was one of the chief features of the New York system. During the year 1898–1899 the program included thirty-six extension lecture courses at twelve different centers. While the courses were considered to be of great pedagogical value, there were many practical difficulties that stood in the way of realizing the objectives of the founders. It was difficult to engage satisfactory lecturers; local communities were often unwilling or unable to lend the necessary financial assistance, and university and college professors found travel and the extra work arduous.

Philadelphia and Chicago were the two other bright spots in the early history of university extension, the American Society in Philadelphia constituting one of the most influential extension organizations in the East and the University of Chicago program, under President Harper, reaching, according to James E. Russell, "the pedagogic high-water mark of university extension in the world." [2]

University-extension courses were first offered at Teachers College, Columbia University, in 1894 and the report of extension activities for that year is in striking contrast to those of recent years. In view of the role which this institution has played in the improvement of teachers in service, and the large numbers of students who have been enrolled in extension courses, the lectures and subjects, together with the average attendance at classes, is given here in full for 1894.[3]

Lecturer	*Subject*	*Average Attendance at Classes*
Pres. Walter L. Hervey	Philosophy of Education	10
Clarence E. Meleney	Science and Art of Teaching	14
Angeline Brooks	Kindergarten (Mothers' class)	19
John F. Woodhull	Chemistry and Physics	30
Anna F. Shryver	Geology	21
Frank T. Baker	English Literature	15
Helen Kinne	Cooking	27
Mary S. Woolman	Sewing	17
Charles A. Bennett	Manual Training (Woodworking)	8
J. F. Lewis	Modeling	7
John H. Mason	Constructive Drawing	3
Ida S. Robinson	Freehand Drawing	15

In only a few instances, however, do we find special attention given by university-extension departments to the training of public-school teachers before 1900. Chicago University worked out a cooperative arrangement with the city board of education and offered seventeen courses of lectures in thirteen different public-school buildings. Such branches of knowledge as history, economics, and political science were included in the extension

[2] Russell, James E., "Extension of University Teaching in England and America," in *University of the State of New York Extension Bulletin*, No. 10 (October, 1895), pp. 182–83.

[3] "Extension Department Report for 1895," in *University of the State of New York Extension Bulletin*, No. 17 (March, 1897), p. 345.

offerings for schoolteachers. In 1898–1899 free lectures for adults were instituted in Philadelphia by the American Society for the Extension of University Teaching in cooperation with the board of education, and were held in well-known school buildings. These lectures were aimed chiefly at public-school teachers and their purpose was to acquaint the listeners with Philadelphia's contributions to art, history, science, literature, jurisprudence, commerce, and philanthropy.

An occupational analysis of those enrolled in extension courses in 1900 would have been helpful in appraising the contribution of university extension to the welfare of various vocational groups and particularly of teachers. Unfortunately, only fragmentary bits of statistical information are available. The subjects offered in university extension were sometimes of such a character as to be of special interest and worth to teachers. For example, St. Patrick's Cathedral, under the auspices of the Cathedral Library in New York City, offered a course on Psychology. Even though the New York State Department of Education had not reported, as they did in 1897, that this course "was largely attended by public school teachers," it might logically have been surmised. M. V. O'Shea gave an extension course in Rochester on Child Study and Frank McMurry one in Methods in Pedagogy. The average attendance in each of these courses was between four hundred and five hundred, larger by far than the other courses offered in Rochester during the same year. Unquestionably, many of those enrolled were schoolteachers. Pedagogical courses did not bulk large, however, in the total offering. Of approximately two hundred and twenty subjects or courses listed in the report of the Extension Department of the University of the State of New York in 1893, only seven were in the field of education.[4]

With the exceptions just noted, university extension did not focus much attention upon the needs of public-school teachers. Courses designed for the latter appear to have been unusual, for the leading discussions of the movement prior to the beginning of the twentieth century are conspicuous by the absence of any mention of the professional improvement of teachers through

[4] *University of the State of New York Extension Bulletin* (1893), p. 1487.

this new medium. That teachers attended and profited by extension lectures in various sections of the country seems likely, but it was not primarily to serve the needs of this group that this institution was originally designed.

There were observers in 1900 who believed that the university-extension movement was a failure and that it had not justified its early promise. With the possible exceptions of Philadelphia and Chicago, the lecturers were something of a disappointment. They had received no special training for this extramural work, and so accustomed were they to imparting information and extracting it from students that they were at a loss in a situation where the audience attended voluntarily, if at all, and responded to questions only because they wanted to. As Lyman Powell so aptly put it, the extension teacher "must be preacher also, driving home his message by the blows of oratory, overcoming inertia the university knows naught of, the inertia of men and women worn and jaded by a day's routine, creating interest where no interest is, leading souls from the lowlands of vulgarity

> High up the mount where guile
> Dissolves in fire that burns the dross away." [5]

There were criticisms also that the "university on wheels" was consuming so much of the time and energy of the staff that its major work at the home office was being neglected. Professors whose academic careers were most promising were being sacrificed to mass education. The extension of the university to rich and poor alike might be sound philosophical doctrine, but until enough teachers could be prepared to staff the public schools university extension looked like robbing children to pay their parents. When confronted with the argument that English experience with university extension had been generally successful, critics answered with the retort that conditions were different in England. There was no shortage of teachers there—public education being a misnomer. To these skeptics, no amount of intellectual stimulation furnished to small bands of individuals here and there could possibly offset the harm which would

[5] Powell, Lyman P., "Ten Years of University Extension," in *Atlantic Monthly*, September, 1901 (Vol. LXXXVIII), p. 395.

result from teachers' neglecting their own classrooms and laboratories for the field.

In 1900, then, there were a few doubting Thomases who presaged an unhappy future for university extension. The optimists, however, were in the majority and their enthusiasm was undiminished, in spite of many weaknesses which had come to the surface since the first extension experiment began in New York State nearly ten years before.

From the standpoint of the popularity of university extension, the decade between 1890 and 1900 was probably superior to the one which immediately followed. At least it was a topic of greater interest to the people in the nineties and created more discussion and comment than at any succeeding period. Figures showing the number of students enrolled in extension courses for these early years are not available and would be difficult to interpret even if they existed. Extension was not limited to lectures. In some states it included study clubs, correspondence courses, traveling schools, and institute work. In fact, almost any activity which could not be classified in a recognized division of a university went under the name of extension, and much of this work was very elementary in character. These varied activities represented different amounts of study and instruction. Comparative statistics on university extension, therefore, have relatively little meaning. Reber reported that fifty-four colleges, universities, and other agencies were doing extension work of some kind in 1910 and that twenty-two of these institutions were offering opportunities to extension students to earn credit.[6]

This is a conservative estimate of the number of institutions that were engaged in extension work at the above date (1910). Chicago stood head and shoulders above any other university in the scope of its extension activities, the number of persons in attendance at lectures exceeding fifty-three thousand in 1907–1908.[7]

The matter of accrediting the work taken in university extension has been a perplexing problem from the beginning and no

----

[6] Reber, Louis E., "University Extension," in Association of American Universities, *Journal of Proceedings and Addresses*, 1910, pp. 57–58.

[7] Extension work by Chicago University in 1907–1908 was carried on in twenty-eight states.

uniform policy exists with regard to it. Individual universities, for the most part, have adjusted the credentials in light of their own campus standards. After-hour classes (those held in the late afternoon, evening, or on Saturday morning) are not technically a part of university extension, since they are held within the walls of the university in contrast to the off-campus courses. The conditions of admission to these classes are the same as those to all other regular university courses. The after-hour class has been especially popular in the large cities and, despite certain obvious limitations inherent in work-study programs of teachers, it has been second only to the summer school as an agency in improving teachers in service.

Both university-extension and correspondence courses have developed rapidly since 1910, which is partially accounted for by the growing tendency of colleges to offer credit for such courses. The United States Bureau of Education reported a total enrollment of 195,549 students in extension courses in 1930, an increase of 179.2 per cent over the preceding ten-year period. An even larger gain was made in the number of students enrolled in correspondence study, the registration advancing from 9343 in 1920 to 88,417 in 1930. These figures do not connote much beyond an expressed interest on the part of citizens to improve their educational background.

The present significance of university extension to teachers is not easy to appraise. On the positive side, the bringing of staff members to the local school system has encouraged many teachers to continue their professional study and has led to numerous modifications in teaching practice.

There are a number of practical courses which can be given much more effectively in the field than at the university, and supervisors and principals can supplement their own efforts to improve instruction with specific extension courses. The local school situation offers, further, a splendid laboratory for weighing theories and experimenting with progressive methods under the guidance of specialists.

Many universities attempt to supply library materials to suit the needs of the various courses. This saves the student's time and simplifies the task of class preparation. There is another feature of university extension which has its advantages. This is the homogeneity of the study groups. Teachers in the same school system have usually had certain experiences in common; they are working toward similar objectives, and are well acquainted with their fellow students and with the resources of the community.

While university extension has thrived because of these favorable conditions, there are many educators who believe that the results have not been altogether salutary. These critics hold that extension standards have been low; that library facilities have been, by the very nature of the situation, pitifully inadequate; that the extension staff is not commensurate in training and ability with the regular faculty members of the university; and that much of the work offered has no relationship to the practical problems of the field and can be given more profitably on the campus than in a local school building. There is a tendency for extension-staff members also to be overworked, fatigued, and ill prepared for the assignments which they have accepted.

Many of the criticisms are valid and constitute a direct challenge to the universities either to curtail their overexpanded programs or to improve the quality of the work offered. At the present time a limited number of field-extension courses can be credited toward a degree in most universities. The balance of the work must be taken either in residence or in after-hour classes. But regardless of these restrictions, there would seem to be no justification for lowering standards for students taking courses for credit. The solution would seem to lie in the limitation of field courses to those which can be given more efficiently off the campus than on and which require high standards of achievement from individuals taking the work. Unless extension directors are vigilant with respect to standards of instruction, the movement will come more and more into disrepute and eventually will fall of its own weight.

TEACHERS' READING CIRCLES

An agency for the improvement of teachers in service which is rapidly passing out of existence is the Teachers' Reading Circle.

This institution seems to have had its origin in a London "society to encourage home study," formed about 1870. Massachusetts experimented with the idea first, in 1873; and it took root in New York in 1878–1879, when the great Chautauqua Literary and Scientific Circle was founded. These societies were not limited to teachers nor were the books selected for reading directed primarily to their interests and needs. The reading circle had such great possibilities for adding both to the cultural and to the technical knowledge of its members that educators looked with favor upon it as an instrument for heightening the understanding of schoolteachers. In Ohio, "a common course of reading" was mapped out for teachers in 1882 and, in order to introduce some uniformity into the program, reading clubs were organized. Wisconsin adopted a similar plan at about the same time, and by 1886–1887 at least a dozen states had formed State Teachers' Reading Circles.[8] It was estimated by the Bureau of Education in 1887 that at least seventy-five thousand teachers in the United States were reading, methodically and systematically, books bearing upon professional subject matter and general culture.

Teachers' reading circles were usually linked up with the state teachers' associations. The latter chose directors and boards of management to lay out the course and direct the work of the circle. It was customary for the controlling board to prescribe a course of study (sometimes four years in length), to secure books at reduced rates, to prepare lists of the best educational publications, to advise as to methods of study, to administer examinations on the reading done, and finally to certificate the progress of students and grant them diplomas upon completion.

The course of study usually appeared in the official organ of the state teachers' association and in the county and local papers. The list on page 392, used in Ohio in 1886–1887, indicates the general scope and character of the studies prescribed.[9]

---

[8] Ruediger claims that in 1888 there were twelve state reading circles, although a U. S. Bureau Report in 1886–1887 estimated twenty.

[9] *Report of the Commissioner of Education, 1886–1887* (Washington, Government Printing Office, 1888), Vol. I, p. 405.

I. Psychology. Sully's *Teachers' Handbook of Psychology.*

II. Literature. "Hamlet" and "As You Like It"; selections from Wordsworth.

III. History. Barnes' *Brief General History of the World,* or Thalheimer's *General History.*

IV. Political Economy. Gregory's *Political Economy,* or Chapin's *First Principles of Political Economy;* with at least one educational periodical.

State examinations of the work covered were given in most states at the end of the course, and certificates and diplomas awarded.

In addition to State Reading Circles, there were a few which claimed to be national in character. One of these, the Teachers' National Reading Circle, was incorporated in New York State and announced its intention of preparing courses, giving examinations, and awarding certificates. While this appeared to be the next logical step to take after experience with state and local organizations, the National Reading Circle never commanded as much interest and attention as the state agencies. Between 1890 and 1910 reading circles were very popular in the United States. Ruediger reported in 1911 that thirty-five states had State Teachers' Reading Circles and two other states, Florida and Pennsylvania, had County Reading Circles. The average membership in twenty-three states for which information was available comprised approximately thirty-one per cent of the teachers, the range extending from four to one hundred per cent.[10]

In most of the states (twenty-seven) the certificates and diplomas earned by teachers in reading-circle courses either counted in teachers' examinations or were recognized by the state department of education in renewing and granting teaching licenses. Six of the states gave legal recognition to these clubs through a mandate to the state superintendent, state board of education, institute director, or other officials, to organize and encourage the formation and operation of reading circles. It was this legal sanction and the recognition given to

[10] Ruediger, William C., *op. cit.,* pp. 92–97.

reading circles in certification regulations which insured the success of the movement.

With the extension of improved teacher-training facilities and the increasing number of teachers attending state teachers' colleges and normal schools, the need for reading circles has been steadily reduced. Institutions of this type, however, have a tendency to persist long after their usefulness has disappeared. This is particularly true of those agencies which have been officially recognized in the law and have become an integral part of the administrative machinery. Reading-circle certificates were honored in many states in renewing teachers' licenses and in issuing certificates. To continue the process was to follow the line of least resistance and to remain popular with that large body of teachers whose training was markedly below standard.

As late as 1925, stimulated by the credit feature included in the arrangement, teachers' reading circles were still thriving in about half of the states.[11] State departments of education either sponsored or conducted the work, assisted by various related organizations such as state teachers' associations, extension divisions of state universities, state library commissions, and state reading-circle boards.

Judging from reading-circle lists, reading for general culture in 1925 had given way largely to reading for professional improvement. Books on psychology, methods, philosophy, school administration, and sociology dominated the prescription lists. With the presses turning off scores of books almost annually in each of these fields since 1920, reading-circle boards have had a difficult time in preparing their lists. Because of the lack of uniformity in procedure and the difficulty of appraising the values derived from reading-circle activities, the practice of renewing teachers' certificates on the basis of reading-circle diplomas has been discontinued in many states. As soon as

---

[11] According to the author's interpretation of Home Education Circular, No. 7, of the United States Bureau of Education, Department of the Interior (March, 1925), *Teachers' and Pupils' Reading Circles*, by Ellen C. Lombard, the following states had State Teachers' Reading Circles or the equivalent in 1925: Alabama, Arkansas, Colorado, Delaware, Florida, Idaho, Illinois, Indiana, Kansas, Kentucky, Louisiana, Michigan, Minnesota, Montana, North Carolina, Ohio, Oregon, South Dakota, Tennessee, Vermont, Virginia, Washington, West Virginia, and Wisconsin.

certification is divorced from reading circles, the latter agency will die.[12]

Reading circles, along with institutes and teacher-training high schools, have served a useful purpose in the education of American teachers. None of these agencies, however, at any time, has been equipped to make a fundamental contribution to the preparation of teachers. They were created to meet temporary emergencies and have either made room or will eventually do so for more permanent training institutions.

SUGGESTED READINGS

ADAMS, HERBERT B., "Educational Extension in the United States," in *Report of the Commissioner of Education, 1899–1900* (Washington, Government Printing Office, 1901), Vol. I, pp. 275–379.

HARRIS, WILLIAM T., "The Place of University Extension in American Education," in *Report of the Commissioner of Education, 1891–1892* (Washington, Government Printing Office, 1894), Vol. II, pp. 743–51.

LOMBARD, ELLEN C., *Teachers' and Pupils' Reading Circles*, U. S. Bureau of Education, Home Education Circular, No. 7 (Washington, Government Printing Office, 1925).

RUEDIGER, WILLIAM C., *Agencies for the Improvement of Teachers in Service*, U. S. Bureau of Education, Bulletin 1911, No. 3 (Washington, Government Printing Office, 1911), pp. 53–59, 93–97.

RUSSELL, JAMES E., "Extension of University Teaching in England and America," in *University of the State of New York Extension Bulletin*, No. 10 (October, 1895).

"Training of Teachers," in *Report of the Commissioner of Education, 1886–1887* (Washington, Government Printing Office, 1888), pp. 404–6.

---

[12] From a questionnaire sent by the author in June, 1938, to twenty states reported by the Federal Office of Education as having State Teachers' Reading Circles in 1931, it appears that only ten states are now using this agency as a means of improving teachers in service. These states are: Colorado, Florida, Idaho, Illinois, Kansas, Nebraska, Ohio, Virginia, West Virginia, and Wisconsin.

XXVIII

The Development of Method

AT the close of the Civil War and for several decades following it, the Oswego plan of object teaching, based on the theories of Pestalozzi, was the prevailing method of instruction in the progressive schools of America. As has been indicated previously, Edward A. Sheldon was the father of this movement and his training and demonstration schools at Oswego, New York, paved the way for the introduction of object-teaching methods. The new theory of instruction spread like wild fire and became, within a few years after its importation from England, the accepted teaching technique in the elementary grades.[1] Real experiences with objects and descriptions of these experiences were the essential elements in the Oswego plan. Sense-perception lessons replaced the dull, uninteresting classroom practices of former years, and oral instruction subordinated or eliminated book study in the lower grades.

The educational significance of the Oswego movement is hard to assay. It is certain that it placed greater responsibilities upon teachers than did the traditional methods of recitation hearing. Since oral instruction was one of the essential features of the Pestalozzian methodology, teachers had to become active instructors of groups of children. Lessons had to be planned in advance, objects selected, purposes conceived, information organized and learned—the teacher, in other words, had to show some initiative and be constantly on the *qui vive* to see that children understood the words used in the textbooks and in the classroom discussions. Methods of instruction in language, elementary science, home geography, and primary arithmetic

[1] The English pattern, a somewhat formalized type of object teaching, rather than the Prussian, was introduced into America.

were either created or greatly improved by the application of Pestalozzian principles.

Object teaching constituted a great advance over the formalism of words, which dominated teaching in the elementary schools during the first half of the nineteenth century. The new procedures, however, were not entirely free of criticism. Tendencies toward formalism appeared even in the work of Pestalozzi and his disciples. It was held, for example, as an inflexible rule that in education we should proceed from the simple to the complex. Teachers, in attempting to carry out this formula, frequently lost sight of children's interests and differences in capacity. Pestalozzi, in his efforts to "psychologize instruction," reduced much of it to a mechanical routine, and in the hands of unimaginative teachers the results were pernicious. Emphasis on the mastery of each step before proceeding to the next led to practices which were equally as harmful as the textbook methods of traditional schoolmasters. Examples of this were the synthetic method of teaching reading, first using drills on the letters, then syllables, words, phrases, etc., and the Grube method of teaching arithmetic in which each number was considered as an individual and all possible operations—addition, subtraction, multiplication, and division—were mastered with it before taking up the next number. It was customary to spend the first year on the numbers from one to ten and the first three years on the numbers up to one hundred.

This process of having the teacher analyze each subject into a graduated series of elements to be learned by pupils in their proper order probably had its advantages in situations where teachers were not slaves to routine. Unfortunately, the training and experience of most instructors led only too naturally to a stilted methodology.

When appraised in the light of twentieth-century standards, the Oswego plan has but little to commend it. Much of it has been demonstrated to be unsound psychologically. Measured, however, in terms of the educational practice and thoughts of Sheldon's generation, the Oswego movement was a marked step forward. Its greatest contribution was the subordination of the textbook and the establishment of a new theory of teaching. A secondary result, which should not be minimized, was the stimulation which Pestalozzi's theories gave to the study of education. Attention was focused upon methodology; theories were challenged and professional interests awakened.

The Oswego plan was an important topic of study in normal schools for nearly thirty years. Critic teachers trained at Oswego were employed by teacher-training institutions all over the United States, and whither they went the gospel of Pestalozzi went also. Here and there voices were raised in criticism, but it was not until about 1890, when the Herbartians came into power in the United States, that the Oswego movement faded into insignificance.

FROEBEL'S INFLUENCE ON TEACHING PROCEDURES

Before turning to the methods expounded by the followers of Herbart, a word needs to be said in behalf of another great foreign educator, Friedrich Froebel, the founder of the kindergarten. His efforts were highly beneficial to American education between 1870 and 1890. It is not within our province to discuss the theories of Froebel except to say that he was an enthusiastic disciple of Pestalozzi and that some of his theories involved metaphysical elements which were never seriously accepted by his most intelligent and successful followers. Froebel was largely responsible for two innovations in practice in the United States, beyond the ones attributed to Pestalozzi. They were: (1) the organization of school training based on motor activity, and (2) the incorporation of active social participation as one of the most prominent phases of school life.

While Rousseau had emphasized the importance of physical activity as a means of child development, it was Froebel who introduced it as the basis of learning. Every child, according to Froebel, "boy and youth, whatever his condition or position in life, should devote daily at least one or two hours to some serious activity in the production of some definite external piece of work." Drawing, domestic activities, gardening, building, paper cutting, modeling, and pasteboard work were means of expression to be utilized in the educational process. Froebel attempted to systematize play activities and organized a series

Harper's, 1878

"THE WINDMILL"

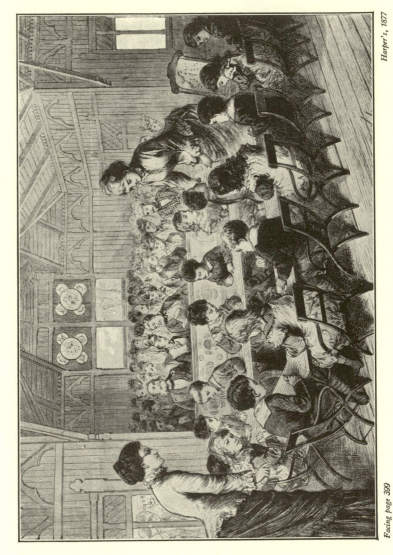

A KINDERGARTEN TRAINING SCHOOL

Harper's, 1877

of playthings which were designated either as "gifts" or "occupations." [2] They included a sphere, a cube, a cylinder, soft balls, small cubes or blocks, sticks, paper, and certain other materials for modeling, weaving, or drawing. According to Froebel, such materials encouraged and facilitated expression.

The kindergarten was also envisaged as a miniature society, in which children learned how to cooperate with one another and how to live together happily and peacefully. Consideration for the other fellow was held to be the chief virtue in such an organization and a sense of responsibility for the welfare of the group was cultivated early. "Learning by doing" was a fundamental concept in the Froebelian philosophy. From the standpoint of method, the contribution of Froebel was not limited merely to the kindergarten. As soon as his ideas began to take form in the lowest grade of the school system, there was a movement to extend them upward; and the effect on methodology was pronounced throughout the primary grades.

The ideas of Froebel were modified by the progressives in the United States before the turn of the century, in keeping with changes in industrial and social conditions and away from the mystical and symbolic aspects of the original program. The most enthusiastic and influential exponent of the kindergarten in America has been Miss Patty Hill, whose name is a by-word with kindergarten teachers everywhere and whose teaching and writing have influenced practice markedly throughout the United States during the past thirty years.

Psychological Theories and Teaching Methods

Teaching methods, when they have any basis in reason at all, are derived from psychological and philosophical principles. Prior to 1890, at the same time that the ideas of Pestalozzi and Froebel were influencing American teaching practice, the prevailing psychology in American normal schools and colleges was the "faculty psychology," in which the soul was a dominant concept and where memory, reason, imagination, perception,

---

[2] For a good discussion of Froebel's mysticism and symbolism, see Graves, Frank P., *Great Educators of Three Centuries* (New York, The Macmillan Company, 1929), pp. 222 ff.

feeling, thought, and will were all separate and distinct faculties to be developed one at a time. The will occupied first place among the faculties and exercised the function of making choices and issuing commands. Memory was an organ of the mind which needed cultivating by appropriate exercises. These beliefs led pedagogues to assign long passages to be memorized by children and to require pupils to learn lessons by heart which had relatively little meaning to either pupil or teacher. Similarly, psychologists concluded that the way to develop reason was to exercise this faculty, and the task of the teacher was to select appropriate subject matter and administer it to whatever faculty of the mind he was intent upon improving. Essentially, the mind was a storehouse and the educator's function was first to reduce knowledge to its lowest terms in the form of rules, definitions, and abstracts, and then to pour this organized knowledge into the appropriate faculty receptacle.

Pestalozzi had only a vague notion of the nature of the human mind, in spite of·the fact that his intuition led him to suggest methods which were in several instances psychologically sound. His followers in American colleges and normal schools sometimes taught his philosophy in one course and faculty psychology in another without seeing any great inconsistency between the two points of view. If Pestalozzi were alive today he would perhaps belong to the Gestalt school, for he was among the first to grasp the idea of organic education. His insistence upon the equal development of all powers (heart, hand, head), so as to produce a harmonious and well-adjusted personality, is indicative also of an organismic slant.

About 1890 there were some fundamental changes introduced into American education. One of them was the importation of the Herbartian theories of education by Charles De Garmo, Edmund James, and the McMurray brothers. These men had sat at the feet of Wilhelm Rein, professor of pedagogics at the University of Jena, and had returned to this country filled with enthusiasm for the ideas of Herbart. They conducted a vigorous campaign in support of Rein's teaching, organized the Herbart Club in 1892, and spoke and wrote widely about German school procedures. At approximately this same time, William James evolved a new psychology and John Dewey advanced a philosophy of teaching, both of which were radically opposed to the doctrines that had dominated the educational scene prior to 1890. The appearance of these new theories was not nearly so sudden, however, as students are likely to think from their reading of educational history. Indeed, the study of psychology and the establishment of laboratories for experimentation had been going on in the United States to some extent since 1875. In that year William James was offering instruction in physiological psychology at Harvard and about this time he made provision for his students to carry on experimental work, presumably in a laboratory. George Trumball Ladd, who is credited with being the first American author of a textbook in psychology, was in 1880, as a professor of mental and moral philosophy at Bowdoin College, studying "the relationships between the nervous system and mental phenomena." His book, the *Elements of Physiological Psychology*, published in 1887, met with a warm welcome in colleges and universities and lived to a good old age. William James, for several decades dean of American psychologists, was the man who introduced experimentalism to America. Historians have pointed out that while James himself was not an experimentalist, and disliked laboratory work, he was the pioneer of the psychological laboratory and the founder of educational psychology.

Most of the important philosophical and psychological ideas that found expression in America in the decade before the century ended came from Germany. Practically every promising student during this period journeyed either to Leipzig to learn from the famous Wundt or to Jena to study under Rein, and returned to America filled with enthusiasm for the new approach to psychology and the ideas of their German professors. A few were influenced by English psychologists and philosophers.

Despite the acknowledged predominance of the German influence on American psychology, a portion of the latter was indigenous, or at least adapted from other schools of thought.[3]

[3] Sir Francis Galton exerted a real influence on American psychology by his development of tests and measurements and his work on imagery.

Its genesis, by 1900, is well summarized by Boring [4] in his succinct statement that "it inherited its physical body from German experimentalism but it got its mind from Darwin."

Classroom methods were not immediately affected by the substitution of functional for faculty psychology in America. The textbooks dealing with the subject were highly academic in character and beyond the comprehension of the average teacher.[5] It remained for later psychologists to interpret the laws of learning in terms that were meaningful to the practitioner.

While psychological and philosophical theories were being formulated and discussed in academic circles, there were a few practical school administrators in America who possessed both the interest and the genius to test out some of the modern principles which had only recently taken form. Of these educators, Dr. William T. Harris and Colonel Francis W. Parker were outstanding. Dr. Harris, as superintendent of schools in St. Louis between 1867 and 1880, introduced the kindergarten into the city schools (1873) and demonstrated more clearly than any other American during the early days the application of Froebel's theories to the education of young children. He rejected much of the faculty psychology and was one of the most constructive educational critics of his generation. Together with G. Stanley Hall, he developed a questioning attitude toward many philosophical principles which were rather slavishly adhered to by educators. Francis W. Parker was also a school administrator. Returning from his studies in Germany in 1875, he became superintendent of schools in Quincy, Massachusetts, and between 1883 and 1899 he was principal of the Cook County Normal School at Chicago. Parker selected educational principles and ideas from various philosophers and psychologists and introduced them into practice in his own schools. He accepted Froebel's principle of self-expression, Herbart's theory of con-

[4] Boring, Edwin G., *A History of Experimental Psychology* (New York, The Century Company, 1929).

[5] John Dewey's *Psychology*, published by Harper and Brothers in 1886 and revised in 1898, is largely an academic discussion of knowledge, feeling, and the will. The carry-over to actual classroom teaching would have required an understanding and appreciation of the implications of Dewey's writing which was quite beyond the interest and capacity of most schoolteachers of 1900.

centration of instruction around a central study, Pestalozzi's method of teaching geography (the local approach), and Spencer's idea of the importance of science in education. His influence, and that of his school, on teaching procedures in the elementary grades was probably greater than that of any other educator prior to 1900.

THE CONTRIBUTION OF HERBART

But to return to Herbart and his American disciples, for it was the theories of this eminent philosopher and psychologist that produced the greatest change in methods in the last decade of the nineteenth century and paved the way for many of the changes which came later. Herbart was one of the first to propose a system of education that was based upon a psychology worked out or subscribed to by the founder. It is not necessary to discuss in detail the philosophical and metaphysical concepts which were a part of the Herbartian creed in order to understand the main elements which composed his system of education and to appreciate their influence upon classroom procedures.

Herbart held that the aim of education was the attainment of character, the making of the morally religious man. To attain virtue it was necessary for the pupil's perception of right and wrong to be in complete accord with his deeds. This was admittedly a difficult assignment for the teacher, particularly inducing the pupil to make the effort of applying the moral principle to his, own life. This ethical theory was clarified somewhat by the formulation of specific moral concepts, of which "efficiency of will" (which includes positiveness of purpose, vigor in action, and harmony with ethical standards), "good will," "justice," and "equity" were the basic considerations.

While to Herbart, the moral and religious aim was the ultimate goal of education, it could be achieved only through instruction; and since teaching involved the use of the mind, psychology became an important factor in the attainment of objectives.

The Herbartian psychology is as difficult to comprehend as faculty psychology and almost as untenable. It assumed an unseen universe composed of "units," called "reals." These "reals" were mere existences whose sole function was to provide a foundation for the development of ideas. Once an idea was formed, it became active and struggled for survival. Related ideas gave each other support and depressed or forced out opposing ones. The fusion of ideas into a homogeneous whole was an essential element in the educational process, and the theory that new ideas are interpreted through those already in consciousness was the central doctrine of Herbartian psychology, known as "apperception." According to this theory, pupils will be interested and will retain in their consciousness any idea or set of ideas which is in harmony with the knowledge which they already possess. Memorization of unrelated facts did not constitute real learning according to this principle. To have meaning, facts must fit into a pattern already established or at least partially formed.

Similarly, "interest," which Herbart deemed essential if learning were to become effective, was dependent upon ideas already existent and the past experiences of the pupil. As Reisner aptly puts it in discussing this point, "many ideas call but only a few are invited to come in." [6] The invitation depends upon how pleasantly the new idea is associated with the ones already incorporated—in other words, how interested the pupil is in acquiring the information.

To many, this principle increased the difficulties of teaching. No longer could instructors impose tasks external to the pupil's interests with justification. It was rather the teacher's responsibility to incite interest, which meant appraising the pupil's present knowledge and experience and so setting the stage that there is a reaching out after more knowledge. Herbart also believed in the development of many-sided interests and held that the pupil should be given as broad instruction as possible— in fact, he wanted the curriculum to cover the entire range of known ideas. In order to maintain unity and avoid the classification and departmentalization of knowledge which a wide range of studies often suggests, Herbart emphasized the principle

[6] Reisner, Edward H., *The Evolution of the Common School* (New York, The Macmillan Company, 1930), p. 469.

of "concentration," [7] in which all subjects were grouped around one common central study, and the accompanying process, "correlation," which attempts to relate the subject matter in the various fields and to insure that each topic studied is strengthened by all the other subjects.

Another Herbartian concept which had considerable influence on American school curricula and method was the culture-epoch theory. This philosophical principle was developed by Ziller, a disciple of Herbart, and was based on the assumption that each child, in his development from infancy to manhood, goes through the same general stages that the race has passed through in its ascension from barbarism to civilization. This hypothesis was supported by biological observations. Since the embryo in the higher animals showed evidence of passing through all the stages of development common to the lower forms of life, it seemed reasonable to conclude that the mental development of the child would follow in its evolution a similar route, passing through all the great culture epochs of the race.

The selection of subject matter suitable for children in various stages of mental development was a problem of great concern to Herbartians. They were interested in the development of character and in the establishment of a pedagogy that was sound socially and ethically. Therefore, with Herbart's three stages of character development to guide them,[8] they classified the literature of the various epochs more or less in order of its complexity, and selected for pupils those historical stories, biographical sketches, and accounts which were most appropriate for their mental development.

The earliest epochs presumably provided the simplest social situations; and since each cultural epoch was built upon the one which immediately preceded it, the problems of life became correspondingly more complex with each succeeding epoch. Herbart himself, in tutoring adolescent boys, selected Homer's *Odyssey* as a beginning point, for he found there, in the descriptions of early Greek life, the simplest of moral and social situa-

[7] For example, central-subject elementary education, with such subjects as geography, history, manual training, and literature grouped around it.

[8] The three stages of character development were: (1) sensation and perception, (2) memory and imagination, and (3) judgment and universal concepts.

tions, comparable to the understandings and ethical levels of his pupils. Herbart's followers introduced children to fairy tales and then made them acquainted with Mother Goose stories, the Old Testament, Greek literature, the New Testament, and finally with modern literature.

One can readily imagine the confusion created by the attempt to introduce this vague generalization of "culture epochs" into American schools. The idea of employing the Jewish and the German historical materials as the basis of the moral training of American children was not well received, and the substitution of American culture epochs was advocated early and actually used in many schools. Several attempts were made by American educators to divide our history into a series of epochs in harmony with the general theory of Herbart, and specific materials were selected for inclusion in the curriculum.

The culture-epoch theory ran its course in a relatively brief period of time; and while a few evidences of its influence still exist, it has only a historical significance for the modern teacher. We no longer believe that children are interested in recapitulating, as they advance from grade to grade, the racial experiences of man from savagery to civilization.

Perhaps the most familiar of all the Herbartian contributions, and the most useful to teachers, are the five formal steps of the recitation which grew out of his theories of teaching method.[9] Since unity of thought was an important objective in education, the technique of achieving it required careful analysis and study. It was the contention of the Herbartians that the instructional procedure should follow the normal avenues by which the mind builds itself up. The formula finally derived included these five steps to be followed in order:

1. Preparation
2. Presentation
3. Comparison and abstraction
4. Generalization or definition
5. Application

[9] Herbart originally suggested four steps: (1) clearness, (2) association, (3) system, and (4) method. His followers substituted preparation and presentation for clearness, and application for method.

Preparation involved getting the pupil's mind in a receptive mood for the new material to be taught. It implied a kind of warming-up process and a focusing of attention upon the aim and direction of the lesson to be learned. The mind required a bit of orientation and a "collecting of thoughts" to be ready to profit most from a new lesson.

Presentation, as the name suggests, was the process of giving out the new information. This was directed toward the understanding of the meaning which the teacher had in mind as the objective of the lesson. There were no specific instructions as to how best to do this, the criterion of successful teaching at this point being the degree to which pertinent facts were exposed.

The next step, comparison and abstraction, was to show relationships between the facts that children already knew and the ones just presented, and also the various connections which existed among those just learned. Of equal importance was the separation of pertinent data from those that were irrelevant to the purpose of the lesson.

The correct understanding having been gained, it followed logically that the meaning of the lesson should be expressed as tersely as possible. It was a common procedure for the class to make up a definition or formula which adequately expressed the central thought in the day's assignment. This fourth step was called "generalization" or "definition."

The final stage was to apply the generalization to some other experience and to use the knowledge that had been acquired. This would definitely fix it in the consciousness of the learner and it would thereby become a part of his mind.

Without question, these five simply stated steps exercised more influence on teaching practice in America between 1890 and 1905 than all other psychological discoveries and philosophical creations combined. The former had the advantage of simplicity and definiteness and lent themselves readily to specific application. Even though the teacher might not comprehend fully the meaning of apperception, she could still follow the procedure recommended for handling a recitation.

Most of the Herbartian principles have undergone serious modification since 1900, and modern teachers seldom associate their practices with the theories of the German philosopher. The McMurrays, during the first decade of the century, continued to spread the Herbartian gospel with some modifications, but it was destined to be overshadowed by more modern and scientific versions.

THE WORK OF G. STANLEY HALL

Before extending the discussion of the philosophical and psychological principles which influenced education beyond the turn of the twentieth century, mention should be made of the point of view represented by G. Stanley Hall. Historians find it difficult to appraise the work of this brilliant educator, for his researches were based largely on a hypothesis that has long been discarded, the recapitulation theory (culture epochs).

Despite the fact that his basic assumptions have been relegated to the dump heap by modern psychologists, Hall's efforts to explore the world of psychic phenomena and earn for himself the title "The Darwin of the Mind" were by no means fruitless. His basic theory was that mental and physical development go along together hand in hand, and that an understanding of the latter is fundamental to an appreciation of mental phenomena. His approach to mental evolution was, therefore, through biology. Hall classified the growth of children into four stages —infancy, childhood, youth, and adolescence—and studied the peculiar characteristics of each classification. It was his judgment that methods of teaching should conform to the psychology appropriate for the age levels or physical development of children. His greatest contribution was his study of adolescence, the results of which were published in two volumes entitled *Adolescence; Its Psychology, and Its Relations to Physiology, Anthropology, Sociology, Sex, Crime, Religion and Education.* This work had a profound influence upon the attitude of teachers, parents, and social workers toward the problems of the adolescent child and paved the way for a reorganization of the secondary school.

A second accomplishment of Hall, which has had a marked effect upon the course of professional education, was his emphasis on studying the reactions of children firsthand. As was mentioned in an earlier chapter, Hall encouraged teachers and those preparing to teach to make their own observations and to test out pedagogical principles by experimentation. He evidently got some of his ideas from Galton, for his techniques of study and analysis bore a close resemblance to those of the English scientist.

The range of the man's interest was astounding and there is scarcely a phase of educational endeavor which did not receive attention by this energetic philosopher. He studied and discussed mental and social hygiene, sex information, abnormal psychology, health and physical education, eugenics and Sunday schools. Many of his ideas were held up to ridicule because they were radical, and he was attacked by religious bigots because he searched fearlessly for the truth. His contribution to American education has been minimized by historians because of the chaff which accompanied the wheat. Hall was a prolific writer and researcher, and his idiosyncrasies led him down many pedagogical blind alleys.

The situation by 1900 with respect to educational methodology is hard to describe. Teachers in the vanguard had departed from faculty psychology, learning from memory, and formal discipline. But these teachers constituted only a small proportion of the total. Most pedagogues either were complacent in their belief that memory and reason needed training, and that the more interesting the subject the less valuable it was for the pupil, or they were terribly confused by the opposing doctrines of German philosophers. Since the educational doctors differed widely among themselves, it is not surprising to discover that teachers were uncertain as to the relative merits of conflicting principles. There has always been a big lag between philosophy and practice, between scientific discovery and the application of it to the solution of problems. This accounts in part for the fact that the formal classroom procedures of Civil War days persisted in many areas throughout the century. Those whose school days go back to the eighteen-nineties and the early nineteen-hundreds can testify in no uncertain terms as to the formalism which dominated American teaching procedure. Many will recall only too vividly the disciplinary measures which were employed to stimulate the learning process and the total absence of any clearly conceived philosophy of education on the part of teachers.

TEACHING METHODS IN THE THREE R's BEFORE 1900

It would require too much space and would perhaps detract from the interest of this chapter to attempt a detailed discussion of the teaching methods commonly employed in each of the various subjects in the curriculum in the latter part of the nineteenth century. In order to visualize the teacher in action, however, it is almost imperative that some specific situation be treated and the teaching procedure described. William T. Harris, probably the most competent observer of the period from 1870 to 1910, in a chapter on education in N. S. Shaler's two-volume work, *The United States of America*, devotes considerable space to the elementary school subjects and touches to some extent upon teaching methods. The author has drawn largely upon Dr. Harris's discussion for information as to the specific practices which were common to American schools in 1894.

During the days of the ungraded school, the alphabetic method of teaching beginning reading was commonly employed. In this procedure the child was introduced to the letters in the order of their appearance in the alphabet, without putting them to any use whatsoever. The use of this method was encouraged by Pestalozzi in his theory of moving from the simple to the complex and in his emphasis upon long drills, first upon letters, then upon forming letters into syllables, and finally in making syllables into words.

The A B C system was followed by the word method, an invention (probably) of Mrs. Horace Mann and her sister Miss Elizabeth Peabody. This method starts the child off with an interesting sentence which has some meaning for him, such as "The boy is playing ball." The pupil learns to recognize these words, not by the letters which compose them but rather by their general shape and appearance. Recognition is followed by an analysis of the words in which the individual letters are learned. The secret of success in this method of teaching reading, according to Dr. Harris, is the restriction of words in the sentence selected for study to those which are already in the child's vocabulary. The pupil knows, for example, what a ball is and what is involved in play and what a boy is like. It was fairly common in the eighties and nineties to confine the first three of a six-book set of readers to colloquial words and then to venture out into the area of unfamiliar words.

One of the aims in teaching reading was to acquaint the child with literary masterpieces during the course of his school days, with the hope that he would come to cherish them as his own. Harris lists several pieces from prose and poetry that, as he puts it, "have passed through the fire of repeated selection and scores of years of use in the schoolroom." Many readers will perhaps recall lessons based on one or more of the following "gems": Webster's *Reply to Hayne*, Campbell's *Hohenlinden*, Jane Taylor's *Discontented Pendulum*, Tennyson's *Charge of the Light Brigade*, Burns's *Bruce's Address*, and Wolfe's *Burial of Sir John Moore*.[10]

The phonic method of teaching reading was also used in several communities. According to this procedure, the teacher took up a single vowel-sound, usually that of a short *a*—heard in hat, sat, rap, etc.—and after the pupil had learned some words in this sound, he was introduced to words with other sounds. This method was followed until the alphabet had been properly exploited. Some of the sentences used to illustrate the use of a particular sound were rather meaningless and absurd, such as "A fat rat had a cap and sat on a mat." However, the tendency by 1890 was in the direction of combining the word with the phonic method. The best way of combining the two methods, the proportion of time to be devoted to each, and the order in which they were to be employed remained unsettled questions in most communities for several years to come.

The persistence of the old alphabetic method is indicated by the following statement taken from the Massachusetts Teachers Association report, *Progress in Primary School Instruction in Massachusetts*, submitted in 1886: [11]

[10] These were cited by William T. Harris in his chapter on "Education in the United States," in Shaler, N. S. (ed.), *The United States of America* (1894), Vol. II, p. 328.

[11] No. 14, p. 23.

It [the old alphabetic method] is too strongly rooted in old custom and tradition to be killed easily. More than forty years ago Horace Mann demonstrated its absurdity; but it has only recently disappeared from some towns, and still flourishes in many more. There are still so many teachers who can teach only as they were themselves taught that another generation or two may pass before the reform is complete.

Reading as late as 1900, then, was being taught in most communities by a combined word and phonic method; the old A B C procedure had disappeared from progressive schools but persisted tenaciously in the classrooms of the more conservative communities, especially where teachers were unacquainted with modern methods.

Spelling had also undergone considerable change by 1900. Perhaps the most notable shifts were from oral to written spelling and from the use of spelling books containing lists of ten to twelve thousand words to spellers made up of selected lists better suited to the needs of pupils. Oral spelling was not abandoned altogether, as the reader is fully aware from his own experience, but the more progressive schools were gradually subordinating it to written spelling before the close of the century.

In arithmetic, the Grube method was popular. This has been mentioned previously but it will perhaps bear amplification. Dr. Harris's definition and illustration follow: [12]

It teaches the four fundamental rules or operations from the beginning commencing with one. It adds and subtracts, multiplies and divides, analyzing thoroughly. Thus taking the number four as an example, its operations are expressed as "four equals three and one or two and two; one from four leaves three; two from four leaves two; three from four leaves one; two times two are four; three times one are four less one; four contains two twice and one four times, and three once with one remainder."

Mental arithmetic was used in many schools in 1890 and, while it did not supersede written arithmetic entirely, it played a very important role in the school curriculum. The problems included in textbooks continued to be obsolete and unrelated to life and consumed more of the pupil's time than was warranted

[12] Harris, William T., *op. cit.*, pp. 326–27.

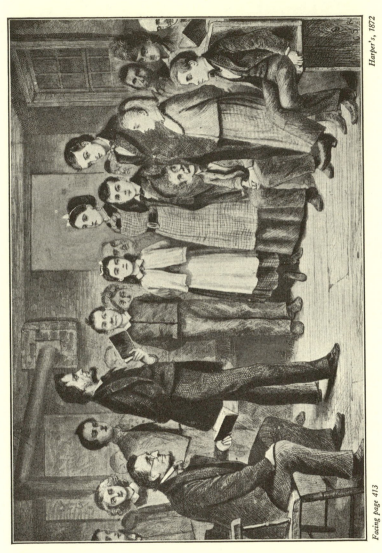

A Spelling Bee

Harper's, 1872

by the facts learned, the skill acquired, or the generalizations formed.

It was contended by an earlier generation that the study of arithmetic was useful because it developed general intellectual power and improved one's logic. By 1900 the progressives had dropped this argument because it belonged with the old faculty psychology, which to them was no longer tenable. Most teachers continued to amble along without fully comprehending what functions arithmetic really did serve, and several decades passed before the textbook writers began to take full cognizance of functional psychology and eliminated impractical problems from their arithmetics.

The Pestalozzian influence on writing was not salutary. In conformity with his general principle of beginning with the simple and gradually approaching the complex, step by step, he gave support to a mechanical technique of teaching writing which tarried with schoolmasters for half a century or more. Each letter in a word was analyzed into strokes—the straight, the outcurved, and the incurved—and before a pupil was ready to write words or sentences he had to drill for weeks upon the strokes.

This analytic method in which children were compelled to spend a long time on the elements of writing gave way to a synthetic method where words were written as wholes without significant loss of quality. Not all schools, by any means, had modified their writing procedure by 1890 but the trend was clearly away from the Pestalozzian theory to one that was less mechanical and dull. Special supervisors and teachers of writing decreased greatly in number during the last two decades of the century, the regular teacher assuming the responsibility for teaching writing.

Teaching methods in other subjects were less well defined and less systematized than in the tool subjects. There was less of a tendency in 1890 to rely upon the textbook in teaching than in 1870, and the topical method was popular where page assignments had existed formerly. Despite the trend away from the slavish adherence to textbook instruction common to an earlier period, the leading educators were slow to make any radical departures in this direction. The textbook represented the instrument by which each individual child might throw off the shackles of ignorance according to his own capacity and effort. It was a democratic tool which savored of rugged individualism and its defenders were both numerous and able.

Teaching in the high school bore a closer resemblance to college instruction than it did to that in the elementary and grammar grades. For the most part, secondary-school teachers had no professional training and they imitated in their teaching the practice of the college or university professors with whom they had most recently studied, using the lecture method to a considerable extent.

Thorndike and the Behaviorists

The modifications in teaching practice in America during the past quarter century are due in no small measure to the work of Edward L. Thorndike and the behaviorists [13] and to the philosophical concepts of John Dewey and his enthusiastic interpreters.

Professor Thorndike's influence upon American education in general and upon the improvement of teaching methods in particular is a topic of such magnitude that the author cannot hope to deal with it adequately in a discussion which attempts to cover the work of a dozen other eminent scientists and philosophers in the same treatise.

Like Hall, Thorndike has spread his efforts over a broad field and his writings and researches are numerous. Both William James and Sir Francis Galton exercised a great influence on the thinking of Thorndike and account, in part at least, for the fact that he has been a pragmatic realist. His three volumes on *Educational Psychology*, published in 1914, constituted the Psychological Bible for educators for nearly twenty years; and while the writings of his disciples were frequently more readable and easier to grasp than his own basic text, the ideas and facts were drawn largely from the latter.

---

[13] Gestalt psychology was born about 1913 but it is still foreign to many American teachers. During the last decade it has gained considerable recognition, and it promises to influence teaching practice rather radically.

Public-school teachers have probably been influenced more in their practices by Thorndike's statement of the laws of learning than by any other single phase of his investigations. The concepts of readiness, exercise, and effect and the S–R bond theory, which was fundamental to them, have modified classroom techniques as well as the nature and arrangement of subject matter. While these principles were not all original with Thorndike, he restated them; and his name is more commonly associated with the laws of learning in the minds of teachers than are those of his professional forbears. Unfortunately, in some instances the Thorndike label has been pasted on indefensible practices which were never implied by the popular laws which he redefined and expounded. This has been caused by a superficial understanding or a total misconception of them.

Of almost equal importance for teaching was his theory of the transfer of training. His conclusion that learning carried over from one situation to another only where there were identical elements present dealt a severe blow to the doctrine of mental discipline.[14] Teachers could no longer impose perplexing mathematical problems on Johnny, nor make him learn a foreign language, nor memorize twenty-seven stanzas of poetry, just in order to discipline his mind.

Thorndike was also one of the earliest leaders in the child-study movement and his *Notes on Child Study*, published in 1901, were decidedly in advance of the work of G. Stanley Hall, who preceded him in exploring this field. He has continually emphasized the existence and importance of individual differences and has been one of the leading spirits in breaking down lock-step

---

[14] Charles H. Judd, recently of the University of Chicago, has consistently differed with Professor Thorndike in the matter of transfer of training. Judd has presented his views in some detail in his *Psychology of Secondary Education*. In brief he holds that "the highest powers of the mind are general, not particular, that mental development consists not in storing the mind with items of knowledge nor in training the nervous system to perform with readiness particular habitual acts, but rather in equipping the individual with the power to think abstractly and to form general ideas."

"When the ends thus described are attained," says Judd, "transfer of training, or formal discipline, has taken place because it is the very nature of generalization and abstraction that they extend beyond the particular experiences in which they originate." (Judd, Charles H., *Psychology of Secondary Education* [Boston, Ginn and Company, 1927], p. 441.)

methods of teaching. Related to this work is, of course, the role which this great educational psychologist has played in the development of tests. Here the influence of Galton and Binet are clearly observable. Beyond dispute, Thorndike has been the leader of the educational-testing movement in America. He and his students have developed numerous intelligence and achievement tests, placing in the hands of the teacher instruments of measurement by which individual differences could be detected and suitable adaptations in method and content provided.

Thorndike's realism is evident in his frequency-count studies and in those which have been carried on by his students, such as word counts for spelling, date and place counts for geography, and fact counts for history. *Use* became the central criterion for including facts and processes in the curriculum. In arithmetic, his investigations led to a shift from concentrating on the forty-five combinations to teaching the one hundred combinations, because he discovered that the bond established in learning the fact that $7 + 9 = 16$ was not the same as $9 + 7 = 16$, and similarly for all the other operations. He has also discouraged the use of crutches in learning, proving by experimentation that writing in the 1's in subtraction and using $+$ and $\times$ to indicate the process to be followed in copying problems do more harm than good, since they build up wrong bonds which have to be unlearned later. These discoveries have influenced teaching largely through the modifications which scientific research has brought about in textbook writing. Arithmetic authors are extremely sensitive to experimental findings and, while the market may be glutted with psychologically unsound texts, the dissemination of research discoveries is fast taking its toll on outmoded teaching devices. Critics have pointed out, and possibly with some justification, that the large number of connections implied in the Thorndike theory have led authors and teachers to overemphasize the parts at the expense of the whole.

In the field of spelling, Thorndike has been influential in consummating the shift from oral to written work, a movement which was well under way in progressive schools by 1900 but which needed further emphasis to insure its completion. He also focused attention upon the infrequency with which many words commonly included in spelling books actually appeared in writing and print, and by his tests of comprehension he scaled word lists to the abilities and achievements of pupils.

From the standpoint of classroom management, his study of "annoyers" and "satisfiers" deserves a prominent place among his contributions. Reduced to its simplest terms, the principle deduced was that punishment is not an effective way of teaching anybody anything; that rewards operate more successfully and to a greater degree in the improvement of the learning process than punishment. This idea is not a new one, but it remained largely a hypothesis until some objective data were assembled to substantiate it. That a negative approach to learning has been used by many teachers in the belief that it was good, sound common sense is undeniable. The fact that Thorndike's work throws doubts on the wisdom of this method, and suggests rather strongly that the more constructive procedure lies in quite an opposite method of treatment, has had an indirect effect upon classroom technique.

There are educators who believe that the contributions of Thorndike have been greatly exaggerated, that his researches have been based upon false assumptions, and that his emphasis upon measurement has resulted in more harm than good. These critics contend that his connectionist theories cannot be reconciled with Dewey's philosophical principles and, therefore, they consider his ideas old-fashioned. The above arguments usually proceed from the mouths of the ardent Gestaltists, who seek the millennium in the organismic approach. Only time can determine the validity of their position. It seems probable that the pendulum will swing wide, during the next decade or so, in the direction of Gestalt theories and will come to rest somewhere between the present position of the behaviorists and the most extreme position of the Gestaltists. Critics of Thorndike frequently attribute tenets to him which he has not held for years, if, indeed, he ever voiced them. The gap, in other words, between the progressive connectionists and the conservative Gestaltists is really much narrower than is commonly believed.

THE INFLUENCE OF DEWEY AND THE PROGRESSIVES

The work of Thorndike in the field of educational psychology has been paralleled by an equally brilliant contribution by Dewey in the realm of philosophy. Dewey has been an eclectic. He was sympathetic toward Froebel's doctrine of social unity; was in his earlier years an adherent of Hegelian philosophy, which emphasized the organismic aspect of society; was a subscriber to Darwin's theories of evolution; and was, in addition, an alert student of social and economic problems.

While influenced by the invasion of Herbartian ideas, Dewey was not blind to the inconsistencies and inadequacies in many of the theories of Herbart's disciples. He considered the mind "a process . . . a growing affair" and knowledge as something dynamic. Education he defined as a reconstruction of experience. He was convinced that methods and materials should be functional, that the school should contribute to the solution of society's problems, and that classroom experiences should be looked upon as life itself rather than as a preparation for life.

The two Froebelian principles of method, self-activity and social participation, stripped of their original metaphysical and religious implications, were accepted by Dewey as sound pedagogical doctrines. Self-activity meant for the child an "opportunity for investigation and experimentation and for trying out one's ideas and things." Such a procedure not only contributed to the well-being and growth of the child himself, but it was also basic to socialization and to democracy.

The school's responsibility was to provide opportunity for real living. This involved making the environment of the school as comparable to life outside the classroom as was humanly possible. Learning to live with others cooperatively, to adapt oneself to new and changing situations, and to solve problems were the central purposes of Dewey's school.

Forcing children to give their attention to tasks had no place in the newer philosophy because the results were not satisfying. It was important that the child should see and feel the relationship between the learning of facts or skills and the purpose which this knowledge had for the welfare of the individual child. The experience must satisfy some more or less immediate interest before its inclusion in the program could be justified. This theory threw into disrepute the practice of awarding prizes, medals, credits, and also the system of imposing penalties. Interest and effort go together. When pupils are interested in performing a task, they will put forth great effort. When they dislike an assignment, no amount of coercion can stimulate an equivalent enthusiasm or effort.

One of the words which became popular as a result of the changed point of view with regard to learning was "motivation." This term implies a purpose on the part of the pupil to learn. If a child really wants to build a boat, he will put forth the effort to accomplish the task because the experience is satisfying. He is motivated to follow the procedure of boatbuilding step by step because it contributes to the realization of his purpose. Just so long as he can see the relationship between what he is doing and the accomplishment of his purpose, the work is motivated. The teacher's task in the process is to assist children in their attempts to realize worthy purposes.

Out of this philosophical theory and functional psychology there developed a wave of so-called "project teaching," which is, in essence, a general method of instruction that takes account of the motives, needs, and purposes of children. The most enthusiastic exponent of this method has been Professor William Heard Kilpatrick. He defines a project as any "unit of purposeful experience, any instance of purposeful activity where dominating purpose, as an inner urge, (1) fixes the aim (or end) of the action, (2) guides its process, (3) furnishes its 'drive,' its inner motivation for its vigorous prosecution."

The process is rather simple. First, there must be present a purpose; second, the children must set up the ends to be achieved and must attain them; third, the teacher must arrange appropriate subject matter and exercise intelligent guidance. Various types of projects have been attempted. Some have been directed toward problem solving; others, toward appreciating or enjoying; others, toward the achieving of ideas; and still others, toward acquiring knowledge or skills which require drill or practice.

The word "project" appears much less frequently in educational literature today than it did a decade ago. The essential principles, however, are practiced in modern schools and motivation is accepted as a prime consideration in the education of children.

The newer methodology has tended to change the position of the teacher drastically. She no longer stands on a dais and rules her subjects with an iron hand. She is more of an interpreter and guide than schoolmistress. She mingles freely with the pupils and her interests are identified with theirs. While, in a legal sense, authority for the government of the class resides with her, she seldom exercises it, the occasion for discipline being symptomatic usually of a dull, uninteresting school program. Critics of this methodology have pointed out with considerable justification that, in practice, it leads to all kinds of absurdities, that it is wasteful of time and effort, and that it is contrary in nature to life outside the walls of the schoolroom. In the hands of the ignorant and unimaginative teachers the above criticisms can frequently be substantiated. But the fault lies with the teacher, not with the method. Most of the objections to the progressive methods growing out of Dewey's philosophy are due to a persistent faith in an outworn psychology. The old discipline inherent in faculty psychology appears more masculine and virile than the "doctrine of interest." Formality and sternness were so closely associated with the otherwise pleasant memories of childhood and school days that many parents and teachers tend to place a halo around the whole system of education which prevailed in their youth. There are other critics who, with the passing of the years, have lost their understanding of children's interests, capacities, and reactions. These individuals are frequently unsympathetic toward self-expression, toward play, toward construction activities—in fact, anything which is related to the immediate interests of children.

The Activity School

Perhaps the best objective illustration of the Dewey philosophy at the present time is the activity school. In many ways this is an extension of the Froebelian principles, originally applied in

EDUCATION THROUGH CHILDREN'S INTERESTS

this country to children in the kindergarten, to include children in all or several of the elementary grades. Its basic principle is self-directed activity. Briefly, the philosophy and procedure are much the same as that associated with the project method. Under guidance, the child chooses an activity in which he wishes to engage, he pursues the activity until he is satisfied, and then he judges of its meaning and worth. The teacher's responsibility is to exercise intelligent guidance but not to compel, to relate past experiences to present activities and point the way to future achievements, and to assist the child whenever guidance and help are really needed. Books and materials are made available for those pupils who feel the need of them in meeting the situation at hand, but pupils are under no circumstances required to consult or use them. Contrary to the traditional notion of "subject-matter-set-out-to-be-learned" the new school has no curriculum as such, the subject matter consisting, as Kilpatrick describes it, of whatever the child "pays attention to or uses in the prosecution of the experience" and "all the learning results of all sorts." [15]

In the most progressive situations, the activity school attempts to take on the quality of the best life outside the classroom and children actually engage in purposeful activity. Under the guiding genius of a competent and enthusiastic principal and a teaching staff of professional artists, the activity program will unquestionably measure up to the highest hopes of its proponents. In a number of schools where a gradual shift to the activity type of curriculum has been attempted and the teachers have shared in the transition and been favorably disposed toward it, the results are promising. Where the traditional philosophy has been deeply entrenched and the faculty are opposed to, or are ignorant of, the psychological and philosophical theories which underlie the activity school, the modifications have amounted chiefly to changes in name rather than in methodology.

As was stated earlier, the Dewey philosophy is the foundation upon which most of our progressive methods of teaching rest. It is a general rather than a special method of approach. Profes-

[15] Kilpatrick, William H., "The Essentials of the Activity Movement," in *Progressive Education*, October, 1934.

sor Horn of Iowa and others contend that there is no such thing as general method. According to these educational scientists, whose work in elementary education has been most noteworthy, each subject demands a special methodology and the approach to spelling should be different from that employed in teaching arithmetic, geography, or history. Until the peculiar elements in each of these subjects are analyzed, it is their belief that no one can suggest a reliable and appropriate teaching procedure.

A compromise position seems most likely of success. The psychological and philosophical principles underlying general method will remain constant throughout the curriculum. They are based on human behavior and are fundamental. Children need motivation in geography as well as in arithmetic. They learn best to do by doing, whether it be baseball or history. Along with learning passages of Shakespeare by heart, there go concomitant learnings, which may be pleasant or unpleasant. This is equally true of the multiplication table. The mastery of facts is always accompanied by other modifications in the human organism.

On the other hand, a teacher fortified with a clear understanding of the principles of progressive education may be very inefficient because in teaching pupils to write she does not know whether or not daily practice periods should be long or short, or whether the use of drill or the teaching of grammar is the more effective method in eliminating errors in language. Experimenters like Horn, Buswell, Gray, Gates, Freeman, Thorndike, and others have uncovered much valuable material in relation to the learning of the fundamental subjects which teachers cannot afford to ignore. The extremists in teacher-training institutions, armed with a smattering of Dewey phrases and a scanty understanding of Gestalt psychology, are sending out graduates whose earnestness and sincerity are commendable but whose ignorance of tested pedagogical theories is appalling.

The Application of Research Findings to Teaching Methods

Specific teaching methods in the fundamental subjects have been based more and more upon the results of scientific research.

The well-informed teacher now has at her disposal an accumulation of objective evidence with regard to the difficulties involved in teaching reading, writing, spelling, and arithmetic. The learning processes related to these subjects have been carefully analyzed and, as a result, suggested procedures have been evolved for teaching them. In reading, considerable knowledge has been brought to light by a process of photographing the eyes of pupils (or light reflected from them) during the act of reading. This type of investigation has revealed eye movements, including speed, regularity of progressions, and efficiency of return. Experiments have also uncovered the types of errors most prevalent in oral reading, the elements in reading selections which are of greatest interest to boys and girls at various age levels, the relationship between speed and comprehension in reading, and numerous facts which give the teacher a more reasonable basis for attacking her problems. Diagnostic tests have been developed for the purpose of discovering reading errors, and special materials have been created and marketed for improving the reading difficulties of children.[16]

Similarly in teaching handwriting, Professor Frank N. Freeman and others have discovered a number of specific methods which have contributed to successful performance. These have grown out of experimental work done on such matters as position assumed in writing, type of movement used, and rhythm—factors which have been demonstrated to affect the speed and quality of handwriting.

In recent years there have been considerable discussion and debate as to the relative merits of teaching manuscript as opposed to cursive writing. The investigations seem to point to several advantages in teaching the former in the earlier grades. Manuscript writing facilitates beginning reading, is more legible, is easier to learn, and removes the disadvantage of two kinds of script with which the child has to contend in learning to read and write.

Research investigations have also had considerable influence

[16] The work of William S. Gray and Arthur I. Gates has been especially noteworthy in the improvement of reading methods. Several other investigators have also made significant contributions to this field.

on the teaching of arithmetic and spelling. Teachers now know, for example, that teaching the combinations as pure abstractions—such as two and two are four—independent of any concrete setting, is an objectionable practice. Furthermore, they have learned that it is inefficient to encourage counting in teaching the combinations. Scores of other illustrations could be given in the field of arithmetic to show how specific methods have been deduced from scientific experiments.

The teaching of spelling has been subjected in a similar fashion to microscopic observation, with the result that a more intelligent and reasonable procedure has been evolved in recent years than that which commonly prevailed. The causes of errors have been isolated; the length of spelling periods in relation to performance has been tested; and the relationship of pronunciation, phonics, meaning and use of words, and rules to spelling efficiency has been studied intensively.

While the philosophers have been theorizing about the implications of their doctrines for specific situations, the educational scientists have been collecting facts showing causes and effects, and providing a wealth of information heretofore unknown to teachers, textbook writers, and school administrators. Diagnostic and achievement tests have developed with the extension of the scientific attack upon educational method. These have constituted the means by which the efficiency of varying procedures could be measured. Following in the wake of these tests has been a flood of practice materials, work books, and remedial equipment of one sort or another.

Many thoughtful observers believe that the scientific movement has not been altogether an unmixed blessing. It is their contention that, in its emphasis upon the parts, the whole child has been forgotten. Teachers have also been led to believe by these more enthusiastic test experts that everything can be accurately measured and that the instruments used in diagnosing the strengths and weaknesses of pupil achievement are as reliable as a metric scale or a doctor's thermometer. There has been a tendency in some quarters, also, for tests to prescribe the aims and objectives of education to the measurable areas of knowledge, and to cause teachers and administrators to lose sight of the less tangible but equally important phases of human achievement. Comparisons between schools and communities of the success of pupils in the Three R's have had unfortunate consequences because of the attention which this procedure focused on the tool subjects.

Despite these criticisms, which have increased in number and intensity during recent years, the movement, in general, has contributed a great deal to the improvement of the teaching profession. It has been possible, because of improved methods, to reduce substantially the amount of time devoted to the Three R's without sacrificing achievement standards. Furthermore, as a result of the work of Thorndike and his measurement colleagues, the teacher's approach to educational problems has become more systematized and objective than it was earlier in the century.

Teaching methods have been greatly influenced over the past century by scientific and philosophical developments, which have suggested in their modifications a different process of learning and thinking than the one or ones commonly subscribed to. During this period, Darwin's notion of the origin of traits and characteristics and his theory of evolution had stimulated the psychologists and philosophers to abandon metaphysics and to look to biology for the explanation of mental phenomena. Faculty psychology, the dominant explanation of the mind and its operations prior to 1890, gave way to a dynamic biological psychology based upon observation and experimentation.

The changes in teaching method which have occurred as the result of this new concept of mental development are too numerous to catalogue if specific techniques are included. In general, the change has been from one in which learning from memory abounded to one where children were encouraged to think; from formal discipline to pupil motivation; from a procedure in which the teacher's position was dominant to one where the child is self-directive and active; from mass education to a consideration of individual differences; from teacher-controlled discipline based on the rod of correction to a pupil-controlled, socially directed form of government; from an autocratic to a democratic approach to school problems.

Perhaps the above claims should more properly be limited to changes in method observable in progressive schools and in the classrooms of those teachers who have kept abreast of the rapidly changing philosophy and psychology of education. Certainly, the vast majority of American public schools have not yet achieved all, or most of, the changes listed in the foregoing paragraph. To assume, however, that the teachers in these schools have not been affected, or their thinking influenced, would be equivalent to charging them with insensitive minds. A transition as great as the one involved in a shift from faculty to behaviorist to Gestalt psychology (where, in the judgment of the author, we are now apparently headed) is of such magnitude as to require years for its complete realization. By that time additional changes will have occurred and a new lag will have appeared between principles and methods, between the psychological findings in the laboratory and the techniques employed in the field.

Suggested Readings

Boring, Edwin G., *A History of Experimental Psychology* (New York, The Century Company, 1929).

Caswell, H. L., and Campbell, D. S., *Curriculum Development* (New York, American Book Company, 1935).

Dearborn, Ned H., *The Oswego Movement in American Education* (New York, Bureau of Publications, Teachers College, Columbia University, 1925).

Eby, Frederick, and Arrowood, Charles F., *The Development of Modern Education* (New York, Prentice-Hall, Inc., 1934), pp. 755–879.

Graves, Frank P., *Great Educators of Three Centuries* (New York, The Macmillan Company, 1929), Chaps. IX, X, XI.

Harris, William T., "Education in the United States," in Shaler, N. S. (ed.), *The United States of America* (1894).

Hissong, Clyde, *The Activity Movement* (Baltimore, Warwick and York, 1932).

Kilpatrick, William H., "The Essentials of the Activity Movement," in *Progressive Education*, October, 1934.

MADDOX, WILLIAM A., "Development of Method" in Kandel, I. L. (ed.), *Twenty-five Years of American Education* (New York, The Macmillan Company, 1924).

REISNER, EDWARD H., *The Evolution of the Modern School* (New York, The Macmillan Company, 1930).

WILDS, ELMER H., *The Foundations of Modern Education* (New York, Farrar and Rinehart, Inc., 1936).

XXIX

Teachers' Salaries

THE Civil War gave strength to the movement, initiated by Horace Mann and his fellow educators, to open wide the doors of the teaching profession to women. When the schoolmasters returned from the battlefields, they found their positions occupied by females who had carried on the work so successfully that many school committees had no desire to replace them. Women had given service in the classroom not only as satisfactorily as men, but at a much lower rate of compensation. As a previous discussion reveals, females received only from forty to sixty per cent as high wages as men teachers, a fact which carried considerable weight with taxpayers. In spite of the apparent lack of public consideration for those schoolmasters who had risked their lives in defense of a great cause, their homecoming was not so unhappy an affair as one might imagine. The abler men went into other lines of work at much higher salaries than they had received for teaching, and the less competent either found business positions suitable to their talents or accepted teaching posts for whatever amount of salary they could extract from local school committees.

The predominance of women had its effect upon the wage rates of both male and female teachers. Since women were able and willing to work for sixteen or eighteen dollars a month, school boards were reluctant to pay men of similar qualifications markedly higher salaries. This competition has resulted in what many educators deem to be relatively low salaries for public-school teachers generally. Differentials, of course, in favor of men have always existed in the teaching profession but the disparity has become progressively smaller with the increase in competition and the wider influence and control exercised by women over public policies.[1]

The economic position of a group of workers, however, cannot be appraised solely by an examination of their weekly, monthly, or annual wage allowances. Their status is influenced also by their length of tenure, pension and retirement arrangements, and the cost of living.

In teaching, as in many other lines of work, turnover has been high and the average length of stay in the profession prior to 1900 would not have exceeded ten or twelve years even in the large cities.[2] Furthermore, the period of service has not always been uninterrupted. Sometimes teachers have been laid off (less then than now) for a year or so, during which time they either engaged in some other occupation or remained idle until a position was found. Similarly in other vocations, wage quotations have been quite incomprehensible to the average citizen because of the seasonal nature of the employment. To say that a bricklayer's wage is twelve dollars a day gives an impression of an exorbitant income until it is qualified by a further statement to the effect that he probably works only a hundred days in the year. The income of prize fighters and baseball players is even more illusory, since their tenure is so precarious. This group of workers must make hay while the sun shines. James Braddock's income was a substantial one as heavyweight champion of the world but his tenure was of short duration.

The regularity of the income is, therefore, an important consideration in judging the relative attractiveness of vocations. Of almost equal importance is protection against sickness and old age. Where individuals are expected to make provision for these exigencies out of their own monthly salary checks or income from business, the rate of compensation must of necessity be somewhat higher than that required to meet the needs of a group for whom public protection has been guaranteed at little or no expense to the individual. A good illustration of this lat-

[1] See Burgess, Warren R., *op. cit.*, pp. 32–33.
[2] According to the National Education Association Report of the Committee on Salaries, Tenure and Pensions of 1905 (p. 160), 48.4 per cent of the teachers in twenty-seven cities of 100,000 population or over had taught less than ten years.

ter point is the provision made by the federal government for army and navy officers. There is no need or incentive for the latter to save money for their old age. To the degree that savings for rainy days, then, are cared for by public agencies, to that extent the employee is freed from setting aside a substantial portion of his annual income for retirement—a responsibility which confronts the rank and file of workingmen in American industry. The United States has been slow in adopting European precedents with respect to pensioning schoolteachers, although the trend in this direction has been noticeable in recent years, as a later discussion will show.

Finally, wage rates cannot be appraised adequately without reference to the cost and standard of living of the group under consideration. Money fluctuates in value from year to year and from place to place. It took $1.70 in 1926 to purchase goods which could have been bought in 1914 for $1.00. Obviously, a teacher receiving $1200 during the latter year (1914) was better off than one receiving $1800 in 1926. Similarly, a rural-school teacher with a salary of $1000 is frequently in a more favorable position economically than a city teacher whose annual salary is $1500, because goods and services cost less in the country than in the urban districts. Another factor which is less tangible but no less real than the purchasing power of the dollar is the standard of living to be maintained. Should teachers be expected to live according to the standards established for American workingmen, or should their standards be higher? This controversial subject has never been squarely faced, partly because it conflicts with traditional economic theories of wages, and partly because it would undoubtedly result in increased taxation. While the public has never deliberately determined the standard of living for teachers, deciding how much should be spent for such items as rent, food, clothing, education, and savings, they have actually done so in awarding them salaries in terms of competition and prevailing rates of pay.

Since the relative attractiveness of teaching from a financial viewpoint is dependent upon actual and real wage rates,[3] tenure,

---

[3] The term "real wage" refers to the purchasing power of the salary paid in contrast to the number of dollars actually awarded, *e.g.*, an actual salary of $1000 in

and pension and retirement provisions, the improvement of the economic status of the teaching profession since 1865 should be reflected in the administrative policies of boards of education and certain other governmental agencies as they apply to the three factors just enumerated.

INCREASE IN TEACHERS' SALARIES, 1865–1890

By virtue of the labors of research workers, we are able to trace rather accurately the average salaries paid to public-school teachers from Civil War days down to the present time. Since methods of reporting statistics, however, varied from time to time and since employment conditions shifted considerably, particularly with respect to the length of the school year and the policy of "boarding round," the author has broken up the discussion into two parts: the first, covering the years from 1865 to 1890; and the second, extending from 1890 to the late thirties of the twentieth century.

Table 14 is a condensation of one taken from Warren R. Burgess's *Trends of School Costs* and shows the average weekly salaries of teachers for each five-year period from 1865 to 1890.

Table 14. Average Weekly Salaries of Public-school Teachers, 1865–1890 [1]

Year	Rural		City	
	Men	Women	Men	Women
1865	$ 9.09	$5.99	$23.15	$ 8.57
1870	10.88	7.53	35.42	11.88
1875	11.46	8.00	36.63	12.69
1880	9.73	7.46	31.36	12.20
1885	10.95	8.23	33.15	13.24
1890	11.30	8.55	32.62	13.16

[1] Adapted from Burgess, Warren R., *op. cit.*, pp. 32–33.

It will be observed that men in both rural- and city-school positions consistently received higher salaries than women but that the increase in women's wages was greater during the twenty-five-year period following the Civil War than that

December, 1922, according to the U. S. Bureau of Labor Statistics, was equivalent to a real wage of $608 (measured in terms of purchasing power of a 1914 dollar).

reported for men.[4] This tends to corroborate the statement, made earlier, that the disparity in salaries between the sexes persisted throughout the period but decreased somewhat in amount.

The average wages reported in Table 14 do not show purchasing power, since the cost of living did not remain constant from 1865 to 1890. Burgess's estimate of the weekly cost of living for a small family in 1865 was $13.54. By 1870 this had decreased to $11.58 and by 1875 it had dropped to $10.16; in 1880 it dipped still further to $8.73 and in 1885 it had shrunk to $8.09, its lowest point during the two and a half decades. Even in 1890 the weekly cost of living ($8.47) was less than it had been a decade earlier and only a few cents greater than in 1885. In other words, the improvement made in teachers' salaries between 1865 and 1890 was much greater than the increases noted in Table 14. The real gains, after proper account has been taken of the increased purchasing power of the dollar, are shown in Table 15.

Table 15. Real Increases in Salaries between 1865 and 1890 (Weekly Rates)

Year	Salary	Rural		City	
		Men	Women	Men	Women
1865	Actual and real	$ 9.09	$ 5.99	$23.15	$ 8.57
1890	Real in terms of 1865	18.08	13.68	52.19	21.05

It is interesting to note that the salaries of all classes of teachers except city men were lower in 1865 than the basic cost of living and that even the latter group, which represented the highest-paid class of teachers, was very close to the subsistence level.

WAGES OF OTHER WORKERS

The relative value placed upon the services of teachers can be judged only by comparing their salaries with the wages paid

[4] The increase in men's weekly salaries in cities was 40 per cent, compared with a 54 per cent increase in women's wages. For rural teachers, the increases were 23 per cent and 42 per cent, respectively.

to other workers. Since country-school teachers received wages which were not greatly different in amount from those paid to common laborers and since artisans enjoyed a status not unlike city teachers, the comparison of these four groups should be quite illuminating. During the twenty-five-year period (1865–1890) included in this discussion, the weekly wages of common laborers decreased from $8.94 to $8.82,[5] and the wages of artisans increased from $14.90 to $15.64. This change is negligible and shows, by comparison, that teachers improved their status more than artisans and far outdistanced common laborers.

There are several explanations for this improvement in economic status. Teachers were better organized and more vocal in 1890 than in 1865; the demand for teachers was also greater during the latter part of the century, due to the extension of public education upward to include the high-school years; and, finally, the qualifications of teachers commanded greater respect, because they were substantially higher in 1890 than at the beginning of this period, despite the fact that many teachers were still without any special preparation for their work.

The wage rate reported for 1890 is obviously too low to warrant the conclusion that teaching was rapidly approaching the state of the learned professions. In fact, the average salary of women teachers was at least thirty per cent lower than that paid to artisans and less than twenty per cent higher than that received by laborers. The teacher's position, therefore, in terms of salary was more nearly comparable to that of a semiskilled workman than that of a professional worker.

SALARY TRENDS SINCE 1890

The economic status of the teacher improved considerably between 1890 and 1937, in spite of temporary reverses due to the World War and the depression. Table 16, adapted from Douglas's study *Real Wages in the United States, 1890–1926*, shows the average annual salary of teachers at each five-year interval beginning with 1890.

[5] Burgess, Warren R., *op. cit.*, p. 71.

Table 16. Teachers' Salary Trends since 1890 [1]

Year	Average Annual Earnings	Approximate Real Earnings Based on 1890–1899 = 100	
1890	$ 256	$246	(104)
1895	289	298	(97)
1900	328	309	(106)
1905	392	341	(115)
1910	492	384	(128)
1915	578	425	(136)
1920	936	320	(286)
1925	1263	526	(240)
1930 [2]	1420	861	(165) [3]
1937 [2]	1325	927	(143) [3]

[1] Figures in this table are taken from Douglas, Paul H., *Real Wages in the United States, 1890–1926* (Boston, Houghton Mifflin Company, 1930), p. 382.

[2] Figures taken from N. E. A. Reports. The average salary for 1926, the last year included in Douglas's study, was $1277 ($529 real).

[3] These figures were obtained by splicing Douglas's index with the Bureau of Labor Statistics index of the cost of all goods purchased by wage earners and lower-salaried workers in thirty-two cities.

The increase in the actual average salaries paid to teachers amounted to $1069, or a gain of 418 per cent during the forty-seven-year period under consideration and approximately 400 per cent between 1890 and 1926. This appears, on the face of it, to be a gigantic increase. Its real significance, however, cannot be understood until the salaries are translated into real wages, with full account taken of the purchasing power of the dollars represented. As the figures in the right-hand column of Table 16 show, the real earnings of teachers also advanced consistently except during the period immediately following the World War, rising from $246 in 1890 to $927 in 1937, an increase of 277 per cent.

In fact, with the exception of one or two depression years, when a phenomenal dip in the cost of living occurred, teachers were enjoying a more favorable economic status in 1937 than at any time in the history of the profession. Whereas Douglas's averages are not broken down to show the differences in salaries paid to rural and city teachers and those paid to men and women, Burgess has supplied us with these data up to and including 1920. For the benefit of those who may be interested in tracing the wages of a particular group of teachers, Table 17 is presented, showing the average weekly salaries of men and women teachers in both rural and urban areas at five-year intervals beginning with 1890.

Table 17. Average Weekly Salaries of Teachers, 1890–1920 [1]

Year	Rural		City	
	Men	Women	Men	Women
1890	$11.30	$ 8.55	$32.62	$13.16
1895	11.70	8.91	31.63	13.40
1900	12.13	8.93	31.54	13.88
1905	14.39	10.15	33.79	14.86
1910	17.11	12.15	36.42	17.38
1915	18.61	13.63	37.15	21.06
1920	26.75	17.68	60.61	35.61
PERCENTAGE OF INCREASE	137	107	86	171

[1] Adapted from Burgess, Warren R., *op. cit.*, pp. 32–33.

The improvement in city women teachers' wages was most striking during this period, which probably reflects the efforts of the feminists to achieve equal pay. For some inexplainable reason, the salaries of rural women teachers did not increase so rapidly as those of rural men and lagged noticeably behind those paid to women in the urban areas.

WAGES OF OTHER WORKERS SINCE 1890

Since teachers have advanced their economic position rather significantly since 1890 and, in fact, have shown a rather steady improvement throughout the period, one might be inclined to congratulate them on their progress and turn a deaf ear to their demands for still higher wages. It is conceivable, however, that the total national dividend has been increasing rapidly since 1890, as a result of technological developments and improved marketing, and that other workers have enjoyed even a greater degree of prosperity during the intervening years than have teachers.

In 1890 the average weekly wage of laborers was $8.82. In 1920 it had risen to $26, an increase of 195 per cent. This, as

Table 17 shows, is considerably higher than the percentage increase in salaries for any group of teachers during the same period of time. Similarly, artisans' wages rose from $15.64 in 1890 to $42 in 1920, representing a percentage increase of 169.[6] This is approximately equal to the gain made by city women teachers and is considerably higher than that achieved by other groups of teachers.

Since 1920, however, teachers have made great strides and their position during the recent depression was more favorable than that of labor. Salaried employees are the last to feel the effects of a business slump and laborers are among the first to suffer reductions in income. The opposite is also true—that labor is the first to profit by a boom and teachers and other salaried groups are among the last.

Authorities are rather generally agreed that teachers' salaries have improved more rapidly during the twentieth century than have the wages of most groups of workers.[7] Such improvement is, of course, encouraging but, judging from the conditions which surrounded the teaching profession in 1890, there was considerable need and opportunity for advancing the economic and social position of the teacher. In the first place, the teacher's average annual earnings of $256 were pitifully inadequate even in 1890. Secondly, the school year at that time consisted of 135 days, whereas now it is well over 170 days. Teachers today are, therefore, working longer for the increased salary. A third factor that cannot be ignored is the marked increase which has occurred in recent years in the preparation of teachers. They have at least twice as much professional training today, on the average, as they did in 1890 and many more years of experience.

THE LIFE EARNINGS OF TEACHERS AND CERTAIN SELECTED GROUPS OF WORKERS

The relative attractiveness of teaching from an economic point of view can be best ascertained by a comparison of the incomes

[6] Burgess, Warren R., op. cit., p. 71.

[7] Ministers' salaries only increased from $731 in 1900 to $1826 in 1926; postal employees from $925 to $2128; salaried workers in manufacturing concerns from $1052 to $2428; railway salaried workers from $682 to $1604. Teachers' wages advanced during this same period from $328 to $1227. (Douglas, Paul H., op. cit.)

of teachers with those of other occupational groups. Professor Harold F. Clark has calculated both the average annual earnings and the average life earnings of workers in selected occupations. These averages are based upon the incomes prevailing in the various vocations between 1920 and 1936, and the estimated life earnings were calculated on the assumption that wage conditions in the future would be comparable to those which existed in the period just mentioned. Table 18 shows income facts and estimates for public-school teaching and for fifteen other occupations in the order of their economic attractiveness.

Table 18. Income in Public-school Teaching and Fifteen Other Occupations,[1]
1920–1936

Occupation	Present Value of Average Earnings for a Working Lifetime in Dollars	Average Earnings in Dollars per Year	Estimates in Percentage of the Limits within Which True Figure Probably Lies
Medicine	$108,000	$4850	±20
Law	105,000	4730	±35
Dentistry	95,400	4170	±25
Engineering	95,300	4410	±20
Architecture	82,500	3820	±40
College teaching	69,300	3050	±10
Social work	51,000	1650	±15
Journalism	41,500	2120	±45
Ministry	41,000	1980	±15
Library work	35,000	2020	±25
PUBLIC-SCHOOL TEACHING	29,700	1350	±05
Skilled trades	28,600	1430	±15
Nursing	23,300	1310	±10
Unskilled labor	15,200	795	±20
Farming	12,500	580	±15
Farm labor	10,400	485	±15

[1] Adapted from Clark, Harold F., *Life Earnings in Selected Occupations in the United States* (New York, Harper and Brothers, 1937), p. 5. Used by permission.

While the figures in Table 18 are, for the most part, only approximations of the true situation, they are the best estimates we have at the present time for appraising the relative economic status of the groups mentioned. Teachers are in eleventh position with respect to value of life earnings and in twelfth place in average annual earnings. From a purely financial point of view, medicine and law are approximately three and a half times as attractive as public-school teaching. Only nurses, unskilled laborers, farmers, and farm laborers fare worse than teachers in earning power, the skilled workers occupying approximately the same position as teachers.

The future of teachers' salaries in America is a highly speculative topic to discuss. The economic prospects of teachers cannot safely be divorced from the general prosperity of the country as a whole. If the total income of the country returns to where it was in predepression days or ascends to new heights, teachers may be expected to enjoy a greater degree of financial independence than they have ever experienced before. If, on the other hand, we linger indefinitely in a slough of business despondency, teachers can scarcely hope to improve their economic status to any appreciable extent. Wages for teachers come from public taxation and the taxpayer's willingness to support generous salary awards as well as his ability to do so are both conditioned by the state of his own pocketbook. The interrelationship between teachers' salaries and the income of citizens generally is too obvious to require lengthy discussion here. Despite the general reservation just made, however, it seems probable that, barring a complete breakdown in our economic machinery, teachers will get a somewhat larger share of the total national dividend than they have been assigned in the past.

This prediction is based on the general trend of the last one hundred years and on the improved political strength of the teaching personnel in America. Until recently teachers have been a rather subdued group in the body politic, playing an inconspicuous role in local and state affairs, displaying in most quarters a timidity which is characteristic of the underpaid and the economically insecure members of society. Many teachers have been transient and poorly trained and, consequently, in no position to press claims for larger rewards. But a professionally trained teacher personnel such as the future promises to witness, protected by tenure legislation and by organized action against intimidation, need not accept the salary ultimatums of parsimonious boards of education and city councils without concerted opposition. Nor need the battle be fought out primarily on local territory by small groups of teachers; rather, it can and probably will be carried to the state legislatures by a strong and enthusiastic lobby, and the particular demands of the profession laid on the doorstep of this representative governmental body, with a warning as to the penalty to be paid in case of unfavorable action. More equitable state-aid programs will be one type of legislation demanded by teachers as a means of raising salaries in the less wealthy school systems. Adherence to salary schedules already adopted and minimum salary legislation designed to safeguard the interests of rural teachers will also be among the objectives of state teachers' associations. By virtue of one million votes, a defensible and clearly defined schedule of wants, and a closely knit professional organization, public-school teachers should be more nearly able to "call the tune" in the years to come than at any time in the history of the profession.

In the hands of an unscrupulous and selfish group, such concentration of power would be an occasion for public alarm. That the real leaders in the profession will not encourage professional vandalism appears certain; whether or not they can curb it if it arises within the ranks of teachers is problematical. In any event, the handwriting on the wall suggests strongly that teachers are going to demonstrate a more questioning attitude toward salary policies and practices than heretofore, and that with improved professional training the tax bill for teachers' salaries will in all probability increase in size.

CHANGES IN THE THEORY AND PRACTICE OF REWARDING
TEACHERS SINCE 1890

The problem of teachers' salaries has received more attention from professional groups and school administrators since 1890 than during any previous period of comparable length. In fact, salary scheduling, with the exception of a few isolated cases, remained in a rather crude state until the second decade of the twentieth century. The explanation of teachers' wages seemed to be based upon an old conception of economics which can be characterized as a theory of "barter and sale." The teacher was asked, "What will you take?" and the employer, "What will you give?" and, after a dickering process, a mutual understanding was arrived at between the school committee on the one hand and the individual teacher on the other. This was related to a second theory which is still propounded today in answer to the puzzling query as to the basic consideration in wage determination. This was the theory of "supply and demand" which, commonly interpreted, meant that when applicants are numerous and vacancies scarce, wages should be low, and vice versa. Since teaching qualifications have been unusually flexible in most states, both from a legal standpoint and in relation to the demands of boards of education, the matter of ascertaining just what the supply is in relation to demand has always been a perplexing one. Unfortunately, this laxity in certification requirements has sometimes led indiscriminating school-board members to employ poorly prepared teachers at low rates of pay, thereby excluding the truly qualified candidates.

In the more enlightened communities, a third consideration entered into the establishment of wage determination, namely, "superficial comparison." Salaries were increased when it was popular to raise them and lowered when neighboring communities found it expedient to curtail expenses. Imitation, then, was the policy which weighed heavily in salary practices.

It would be unfair to the educational statesmen of the last century, however, to ignore certain features of salary scheduling which were destined to become a pattern for future years. Dyke,[8] in one of the earliest comprehensive studies of teachers' salaries in America, listed the provisions for the cities which he deemed to have the best schedules in 1898.[9] For most of the positions included in these schedules a minimum salary was indicated and for at least half of them an annual increment was stipulated. A stated maximum appears to have been common to all the schedules, varying in amount with size of city and position held.

[8] Dyke, Charles B., *The Economic Aspect of Teachers' Salaries* (New York, Columbia University, Contributions to Philosophy, Psychology and Education [1899], Vol. VII, No. 2).

[9] St. Louis; Boston; New Bedford, Mass.; Somerville, Mass.; Taunton, Mass.; Cleveland; Columbus, Ohio; Providence; San Francisco; Oakland; Los Angeles; Milwaukee; Louisville; Nashville; Grand Rapids; New York; Chicago.

The number of annual increments for classroom teachers ranged from three to sixteen, the average being approximately six in the high school and seven in the primary and grammar schools.

The framework of the modern salary scale was obviously present in the above city schedules; and while the minimum and maximum salaries were not based upon any careful study of cost of living nor the qualifications of the teaching staff, they had the merit at least of being definite and understandable. Presumably teachers in the primary grades, in accordance with their rank, began teaching at a specified minimum and proceeded according to a series of steps to a predetermined maximum.

Men and women were sometimes classified separately in the high-school schedules, the former enjoying a substantial differential throughout their period of employment. Schedules for elementary teachers were more numerous than for high-school teachers, boards of education finding it more convenient in the case of the latter to adjust salaries according to the position to be filled and the sex and qualifications of the individual applicant rather than in conformity with any prescribed plan.

While the influence of certain progressive administrators on salary practices throughout the country was probably considerable, there was no significant leadership exercised until the professional associations took up the problem on a national scale shortly after the turn of the century. The way to improvement had been paved by men like William McAndrew and Charles Dyke, through speeches and writings. McAndrew, in 1898, made a brilliant address before the New York State Teachers' Association in Rochester on the topic "Theories of Salaries Discussed," in which he assailed the individual bargaining procedures of boards of education and made a plea for salary schedules based upon cost of living and the professional needs of teachers. Dyke's contribution was even more significant, for it was the most thorough study of the problem that had yet been made. Not only did he make a clear exposition of the economic theory of teachers' salaries, but he explained the reasons why they were low, citing tradition, sentiment, public ignorance, public indifference, inefficiency of teachers, and the sex of teachers as the chief causes of the lowly state of the profession.

This study marked the beginning of a series of objective treatises on the economic status of teachers.

In 1903 the National Education Association appointed a committee to "inquire into and report upon salaries, tenure of office, and pension provisions of teachers in the public schools of the United States." This committee employed an expert statistician, Mr. Charles H. Verrill, to collect and interpret the facts on teachers' salaries. The report which the committee made as a result of Verrill's study was published in 1905. It contained a mass of statistics and was a source book on those interested in knowing what their neighbors were doing by way of rewarding teachers. It was purely a fact-finding committee and the report contained no suggestions of principles or procedures to be followed in drafting schedules.

In 1913, under the direction of Professor Robert C. Brooks of Swarthmore College, the National Education Association made another report on salaries, devoting the major portion of the study to facts bearing on cost of living. This helped to focus the attention of teachers and boards of education upon the relationship of salaries to the professional and economic needs of teachers—a consideration which McAndrew in 1898 had clearly pointed out, but which had been treated as an impractical platitude by most schedule makers.

The types of schedules described by Brooks in the 1913 study do not show any material extension or improvement over the ones listed in the 1905 report. Apparently the measurement movement was beginning to have some effect upon administrative policies, for Elliott's "Tentative Scheme of Measurement of Teaching Efficiency" was reproduced in this report as an illustration of an objective approach to the administration of salary schedules.

The next important study of teachers' salaries made by a National Education Association committee was published in 1918, just before the close of the war. The cost of living had risen rapidly during the war period and teachers' salaries had lagged behind. The tone of this report is somewhat bolder and sharper than former ones. The reader is led to believe from this 1918 study of *Teachers' Salaries and Cost of Living* that immediate action was imperative and that in the minds of the committee unless something were done to elevate the economic position of teachers, the American public would "kill the goose that lays the golden eggs." The sympathies of the committee toward the efforts, if not the methods, of teachers' unions in securing more equitable salary arrangements is indicative of the feeling of injustice which prevailed and is evidenced by such statements as the following: [10]

While many of us are strongly inclined to favor agitation within strictly professional lines rather than along the lines associated with the labor movement, we must recognize, however, that in certain communities the union method may be the better method. At least we must be prepared to welcome the cooperation of the new method in every feasible way.

The following year (1919) Professor E. S. Evenden, under the auspices of the National Education Association's Commission on the Emergency in Education, published a comprehensive study on *Teachers' Salaries and Salary Schedules in the United States, 1918–1919.* This was supplementary to the work done by the Committee on Salaries, Tenure and Pension and constituted a landmark in the development of salary principles and policies.

Evenden evolved, from his study of best practice and from his own thinking about possible procedures, a rather definite plan of setting up and operating a salary schedule. There had been no clear philosophy underlying most salary schedules heretofore and no reasonable defense for practice. Procedures had grown up like Topsy. Evenden provided a rational explanation for his proposals. He urged the adoption of the single-salary schedule and suggested specific standards for the administration of schedules. His recommendations carried great weight in the many debates of salary issues engaged in by teachers and school boards during the next decade.

The National Education Association Salary Committee followed up Evenden's historic study with a similar investigation four years later and published a report, entitled *Teachers' Salaries and Salary Trends in 1923.* This bulletin contained comparative

[10] *Teachers' Salaries and Cost of Living,* National Education Association, The Report of the Committee on Teachers' Salaries, Tenure and Pensions (July, 1918), p. 21.

information on salaries of school employees in cities of various sizes, data on cost-of-living trends, salary-schedule provisions, and a chapter on "Principles and Standards in the Making and Administration of Teachers' Salary Schedules."

One of the interesting disclosures of this report was the number of communities operating single-salary schedules. Whereas in 1918–1919 there were no salary scales embodying all the principles which are ordinarily understood to be included in a single-salary schedule, in 1923, 154 or 16 per cent of all American cities were operating schedules of this type.

According to the findings of this study, 57 per cent or 538 of the cities reporting rated the quality of the teaching service, but in most instances the ratings did not affect salaries directly. Just what proportion of the cities could be classified as using merit-type rating schedules cannot be deduced from this investigation. It is apparent, however, that ratings were most commonly used as supervisory devices to improve teaching technique.

Among the recommendations of the committee was one which has played a very important part in salary scheduling and which in recent years has proved to be ill adapted to the current situation. It was laid down as a sound principle that the annual salary increment should approximate 10 per cent of the salary. Thus, if a teacher's minimum wage were $1500 a year, the increment would be $150, whereas if it were only $900, it would be correspondingly reduced to $90. In 1923 a 10 per cent increment was considered conservative since, in the words of the committee, "it stands not only for interest upon his [the teacher's] investment in training but also for the increased earning power resulting from successful experience." [11]

Hindsight is always better than foresight. Experience has demonstrated that, despite the theoretical arguments which were advanced in support of a 10 per cent annual increase in salary, it was a more rapid rate of progress than the taxpayers were willing to grant to the rank and file of the teaching profession. The practice today is far less generous than the one recommended in this 1923 report and, except for a few of the wealthy school

[11] *Teachers' Salaries and Salary Trends in 1923*, National Education Association, Research Bulletin (May, 1923), Vol. I, No. 3, p. 75.

districts in which schedules were introduced during the heydays of the twenties, annual increments for classroom teachers seldom exceed $125, regardless of basic salary.

From 1923 to the present time the National Education Association has continued its leadership in this important field of teachers' salaries. Not only have they collected and made available to the profession and the public statistical information as to current practices, but they have evolved principles and encouraged pioneer efforts in salary scheduling, until today superintendents of schools, teachers' organizations, and lay boards of education have for their guidance an imposing array of precedents, principles, and procedures.

Probably the most unique service the National Education Association renders in the improvement of the economic status of teachers is the biennial collection and tabulation of facts on teachers' salaries for cities ranging in population from twenty-five hundred to one hundred thousand and over. This work was begun in 1924–1925 and has been generally approved by teachers and school-board members because of its practical utility in appraising and reorganizing salary levels.

Over and above the attention given to salaries by the staff of the Research Division, special committees of the National Education Association are still chosen from time to time to study and report on problems related to the economic welfare of the classroom teacher. In 1935 a committee, of which B. R. Buckingham was chairman, submitted a report which was issued as a Research Bulletin of the Association on *The Teacher's Economic Position*.[12] This report has been used as a source of reference by nearly every local salary committee in America and is looked upon as an authoritative document by members of the profession.

State and local associations have also contributed to the improvement of the teacher's economic welfare. They have encouraged the collection of facts, and in those states where the association maintains a research department they have actually carried on intensive salary studies in the interest of the teaching profession. Similarly, local associations have employed expert

---

[12] *The Teacher's Economic Position*, National Education Association, Research Bulletin (September, 1935), Vol. XIII, No. 4.

assistance in analyzing their salary problems and in several instances have made the matter one for committee study and investigation.

The American Federation of Teachers has been particularly alert to salary injustices since its organization in 1916. At the annual convention in 1931 the Federation went on record as favoring a two-thousand-dollar minimum salary for teachers. As modest a stipend as this may have appeared to be to representatives from New York City and Chicago, it was looked upon as a wild dream by school boards and educators in the majority of American communities. The point of view represented by the Federation has been much more radical with respect to salaries than that of the National Education Association and its affiliated state and local organizations. In most communities, the number of teachers belonging to the American Federation has been too small to carry great weight with boards of education and, even though theoretically they are allied closely with labor, the results have not been so spectacular as one might expect from the potential strength implied in such a union.

State departments of education have also been favorably disposed toward the improvement of teacher welfare, and the leadership exercised by state superintendents and their associates through public reports, addresses, and general advisory relationships has been beneficial.

Educators have not stood alone in their efforts to wrest a living wage from the watchdogs of local treasuries. An ally which has rescued them from defeat on many an occasion has been the parent-teacher association. While this organization has not pursued any consistent policy with respect to teachers' salaries and has not been active in studying the problem, it has been, on the whole, friendly toward the general movement to raise the economic and social level of teachers.

It may appear to the reader from the foregoing discussion that teachers and educators have organized themselves over the years into a pressure group to promote their own interests rather than those of children. That the national and state associations just mentioned constitute pressure groups is, in the judgment of the author, an undeniable fact; that their interests are selfish in the narrow sense of the term does not follow. American life consists of myriads of organizations whose purposes range from the purely altruistic to the diabolical. In the educational world, taxpayers' leagues and associations are bobbing up periodically to harass public-school officials with accusations of extravagance and waste. These organizations collect statistics; they frequently disseminate half-truths and, in some instances, they wield big political sticks in an effort to curtail budgets and keep taxes low. Salaries, since they usually account for three quarters of the current school budget, are likely to be the major object of attack. For teachers to sit idly by like Pontius Pilate and wash their hands of the whole matter would be to sacrifice professional standards which have taken decades to achieve and which over a period of years are closely related to the welfare of children. It is a truism that in the long run the wage rate determines the quality of the service rendered and it is only natural that teachers should be equally as alert to this fact as taxpayers. To protect the interests of the service to which they have consecrated their lives is not a selfish objective; and while individual teachers here and there and perhaps groups of teachers sometimes may be selfish and unworthy of the rewards which the public has provided them, this in no way denies the validity of the argument that teachers, through their associations, should protect their members against unjust salary practices and should employ pressure methods when necessary to defend a just cause.

RECENT APPROACHES TO THE SALARY PROBLEM

The approach to the salary problem in recent years has been quite different from the superficial methods employed prior to 1900. As was pointed out previously, salaries were largely determined in these early years by one of two methods: comparison with other communities or by an individual bargaining procedure. The former technique was superior to the latter, although little defense could be made for either of them. No serious attention was given to the cost or standard of living of teachers. Apart from the perennial complaints of members of the profession about the economic plight of the schoolteacher, professional and economic needs seldom entered into the discussions of salary problems. School surveys were unknown and expert opinion, had there been any available, would not have been favorably received by local school boards, who considered it *their* right and prerogative to determine the salaries and hire the teachers. Reliance was commonly placed upon the mystical law of supply and demand to somehow adjust salaries to appropriate levels. This theory served as a final answer to all who questioned the "reason why." The older and more advanced the pupil taught, the higher the wage of the teacher. Men, by virtue of their masculinity, and in some instances for sounder reasons, were universally accorded higher remuneration than women. Some attention was focused upon the qualifications of teachers within the same unit of the school system and such designations as first assistant, second assistant, and so on implied different qualifications and different salary awards.

Cost-of-Living Standards and Wages in Other Vocations. Largely as a result of the studies and efforts of the National Education Association and the work of individual educators here and there, the problem of salaries and salary scheduling has been attacked in recent years in a more thorough and scientific fashion. In the first place, it has become an accepted principle in socially minded communities that salaries should be high enough to enable teachers to maintain a dignified scale of living. With this principle in mind, schedule makers now collect detailed figures on cost-of-living and translate the basic needs of teachers into minimum and maximum salaries. This task consumes a great deal of time and requires extraordinary judgment if sound proposals are to be derived from the process.

Paralleling the cost-of-living analysis go comparative studies of salaries and wages of workers in vocations demanding equivalent qualifications to those required of teachers, and of the salary policies affecting teachers in communities of similar type and size. These studies focus attention upon the value placed by society upon intelligence, training, and personality in other walks of life and show how generous or niggardly other communities are in the remuneration of schoolteachers. While common practice is not in and of itself a sound criterion by which to judge the acceptability and soundness of a policy, it is well for those establishing salary schedules to know the degree to which they are departing from the norm. Furthermore, comparative studies enable the schedule maker to take some account of the elusive law of supply and demand.

The Single-salary Schedule. Along with a more thorough and comprehensive attack upon the problem of basic wage rates, there seems to be developing a number of changes in the structure of the schedule itself which merit some consideration here. By far the most drastic modification is the substitution of the single-salary schedule for the traditional position-type scale. Despite the present superiority in numbers of the position-type schedule, the practice of rewarding high-school teachers, regardless of qualifications, more generously than elementary teachers is fast losing ground.

Educators have realized for years the fallacy of this tradition, even though communities have been loath to modify their former practices. State departments of education have rapidly increased the training requirements for elementary teachers. Universities and teachers' colleges have made corresponding changes in their curricular offerings; in fact, only the uninformed or the uneducated still think of the difficulty or importance of the teacher's task in terms of the size and age of the youngster to be taught. It seems inevitable, therefore, that a type of schedule will soon be generally adopted wherein years of training and experience, rather than the outmoded criterion of subject or grade taught, will determine the salaries of teachers.

Merit Ratings. A second trend in the administration of salary scheduling is in the direction of discarding all attempts to reward teachers according to subjective ratings of efficiency. With the development of the measurement movement in the United States during the first two decades of the century, there arose a hue and cry for some kind of a measuring rod that would appraise accurately the effectiveness of teachers. Rating scales of various types were drafted and a large number of communities attempted to pay their teachers in accordance with their scores on these newly created devices. The procedure never met with the approval of teachers and this fact, coupled with the demonstrated unreliability of the ratings secured, has brought the scheme into disrepute as a factor in salary scheduling.

To the businessman accustomed to the idea that promotions should be based solely on merit, this trend has appeared irrational and hence indefensible. To those who are closest to the problem, however, the harmful effects on teacher morale of applying rating devices appear to more than offset the good that is derived. In fact, it is the judgment of many school administrators that the total educational product of a school system is greater where teachers are paid according to years of training and experience than where they are rewarded on the basis of efficiency ratings. These superintendents contend that wise selection and intelligent leadership are far better methods of improving the quality of instruction than is the holding of a club over the heads of teachers in the form of a rating scale.

There appears to be no good reason, also, for assuming that a merit type of salary schedule deals more justly with teachers than do the automatic scales. The total contribution of an individual teacher to the development of a particular child cannot be measured accurately. For this reason, superintendents and boards of education should be exceedingly skeptical of the validity and reliability of instruments, the purpose of which is to classify teachers according to merit.

To many modern educators, there is still a further criticism of merit rating which is perhaps more fundamental than any of the other objections which are commonly advanced against it. This is the matter of stimulating a competitive spirit among individuals whose only hope of successful achievement lies in cooperation. The education of children is a group project, not an individual one, and any spirit of rivalry which is developed to speed up competition is likely to prevent gains which would otherwise be made. Since rating tends to accentuate rivalry, it is, therefore, regarded as a destructive device to use in rewarding teachers. While the trend is clearly away from the general employment of rating schemes in connection with salary schedules, administrators frequently withhold annual increments from teachers whose services are clearly unsatisfactory. The status of the profession has not yet reached the place where all its members are motivated by high ideals of service; and despite the theoretical desirability of removing all administrative goads and whips, it has not been deemed practical by many educators to do so. Tenure laws have further complicated the matter by the degree of protection which they guarantee to even the lazy and indifferent teachers. Accompanied by an automatic-promotion-type salary schedule, the only recourse for school boards is to bring these malingerers up on charges of incompetency and attempt to oust them from their positions. The bitterness engendered by this process, despite its acknowledged justification, has led most school administrators to close their eyes to incompetency in teaching and follow the course of least resistance. The only other alternative is to pay teachers according to an efficiency-rating plan.

Equal Pay and Family Allowances. A third factor in modern salary scheduling which has experienced considerable change over the past twenty-five years is the "equal-pay" provision enforced in ten states [13] by law and in the majority of communities operating salary schedules by the rules and regulations of boards of education.

The feminist movement in the United States accounts for the legal enactments on equal pay, all of which have occurred since woman suffrage in 1920. The equal-pay controversy is not of recent origin, however. As was indicated in an earlier chapter, the topic was discussed frequently at teachers' institutes and at association meetings prior to the Civil War. The arguments advanced both in support of equal pay and against it have not varied much throughout the years. Those who have favored it have pointed out the obvious justice of paying women the same wage for making the same, or an equivalent, contribution to society as men. Those who have opposed it have done so on the ground that such practice was incompatible with the operation of the law of supply and demand; that equal pay would result either in driving men out of the profession altogether or in attracting to it only those who were woefully unfit for the task; and, finally, that it did not operate in the business and industrial

---

[13] In 1930 equal-pay laws were in effect in the District of Columbia and the following ten states: California, Louisiana, Maryland, Nevada, New Jersey, New York, Oregon, Texas, Washington, and Wyoming. Summaries of state school legislation since 1930 make no reference to any recent laws requiring equal pay.

world and was, therefore, unsuited to the conditions prevailing in teaching.

The influence of equal pay on the profession is certainly a debatable issue. To some observers, it appears that the new provision has tended to weld together the personnel into a more cooperative and efficient whole; that, where before there was jealousy and bitterness on the part of the women teachers because of the disparity in salary and a tendency to draw lines in supporting and opposing issues in their association meetings on the basis of sex rather than according to intellectual belief, now there is a feeling of equality which is essential for the success of any democratic undertaking; that, from the standpoint of mental hygiene, equal pay has returned big dividends in removing feelings of inferiority which have been a characteristic trait of women for generations. Equal pay, then, constituted the destruction of one more fortress in this *man's* world.

These observations cannot be dismissed lightly. They represent the opinions of the vast majority of schoolteachers and of women generally. Nor are the men united in their opposition to the principle; otherwise, there could not be ten laws on the statute books upholding women's rights to wage equality. To the dispassionate student of the problem, however, the provision of equal pay has not been considered an unqualified blessing. Not only does it ignore the fact that the relationship of wage conditions outside of the public service to teachers' salaries has a profound effect upon the supply and demand of men teachers, but it overlooks entirely the economic problem confronting married men and especially those with dependent children. It suggests, in effect, that the services of the married woman in the home, rearing children and providing for the comfort of her husband and family, are not worthy of any financial recognition by society. It is obvious to the most casual observer that a married man cannot adequately provide for himself, his wife, and two children on a salary that is just sufficient to meet the needs of a single man or woman. It seems equally unreasonable that boards of education should establish salary schedules designed for families of four when eighty per cent or more of the profession are single and without legal dependents. If the salary is based on the cost of living of single women teachers, then either the ablest of the men will not enter the field of teaching or, if they do, they will be forced to supplement their income by earnings outside of the profession.

Equal-pay legislation is desirable and justifiable only when it is accompanied by a system of family allowances. Such a plan does not differentiate in salaries on the basis of sex but, like income-tax regulations, takes account of the larger responsibilities of the married man and the widow with dependent children.

There are a few communities in the United States which have adjusted salaries within the last few years in keeping with this general idea, the most notable of which are Grand Island, Nebraska, and Garden City, Long Island, New York.[14]

As plausible as such an arrangement appears, it is most difficult to persuade boards of education to adopt it. To them it connotes socialism, communism, Townsendism, or some other share-the-wealth *ism* and seems wholly inconsistent with the American way of doing things. The educational significance of the plan has not penetrated deeply into their minds.

While predictions sometimes prove to be embarrassing, the author is willing to venture the guess that the principle of family allowances will eventually become an integral part of state-aid regulations, thereby encouraging the employment of teachers on a basis of merit without regard to their marital status or the amount of dependency. In the meantime, some experimentation with family allowances will not come amiss in demonstrating its effectiveness on the morale of the teaching staff and in discovering the relative cost of operating such a plan.

Annual Increments. Perhaps the issue which is of greatest financial concern is the matter of the number of annual salary increments to be awarded. In the older schedules, it was common practice to provide relatively few increments. Under this ar-

[14] The provision in the original Garden City schedule reads as follows: "Upon application to the Superintendent (form to be supplied by the Board) and with the approval of the Board of Education, a family allowance may be granted to any classroom or special teacher under conditions such as, to a married teacher with wife or to a widow with dependent children, where a maximum of $300 for such dependent wife and a maximum of $100 for each child under 18 years of age may be allowed. No application will be considered where the yearly income of the dependent or dependents is more than $300."

rangement, many teachers arrive at the maximum salary by the time they are thirty-four or thirty-five years of age and expect to remain at this vantage point for another thirty or thirty-five years until forced out by retirement. As long as teaching was a peripatetic profession, communities could count on enough turnover to offset the high cost of maintaining the few whose tenure equaled or exceeded the number of increments allotted. Unfortunately, or fortunately (depending on how one views it), teachers now are looking at teaching as a life career rather than as a stopgap until marriage or as a steppingstone to some other profession, with the result that their average tenure has more than doubled in many sections of the country within the past decade. If this trend continues, the proportion of teachers who will achieve the highest rung of the salary ladder will increase drastically and salary budgets will mount accordingly.

In one metropolitan-area community whose schedule for elementary teachers called for ten annual increments, sixty-five per cent of the personnel had reached the maximum salary in 1936–1937, and ninety-one per cent were at or near this point on the scale. Even when due consideration is made for the separation of teachers from the school system because of death, retirement, and withdrawal for other causes, the group receiving the maximum salary in this city will remain disproportionately large for several years to come. If the scale is totally inadequate, such a condition may not constitute a serious drain on the municipal treasury. On the other hand, if the maximum has been established with some reference to sound principles of salary scheduling and proper consideration has been given to living expenses, the costs are likely to arouse the ire of taxpayers and serve as a boomerang to the schools.

A further weakness in such an arrangement lies in the absence of financial incentive for teachers who survive beyond this brief decade. A thirty-five-year-old teacher with no further monetary worlds to conquer is likely to lose some of her zest and enthusiasm. The time may come when teachers are paid a "single wage" and when salary increments will no longer be considered necessary for stimulating professional growth. When that day arrives, if ever, American psychology will have been radically modified and other equally potent substitutes will have been created for money. At the present time, the practice of limiting increments to eight or ten is neither financially sound nor can it be defended by practice in other professions. The newer schedules for teachers must unquestionably provide longer spans between the minimum and maximum. It seems probable that eighteen to twenty-five years will be the usual length of time required for a beginning teacher to arrive at the highest point on the salary schedule.

OTHER CURRENT SALARY PROBLEMS

There are many other matters pertaining to teachers' salaries, in addition to those just discussed, which might be of interest to those who are confronted with salary problems; but only two or three will be mentioned here, because this is not intended as an exhaustive treatment of the topic. Until our antiquated tax machinery and formulas for distributing state aid are reconstructed, there will always be communities which cannot afford to reward teachers adequately. No matter how one rearranges a schedule, if the salaries awarded are too small, the results will be most disheartening to teachers. Fortunately, the profession is gradually awakening to the importance of sound tax plans and state-aid regulations, and considerable revision is already under way. If, in addition, the federal government moves soon in the direction of granting support to public education in accordance with state needs, the problem of ability to pay will no longer assume its present proportions.

Perhaps the most difficult task confronting schedule makers is that of enlisting the support of teachers, taxpayers, and school-board members in any salary proposal designed to serve the best interests of school children. Facts fall down like wooden soldiers before the onslaught of emotions and the salary question inevitably stimulates an emotional response, since to both teacher and taxpayer it is a highly personal matter.

The past few years have witnessed more vocal opposition on the part of teachers to board-of-education policies and traditional administrative techniques than heretofore. This is especially true in states having teacher-tenure laws, where security in position strengthens courage and permits a freer expression of opinion than is otherwise the case. Teachers' organizations are particularly active in salary campaigns, and the political and moral pressure which they exert cannot be dismissed lightly. On the other hand, there are strong taxpayers' groups which see this matter in quite a different light. As self-constituted watchdogs of municipal funds, they view with alarm any plan which promises to increase the tax millage.

The solution to this controversy does not appear imminent, but in the author's opinion it lies in a more democratic procedure in establishing wage and salary policies. Salary scheduling is not a one-man job; it is, rather, a matter to be undertaken cooperatively by all parties concerned. A few communities have already recognized the efficacy of this method and have submitted the whole problem to representatives of the teaching group, the administrative and supervisory staff, taxpayers, and board members. While the amount of time and patience required to establish schedules through such a procedure will unquestionably be great, the friction resulting from the traditional methods so commonly used should be considerably reduced.

Suggested Readings

Burgess, Warren R., *Trends of School Costs* (New York, Russell Sage Foundation, Education Monographs, 1920).

Douglas, Paul H., *Real Wages in the United States, 1890–1926* (Boston, Houghton Mifflin Company, 1930).

Elsbree, Willard S., *Teachers' Salaries* (New York, Bureau of Publications, Teachers College, Columbia University, 1931).

History of Wages in the United States from Colonial Times to 1928, U. S. Department of Labor, Bureau of Labor Statistics, Bulletin No. 499 (1929).

The Preparation of Teachers' Salary Schedules, Part I and II, National Education Association, Research Bulletins (January and March, 1936), Vol. XIV, Nos. 1 and 2.

The Teacher's Economic Position, National Education Association, Research Bulletin (September, 1935), Vol. XIII, No. 4.

XXX

Teachers' Pension and Retirement Systems

THE problem of the superannuated teacher is as old as the American school system itself. In the absence of retirement regulations, the earliest schoolmasters continued to "keep" school as long as their strength would permit and, unless they absented themselves frequently and for long periods of time, the colonial towns were reluctant to compel them to resign their duties to make way for younger teachers. There is a case on record of a Massachusetts schoolmaster who was voted a pension as early as 1671, and Kilpatrick reports an instance in New Netherland around 1770 in which the widow of a schoolmaster was given an annual pension of twenty pounds by the Dutch Reformed Church.[1]

However, these were the exceptions. General practice did not concede schoolmasters any advantages of this nature over private citizens. Like nearly everyone else, they were expected to make their own provisions against the vicissitudes of old age by exercising extreme care and wisdom in the management of their resources. If they landed in the poorhouse or spent the last days of their life in a poverty-stricken environment, it was not a matter of great concern to the public at large. More usually, friends and relatives came to the support of the aged and eased their burdens by contributions and direct aid.

Obvious as the need was for some kind of organized attack on this old-age problem, it did not receive any public attention to speak of prior to 1869, when the New York City Teachers Mutual Life Assurance Association was formed. Pensions for policemen were introduced in the larger cities in America as

---

[1] Kilpatrick, William H., *The Dutch Schools of New Netherland and Colonial New York*, p. 157.

early as 1859; and at a somewhat later date firemen were made eligible for pensions, either at the expense of the taxpayers alone or through some other financial arrangement. While the idea of pensioning teachers would have been called to public attention soon after the inauguration of retirement plans for policemen and firemen simply because it presented an analogous situation, it did not, for some strange reason, spring primarily from this source. The foundation for a system of pension and retirement allowances for schoolteachers was laid in New York City. Several times during the year 1869 collection lists were circulated among the teachers in one of the large schools in New York, with an appeal to them to contribute to the burial expenses of an associate who had died without leaving any funds. This procedure led one of the schoolmasters, a Mr. Vanderbilt, to organize an association for the mutual protection of teachers. It was this young man's idea that each teacher would contribute one dollar whenever death knocked at the door of an associate, with the understanding that he would be assured of similar consideration in the event of his own death. The response to his proposal was favorable and, as a result, the New York City Teachers Mutual Life Assurance Association was established (1869). This was followed, two years later, by a similar organization in Brooklyn. The scheme apparently did not stir the imagination of teachers generally, for it was nine years before a third association was formed by Jersey City teachers; and the next one to follow it was in Camden, in 1885.

These associations were obviously very loosely organized. They had no capital; there were no annual dues, only assessments on call; no sick benefits were included in the provisions; and death benefits were by no means uniform, ranging from $120 in Camden to $500 in the New York association.

Despite the absence of actuarial data and mortality tables, the older teachers lent enthusiastic support to the mutual-aid societies. They welcomed the protection which was promised by such an arrangement. On the other hand, the younger instructors resented the assessments and considered them burdensome. Since death to them seemed a long way off and since many of them planned to marry or leave the service for other reasons, their interest in mutual aid was at no time great.

However relieved the older teachers may have felt because of the death benefits which were guaranteed by the mutual life-assurance associations, they were still worried and harassed by the thought of long, unexpected illness. This problem began to command the attention of public-school teachers by 1880, and most of the associations established after this date included sick benefits payable for certain limited periods. These were unlike the lump-sum death benefits. The former had to be paid day by day and the principle of assessments on call gave way to a system of regular annual dues. The extension of the benefits, therefore, produced some improvement in the methods of financing the associations. Since the whole scheme was not based on any actuarial calculations, however, all these early associations were financially unsound.

With death benefits provided by life-assurance associations and temporary illness cared for by sick-benefit associations, there remained only old-age and permanent-disability annuities to give the teacher as high a degree of security against misfortune, accident, and superannuation as any professional group of workers could hope for. The teachers of New York City and Brooklyn established the first voluntary annuity associations in 1887. The annual contributions of members in the New York society amounted to one per cent of salary and the maximum annuity after thirty-five to forty years of service was six hundred dollars. Teachers were eligible for disability benefits after five years' membership in the association. The requirements and provisions of other city benefit societies were similar to those listed above. Women were commonly allowed to retire with fewer years of service than men, a privilege which has since been demonstrated to be quite unsound actuarily. In fact, studies have shown clearly that the life expectancy of women at sixty-five is considerably greater than that of men; hence, if either sex should have been favored by a shorter service requirement, it should have been the male.

A few of the associations combined life insurance with sick benefits and annuities, although the amount of the death benefits in all instances was markedly small.

The chief problems confronting all the early associations were financial ones. Promoters were distraught over the indifference of the younger teachers toward joining the system. To these youthful pedagogues, old age, disability, and death seemed too remote a matter to warrant sacrificing the immediate use of any part of their monthly wage. The membership was, therefore, restricted to a considerable extent to the older and feebler individuals in the teaching staff, many of whom were extremely poor risks. When the associations got well under way and it was discovered that the costs exceeded all expectations, it was necessary to devise ways and means of balancing the budget or else to close up shop. Some of the associations were quite proficient in raising money through bazaars and private donations. However, this soon became tiresome to the public and embarrassing to the promoters, and most of these early associations found it impossible to meet their promises. In order to carry on at all, they were compelled to prorate benefits. The realization by teachers that the annuity associations could not meet their obligations had an effect comparable to a loss of confidence in a bank. The young members hastened to withdraw from the associations, thereby causing a panic among the whole membership. The result was the collapse of most of the societies.

Publicly Supported Pensions

Somewhat discouraged but not wholly dismayed, the teachers' pension enthusiasts cast around for a solution to their perplexing problem. It seemed reasonable that some provision should be made for the retirement of superannuated teachers, and the precedent established by the municipalities in granting old-age benefits to firemen and policemen served as a lead to the ardent supporters of the pension movement. Perhaps the government would bear the burden of pensioning schoolteachers. Efforts were made to secure such legislation in New York City and, after several years of fruitless toil, the friends of the movement succeeded in getting a rather innocuous bill through the state legislature in 1894; this provided for a pension fund, the resources of which were to be derived from deductions made from the salaries of teachers because of absence. There was to be no assessment against the salaries of teachers; on the other hand, no provision was made in the law for using tax moneys to supplement the income from absence deductions in case this fund proved inadequate.

The legislative enactment was conveniently vague and general. The New York City Board of Education was given full control over the fund, and pensions of one half of the final salary, not exceeding one thousand dollars, could be granted to teachers who were mentally or physically disabled. The service requirement was thirty-five years for men and thirty years for women.

Inadequate and unsound as this first legislation was, it aroused teachers to action in several other cities throughout the country and within two years at least eight such pension funds had been established.

The First State Retirement Systems

Following closely in the wake of these municipal enterprises was the creation of a mutual old-age and invalidity insurance association in New Jersey in 1896, with the state acting as custodian and administrator of the funds. Members of this association were to contribute one per cent of their salary and were to receive on disability after twenty years of service an annuity of one half of their salary with a minimum of $250 and a maximum of $600. This principle of relating benefits to salary had been used by the Brooklyn Aid Association earlier and was soon to be employed rather universally. New Jersey, therefore, is credited with having established the first state-wide teachers' pension system in America (1896).

The development of state-wide retirement systems was exceedingly slow, New Jersey, Maryland, Rhode Island, and Virginia comprising the only states to institute such arrangements for teachers before 1910. In contrast to this retarded growth, the local teacher-pension movement spread rapidly, and between 1905 and 1914 sixty-five cities had established retirement plans.[2]

The trend after 1910, however, was away from the organization of local to the creation of state systems, and not uncommonly

---

[2] Palmer, Nida Pearl, *Pension Systems for Public School Teachers*, U. S. Bureau of Education, Bulletin 1927, No. 23 (Washington, Government Printing Office), p. 4.

the former pension funds and obligations were absorbed by the larger state system to the advantage of all parties concerned. Teachers protected under local retirement systems could not transfer to other teaching posts, even within the same state, without loss of benefits. Furthermore, the cost of operating a small pension system was proportionally greater than administering a state one. So the absorption of local retirement funds and the assumption of the financial obligations by the state systems were really to the economic advantage of both teachers and school districts. The state welcomed the larger membership, since it tended to reduce the per capita costs of administration.

Most of the local and many of the state pension systems formed before 1915 were unsound financially and continued their existence only by shifting their deficiencies ahead year by year. Adequate reserves were almost never provided and the liabilities were considerably greater than the assets. In the old New York City system, for example, an actuarial investigation in 1914 showed a deficiency of more than fifty-four million dollars, the result of an insufficient income over its twenty-one-year period of operation.

It is difficult to understand how intelligent individuals organizing an insurance enterprise would fail to see the inconsistency of promising benefits beyond those earned by the accumulated income of the fund. But that is just exactly what happened. The embarrassing situation which confronted several of these early pension systems led to a great deal of discussion about retirement legislation and eventually to a more businesslike approach to the handling of the funds. The leadership for the establishment of the more recently created state systems has been provided by the Carnegie Foundation for the Advancement of Teaching and by the National Education Association.[3] These two organiza-

---

[3] The Department of Superintendence of the National Education Association recommended the enactment of laws in the several states "to permit and to regulate the retirement and pensioning of teachers" as early as 1891. Not until 1911, however, did a committee of the National Education Association actually report on existing pension systems and then only in a superficial way. In 1916 the Teachers' Salaries, Tenure and Pensions Committee reported that it had arranged with the Federal Bureau of Education and the Carnegie Foundation for the Advancement of Teaching for a study of the pension problem. This study, which was a comprehensive treatment of pension practices and philosophy, was published by the Carnegie

tions have both devoted a great deal of time and money to research in this field and, as a result of their efforts, a sound program of pension and retirement for public-school employees has been evolved.

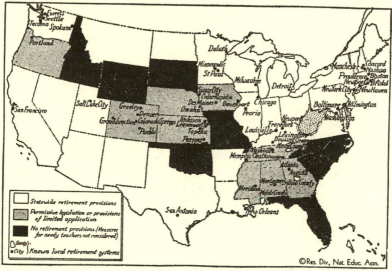

FIGURE II. STATE AND LOCAL RETIREMENT SYSTEMS [1]

[1] Taken from *Teacher Retirement Systems and Social Security*, National Education Association, Research Bulletin (May, 1937), Vol. XV, No. 3, p. 99.

By 1937 state teacher retirement laws had been enacted in twenty-eight states, Hawaii, the Panama Canal Zone, and Puerto Rico.[4]

Foundation in 1918. Five years later the National Education Association appointed a Committee on Retirement Allowances. This committee, in cooperation with the National Council of Teachers' Retirement Systems and the Research Division of the National Education Association, was active in promoting sound retirement principles. In 1937 a new association, the result of a merger between the Committee on Retirement Allowances and the National Council of Teacher Retirement Systems, was formed and is called the National Council on Teacher Retirement of the National Education Association.

[4] The states having retirement systems in 1937, together with the dates of enactment of laws are as follows: Arizona (1912), Arkansas (1937), California (1913), Canal Zone (1926), Connecticut (1917), Hawaii (1926), Illinois (1915), Indiana (1921), Kentucky (1928), Louisiana (1936), Maine (1924), Maryland (1927), Massachusetts (1914), Michigan (1915), Minnesota (1915), Montana (1915–1937), Nevada (1937), New Jersey (1919), New Mexico (1933–1937), New York (1921), North Dakota (1913), Ohio (1920), Pennsylvania (1919), Puerto Rico (1928),

Local retirement systems are still fairly numerous, in spite of the pronounced trend toward state-wide systems. The former may be classified into three types: (1) those operating within, but independent of, a state-wide system, such as New York City, San Francisco, and Chicago; (2) those based on a state law providing for teacher retirement in a certain class of community, such as Wilmington, Delaware; Atlanta, Georgia; and Omaha, Nebraska; and (3) those based on general permissive legislation, such as Colorado Springs, Colorado; and Des Moines, Iowa.

As indicated by Figure II on the preceding page, neither state nor local retirement systems are limited to any single section of the United States.

Approximately sixty-five per cent of the teachers in the United States were protected by some kind of state or local retirement system in 1937. Unfortunately, however, the benefits provided in many of these systems are quite inadequate to care for the needs of the members retiring.

As Figure III shows, when only those teachers are considered who can look forward with some assurance to a retirement allowance, the number and proportion who expect fifty dollars or less a month is disproportionately large, comprising as it does approximately 275,000 teachers or slightly less than half of the total number who belong to retirement systems. While the proponents of pension and retirement allowances have never claimed that the protection guaranteed under retirement systems obviated the necessity for personal savings on the part of teachers, the fact still remains that thousands of teachers, for apparently good reasons, arrive at the compulsory retirement age without any income or savings apart from their pension and retirement allowance.

The extension of retirement systems to include sixty-five per cent of the teaching personnel is a most encouraging fact, although the situation is not quite so hopeful as it appears to be at first glance. Several of the systems are based upon principles which are actuarily unsound. In some instances, benefits are promised which bear no relation to the annual deposits of mem-

Rhode Island (1908), Texas (1937), Utah (1935–1937), Vermont (1919), Virginia (1908), Washington (1923–1937), Wisconsin (1921).

bers. The Virginia system, established in 1908, is an example. It provides for an annuity equal to one half the average salary of the teacher during her last five years of service, with a maximum allowance of $400 unless salary equals $1000, then a maximum of $500.[5] The teacher's deposit in the above system is one per cent of salary and the state's contribution is "such sums as may be appropriated for the benefit of the retired teachers' fund." While potentially the state has the financial resources to supplement the teacher's deposit to the extent of guaranteeing a $400 allowance, there is no provision in the law calling for an annual appropriation to meet the costs of the system. In other words, it is not a clear contractual relationship between the teacher and the state; and in case the legislature should fail to take the necessary steps to make the fund solvent, the teachers would lose their equity.

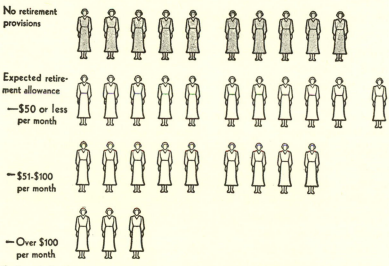

No retirement provisions

Expected retirement allowance
—$50 or less per month

—$51-$100 per month

—Over $100 per month

Each symbol represents 25 000 teachers.   Based on data from 50 state and local government systems

FIGURE III. TEACHERS AND ECONOMIC SECURITY[1]

[1] This figure does not include teachers who are under new or inoperative systems. Adapted from *Teacher Retirement Systems and Social Security*, National Education Association, Research Bulletin (May, 1937), Vol. XV, No. 3, p. 143.

[5] *Teacher Retirement Systems and Social Security*, National Education Association, Research Bulletin (May, 1937), Vol. XV, No. 3, p. 104.

There is relatively little uniformity in the regulations of the retirement systems established before 1920, and even within the last fifteen years wide variations are observable among the principles underlying retirement legislation. It is now generally conceded that teachers' pension and retirement systems should be financed jointly by teachers and the state or municipality. The theory upon which this principle is based is that both parties are benefited by the arrangement and should therefore contribute. It has been further demonstrated that where the state finances the whole enterprise the pension is too small to satisfy the economic needs of teachers, and that only through joint contributions will adequate pension and retirement allowances be provided.

In spite of the acknowledged superiority of the joint-contributory plan, Arizona, New Mexico, and Rhode Island require no deposits by teachers and Michigan teachers expect none from the state. In California, Illinois, and Indiana, teachers contribute a flat amount annually to the retirement fund; in the other contributory systems, the teacher contributes a per cent of his salary.

Service requirements for retirement also vary widely, the range extending from none to forty years. In a few states, all the service must be in the state from which the teacher hopes to get her retirement allowance. In others, part of the service requirement may be met by years taught in other states.

Only eleven states set the age for compulsory retirement. Sixty years of age is usually set as the date for optional retirement, which may be in addition to a service requirement or without reference to it whatsoever.

Most state systems now pay an annuity to retired teachers based upon their annual deposits to the retirement fund. The annuity is supplemented by an allowance derived from the state appropriation, which is referred to as a pension.

Disability benefits are quite commonly provided in state retirement systems to teachers who find it necessary to withdraw from active service prior to the time set for regular retirement. In the more recently adopted plans, the disabled teacher is provided with an annuity representing the actuarial equivalent of his accumulated deposits, together with a pension from the state to bring the total up to an amount proportional to the length of service, but not exceeding the allowance which he would have received upon regular retirement. Usually, the applicant for disability benefits must have served a minimum of ten to fifteen years in order to be eligible for a retirement allowance.

The lag between practice and theory is particularly noticeable in an examination of retirement provisions. For several years the National Education Association has published bulletins on teacher pension and retirement systems and has formulated principles which have the support of experts in this area of finance. Notwithstanding all the literature and research, however, the antiquated systems are retained and, what is even worse, new systems are sometimes inaugurated which embody outworn principles.

Some significant gains have been recorded over the years, in spite of the inexcusable practices which still prevail. Legal sanction has been given to the retirement principle; state systems are definitely superseding the small local systems; the local and state governments are now commonly appropriating funds and lending their support to the financing of teacher retirement, whereas in the earlier days benefits depended upon private charity, bazaars, and the insignificant contributions of teachers. An improvement which is of equal or greater importance to those just enumerated pertains to the control and management of the retirement fund. Here legal safeguards comparable to those governing trust funds generally have been established and a thoroughly democratic board of trustees set up to administer the affairs of the retirement association. Finally, communities and states which contemplate the creation of a teachers' retirement system now seek competent actuarial advice in drafting proposed legislation governing pension and retirement, thus avoiding the glaring mistakes in the early laws.

An extended literature has been developed by the National Education Association and the Carnegie Foundation for the Advancement of Teaching covering practically every phase of the retirement problem, from the philosophy which underlies the whole program to the detailed procedures for administering the funds. The following principles formulated by the Committee on Retirement Allowances of the National Education Association are indicative of the thought and study which have been given to the matter of teacher retirement by the profession itself:[6]

1. Membership required of new teachers; optional for those in service.
2. Guarantees to both teacher and public.
3. Costs shared by teachers and public.
4. Amount of deposits and payments stated.
5. Deposits of teacher and payments by state concurrent with service.
6. Individual accounts kept.
7. Retirement system on a reserve basis.
8. Periodic actuarial investigation.
9. Disability provided for.
10. Teachers' accumulated deposits returnable in case of withdrawal from service or death prior to retirement.
11. Choice of options offered upon retirement.
12. Credit should be allowed for past service.
13. Rights under previous retirement systems safeguarded.
14. Reciprocal relations between states.
15. Retirement board in control.

The social justification for teachers' pensions has never been fully understood or appreciated by the American public. This is not surprising, since every conceivable argument, from the economic needs of teachers to the welfare of children, has been used to win public support for teacher-retirement legislation. Most citizens accept the principle of teachers' pensions and retirement on the grounds that teachers are civil servants and as such are entitled to the same considerations as those granted to other governmental workers, including a pension upon retirement. As mentioned previously, we began early in this country to pension policemen and firemen as well as soldiers and sailors; and the extension of this policy to other civil employees was but a natural step, even though most states have been slow to take it. It was argued by the proponents of teachers' pensions that

[6] *Ibid.*, pp. 96–97.

the salary of teachers was relatively small and that it was unfair for the public to exploit a professional group throughout the best days of their life and then leave them unprotected and without resources during the last few years of their earthly journey. Statistics were compiled by local and state teachers' associations which demonstrated rather conclusively the impoverished state of the superannuated teacher. This portrayal won public sympathy, but it did not appeal to the more discriminating minds as the soundest argument for teachers' pensions.

The most powerful of all the claims made for special legislation in the form of pensions for teachers has been the advancement of the true interests of public education—the improvement of child welfare. Scientific evidence has not yet been assembled to demonstrate this thesis. It still has to be accepted on faith, although it is argued, and with considerable force, that the removal of financial worries which a pension system at least partially insures makes for better teaching, and that the retirement of teachers before the enfeeblement of old age has crippled their efficiency is beneficial to society generally.

The peculiar nature of teaching as a vocation, along with the civil service, has made it highly important for society to provide the members of these groups with protection against the hazards of old age. In teaching, it is important that the teacher shall devote her full time to the professional task for which she is employed. For her to divert her thought and effort to ways and means of building up a competency is to detract seriously from her efficiency as a teacher and is opposed to the best interests of the children in her classroom. It is, therefore, economical, in terms of the results sought, for the public to provide the pension and encourage the teacher to give her undivided attention to her professional work.

The skeptics in the profession have held that the teacher pays the pension bill in the form of a reduced salary; that the taxpayers are willing to spend just so much for education and no more; that if pension laws are passed calling for increased revenue, the public then diverts salary moneys to pay the bill, which practice in the long run results in lower salaries. In the case of local retirement systems, there may be some basis for this suspicion, since the taxpayers are exceedingly conscious of the composition of the tax dollar, although such a conclusion has never been objectively substantiated. Where state systems are concerned, there is every reason to believe the contention is unsound. Apparently, high salaries and pension provisions go along together, as any careful examination of state school statistics will reveal; and if the public has subtracted from wages in any of the teacher-pension states to increase the retirement funds, they have achieved this transfer without notice or objection from the teaching body. As for the future of teacher retirement, the experience of the past two or three decades would lead one to conclude that teachers are likely to enjoy a greater amount of protection than ever before and that state-wide systems will supersede local provisions, except possibly in the cases of large cities like New York and Chicago.

It also appears likely that the financial soundness of future retirement systems will be considerably enhanced by a strict adherence to insurance principles and that the size of the benefits will be augmented by larger contributions from both teachers and the public. Some arrangement will also be worked out whereby reciprocal relations will be universal. In all probability, a higher degree of uniformity will be achieved among the states with respect to benefits, service requirements, and the general principles underlying the systems.

In some respects, the widespread feeling of insecurity which dominated the depression years, and which included practically all groups of workers in its wake, impeded the progress of the teacher-retirement movement. As salaried workers with a high degree of tenure, teachers were considered especially fortunate, even though their old age remained, in many cases, unprovided for. Thousands of individuals who commonly enjoyed a superior financial status to that held by teachers were denied the opportunity of continuing in their jobs, not to mention forfeiting their rights to future pension allowances. During such an economic lapse, the public was not in any mood to feel sympathetic toward those who appeared relatively well to do. Paralleling this somewhat envious attitude of certain groups toward the economic welfare of teachers, there has developed a social philosophy which has as one of its major aims a greater degree of economic security for everybody. There is, in this point of view, a rejection of the notion that every individual should be expected to save for the proverbial "rainy day," partly because it simply cannot be done in modern economic life and partly because it leads to unfortunate maladjustments in the economic scheme. During the days of the frontier, when there was work for everyone and when the relationship between one's effort and one's reward was direct and measurable, the need for old-age and unemployment insurance was hardly observable. But technological development has thrown the old order out of gear. The individual today is powerless to protect himself in a world that is as unpredictable economically as the present one, and some mutual plan of safeguarding the interests of all worthy members of society appears to be a goal toward which our most intelligent reformers are working. From this angle, then, the depression has created a more favorable attitude toward the economic protection of all citizens, including teachers.

SUGGESTED READINGS

HOUSMAN, IDA E., *Pension Facts in New Jersey* (New York, American Book Company, 1938).

PRITCHETT, HENRY S., *The Social Philosophy of Pensions*, Carnegie Foundation for the Advancement of Teaching, Bulletin No. 25 (1930).

STUDENSKY, PAUL, *Teachers' Pension Systems in the United States* (New York, D. Appleton and Company, 1920).

Teacher Retirement Systems and Social Security, National Education Association, Research Bulletin (May, 1937), Vol. XV, No. 3.

XXXI

Tenure of Office

O F almost equal importance with salary in choosing a vocation is the matter of security in position. Individuals who
can look forward to steady employment, where the pay check
comes along with clocklike regularity, have little occasion to be
envious of their more highly paid confrères in occupations where
the hazards of unemployment are great.

It is difficult to appraise the vocation of teaching with respect
to the opportunities which it presents for permanent and continuous employment, since the causes of turnover are so numerous
and complex. Composed as the profession is of a large proportion
of women, the reasons for withdrawing from the service are frequently of a personal nature and by choice of the individual
rather than by any coercion from the employing agency. Therefore, to charge the high degree of instability which has characterized public-school teaching in America since its inception
wholly to policies and practices of boards of education and school
administrators is to ignore the voluntary separations which constitute by far the largest proportion of the turnover. Marriage
among the women teachers has been the greatest single cause of
turnover. To be sure, a considerable part of this loss to the profession could be salvaged by lifting the ban which many local
boards of education have placed on the retention of married
women teachers.[1]

But even if this restriction were removed, there would still be,

---

[1] A survey made by the National Education Association in 1928 showed that of
1532 cities of more than 2500 population, 25 per cent required teachers who married to resign at once and 25 per cent more dropped them at the end of the year.
Of 66 cities with more than 100,000 population, 23, or 35 per cent required instant resignation. In 1931 another survey by the National Education Association
revealed similar conditions.

during normal economic times, a relatively large number of resignations because of marriage alone. Many women use teaching as a stopgap until matrimony and have never seriously entertained the idea of making it their lifework.

A second cause of instability has been the wide differences in wage rates which have prevailed in American communities. Teachers' salaries have been closely related to size of community, the larger cities providing the more generous rewards. This hierarchy of salary levels has led to a constant shifting of teachers from smaller to larger school districts, with the result that the average tenure of teachers in any single position has been singularly low in all except the large cities.

The American tradition of encouraging local initiative and leaving the determination of teachers' salaries to the individual districts has stimulated a tremendous amount of competition among school boards for teachers. This policy is partially responsible, also, for the wide variations which sometimes exist between salary policies in communities of the same size, the wealthier cities finding it comparatively easy to establish rates of pay above those of their less fortunate neighbors. While there are unquestionably many advantages inherent in the relatively large amount of local control which has always obtained in American education, there can be no denying the fact that this policy is responsible for a substantial portion of our teacher transiency.

Local boards of education have also exercised control of the "hiring and firing" of public-school teachers, employing them, for the most part, on a yearly contract basis, the board sometimes basing their actions upon the recommendation of a professional adviser and often themselves attempting to appraise the qualifications of the individual teacher, either for appointment to a position or for retention in the school system.

Stories of political favoritism in the employment of teachers are fairly common in the history of the profession. Wholesale dismissals have taken place, in some cities, to make room for the needy relatives of local politicians and, occasionally, to purge the community of teachers whose social or religious views did not conform to those of school-board members. The actual extent of this practice is unknown. It seems improbable, however, that it has ever been as widespread as our most ardent tenure proponents are prone to imply, or that it prevails to any appreciable degree in city school systems today. The management of rural schools, however, has been so pitifully inefficient and inadequate that every conceivable type of motive has figured in the appointment and dismissal of teachers. Local trustees have dismissed teachers because they boarded at the wrong place, attended the wrong church, and kept company with the wrong young men. In many of these sparsely populated districts, teachers, regardless of their qualifications, have found it exceedingly difficult to hold on to their jobs for any considerable period of time.

While the majority of school boards in the United States have been actuated by high ideals of public service, and while their policies and practices have been free from political influence, the exceptions have been most conspicuous and have served to focus public attention upon the importance of keeping the schools out of politics and putting the interests of the child above every other consideration. Experience with the "spoils" system in other phases of government activity sensitized the public mind to the issues involved in tenure. In fact, the Pendleton Reform Bill, passed in 1883, which established standards for the selection of civil employees and purported to remove appointments and dismissals from political considerations, was essentially the basic idea behind teacher-tenure legislation.

As Professor Scott has pointed out, civil service antedated indefinite teacher-tenure laws in all states having both types of legislation, save for two exceptions—Oregon and Maryland.[2] While a cause-and-effect relationship cannot be incontrovertibly deduced from this situation, it seems highly probable that those states which have tried civil service are more favorably disposed toward the extension of the principle to public-school teachers than are other states.

No one seems to know just how unstable the profession of teaching has been at various stages in its history; and even if

---

[2] Scott, Cecil W., *Indefinite Teacher Tenure* (New York, Bureau of Publications, Teachers College, Columbia University, 1934), p. 10.

accurate facts on turnover were available, the particular influence of tenure legislation could scarcely be divorced from numerous other stabilizing influences, such as salary-improvement and higher-training qualifications. A rough approximation of the relative instability of the teaching profession can be had by examining the age statistics reported in the United States Census. According to this authority, the proportion of teachers above forty-five years of age has increased considerably within the past fifty years. In 1890 only 8 per cent of all the public-school teachers in the United States were forty-five years of age or over; by 1910 this had risen to 11 per cent, and in 1930 it reached 17 per cent. Even with this indicated increase in maturity, the reader will probably be surprised to learn that the median age of 943,683 white teachers in 1930 was only 29.1 years. The business of teaching, therefore, is still largely in the hands of young women.

INFLUENCE OF TEACHERS' ASSOCIATIONS ON THE EXTENSION OF TENURE

The National Education Association and the individual state teachers' associations have been largely responsible for the extension of the tenure movement. As early as 1887 a committee of the National Education Association made a report on tenure in which they pointed out the lack of permanence in teaching and urged an exposition of the evils of the current system. Apparently nothing was done about this, and the next time the association displayed any interest in this topic was in 1905, when the Committee on Salaries, Tenure of Office, and Pension Provisions of Teachers reported. While the reader might logically conclude, from the name of the foregoing committee, that tenure would be treated at some length, it received no attention whatsoever. The association, while sympathetic toward a greater degree of permanence in the profession, did not, apparently, commit itself to protective-tenure publicly until 1915.[3]

The committee on teachers' salaries, tenure, and pensions, after several years of concentration on salaries and pensions, concluded in 1920 that tenure was a topic which also deserved

[3] National Education Association, *Addresses and Proceedings* (1915), Vol. LIII, p. 29.

the committee's attention. As a result, subcommittee reports appeared, during the next few years, containing discussions of the history of tenure, the conditions in the profession with respect to job security, and an analysis of tenure laws.

In 1923 the Tenure Committee of One Hundred, which still functions today, was created. This committee has made several investigations of teacher turnover and tenure and has fought vigorously for protective legislation. Most of the credit for the latter, however, must go to the state teachers' associations. The active campaigns waged by the teachers in New Jersey, California, Indiana, and certain other states have been determining influences in the passage of tenure laws.

While the profession has not stood solidly behind the tenure movement, the dissenting minority has been neither large nor vocal. Nearly every type of teachers' association has officially included tenure among the planks in its platform. Prominent among these has been the American Federation of Teachers, which has advocated it since its organization in 1916 and has used its official organ, the *American Teacher*, to expose unjust dismissals of teachers.

Growth and Extent of Teacher-tenure Legislation

Notwithstanding the continuous efforts of teachers over a period of thirty years to secure tenure protection for their own group, progress has been painfully slow. The District of Columbia, in 1906, was apparently the first governmental unit apart from municipalities to grant teachers security in their positions during good behavior and efficient service. The extent to which this action of the federal government influenced the attitude of state legislatures toward the problem is not known. It certainly provided the tenure advocates with an additional talking point. On the other hand, the fact that only two of the states, New Jersey and Wisconsin, enacted similar laws within the next five years (1906–1911) suggests that the action of the Capitol City was not an important factor in the extension of tenure legislation.

As Table 19 shows, there has been no tendency for tenure legislation to spring forth in response to economic depressions or to any discernible nation-wide influence. Its development appears to have been haphazard and sporadic.

Table 19. Dates of Enactment of Indefinite Teacher-tenure Laws

State	Date of Enactment
District of Columbia	1906
New Jersey	1909
Wisconsin	1909
Oregon	1913
Massachusetts	1914
Maryland	1916
New York	1917
Illinois	1917
California	1921
Colorado	1921
Louisiana	1922
Indiana	1927
Minnesota	1927
Florida	1937
Pennsylvania	1937
Kansas	1937
Michigan	1937
Oklahoma	1937

Not only has the tenure movement progressed slowly, but the legislation enacted has not been uniform in character save in the one general provision of granting a rather large degree of security to teachers. Only four of the eighteen laws enumerated in Table 19 are completely state-wide in application, although two others are practically so. In ten states, the tenure law applies only to certain districts; in one state, the matter is optional with the local voters.[4]

The number of teachers in 1938 who were affected by these various types of state tenure laws is shown in Table 20 and illustrated graphically in Figure IV. Two facts stand out clearly: first, the large number and percentage of teachers that are still unprotected in their positions by any legislation whatsoever, or at most by an annual contract; and second, the lack of uniform-

[4] The four states which have laws that are state-wide in application are: Louisiana, New Jersey, Pennsylvania, and Wisconsin. Two that are practically so are Maryland and Massachusetts. The other states in Table 19 have laws which apply to cities at and above a stipulated population. In Michigan, the law is applicable only after local voters have approved it.

ity in the type of tenure legislation applicable to the teachers who enjoy some measure of job security.

Table 20.   Number and Per Cent of Teachers Affected by Various Types of State Tenure Laws, July, 1938 [1]

Type of Law	Number of Teachers	Per Cent
Teachers in states without tenure legislation of any type; or annual-election plan..........................	340,908	38.0
Teachers entitled to tenure after a probationary period or upon appointment	334,968	37.4
Teachers under continuing contract laws.............	50,045	5.6
All others, including teachers in districts which may legally issue contracts for more than one year.............	170,282	19.0
Total...	896,203	100.00

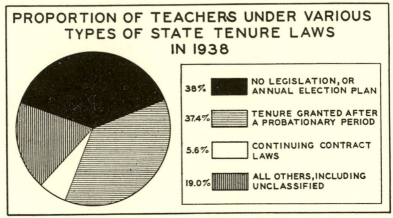

PROPORTION OF TEACHERS UNDER VARIOUS TYPES OF STATE TENURE LAWS IN 1938

38% NO LEGISLATION, OR ANNUAL ELECTION PLAN

37.4% TENURE GRANTED AFTER A PROBATIONARY PERIOD

5.6% CONTINUING CONTRACT LAWS

19.0% ALL OTHERS, INCLUDING UNCLASSIFIED

Figure IV.   Proportion of Teachers under Various Types of State Tenure Laws in 1938

[1] Adapted from *Handbook on Teacher Tenure*, National Education Association, Research Bulletin (September, 1936), Vol. XIV, No. 4, p. 177.

The Operation of Tenure Laws

Legal tenure involves a number of factors and provisions which have come up for considerable discussion and criticism. Since an exhaustive treatment of these issues would constitute a large volume in itself, and since several books and bulletins have already been issued dealing with them, the author has elected to discuss briefly at this point only the chief tenure practices and to state without undue elaboration what appears to be the probable trend in tenure legislation.

With the exception of Pennsylvania, where a teaching contract entitles one to tenure protection immediately, it is common practice to require teachers to serve a probationary period varying from two to five years before permanent appointment can be made. The arrangement also provides that teachers who have earned tenure privileges cannot be dismissed for personal or political reasons; at least, this is the intent of the law. Teachers under tenure can be dismissed for incompetency, immorality, insubordination, and conduct unbecoming a teacher (or words and phrases conveying similar meanings).

Tenure protection is usually restricted to teachers, principals, and supervisors. Superintendents of schools are not eligible for tenure in most states, the law excluding them on the theory that as executive heads of school systems their tenure should be subject to the wishes of the people's representatives.[5] So long as the position of superintendent of schools carries with it the responsibilities and duties now commonly attached to the office, school administrators will face a relatively high degree of insecurity in their jobs. The dominant theory of public-school administration in the United States has placed upon the shoulders of the superintendent almost full responsibility for the success of the educational enterprise. He is expected to formulate policies and see to it that the ones finally adopted by the board of education are carried out. He represents the board and he heads the instructional staff. As superintendent he must be impersonal, objective, and wholly professional in his relationships. If his administration is offensive to the teachers, his leadership will be ineffectual; if his actions are displeasing to the board and the public at large, his efforts will be fruitless. Therefore, with so many possibilities for strained relationships, any or all of which would seriously impair the success of the educational program, most legislatures have deemed it unwise to include superintendents in the group for whom tenure legislation has been designed.

[5] The exceptions to this rule are Massachusetts, California, Indiana, and supervising principals in New Jersey.

Principals and supervisors have usually been accorded the same tenure privileges as teachers, the criterion for classification being, apparently, whether or not the work of the individual was directly related to classroom instruction. While long-term contracts, which constitute a limited form of tenure legislation, are countenanced for superintendents of schools in some states, the period covered seldom exceeds four years and the arrangement has few of the implications embodied in indefinite tenure laws.

Tenure in Rural Districts

Experience with tenure in the rural areas has not been uniformly satisfactory. Both California and Indiana have modified their original laws, the former state making tenure optional with rural districts (average daily attendance, eight hundred and fifty or less) and the latter exempting all individuals teaching in townships. The smaller the unit of administration, the more difficulties encountered in the operation of tenure. There is little or no opportunity in the rural districts for the transfer of teachers from one school to another in cases of maladjustment and dissatisfaction. Furthermore, supervision and educational leadership in small school systems are usually less adequate than in the cities, and teachers who might succeed under favorable conditions are likely to fail when left to their own resources for inspiration and guidance. Students of the problem now generally concede the importance of establishing large units of administration if tenure is to serve the best interests of education.

Absence of the Merit Principle

A marked weakness in both past and present tenure laws has been the total absence of any qualifying requirement save successful teaching experience. With the passage of a tenure law, every teacher, regardless of her training, who was retained by a local board of education long enough to satisfy the probationary service requirement has been granted tenure protection. This situation accounts for the fact that literally thousands of American teachers are on tenure whose training is little if any above high-school graduation. Just what justification there is for civil service (and that, we assume, is what tenure is intended to be) without the merit principle is a question which perplexes many intelligent educators as well as laymen. The more thoughtful members of the teaching profession are now urging their associates to support the inclusion of a training qualification when future tenure legislation is being considered.

THE DISMISSAL PROBLEM

The protection of teachers against dismissal for unjust reasons has been the basic argument for tenure legislation. Unfortunately, it has been difficult if not impossible under past tenure arrangements to protect the strong without at the same time safeguarding the weak. The chief criticism against tenure in office is that the incompetent, the neurotic, and the lazy all enjoy protection in their positions along with the ablest teachers in the profession. Holmstedt's intensive study of the operation of the New Jersey tenure law disclosed, among other things, that the dismissal of unsatisfactory teachers was the greatest and most aggravating problem confronting school officials in New Jersey.[6]

While technically the law provides for the removal of these unsatisfactory members of the profession, actually school administrators and boards of education have found it inexpedient and unwise to take advantage of their legal rights to oust the weak and incompetent teachers. The proceedings required to dismiss them from office have apparently been so disagreeable to school officials, and the attendant publicity so unpleasant, that only the most flagrant violations of the moral code, or total mental disability, are made the occasion for dismissal charges. Scott's findings with respect to the dismissal of teachers in Newark and Trenton, New Jersey, tend to corroborate this statement. During the five-year period ending June, 1931, only one teacher had been dismissed, this removal having occurred in Newark.[7] A similar situation was reported for Chicago, where, during the twelve-year period from 1920 to 1931 inclusive, only fourteen educational workers were dismissed, of whom nine were on tenure. It seems almost inconceivable that so few teachers in these

---

[6] Holmstedt, Raleigh W., *A Study of the Effects of the Teacher Tenure Law in New Jersey* (New York, Bureau of Publications, Teachers College, Columbia University, 1932), pp. 100–2.

[7] Scott, Cecil W., *op. cit.*, p. 52.

large cities, over such an extended period of time, could have failed. Conditions in other large cities are not unlike those in the three just cited.

Equally harmful, but in the opposite direction, has been the high rate of dismissal which occurs in many tenure states among teachers who have not yet earned tenure protection. Fearful lest the candidate may not prove entirely satisfactory over a long term of years, boards of education resort to dismissal at the end of the first, second, or third year of the probationary period, thereby producing an inordinate amount of turnover and frequently doing a serious injury to the dismissed teacher. In the rural areas of tenure states, this practice has been a common one and in some instances all teachers about to qualify for tenure have been dismissed in order that the board of education might avoid any possible future embarrassment. These inexcusable practices and evasions of the tenure principle have led many educators to question the efficacy of the probationary period, and one state (Pennsylvania) has recently enacted a tenure law which provides protection to teachers against unjust dismissal from the time their contracts are signed.

The Psychological Factors Related to Tenure

While the number of unwarranted dismissals in the case of probationers suggests that tenure may not be altogether an unmixed blessing, the psychological effect of tenure protection on those who survive the trial period has led many disinterested observers to acknowledge its superiority to the traditional annual-contract arrangement. Worry and fear are not conducive to efficiency. The removal of the feeling of insecurity, which is rather widespread even among teachers of long experience in nontenure states, decreases emotional tension and makes for poise and confidence. To some boards of education the degree of independence which tenure accords teachers is abhorrent, because bootlicking and fawning are no longer necessary for job security. Teacher tenure is equally repellent to certain administrators of the Fascist type, who protest against it because it necessitates the alteration of their methods of dealing with the teaching personnel. To work successfully with teachers freed from the constant threat of losing their positions requires the substitution of administrative leadership for authority.

The author has observed a pronounced difference between teachers in tenure and nontenure states in their willingness to speak frankly and directly to their superior officers and to the board of education about salary matters and working conditions. When protected by tenure, they express themselves courageously. While the reverse is not always true in situations where tenure does not apply, there is a noticeable hesitancy on the part of most teachers, because of fear of retaliation, to assert their rights.

DISCRIMINATION AGAINST MARRIED WOMEN

Tenure has aggravated the problems of married women teachers. Even in nontenure states, the public has been prejudiced against the employment of married women, on the grounds that two incomes in a family are neither necessary nor socially desirable; that jobs should be reserved for the single women; and that, from the standpoint of the welfare of the race, the place for a married woman is in the home, rearing a family. In tenure states, the situation is much worse for those women teachers who are already married when they apply for a position or for those teachers who are unfortunate enough to marry during the probationary period. Boards of education are almost universally disposed to "let out" these teachers before they are eligible for tenure.

From another angle, tenure has been a professional lifesaver to many women who wanted to marry. The courts, in most states, have held that marriage does not constitute a sufficient cause for dismissal and that, after having earned tenure, a teacher can marry and the school board be damned. Whether or not the courts will continue to uphold married women in their rights to teach is problematical in view of certain recent decisions, although common sense and reason would seem to answer the question in the affirmative.

RELATION TO SALARY AND RETIREMENT LAWS

Protection against dismissal is rather useless to teachers if the employing board can lower salaries without the interference of the courts. To safeguard the profession against any such evasion of the tenure principle, minimum salary laws and legally graduated salary schedules are necessary. Controversies resulting from decreases in salary in three tenure states show quite a variation in the interpretation given by the courts. In California, the Appellate Court has held that the trustees of local school districts had the power to regulate the compensation of teachers either upward or downward, providing the salary finally fixed constituted reasonable pay for the services to be performed.

In Massachusetts, the school code provides that reduction of salary is possible only when a general revision applying to all teachers of the same class or grade is made. Within these limitations, the courts have held that local trustees were quite within their rights in reducing salaries. In New Jersey, teachers' salaries (either individual or group) cannot be reduced legally.

While, at first glance, a mandatory salary law such as the one just referred to in New Jersey appears to be to the decided advantage of the teachers, there is one objectionable feature to it which is frequently overlooked. Boards of education will tend to establish salary levels as low as possible because of the realization that they can never lower a salary once a teacher has received it. The Massachusetts provision is superior to the inflexible type just described. That some regulation of salaries is imperative if tenure is to be effective is now generally admitted.

Pension and retirement laws should also parallel or precede protective tenure legislation. Otherwise, teachers will be forced to continue in service long after their strength has failed them, to the detriment of themselves and the children in the schools. In the absence of a specified retirement age, teachers on tenure can hold on to their jobs until they are physically or mentally incapacitated. Experience in some states indicates that the compulsory retirement age should not be above sixty-five if tenure is to serve the best interests of children.[8]

The extension of tenure legislation in the United States will probably proceed slowly, since the public is still rather skeptical

[8] In New York State cities, the proportion of teachers between sixty-five and seventy years of age who are considered unfit for classroom service by superintendents of schools is considerably higher than for younger-age groups.

of the claims made for it. Nor does it seem likely that objective evidence can be assembled to demonstrate beyond the shadow of a doubt the superiority of protective tenure over the annual-contract system. Most of the important considerations are un-measurable. One cannot show precisely the influence of fear on teaching efficiency, yet the removal of worry and fear is a highly important factor in support of teacher tenure. If the latter is to become a reality, therefore, in the forty-eight states, it will have to be accepted because of its theoretical soundness.

The basic arguments will be that tenure contributes to child welfare through the freedom of thought and action which it gives to teachers; that it removes fear and worry over insecurity; that it protects teachers, and consequently children and society, against the "spoils system"; that it is consistent with civil-service principles to grant tenure of office to teachers, since they are state employees and as such should be safeguarded against local prejudices and petty politics; and, finally, that tenure is in harmony with our more recent theories of social justice, which in essence suggest that the individual should be protected against powerful forces over which he has but little or no control. In other words, tenure is but another evidence of the need for collective action in safeguarding the individual's right to live, to work, and to be happy. Comparable types of legislation are un-employment insurance, workmen's compensation, and old-age pensions. If and when the public comes to accept this broad social philosophy which grows rather logically out of the machine age, job security for teachers will become a commonplace.

SUGGESTED READINGS

A Handbook on Teacher Tenure, National Education Association, Research Bulletin (September, 1936), Vol. XIV, No. 4.

HOLMSTEDT, RALEIGH W., *A Study of the Effects of the Teacher Tenure Law in New Jersey* (New York, Bureau of Publications, Teachers College, Columbia University, 1932).

SCOTT, CECIL W., *Indefinite Teacher Tenure* (New York, Bureau of Publications, Teachers College, Columbia University, 1934).

XXXII

Teacher Health and Sick-leave Provisions

THE health of schoolteachers is a vital factor in the efficiency of American public schools. Statistics have tended to show that teachers as a group enjoy a degree of health somewhat above that of the average citizen, and that there are few, if any, diseases which are peculiar to the profession. It was quite commonly believed a few decades past that teachers were more subject to tuberculosis than outdoor workers, and that the hazards of the office were greater than those confronting individuals in other vocations. This belief was never substantiated by the facts. On the contrary, according to the reports of physicians, nervous diseases and those pertaining to the heart and circulatory system have been found to be even more prevalent among teachers than have respiratory diseases.[1] Apparently, teachers have been more health-conscious than the general public, and better informed about health habits, for the facts indicate that they are absent from their work because of illness less frequently and for shorter periods of time than most other workers.[2]

Despite their superior health status, however, research students tell us that twelve thousand teachers are absent each day from their work because of illness, and that during a single school year American public-school teachers lose time totaling no less than two million days.[3]

Schoolwork is thus interrupted. Substitute teachers are commonly employed to carry on, although the task of teaching re-

---

[1] "Fit to Teach," in National Education Association, Department of Classroom Teachers, *Ninth Yearbook* (1938), p. 31.

[2] Rogers, James F., "The Health of the Teacher," in *School Health Studies*, U. S. Office of Education, Bulletin No. 12, 1926, pp. 2 ff.

[3] National Education Association, Department of Classroom Teachers, *Ninth Yearbook*, p. 1.

quires a degree of continuity in method and program which cannot be preserved when substitutions are made. In addition to the educational loss, there is also an economic one. Many of the absent teachers lose part or all of their wages for the period of their illness. In some instances, more than formerly, the school districts pay the substitutes and the absent teacher does not lose her salary. Unfortunately, sick-leave provisions among American communities are not uniform, and many school boards have found it relatively easy to justify their niggardly practices because of the absence of any commonly agreed upon sick-leave policies within a state or section of the country.

This chaotic condition is not due to the recency of the problem, for as early as 1849 some of the more progressive school systems had incorporated sick-leave provisions into their rules and regulations. Among these was the Boston School Committee, which provided as follows: [4]

Whenever any instructor shall be absent from School, and a temporary instructor rendered necessary, the amount required for said substitution shall be withdrawn from the salary of the absentee; unless upon representation of the case by petition, the Board shall appoint a special committee, upon whose report to the effect an allowance may be made.

This rule is particularly interesting because both provisions—the deduction of pay for the substitute, and a special action of the board for salary allowance—are typical of the early rules adopted by school boards to care for this problem.

Only a short time after Boston adopted the regulation just quoted, New York City followed with a similar provision (1855) and limited the amount of absence with pay to one month, except for special leaves, which had to be confirmed by the Board of Education.[5] Newark, in 1857, placed the responsibility on the teachers for "providing a satisfactory substitute to discharge their duties during such absence, which substitute shall be a pupil of the Normal School or a practical teacher." [6]

---

[4] *Rules of the School Committee and Regulations of the Public Schools of the City of Boston* (Boston, Mass., printed by J. H. Eastburn for the School Committee, 1849), p. 18.

[5] *Manual of the Board of Education of the City and County of New York* (New York, printed by Edward O. Jenkins for the Board of Education, June, 1855), pp. 69–70.

[6] "Regulations of the Board of Education of the City of Newark, Relating to the

During this early period some cities mentioned sickness in the rules and regulations of the board of education but made no provision for deduction, or payment in full, of the salary. Thus, in the case of Cleveland in 1862, the Annual Report of the Board of Education stated: [7]

No teacher is authorized to dismiss his or her school . . . except from illness or unavoidable necessity, without the consent of one or more of the officers of the Board of Education. In any case, immediate notice must be given to the Superintendent, that a substitute may be provided if possible.

Another system which permitted dismissal of school in case of the teacher's sickness but made no provision for sick pay was Syracuse in 1869.[8]

During this same year Cincinnati provided for payment of the teacher for three days in case of sickness, and for a longer period of time if necessary. Although this was a step in the right direction, the board still passed on the merits of every individual absence. When no reference was made to pay, it is probable that the teacher was required to compensate the substitute, either directly or through a reduction in salary. Many large cities, during the last half of the century, provided specifically for the payment of substitutes through the salary deductions of absent teachers. This was the case in Milwaukee in 1871,[9] Jersey City in 1876,[10] and Cincinnati in 1887.[11]

As improved methods and schedules for hiring and paying

Organization and Government of the Public Schools," in *First Annual Report of the Board of Education of the City of Newark for the Year 1857* (Newark, N. J., printed by the Daily Advertiser Office for the Board of Education, 1858), p. 41.

[7] *Twenty-sixth Annual Report of the Board of Education for the School Year 1861–1862* (Cleveland, Ohio, Fairbanks, Benedict and Company, 1863), p. 104.

[8] *Twenty-first Annual Report of the Board of Education of the City of Syracuse, 1869* (Syracuse, B. Herman Smith, 1869), p. 124.

[9] *Annual Report of the Board of School Commissioners for the Year Ending August 31, 1872* (Milwaukee, published for the Board by the Milwaukee News Company, 1872), p. 16.

[10] *Annual Report of the City Superintendent of Public Schools of Jersey City, N. J., for the Year Ending November 30, 1876* (Jersey City, published for the Board by Pangborn, Dunning and Dear, Printers, 1877), pp. 110–11.

[11] *Fifty-eighth Annual Report of the Public Schools of Cincinnati,* "A Handbook for the School Year Beginning September 1, 1887" (Cincinnati, published for the Board by the Ohio Valley Publishing and Manufacturing Company, 1888), pp. 194–95.

substitutes were developed, many school systems began to deduct a certain percentage from the teacher's salary, the board of education, rather than the teacher, then making full provision for the substitute. In most cases of this kind the teacher was allowed half pay. When salary was paid on a percentage basis, there was usually a time limit, after which no pay at all would be allowed.

The development of sick-leave provisions in large cities was well under way by 1900. Unfortunately, policies in the small municipalities and in the villages were less standardized, and frequently less generous, than those cited in the previous pages. The more typical procedure for the period up to 1900 is probably that described by Clark in the following paragraph: [12]

> Many of us who, as children, went to school in small towns, remember that the announcement that the teacher was sick filled us with unholy glee. It meant that school was closed until she recovered, or until a new teacher was found. Somehow, even though we liked her, we just couldn't make ourselves feel depressed. The superintendent permitted her to "keep school" on Saturdays to make up the time lost. If this was not done, the pay for the days missed was deducted from her wages. At that time and in these places teachers were employed for the term, and were paid at the end of it on the basis of the number of days taught.

Although the more progressive school systems were making some effort to meet the problem of sick leave, even here absence deductions were sufficient to be included as one of the methods of supporting the retirement funds. Thus the New York City pension plan was supported entirely by "absence deductions, gifts, etc. (no public support)" from 1894 to 1904.[13] In 1907 "deductions on account of teachers' absences" were one of the major means of supporting the retirement funds in Philadelphia, Detroit, and San Francisco.[14] And in 1913 at least some of the money for retirement funds was secured from absence deductions

[12] Clark, R. C., "When the Teacher Is Sick," in *American School Board Journal*, June, 1930 (Vol. LXXX), p. 68.

[13] Palmer, Nida Pearl, *Pension Systems for Public School Teachers*, U. S. Bureau of Education, Bulletin 1927, No. 23 (Washington, Government Printing Office, 1927), p. 11.

[14] Keyes, Charles H., "Teachers' Pensions," in National Education Association, *Addresses and Proceedings* (1907), p. 106.

in the following cities: Lynn, Massachusetts; Albany, New York; New York City; Syracuse; Troy; Yonkers; and Salt Lake City.[15]

The Influence of European Practices

Some of the European countries had made considerable progress in providing for sick leave even before 1900. Practices abroad no doubt had their part in making boards of education and teachers in this country conscious of the need of some kind of provision to meet sickness. In speaking before the Department of School Administration in 1896, John E. Clark, ex-president of the Board of Education of Detroit, asserted: [16]

> The success of the school systems of Germany is universally attributed by her own educators to her school laws; especially those which relate to the teachers. The provisions respecting teachers may be summed up as follows . . . A pecuniary allowance when sick, and a provision for years of infirmity and old age, and for their families in the case of death.

Less than a year later the Annual Report of the Commissioner of Education quoted Dr. Schlee of Altoona as observing that it was impossible to compare the salaries of the American teachers with those of their colleagues in Europe, since the latter enjoyed the additional benefits of generous pensions and sickness allowances.

The results of this propaganda were effective and a number of voluntary mutual-benefit associations were formed. In fact, ten of these were already operating in 1896.[17]

The nature of these societies was discussed by the Commis-

---

[15] "Retirement Allowance Systems of the Public Schools," in *Report of the Commissioner of Education, 1913* (Washington, Government Printing Office, 1914), Vol. II, pp. 37–42.

[16] Clark, John E., "Shall Teachers Be Pensioned?" in National Education Association, *Addresses and Proceedings* (Chicago, published for the Association by the University of Chicago Press, 1896), pp. 990–91.

[17] Baltimore, St. Louis, Cincinnati, Cleveland, Detroit, Chicago, Buffalo, San Francisco, St. Paul, and one interstate association. In addition to the ten associations existing for temporary aid only, there were four others which provided "both temporary aid and annuity." These were Hamilton County (Cincinnati), Philadelphia, Brooklyn, and the District of Columbia. ("Teachers' Pension and Mutual Aid Societies," in *Annual Report of the Commissioner of Education, 1896–1897*, Vol. II, p. 1533.)

sioner of Education in his annual report for 1898–1899. He described the system in Charleston as follows: [18]

> There is a local teachers' benefit association whose object is to relieve sick teachers by the payment of 75 cents a day for ten school days, and 50 cents a day for the remaining ten days of a school month, should the sickness continue for that period.

The development of these associations was important, because the members became active in educating the public to the needs of the teachers, and because they went even further and campaigned to get boards of education to supplant their funds with public aid. During the next decade the movement to provide temporary aid to teachers, especially during sickness, became widespread, and local teachers' associations in the larger cities were engaged in promoting and administering mutual-benefit associations. [19]

While there is a rather marked tendency at the present time for boards of education to assume the responsibility of providing substitutes for teachers who are ill, and thereby to relieve the teaching staff of this one-time commonly imposed burden, the number of mutual-benefit associations has increased rapidly. In 1930 of seventy-three selected cities, most of which had a population of one hundred thousand or over, twelve reported health and accident insurance for teachers (in all but one case managed by the teachers themselves), while two others indicated both health-accident and life insurance. [20]

As Table 21 shows, similar results were reported by the Department of Classroom Teachers of the National Education Association in 1931.

[18] "Teachers' Pensions and Annuities," in *Annual Report of the Commissioner of Education, 1898–1899* (Washington, Government Printing Office, 1900), Vol. II, p. 1480.

[19] In 1910 work of this sort was being carried on in Baltimore; Boston; Buffalo; Canton, Ohio; Chicago; Cincinnati; Denver; Detroit; Grand Rapids; Harrisburg; Indianapolis; Jersey City; Louisville; Nashville; New York; Paterson, N. J.; Philadelphia; Rochester; St. Louis; St. Paul; San Francisco; Topeka; Washington. (Alexander, Carter, *Some Present Aspects of the Work of Teachers' Voluntary Associations in the United States* [New York, Bureau of Publications, Teachers College, Columbia University, 1910], pp. 50–51.)

[20] Fox, Guy, "Group Insurance in Public School Districts in Cities of 100,000 Population and Over" (Denver Public Schools, Department of Research, May 21, 1930), 4 pp. (mimeographed).

Table 21.   Number and Per Cent of Local Teachers' Organizations Reporting Mutual Benefit Plans Available to Their Members, 1930–1931 [1]

| Type of Association | Mutual Benefit Association in Operation | | | | | | No Definite Report |
| | Yes | | No | | Total | | |
	Number	Per Cent	Number	Per Cent	Number	Per Cent	
City associations:							
Below 100 in membership....	1	2	50	98	51	100	6
100–299 in membership......	15[a]	14	94	86	109	100	2
300–499 in membership......	15[b]	29	37	71	52	100	—
500–999 in membership......	12	39	19	61	31	100	2
1000 or more in membership.	16	42	22	58	38	100	1
County associations..........	4	11	32	89	36	100	2
Miscellaneous associations.....	2	15	11	85	13	100	—
TOTAL.....................	65	20	265	80	330	100	13

[a] Three of these associations reported that the benefit plan is administered by the local board of education.

[b] Two of these reported that the plan is administered by the local board of education.

[1] Taken from "The Economic Welfare of Teachers," in National Education Association, Department of Classroom Teachers, *Sixth Yearbook* (1931), p. 81.

SICK-LEAVE PROPAGANDA AND HEALTH STUDIES

During this period when teachers' associations were trying to provide sick leave, and at a later date when they were attempting to shift this burden to boards of education, public attitude was changing gradually with respect to the importance of health as a factor in teaching efficiency. This is reflected in the writings and addresses of educators. Thus in 1910 W. S. Small asserted: [21]

To win the general attention from parents to the importance of protecting the health of teachers—which of course is the end of investigation—it must be shown that teachers of subnormal health are a menace to children; or, at least, that the value of the school to the children varies directly with the health and vitality of the teacher. This will hardly be questioned by competent school and medical men; but about the best that can be done at present, in presenting the matter to the public, is merely authoritative general statement.

[21] Small, W. S., "The Health of Teachers," in *Pedagogical Seminary*, March, 1910 (Vol. XVII), pp. 78–80.

In 1913 Terman's oft-quoted book, *The Teacher's Health*,[22] made its appearance, emphasizing the importance of safeguards that would protect the teacher's health. In addresses to the National Education Association in 1914 Scott Nearing [23] and Walter Hamilton [24] both called attention to the necessity of provisions for sickness.

The growing interest in the health of the teacher was also shown by Dublin's magazine article on the "Physical Disability of New York City Teachers." [25] During the same year, 1916, the Commission on the Welfare of Teachers recommended that there should be a "decrease of worry of teachers regarding financial matters by . . . arrangement for health insurance, sick leave, etc., if needed during the term of service." [26] Similarly, the Committee on Health Problems in Education directed their attention to the health and welfare of teachers.[27] It must not be assumed that all the ideas presented on sick leave during this time were progressive. The following statement by William C. Prosser, who was then Assistant Commissioner of Education in Boston, Massachusetts, illustrates this point: [28]

Teachers appear to derive practically all the benefit from protection against temporary disability due to sickness or accident. Whatever benefit the public receives seems small and remote. It would probably be equitable for the teachers to support, unaided by the public, these two risks, if compulsory insurance seeks to cover them.

As late as 1917 Clyde Furst argued that: [29]

[22] Terman, Lewis Madison, *The Teacher's Health* (Boston, Houghton Mifflin Company, 1913).

[23] Nearing, Scott, "The Public School Teacher and the Standard of Living," Report of the Committee on Teachers' Salaries and Cost of Living, in National Education Association, *Addresses and Proceedings* (1914), pp. 78–90.

[24] Hamilton, Walter I., "Teachers' Retirement Allowances," in National Education Association, *Addresses and Proceedings* (1914), pp. 71–78.

[25] Dublin, L. I., "Physical Disability of New York City Teachers," in *School and Society*, October 7 and October 14, 1916 (Vol. V), pp. 564–69, 602–7.

[26] Wood, Thomas D. (chairman), "Health of Teachers," in *Report of the Commission on Welfare of Teachers* (New York State Teachers' Association, 1916).

[27] Keyes, Charles H., "Report of Committee on Health Problems in Education," in *Journal of the National Education Association*, November, 1916 (Vol. I), p. 285.

[28] Prosser, William C., "Teachers' Compulsory Insurance," in *Teachers College Record*, November, 1910 (Vol. XI), p. 328.

[29] Furst, Clyde, "Pensions for Public School Teachers," in *Journal of the National Education Association*, October, 1916 (Vol. I), p. 137.

A relief system must be planned with special reference to the group it is intended to serve. Among railroad employees the risk of accident is greater than among teachers. Sickness is a risk common to teachers and railroad employees, but teachers are better able to deal with it as individuals. In general, a relief system will undertake only those capital risks of life which can best be met by cooperative effort. In the case of teachers, death, dependence in old age, and disability are such risks.

Thus during this period there was some opposition to sick leave voiced by leaders in the profession.

A number of studies have been made of the amount and causes of absence, and of the sick-leave policies of boards of education during the past two decades. In 1921 a study by N. L. Engelhardt and E. L. Baxter showed that current practice varied all the way from "no pay granted" to "full pay for indefinite time." [30] These investigators reported that in the three hundred and thirty-two American cities having a population of eight thousand or more there were two hundred and nine different regulations. The Research Division of the National Education Association conducted similar studies, published in 1922 and 1923, in which they also portrayed the chaotic situation with respect to sick leave. [31]

An excellent summary of conditions in 1926 appeared in one of the publications of the Bureau of Education. [32] This is especially interesting because it points out that some systems were still deducting for the pay of the substitute in 1926, while others were still allowing only a fraction of the teacher's salary, usually one half. These provisions appeared in some of the regulations of city boards of education prior to 1870.

Another apparent tendency in recent years has been the increased application of the cumulative principle. [33] Cumulative

[30] Engelhardt, N. L., and Baxter, E. L., Table Showing the Pay Granted to Teachers during Absence on Account of Sickness in American Cities of 8,000 Population and Over (1921, mimeographed), in Carrothers, George E., The Physical Efficiency of Teachers (New York, Bureau of Publications, Teachers College, Columbia University, 1924), p. 61.

[31] National Education Association, Research Bulletin, November 3, 1923 (Vol. I).

[32] Pay Status of Absent Teachers and Pay of Substitute Teachers, U. S. Bureau of Education, City School Leaflet, No. 21 (April, 1926), p. 1.

[33] The cumulative plan provides that unused absences can be carried over to the credit of the teacher from year to year and applied to long illnesses. To illustrate,

sick leave had been adopted by many cities early in the nineteen-twenties. A Research Bulletin of the National Education Association appearing in 1932 showed that in 1928 there were seven and nine tenths per cent of the cities with cumulative pay, as compared with fourteen per cent in 1931. The comparative figures for cities of various size are given in Table 22.

Table 22. Frequency of Cumulative Sick-leave Plans, 1927–1928 and 1930–1931 [1]

Sick Leave with Pay Cumulative	Cities over 100,000 in Population		Cities 30,000 to 100,000 in Population		Cities 10,000 to 30,000 in Population		Cities 5000 to 10,000 in Population		Cities 2500 to 5000 in Population		All Cities Reporting	
	1928	1931	1928	1931	1928	1931	1928	1931	1928	1931	1928	1931
1.	2	3	4	5	6	7	8	9	10	11	12	13
Number of cities.......	7	18	23	41	37	56	16	35	10	27	93	177
Per cent of cities.......	9.6	23.1	14.0	24.1	10.9	15.7	5.1	10.0	3.5	8.7	7.9	14.0
TOTAL NUMBER REPORTING...	73	78	164	170	339	356	316	349	285	311	1177	1264

Read table as follows: Of the 73 cities over 100,000 in 1927–1928 which reported sick leave with pay and also answered the question regarding cumulative leave, 7, or 9.6 per cent, used the cumulative plan. Of the 78 cities over 100,000 in 1930–1931 which reported sick leave with pay and also answered the question as to cumulative leave, 18, or 23.1 per cent, used the cumulative plan. Similarly read figures for other population groups.

[1] *The Retention, Promotion, and Improvement of Teachers,* National Education Association, Research Bulletin, No. 2 (March, 1932), Vol. X, Pt. ii, p. 57.

In recent years the trend toward the cumulative plan has been equally as pronounced. Despite the growing popularity of this type of sick-leave plan with boards of education, it has been severely criticized by many students of the problem. The cumulative plan rewards most those who are absent least and places a premium upon the teacher's being in the classroom whatever the condition of her health. This is opposed to the best interests of children and is not in harmony with the commonly accepted purposes of sick leave. Kuhlman, in his comprehensive study

if teachers are allowed five days of absence a year under the cumulative plan, a teacher who was absent only one day during the first year would be permitted to take nine days the following year without loss of salary. Frequently a maximum accumulation is stipulated, such as fifty days.

of *Teacher Absence and Leave Regulations* in 1933, rejected it and proposed as a substitute a cooperative plan for meeting the extra costs of absence (costs above normal years). He suggested an arrangement whereby teachers would share in the cost whenever the average number of days of absence of teachers exceeded a figure established by the board of education.[34] While relatively simple to operate, Kuhlman's proposal apparently involves too much calculation to be acceptable to most boards of education, and thus far has not been employed to any extent.

Rogers also studied sick-leave practices. He found that in 1934 there were still about seven per cent of the larger cities, and twenty-five per cent of the cities between five thousand and ten thousand population which had no arrangement for granting sick leave.[35] He also reported that there were at least five cities granting unlimited sick leave at full salary, and that in Bristol, Rhode Island, where this plan of leave had been in operation for more than ten years, there was the lowest average absence of teachers because of illness of which the Office of Education had record, the average loss of time for the eighty-five teachers in that city being only 1.17 days.[36]

Although there has been a gradual improvement of sick-leave plans throughout the years, conditions are still far from ideal. Table 23 shows the number and per cent of cities which granted sick leave to teachers in 1938.

While the facts in Table 23 are encouraging, they indicate that eighteen per cent of the cities included in the study still do not provide even part pay during sick leave. Even when they grant sick leave, boards of education are not always generous in the amounts allowed. Of one hundred and thirty-seven cities reporting on this matter in 1938, forty-four granted five days' leave, forty-four allowed ten days, and fifteen provided for twenty days. The remaining cities were operating other sick-leave plans.[37]

[34] Kuhlman, William D., *Teacher Absence and Leave Regulations* (New York, Bureau of Publications, Teachers College, Columbia University, 1933), p. 56.

[35] Rogers, James F., *op. cit.*, p. 58.

[36] *Ibid.*, pp. 60–61.

[37] National Education Association, Department of Classroom Teachers, *Ninth Yearbook*, p. 165.

Table 23. Number and Percentage of School Systems Granting Sick Leave to Teachers, 1938 [1]

Health Service	Number of Cities			Per Cent of Cities		
	Over 100,000	Under 100,000	Total	Over 100,000	Under 100,000	Total
1	2	3	4	5	6	7
Sick leave with part or full pay....	41	121	162	80	83	82

Based on questionnaire replies from superintendents of schools in 197 of the 220 cities included in this study—146 under 100,000 in population; 51 over 100,000.

[1] National Education Association, Department of Classroom Teachers, *Ninth Yearbook*, p. 164.

Similar progress cannot be reported for the rural areas. The practice of districts which have the one-room rural school is usually to close the school during the absence of the teacher. In some cases substitutes are employed by the absent teacher and paid by her, and in others the regular teacher is paid the full salary by the school board.[38]

Thus the development of sick-leave provisions has been a slow, evolutionary process. The philosophy underlying the practice of granting sick leave to public-school teachers has been rather clearly defined by educators. It has not been so readily accepted by the public, in spite of numerous precedents in the civil service and in related occupations. The efficiency argument, or the welfare of the child, while theoretically sound, is difficult to demonstrate. In a few instances, teachers appear to have taken advantage of generous sick-leave provisions. In these cases the black sheep in the teaching staff have provoked boards of education to adopt niggardly policies. Only when the public is fully assured that teachers are thoroughly professional in their attitude toward their work, will they guarantee them full protection during illness.

Coupled with the matter of sick leave is the more fundamental problem of promoting and preserving teacher health. Relatively

[38] Fischer, Fred C., and Le Cronier, Russell, "Sick Leave for Teachers," in *Michigan Education Journal*, March, 1938 (Vol. XV), p. 328.

few constructive efforts have been made in this direction by boards of education. It is partly a matter for school administrators to consider in arranging schedules and in providing attractive and comfortable surroundings for the school personnel, and partly a responsibility of teachers in exercising intelligence in the management of their own lives. Teachers are in a favorable position to know about health habits; in fact, the acquisition of such knowledge is a responsibility which they cannot rightfully dodge if they are to fulfill their function as teachers. If health standards are maintained by teacher-training institutions in the original selection of teachers, and public-school systems encourage frequent medical examinations for those in service, there is good reason for believing that schoolteachers will continue to hold their favorable position with respect to health.

Suggested Readings

"Fit to Teach," in National Education Association, Department of Classroom Teachers, *Ninth Yearbook* (February, 1938).

Kuhlman, William D., *Teacher Absence and Sick Leave Regulations* (New York, Bureau of Publications, Teachers College, Columbia University, 1933).

Practices Affecting Teacher Personnel, in National Education Association, Research Bulletin, No. 4 (1928), Vol. VI, pp. 233–37.

Rogers, James F., *The Welfare of the Teacher*, U. S. Office of Education Bulletin 1934, No. 4.

XXXIII

Teachers' Voluntary Associations

TEACHERS' associations have played a unique part in the improvement of the teaching personnel and in the advancement of public education. While their efforts have been devoted largely to the economic and social betterment of their own members, they have championed many causes purely in the interests of child welfare.

The development of teachers' organizations was a gradual one between 1865 and 1900. The enthusiasm which marked the rise and growth of the educational associations in the thirties and forties was not observable in the voluntary societies formed later by teachers alone. Public education, at least in principle, was an accepted fact after the Civil War. There was not the same occasion for becoming militant about the ignorance of the masses or the fate of democracy as in the earlier decades of the century. While admittedly, in 1865, the American school system was still in its infancy, and only the scaffolding of the building had been erected, the task of completing the structure was apparently not so soul-stirring nor thrilling as the pioneer undertaking of making schooling a privilege, in theory at least, of every child in the country. Furthermore, the old educational societies had included in their membership many of the nation's ablest laymen, who, by virtue of their wide influence and vision, accomplished more spectacular results than the less colorful and more humble pedagogues.

Another difference between the work and prestige of the old education associations as contrasted with the newly created teachers' organizations was in the nature of their objectives. Before the days of the city and state superintendent of schools, there were many educational problems which commanded the attention and effort of the education societies because there was no legally constituted school officer to assume the leadership in solving them. For this reason, greater emphasis was placed on broad educational questions in the early associations than upon the economic improvement of teachers themselves. Later this situation was reversed, educational problems being handled to a larger extent by school superintendents and supervisors.

From a historical standpoint, the programs and activities of the National Education Association and those of state teachers' associations are far more important than the work of local societies or even than that of the American Institute of Instruction, which was a thriving sectional organization between 1865 and 1900. The National Education Association experienced such a metamorphosis during its early history that a description of its influence and activities is exceedingly difficult to give without burdening the reader with many details. Until 1870 the association was called the National Teachers Association. Its membership was small and the annual meetings were general in character, all topics being presented to the association assembled as a whole. As late as 1872 the total membership was slightly less than three hundred. In 1870 the name of the association was changed to the National Educational Association.[1] During this year it began to absorb certain relatively small societies of schoolworkers whose interests and objectives were similar in nature to those of the larger organization, and to departmentalize the work of the association by encouraging the creation of specialized divisions within the National Educational Association itself. The American Normal Association and the National Superintendents Association were the first to unite with the National Educational Association, and within a few years a number of other divisions and departments were either organized or absorbed.[2] Among these were the departments of (1) higher instruction, (2) elementary instruction, (3) industrial education, (4) the National Council of Education, (5) the kindergarten,

---

[1] This was not made official until 1886, when Congress changed the name to National Educational Association.

[2] In 1866 the superintendents and the normal-school group withdrew from the National Teachers Association to form separate groups and were readmitted in 1870.

(6) art education, (7) music instruction, and (8) secondary instruction.

The establishment of these special departments was the outstanding achievement of the association during the last three decades of the century, for it provided an opportunity for all types of teachers and educators to serve their own immediate interests and at the same time to be affiliated with the larger work of the association. It also led to a marked change in the nature of the programs presented at the annual meetings. Where, before, undue emphasis had been placed on the personal character of the teacher, the speaker finding it necessary to choose a message of equal implication for all members attending, there now appeared a more practical selection of topics dealing with problems of immediate interest and worth to particular groups.[3] The music-instruction division confined its attention largely to matters which pertained to music; the superintendents discussed administration and supervision; elementary teachers concentrated on methods and problems primarily related to the first eight grades; and, in turn, other groups focused the attention of their members upon practices and procedures that were associated with everyday experiences. Coupled with this specialized offering, the national association provided some general meetings of an inspirational character, which served to bring the whole membership together in close harmony. This policy proved so successful that it has been continued and extended. Today the National Education Association maintains twenty-four departments.

In spite of the stimulation which the absorption and creation of special divisions provided, the association was confronted with serious financial problems in the early eighteen-eighties. On July 1, 1882, the accounts of the National Educational Association were overdrawn $557; and by July 1, 1883, the deficit had increased to $660. Somewhat alarmed over the possibilities of an expanding deficit, the leaders in the association cast around for a promoter—someone who could plan the next annual con-

[3] Under the old regime such topics as the following appeared frequently in the programs of the association: "The Teacher's Motives," "The Teacher and His Work," "The Causes of Failure and Success in the Work of the Teacher," "The Teacher's Idea."

vention in such a way as to increase membership and one who would breathe new life into the association. They were fortunate in locating an individual who had all the qualifications necessary for the successful performance of this difficult task. The Honorable Thomas W. Bicknell of Massachusetts had already rescued the American Institute of Instruction from what appeared to many educators to be certain death, and his accomplishments had so aroused the admiration of his associates and had been heralded so universally that his election to the presidency of the National Educational Association was assured. Mr. Bicknell's arrangements for the Madison, Wisconsin, meeting in 1884 were so efficient and so well advertised that the attendance exceeded all previous records. Nearly three thousand members, in addition to thousands of visitors,[4] attended this convention. Through his leadership the membership increased to the point where the association was able to wipe out the deficit and to deposit a substantial surplus in the treasury against any future embarrassments that might arise.

The active members of the National Educational Association increased in number from approximately 300 in 1872 to 2322 in 1900. While the percentage gain is indeed striking, the proportion of the nation's teachers enrolled in this national society in 1900 was pitifully small. One of the most interesting facts about the total membership (both active and associate) during the last sixteen years of the century, as the reader will observe in Table 24, was its lack of stability.

The achievements of the National Educational Association between 1865 and the turn of the century are hard to assay. As far as their influence in securing desirable school legislation is concerned, it does not appear to have been great. The membership was small and unstable, and the interests of teachers were not closely enough identified with those of the association to lead to any unified action. Furthermore, communication between the leaders of the society and the members was infrequent and the relationships were somewhat remote. Politically, the National Educational Association was unimportant before

---

[4] The largest attendance of auditors at the Madison meeting was approximately ten thousand.

1900 and legislatures were not afraid of antagonizing this group whose membership was unimpressive in size and whose influence was insignificant. On the other hand, the association kept many important issues alive and directed the public's attention and that of the profession to needed reforms. This was a distinct service to education.

Table 24. Record of Membership [1] *in the National Educational Association for Each Year from 1884 to 1900 Inclusive* [2]

Year	Membership
1884	2,729
1885	625
1886	1,197
1887	9,115
1888	7,216
1889	1,984
1890	5,474
1891	4,778
1892	3,360
1893	no meeting
1894	5,915
1895	11,297
1896	9,072
1897	7,111
1898	10,533
1899	13,656
1900	4,641

[1] Includes both active and associate members.
[2] National Education Association, *Journal of Proceedings and Addresses*, Vol. XXXIX (1900), p. 801.

An analysis of the association's resolutions during the thirty-five-year period (1865–1900) shows a wide variety of interests. Among other things, the National Educational Association favored the establishment of a national university, the inclusion of Bible study in the schools, the extension of federal aid to education, the work of the National Bureau of Education, the establishment of chairs of pedagogics in universities and colleges, instruction in public schools on the effects of alcohol upon the human system, a more stable tenure of office for teachers, the extension of the school year, the retirement of meritorious teachers, the adoption of laws forbidding the sale of tobacco to youth, the kindergarten, the education of the Indians and the Alaskans, all rational efforts to train the youth of the country in an intelligent and pure patriotism, the promotion of Americanism in the public schools, and moral training.

The research efforts of the association and the special investigations of committees were relatively insignificant before 1890. During the last decade of the century, however, there were a number of comprehensive studies made by committees under the sponsorship of various divisions of the National Educational Association which are worthy of mention.[5] Some of these studies were financed, in part at least, by the association, although the amount of money granted was in no instance large.

One of the earliest committees to receive a substantial grant (one thousand dollars) from the National Educational Association for research and investigation was the Committee of Fifteen, who were appointed in 1893 to investigate the organization of school systems, the coordination of studies in primary and grammar schools, and the training of teachers. The report which appeared in 1895 was based to a considerable extent upon a questionnaire submitted by the committee to "all persons throughout the country whose opinions might be considered as of value." The contribution lay chiefly in setting forth standards defining educational values and in furnishing broad grounds for future planning.

A second study of considerable size and import was the one made by the Committee of Twelve on rural schools. This was launched in 1895, and included an investigation of school maintenance, supervision, supply of teachers, and instruction and discipline. The final report of the committee was presented at the annual meeting in 1897, and comprised approximately two hundred printed pages of data and discussion bearing on rural-school problems.

At least two other research projects deserve comment, one made by the Committee on College Entrance Requirements and

---

[5] The National Educational Association had twelve standing committees in 1894 as follows: on state school systems; on city school systems; on higher education; on secondary education; on elementary education; on normal education; on technological education; on pedagogics; on moral education; on school sanitation, hygiene, and physical training; on psychological inquiry; and on educational reports and statistics.

another carried on by the Committee on Normal Schools. Both of these reports appeared in 1899 and were widely discussed in educational circles. The former report was a scholarly treatise on the problem of college-entrance requirements, and led to a greater degree of cooperation between the secondary schools and the colleges. The normal-school study dealt with the functions, administration, and special problems of teacher-training institutions. The work of these committees stimulated an interest in educational research and gave rise to many studies which were national in scope and which would not have been undertaken at that time by any other existing body of educators.

For the most part, the association enjoyed good leadership. Men like William T. Harris and Nicholas Murray Butler were numbered among the presidents of the society and participated for years in the management of its affairs. By 1900 the prestige of this national organization was sufficiently high to insure its continuance, and while the total membership was only 2300, or about one half of one per cent of the total number of teachers in the United States, the influence which it wielded was far greater than one might expect from the size of the organization. Some of the best minds in the profession were represented in the association, and the opinions expressed by these leaders carried great weight in the determination of practice. Unfortunately, the rank and file among the classroom teachers exercised relatively little influence in this national society before 1920. School administrators in the early days controlled the policies either directly or indirectly and assumed the general leadership of the association. Furthermore, women teachers played only a small part in the affairs of the association. Ella Flagg Young was the first woman to be elected president (1911) and up until 1920 only *two* women had served as the chief executive officer of the association. In recent years the presidency has alternated between men and women.

Between the turn of the century and 1919 the National Educational Association grew slowly from an enrollment of just over 2000 to nearly 10,000. While this growth was encouraging, it was in no respect phenomenal. Between 1919 and 1921 the society [6] added more than 40,000 to its membership and during the next two years it gained 60,000 more, making a total of 118,032 on January 1, 1923. The sensational rise occurred during the next decade, the registration in 1932 reaching 220,149, the highest enrollment attained up to the present writing.[7]

Part of the increase during the past two decades has been due to new promotion activities and techniques employed in obtaining members, but mostly the increase was related to a more representative plan of governing the association which was introduced in 1920. Prior to this date, members present at an annual meeting determined the policies and controlled the election of officers. This meant that teachers residing in or near a convention city could manipulate elections and put through measures to suit themselves, without deference to the wishes of members from a distance who were unable to attend and who, therefore, could not participate in the management of the association. The newer type of organization provided for government by representative assembly, composed of delegates selected by affiliated local and state organizations. It stimulated membership because it narrowed the gap which had existed between the interests of the classroom teacher and the activities of the headquarters' staff. The latter are determined largely by the policies adopted by the representative assembly.

The rapid expansion in the number of members has increased the income of the association markedly and has led to a corresponding improvement in services. Not only has the National Education Association continued its research activities through specially appointed committees, but since 1922 it has maintained a research division whose investigations and reports have been among the most outstanding contributions of the association.

The bulletins published by this division have treated a variety of topics in a rather scholarly fashion. The following titles were selected from a large list of research-division booklets and

[6] The name was changed from National Educational Association to National Education Association in 1907.

[7] The membership of the National Education Association was 181,228 on May 31, 1937, or approximately 20 per cent of the total teaching personnel in the public schools.

pamphlets to give the reader some appreciation of the nature and scope of the research undertakings of this association:

> *Crime Prevention through Education*
> *The School Board Member*
> *Facts on School Costs*
> *Vitalizing the High School Curriculum*
> *Creating Social Intelligence*
> *Better Reading Instruction*
> *Education for Character*
> *The Teacher's Economic Position*

In addition to the publications of the research division, the association issues a fifty-six-page monthly *Journal*, the annual *Addresses and Proceedings*, and various yearbooks and committee reports. While these publications have not been of equal value, they have all served a very useful purpose in American education. Many of the studies reported are national in scope and the topics treated are frequently those which local agencies cannot deal with so intensively for lack of staff and funds. Other important activities of the National Education Association include the preparation and distribution of material related to American Education Week, the presentation of radio broadcasts, and the preparation and distribution of news releases pertaining to education.

In 1919 a large and commodious building in Washington, D. C., was purchased for use as the headquarters of the National Education Association. This has been a factor in raising the efficiency of the organization and has lent considerable prestige to the society.

While an association with 200,000 members and a potential representative assembly of 2000 delegates is bound to be unwieldy, the affairs of the National Education Association have been handled with a minimum of friction and delay. The annual meetings of most departments of the association are held at the big summer convention.[8] The programs are built around some general theme, such as "The Relation of Schools to Busi-

---

[8] The Association of School Administrators is the most notable exception to this rule. They meet in February.

ness," "Looking Ahead in Education," or "The Responsibility of Education in Promoting World Citizenship." Since 1920 there has been a tendency for the addresses and discussions of the National Education Association to lose some of their former resemblance to religious and political exhortations and to take

National Education Association

THE HOME OF THE NATIONAL EDUCATION ASSOCIATION

on a more practical bent. The presentation of critical issues supported by evidence and logic is gradually supplanting the inspirational discourses which were so common in the association's conventions before the World War. The resolutions also reflect the practical aims of the national organization. Those adopted in 1923 are fairly typical of the professed objectives of the association in recent years.[9] They were essentially as follows:

[9] The Committee on Resolutions in 1938 reported to the Representative Assembly of the National Education Association in favor of (1) federal aid for education, (2) tax education, (3) teacher tenure, (4) teacher credit unions, (5) guidance program for youth, and (6) international good will. They went on record as opposing constitutional tax limitations, teaching without pay, and teachers' oaths.

1. Political sniping was condemned.
2. The Towner-Sterling Bill (for federal aid in the financing of education) was endorsed.
3. A child-labor amendment to the Constitution of the United States was favored.
4. A policy of developing a model system of schools in the city of Washington was approved.
5. The following items were "emphasized" with regard to improving the status of the teacher:
   (1) Salaries adequate to attract high-minded and well-educated youth into the profession.
   (2) Promotion on merit alone.
   (3) Tenure while teachers render satisfactory service.
   (4) Adequate retirement annuities and pensions, so as to remove fear of destitution.
   (5) Recognition of teacher's right to express professional opinions and to develop personal initiative.
   (6) Equipment and support of more and better teacher-training schools and colleges.

In 1935 the association, aided by a generous grant from the General Education Board, organized an Educational Policies Commission which promises to have a most salutary influence on American education. Some of the ablest men and women in the profession and in related fields are serving either as members of this commission or as consultants to it, and the problems attacked thus far have been fundamental in character and broad in scope.[10] The following publications of the Policies Commission reveal the nature of their efforts: *The Unique Function of Education in American Democracy, A National Organization for Education, Research Memorandum on Education in the Depression, Education for Democracy, The Structure and Administration of Public Education in the United States, The Effect of Population Changes on American Education.*

The commission also issues a bimonthly leaflet, entitled *Educational Policy*, for the purpose of keeping consultants and other members of the profession informed about its work.

[10] The Policies Commission is composed of twenty members, thirteen of whom were appointed at large. The ex-officer consultants number some twenty-two hundred officials of educational and related organizations.

To discuss all the present activities of the National Education Association would require greater space than can well be devoted to the topic in this book. There is scarcely any phase of public education in which this great organization is not providing some leadership and, on the basis of its past record of service, the future of the association appears hopeful and promising.

THE AMERICAN FEDERATION OF TEACHERS

Because of differences in point of view, no one association can hope, in a country as large as the United States, to enlist the support of all public-school teachers. It is, perhaps, fortunate that this is so, since through experimentation and exchange of ideas institutions are stimulated to put forth greater effort and to improve their programs.

The American Federation of Teachers has a rather brief history. It was organized on April 15, 1916, and it formally affiliated with the American Federation of Labor on May 9, 1916. Prior to this year (1916) there were only a few local teachers' unions in the United States, the one in Chicago laying claim to the largest and most active enrollment. The influence of the American Federation of Teachers has always been greater than its membership implies. The eight local unions which united to form the federation in 1916 comprised only 2800 teachers; and while the membership increased by leaps and bounds during the next four years, reaching a total of 12,000, it did not include any sizable percentage of the teaching personnel. Even as recently as 1934 the reported membership of the federation was only 13,000.[11]

Between 1934 and 1938 there was a marked increase in the membership of the teachers' union, the total number reaching 30,000. The failure of the union to attract into its ranks a large segment of the teacher personnel can be attributed in part to the opposition of educators and school-board members to teachers joining a trade-union movement. While labor has never dictated the policies of the teachers' federation, and while the strike has not been accepted as an appropriate weapon for forcing recalcitrant school boards to come to terms, the phrase "teachers'

[11] The total number of locals in 1934 was reported to be 125.

union" still causes many pedagogues, as well as citizens, to raise their eyebrows and to view its purposes with alarm. There are instances in which teachers have been discharged for belonging to a teachers' union.[12] While the courts have held that membership in a union does not constitute a crime and is not a sufficient reason in a tenure state for dismissing a teacher, the public has never looked with favor upon "unionism" for teachers.

The activities of the American Federation of Teachers have been largely in the field of public opinion and legislation. The typical local teachers' unions do not hesitate to investigate problems which face public education, and then to widely publicize their recommendations and lobby actively for desired legislation. Matters such as tenure, pensions, salaries, and academic freedom have been the focus of continual activity by these organizations. The American Federation of Teachers is considered, because of its activities and the reputed point of view of its members, to be a radical organization. There are those who assert that it is composed chiefly of malcontents, that it is a house of refuge for the oppressed and for the revolutionary spirits in the profession. Although the teachers' unions in large cities undoubtedly have within their membership various minorities of different shades of political opinion, the most extreme stands which these unions have taken are typified by the following: opposition to war as a means of settling international disputes, advocacy of the recognition of the Soviet Union, approval of the abolition of child labor, opposition to exploitation of workers for the sake of profit, attack upon bankers for their attitude toward public education,

[12] In Seattle, Washington, more than a score of teachers in 1928, as a result of a salary controversy, allied themselves with the local labor union, under the name American Federation of Teachers. The school administration disapproved the action of the teachers, believing that it was not in the interests of the school system for public-school teachers to place themselves under an authority other than that of a board of education. In accordance with this belief, the board of education unanimously adopted the following resolution:

"Resolved: That no person be employed hereafter or continued in the employ of the district as a teacher while a member of the American Federation of Teachers or any local thereof; and that before any election shall be considered binding, such teacher shall sign a declaration to the following effect:

"I hereby declare that I am not a member of the American Federation of Teachers, or any local thereof, and will not become a member during the term of my contract." (*School Board Journal*, June, 1928, p. 28.)

and advocacy of a nationalized system of banks and control of credit.

The slogan of the American Federation of Teachers is "Democracy in Education; Education for Democracy." For the information of its members, the society publishes a thirty-two-page journal, called the *American Teacher*, which appears five times a year. It contains news of the federation's activities and interpretive articles of general interest. The federation does not engage in educational research. The only meetings of the federation are the annual conventions, which are usually held in the summer months and consist of accredited delegates from the locals.

Judging from the strides made by American labor in recent years and from the influence which the labor movement is now wielding upon our life and institutions, one might be disposed to presage an enviable future for the American Federation of Teachers. Logic would at least suggest that this branch of the labor federation bids fair to increase its membership markedly in the immediate future. Despite the reasonableness of this assumption, there is no indication at present that the rank and file of American schoolteachers are greatly interested in the peculiar functions which the union professes to serve. It seems probable that the society's contribution in the future is going to continue to be that of a minority group, stimulating and spurring on to action larger professional associations.

The Progressive Education Association

Like the American Federation of Teachers, the Progressive Education Association is a relatively young organization. It was formed in the winter of 1918–1919 in Washington, D. C., by Stanwood Cobb, headmaster of the Chevy Chase Country Day School, in cooperation with a small group of teachers and laymen interested in the newer types of education which were springing up in various parts of the country. This study group, under Cobb's direction, organized themselves into an association for the purpose of appraising the more promising school experiments and of interpreting the scattered efforts of educational reformers.

The association had its roots in the philosophy and experiments of Colonel Francis Parker and John Dewey. The progressive movement was profoundly influenced by the formalism and regimentation which were the two chief characteristics of the public schools of the early nineteen-hundreds. The formation of the association represented a reaction against the standardized subject matter of the typical school, with its rigid system of grading and its emphasis upon repressing the natural impulses of the child. Parker and Dewey, imbued with the philosophical concepts of reformers from Socrates to Froebel, had laid the foundations for a revolutionary change in school management and in methods of teaching. It remained now for some intelligent and energetic professional body to interpret and give expression to the principles evolved by these educational philosophers before any significant progress could be looked for in the schools of the country generally. This task the Progressive Education Association accepted as one of its primary responsibilities.

The original platform of the association included the following general principles:

1. Freedom to develop naturally
2. Interest, the motive of all work
3. The teacher a guide, not a taskmaster
4. Scientific study of pupil development
5. Greater attention to all that affects the child's physical development
6. Cooperation between school and home to meet the needs of child life
7. The progressive school, a leader in educational movements

Since 1924 the Progressive Education Association has issued a journal entitled *Progressive Education*. This magazine carried articles designed for both professional and lay readers and emphasized the pioneer efforts of individuals and schools to break with traditional practices. During the earlier years of the association's life, considerable attention was focused upon developing methods and techniques that would encourage the natural unfolding of child nature. Elementary education, therefore, received the most consideration. Since it was deemed quite impracticable to alter the practices of high schools because of the control exercised by the college entrance boards through their examinations, relatively little attention was devoted by the association to secondary education during the first decade of its history.

The membership of the Progressive Education Association has never been large, the total number enrolled in 1938 being approximately ten thousand. At first it consisted chiefly of parents and teachers connected with private schools. In recent years the number of public-school teachers, professors, and educational workers in public institutions who have enlisted in the association is a substantial one and gives promise of increasing as the work and influence of the association is brought more directly to bear upon the improvement of public education.

Since 1929 the association has shifted its emphasis somewhat from the problems of child growth to a consideration of socio-economic problems and their relation to education. The association has issued no statement of its philosophy, and the economic and social, as well as the educational, views of its members unquestionably range from mildly conservative to extremely liberal.

Some of the recent activities of the association include summer workshops, in which students and teachers interested in progressive education are given an opportunity to study intensively, for six weeks, definite problems growing out of their schoolwork. It is a variation from the typical summer-school procedure. Four of these workshops were held in the summer of 1938. In addition to the workshop development, the Progressive Education Association holds regional conferences in connection with the regular summer-school programs in selected colleges and universities. In 1937 three were held in cooperation with Colorado State College of Education, Ohio State University, and Harvard University.

The most significant work of the association has been done through committees and commissions. The committees that were active in 1928 included the following:

The Committee on Progressive Education in Rural Schools
The Committee on Community School Relations
The Committee on Experimental Schools

The Committee on Child Development, and the Preschool
and Elementary Curriculum

The Committee on International Relations

The scope of the commissions' activities was as broad as that
of the committees just listed. The Commission on Educational
Freedom, appointed in 1935, has as its objective the giving of
vigorous support to the protection of the educational freedom of
teachers and students. A second commission is the Commission
on Intercultural Education. Three other commissions are working primarily with secondary education. They are the Commission on the Relation of School and College, the Commission
on the Secondary School Curriculum, and the Commission on
Human Relations. It is too early to attempt an appraisal of
the Progressive Education Association and its work or to foretell,
with any assurance of accuracy, its future destiny. Thus far it
has served as a goad to other teachers' associations and to the
profession generally. It has supplemented the research activities
of certain educational agencies and has lent considerable support to pioneer efforts. Its leaders, for the most part, have been
men and women of considerable prominence in the educational
world who were highly respected by their colleagues. The contribution of the association, while questioned in some quarters,
has been conceded by most thoughtful educators to be a significant one; and its aims and purposes have been silently endorsed by thousands of teachers who have not enrolled, but
whose sympathies are unmistakably with the progressives.

State Teachers' Associations

State teachers' associations have played a more active part in
the improvement of teacher welfare than any other single agency.
Between 1845 and 1900 there was a steady increase in the number
of state teachers' organizations, as is shown in Figure V.

At the present time there is a state teachers' association in
every state. What has been even more phenomenal is the growth
in membership within the state associations themselves. In 1907
only 14.7 per cent of the country's teachers were members of
state teachers' associations; in 1916 this percentage had been

raised to 34.1; by 1923 it had reached 61.5 per cent; and in 1937 slightly more than 70 per cent of the nation's teachers were enrolled in state teachers' associations. This increase in membership over the past quarter century has been achieved by a variety of means, some of which are scarcely defensible. It has been customary in some states for many local superintendents to coerce

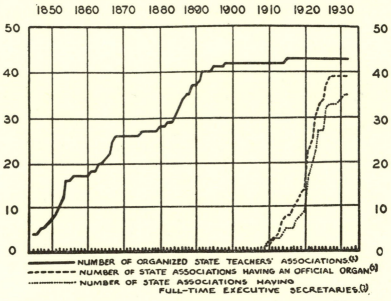

FIGURE V. DEVELOPMENT OF THE STATE TEACHERS' ASSOCIATION MOVEMENT
IN THE UNITED STATES

[1] Based on the date of organization of the now dominant association in each of 43 states, as given in Crawford, Albert Byron, *A Critical Analysis of the Present Status and Significant Trends of State Education Associations of the United States*, p. 12 (Bulletin of the Bureau of School Service, Vol. IV, No. 4, College of Education, University of Kentucky, Lexington, Ky., 1932). Data for five states missing.

[2] According to Brewton, J. E., "The Functions of State Education Association Journals," p. 14 (unpublished doctor's thesis, Peabody College, 1933). Data for only 39 states.

[3] According to Crawford for 32 states and to Brewton for three states.

teachers to join the state teachers' associations through one hundred per cent membership campaigns. Fearful lest they be deprived of their jobs or be in disfavor with the administration, hesitant teachers, when appealed to by their superior officers, are moved to join the state association without further delay.

This practice has led to considerable teacher criticism of the management of state teachers' organizations by school administrators who have played an important role in the activities of the association from its earliest beginnings. Until recently state superintendents of instruction, local superintendents of schools, and the members of college faculties have practically controlled teachers' organizations. These individuals have been better able to attend the conventions than teachers, because of the more generous salaries awarded to them, and are more experienced in managing affairs of this nature than classroom teachers. Furthermore, teachers have been untrained, transient, and frequently indifferent toward professional matters outside of their own bailiwick. It is not to be wondered at, then, that the leadership in the associations has rested largely in the hands of administrators, and that the latter have brought pressure to bear upon teachers to join.

A second reason for the increase in the membership of state teachers' associations has been the improvement in the services rendered to classroom teachers. The recognition by the rank and file of classroom teachers of the achievements of the association and its potential strength in securing for them greater security and a better economic status has brought many members into the fold. Tenure laws, pension and retirement legislation, and minimum-salary laws have all been enacted, largely through the efforts of the state teachers' associations.

In recent years teachers have also been stimulated to join the associations by direct appeals from executive secretaries.[13] Most of the state associations employ an officer, called "executive secretary," whose functions are to keep the membership and financial records, to act as editor or editorial adviser for the official journal and other publications, to take charge or assist with convention arrangements, to act as publicity agent with respect to both association activities and the public schools of the state, to serve as legislative representative and make studies pertaining to legislative problems, and to do everything he can

---

[13] The movement to establish executive secretaries began about 1909. During the years 1921–1924 eighteen states engaged full-time executive secretaries. By 1933 thirty-five state associations were operating with such a secretary.

to increase the membership and improve the services of the association.

Modern methods of communication and travel are making it increasingly easy for teachers to know what their association is doing. It is quite practicable now for teachers to participate actively in the work of state committees without undue cost to themselves or the association. Increased participation will undoubtedly strengthen state teachers' organizations and make them even more popular than they are now.

Most state associations are organized on a departmental basis, similar to the National Education Association. In several of the states the constitutions of the associations specify what departments should exist. The most common one is the kindergarten or kindergarten-primary. Others include the elementary, the high-school, the music department, the rural or rural-primary, and the higher-education department. Similarly, certain annual committees are quite frequently specified, such as a resolutions committee, a legislative committee, an auditing committee, and a committee on necrology.

The budgets of some of the state associations are relatively large, the total annual income for all the organizations amounting to approximately $1,800,000 in 1928–1929. The sources of revenue are membership dues, which account for about fifty per cent of the income; advertising in the association publications, which amounts to more than twenty per cent of the revenue; and income from reading circles, fees, receipts from placement bureaus, subscriptions, commercial exhibits, subsidies, and miscellaneous sources.

In several of the states there are minor associations of teachers which have been created to serve the interests of special groups. The most important of these are the separate organizations for Negro teachers which have been established in many of the Southern states.

State associations will continue to exercise a powerful influence upon educational policies and administrative practices. Experience has demonstrated the usefulness of this organization as an agency of the teaching profession. The state appears to be the optimum unit for teachers' associations when judged by actual achievements. While administrators have tended to dominate state teachers' organizations in the past, there are some indications that teachers are gradually taking over the leadership and that merit, rather than position, is likely to become the determining factor in the election of association officers.

LOCAL TEACHERS' ASSOCIATIONS

A history of local teachers' associations in the United States would unquestionably throw considerable light on the problems which have been of greatest concern to the teaching profession during the past seventy-five years. Local organizations of teachers have been primarily interested in matters which were directly and immediately associated with the economic and professional welfare of their own members. Unfortunately, the records of these associations have never been studied in any comprehensive fashion, and only isolated bits of evidence are available for readers who are interested in a chronological account of the activities of classroom-teacher organizations. Most of the local associations established prior to 1900 were either disbanded or reorganized, so that the number of present societies which have enjoyed a continuous existence of fifty or more years is strikingly small, as Table 25 indicates:

Table 25. Local Teachers' Organizations Established since 1870 Which Are Still in Existence [1]

Date Organization Was Established	Number of Local Associations
1870–1879	5
1880–1889	2
1890–1899	7
1900–1909	37
1910–1919	84
1920–1929	45
1930–1936	33
TOTAL	213

[1] Adapted from National Education Association, Department of Classroom Teachers, *Teachers' Local Organizations—A Manual for Leaders* (February, 1937), p. 4.

It is clear from Table 25 that the decade 1910–1919 witnessed the largest growth in the establishment of local teachers' associations of any ten-year period since 1870, and that a marked drop in the number of new associations followed this temporary spurt. Prior to 1900 teachers either looked to other agencies for the promotion of their welfare and for intellectual stimulation, or were indifferent to many problems which in recent years have constituted real challenges to the profession. Higher standards of training and greater tenure have increased the span of interest of teachers and have led them to take a longer view when considering educational policies.

It is obviously beyond the scope of this discussion to record the struggles and achievements of the two hundred and thirteen local teachers' associations included in Table 25. There are only a few associations for which adequate published records are available, and these are seldom in such form as to render a continuous account of the organizations' activities possible. In order to make an accurate appraisal of the programs of local teachers' associations, it would be necessary to go directly to the minute books of the various societies. This task, while offering a promising area for research, must be left for some enterprising student to undertake.

Fortunately the history of one of the oldest and most active city organizations of teachers, the Brooklyn Teachers Association, has been compiled and, while it is admittedly not representative of local associations generally, it is interesting and enlightening because of the nature of its program and the wide range of activities in which its members engaged.

The Brooklyn organization was formed in 1874. The features emphasized by the founders in their first appeal for membership included: [14]

Four entertainments similar to those already given by the Principals Association to the teachers of the city.

Two or more first class lectures by prominent educators.

One or more social entertainments.

Admittance to all of these to be by tickets issued to members.

---

[14] Taken from a circular sent to thirty-eight schools in Brooklyn on February 24, 1874.

The aims of the association, judged by the activities pursued, were professional improvement and increased opportunities for social intercourse. Debates and discussions on current educational problems were held during the earlier years of the association. In 1874 the question for debate was: "Resolved, that the detention of pupils beyond the regular school session is detrimental to the interests of both pupils and teachers." The decision was for the negative. A few months later (September, 1874) the topic "Resolved, that the educational necessities of Brooklyn demand the establishment of a high or normal school" was debated, the affirmative side carrying off the honors. Such innovations as "Drawing in the Public Schools" were vigorously discussed at regular meetings of the association. Literary and musical programs were also commonly presented, as the following digest of the association's activities for 1875–1876 shows: [15]

Record of Lectures and Entertainments, Given by the Brooklyn Teachers Association, 1875–1876

1. Social Entertainment at Association Hall, June 19, 1875. A short literary and musical programme occupied the early part of the evening including
   Readings by Mr. W. M. Jelliffe
   Song by Mrs. E. J. Whitlock
   Recitations by Mrs. Braman, and
   Instrumental Music by Mr. and Mrs. Henry Ahlers.
   The remainder of the evening was devoted to promenades, dancing and social intercourse.

2. Social Entertainment at Novelty Hall, November 13, 1875.

3. January 21, 1876, Association Hall
   Lecture by Professor Thomas M. Sprague—"Gesture."

4. February 25, 1876, Social Entertainment at Apollo Hall

5. March 29, 1876, Association Hall
   Lecture by Rev. R. S. Stows, D. D.—"The Times of Robin Hood."

The educational work of the association was a prominent feature from the very beginning, and it is doubtful if any teachers' association surpassed the Brooklyn organization in its pro-

---

[15] Brooklyn Teachers Association, *Fiftieth Annual Report* (September, 1924), p. 79.

vision of professional lectures and courses of study for members. In 1882 a series of lectures designed to improve classroom methods was instituted, and included such topics as "Primary Reading," "Decimals," "Percentages and Their Applications," and "Ratio as Applied to Business Arithmetic." In 1886 Dr. Nicholas Murray Butler conducted a class in psychology under the auspices of the Brooklyn Teachers Association, and a report made in June, 1887, "brought out the fact that two hundred forty-eight lessons had been given by talented instructors during the year," at an expense to the associations of six hundred and fifty dollars. These included, in addition to the class in psychology, lectures in English literature, penmanship, Latin, French, German, and physical training.

A class in pedagogy and one in natural science were recommended to the association about this time, and by 1893 the society's course of study included principles of education, methods of teaching, psychology, and school government, in addition to subjects of a more academic nature. Apparently the courses were popular, for the average attendance of one hundred and sixty-one lessons in 1892–1893 was thirty-eight.

In 1898 the association was granted a charter under the Regents of the State of New York and given power to issue certificates to teachers for course work offered under the direction of the association. The fact that the superintendent of schools placed his stamp of approval upon these certificates is indicative of the high professional character of the courses sponsored. By 1904, however, the Board of Regents had changed their minds about the policy of approving or registering pedagogical courses by which exemption from certain examinations was sought. To meet this situation the association, in 1905, reorganized their procedure somewhat and provided five extension courses of thirty hours each in local colleges, for which credits were given by the Board of Examiners, the Regents, and the colleges. The interest of the association in professional study has remained unabated throughout the years, and the encouragement offered to teachers to keep abreast of educational thought has been unexcelled.[16]

[16] In 1936 Wattenberg wrote about the Brooklyn Teachers Association: "The

Cultural Activities

Related to the organized course work which was offered under the auspices of the Brooklyn association were the arrangements made by officers and committees of the association for increasing the cultural opportunities of members. A committee which was appointed in 1879 to formulate a program for the future recommended among other things that "at least one concert" be held annually.[17] The entertainments, which were an integral part of the association's program, consisted frequently of musical and literary performances by talented artists. Numerous excursions were made by members to points of interest in the New York metropolitan area and, judging from the enthusiastic reports contained in the minutes, these trips were thoroughly enjoyed.

Promotion of Teacher Welfare

In addition to the opportunities provided by the Brooklyn association for cultural and professional growth, the organization was active in protecting and promoting the economic welfare of classroom teachers. In 1877 the association appointed a committee to protest the salary cuts proposed by the Board of Estimate. One objector decried this move, saying it marked the "entry of the teachers into politics." For the most part the association worked harmoniously with the board of education and was extremely cautious about taking any action which might embarrass the members of this latter body. At times, however, differences of opinion arose over policy. In 1894 the teachers' association passed the following resolution: "Resolved, that the resolution of the Board of Education in assessing a fine upon teachers of 50 per cent of their salary for absence is a seemingly unfair discrimination in that it does not include all employees of the Board."[18]

Association has a school offering more than one hundred courses, most of which can be counted as credits to meet the alertness requirements for salary increments. Members receive a discount of $1.50 a year on these courses." (Wattenberg, William W., *On the Educational Front* [New York, Columbia University Press, 1936], p. 47.)

[17] *Ibid.*, p. 82.

[18] Brooklyn Teachers Association, *Fiftieth Annual Report*, p. 102.

Similarly, the association voiced their opposition to the appointment of two primary supervisors, in 1895, as not in the best interests of the schools and contested a proposed amendment of the board's rules to the effect that all certificates of teachers less than five years in service would be canceled and new ones required. The teachers fought centralization and what they deemed to be excessive supervision. In 1897 the association went on record as favoring:

1. A board of education of forty-five
2. Well-defined powers of the city superintendent

The following year the Brooklyn teachers recommended a salary schedule to the board of education. This was not accepted in its original form, although it received consideration by the board of education.

In 1899 the first Committee on legislation was appointed, and in future years every proposal in the legislature which had any bearing on education in New York City was made the subject of study and investigation by this committee. Teachers were kept informed of the implications of the various proposals, and in some instances endorsements by the association were secured and forwarded to the appropriate individual or agency; in others, a record of the organization's opposition was placed before the proper authorities.

Retirement allowances was another topic of considerable interest to the association. Detailed provisions such as the following became planks in the platform of the association: [19]

1. Optional retirement after thirty years
2. Half pay when retired
3. Proper care of teachers after twenty years' service
4. No direct tax on people to make up deficiencies

Many of the measures supported by the Brooklyn Teachers Association appear to have been educationally desirable and were later adopted by the board of education. Equal pay was favored as early as 1907, although it later became a point of controversy; tenure legislation was actively sponsored. In 1910

[19] *Ibid.*, p. 110.

the association adopted the following principles, which represented its educational platform: A smaller independent board of education; protection of the teacher in trials and transfers; protection during good behavior of the members of the Board of Examiners; curtailment of the excessive powers of the superintendent of schools although retaining expert initiative in professional matters; a minimum three-mills tax provision; and tenure of office for district superintendents.

Most of these recommendations were adopted during the decade which followed. The achievements of the Brooklyn organization cannot be assayed accurately, because in most instances there were other agencies and forces pressing for positive action on the measures in question. The Problems Committee of the association conducted several investigations, including a study of Promotion and Rating of Teachers, the Health of Teachers, Causes of School Absences, and Grading and Promotion of Pupils. These professional reports unquestionably influenced school policy. The Brooklyn association must have contributed greatly to the happiness of individual members. Not only has the organization fought consistently for the rights of classroom teachers throughout the years, but through organized efforts it has extended to members many privileges and opportunities which would have otherwise been denied them. Lectures, study courses, excursions, entertainments, group health and accident insurance, cooperative purchasing,[20] and a cooperative camp are among the special services which the association has provided. To these advantages there must be added all increases in salary or pension allowances resulting from the united support of the association. While not a militant organization, the Brooklyn association has not been hesitant in making the wants of its members known to responsible authorities. The influence of the association has increased markedly with the growth in membership. In 1875 the total number of members was 329; within fifty years it had reached 7000, and in 1928 the maximum membership totaled 9171.

[20] The Committee on Cooperation reported sales for 1920 as follows: eggs 5500 dozen; butter 4250 lbs.; cocoa 3500 lbs.; bacon 3000 lbs.; coffee 1400 lbs.; tea 750 lbs.; ham 800 lbs.; canned fruits 85 dozen.

One cannot safely generalize from the achievements and activities of the Brooklyn Teachers Association. It is a large organization and its program is more varied and extensive than that of smaller local teachers' societies. The association's generous provision of study opportunities for members appears to have been unusual. A history of the Educational Club of Philadelphia, an association of public-school men, shows no comparable course work for those enrolled. According to a résumé of the achievements of the decade 1892–1902, the Philadelphia society held fifty-seven scientific lessons, at which questions connected with the theory and practice of education were considered. Yet as significant as this record is, it does not compare in magnitude with the professional work of the Brooklyn association during the same decade.[21]

The Philadelphia club resorted chiefly to round-table discussions and an annual conference for professional stimulation. In cooperation with other associations they brought in as lecturers on special occasions nationally prominent educators. Apparently the Philadelphia schoolmen were somewhat hesitant about entering the field of politics, for the Committee on Publication, in sketching the history of the club, stated that "the professional nature of the organization has justified a natural reluctance to engage in a public agitation for men or legislation."[22]

Despite this point of view, the executive council of the Philadelphia association in 1897 endorsed a bill for a lengthening of the minimum school term from six to seven months; and in 1901 resolutions were adopted, formally commending the administration of the state superintendent of instruction and urging his reappointment.

While the activities of the Brooklyn and Philadelphia associations are not representative of the vast majority of local teachers' associations, they do suggest the type of work undertaken by city teachers' organizations generally. The chief aims which appear to have dominated most of the local associations are professional improvement of members, the advancement of

[21] *Handbook of the Educational Club of Philadelphia, 1892–1902* (Philadelphia, The Educational Club, 1903), p. 5.

[22] *Ibid.*, p. 8.

pupil and teacher welfare, and service to the community. In some societies the promotion of the economic status of teachers has been the chief goal of the association. Where this situation prevails, the public has been extremely critical of teachers and their activities. The stronger associations have adopted platforms which are rather broad in scope and reasonably unselfish in purpose.

PRESENT-DAY ASSOCIATIONS

Local associations in large cities are numerous. Wattenberg reported that New York City had more than one hundred and sixty different teachers' organizations in 1936 and Chicago at least twenty-nine.[23] The variation in the aims of these societies within a given city is sometimes wide. In New York City, for example, the associations range from one with opposition to Fascism as a dominant purpose, to organizations concerned primarily with academic problems. The vast majority of these specialized associations are connected only in the slightest way, if at all, with the dominant state and national societies.

In a study by Hoffman [24] of eighty-one associations in cities of one hundred thousand population or more, the most frequent type of activity was found to be lectures, 84 per cent of the cities reporting indicating that they provided lectures for members, and frequently for the public, on one or more of the following topics: art, travel, civics, current events, music, other cultural subjects, or professional matters. The operation of university-extension courses, or other courses, was the next most common type of activity, with 35 per cent of the organizations engaged in such projects. Research was claimed to be an element in the program of 32 per cent of these large city associations, and reading- and discussion-group meetings were carried on by 30 per cent. A few societies hold institutes and conferences and occasionally a group attempts to carry on some type of educational experimentation.

This same study of Hoffman reported that local associations

[23] Wattenberg, William W., *op. cit.*, p. 41.
[24] Hoffman, M. D., *Status of Voluntary Teachers' Associations in Cities of 100,000 Population or More*, U. S. Office of Education, Bulletin 1930, No. 36 (Washington, Government Printing Office, 1931).

were actively seeking to change a number of school policies, the most commonly mentioned of which was teachers' salaries. Curriculum revision, sabbatical leave, school publicity, teacher rating, absence and sick-leave regulations, and teacher qualifications were all listed among the items with which teachers' associations were vitally concerned. In fact, in recent years there has scarcely been a phase of school administration which has escaped the attention of local teacher groups.

The legislative activity of local associations has been confined chiefly to pension and retirement laws, tenure and salary laws, and legislation pertaining to the distribution of state aid. In a few situations, proposed certification changes and administrative reorganization have been the objects of attack or support. The success of local associations in promoting legislation is difficult to determine. More than half of the desirable measures which large city associations have actively supported have been adopted. To what extent the passage of the various bills included in the above contention was due to the support of teachers' associations, rather than to other agencies, is a matter of speculation. In smaller communities, local associations have been somewhat reluctant to engage in legislative activities.

Welfare measures constitute an important part of the program of local teachers' associations. Aid to needy teachers; scholarships for deserving students, group-insurance arrangements; the administration of funds for sickness, accident, and hospitalization; and the management of travel parties—all these activities are engaged in by teachers' associations.

The establishment of credit unions among teachers has taken place rapidly since 1930. These unions are mutual savings and loan organizations which operate by legal charter and are under the supervision of the state banking departments. They offer credit to members at rates substantially below the usual commercial ones.

Most local teacher groups are not able to support, easily, a newspaper or journal and they resort to a more personal type of communication with their members and friends. In the larger associations, however, there are well-established journals. Some of the New York organizations have full reports of their meetings published regularly in each of several metropolitan newspapers.

In carrying out their programs, the officers of local teachers' associations are often assisted by suggestions from the National League of Teachers Associations and the Department of Classroom Teachers of the National Education Association. A recent bulletin by the former organization reviewed for the benefit of local associations a number of problems, including professional ethics, teacher rating, tenure, teachers' councils, the single-salary schedule, and several other important current issues. The yearbooks of the Department of Classroom Teachers have dealt with topics which were of immediate concern to teachers' associations. The leadership exercised by this national body has served as a real boon to local societies.

Probably the most commonly voiced criticism of teachers' associations in the United States is that they degrade themselves by entering upon or continuing in "unprofessional" activities. The definition of "unprofessional" in the minds of many administrative officers, and others whose opinions they voice, has sometimes been extended to include practically all matters except those having to do with teaching techniques. Interest of teachers in better salaries, in tenure, in pensions, and in academic freedom has been severely criticized as being selfish and unbecoming. With the present tendency for teachers to take a real share in the control of their organizations, however, this attitude will probably be given less heed than formerly.[25]

More justified than the foregoing are the following criticisms: Teachers' associations, in general, are loose groups of transient workers who can hardly be said to have that unity of interest and that common body of professional traditions characteristic of long-established professions. The membership is predominantly feminine, but the leadership is largely masculine. The organizations are cooperative in spirit, but mostly without specific objectives and practical programs. They are nonmilitant and nonpolitical. Their government is nominally representative, but not so in actuality. The positions of leadership have been

---

[25] Some of the material on local associations appears in the section "United States" of the *Educational Yearbook of the International Institute of Teachers College* (New York, Bureau of Publications, Teachers College, Columbia University, 1935).

occupied more often by impractical, would-be reformers than by practical realists, and the leaders themselves have been uncertain of their own goals. The control has been largely in the hands of administrators, whose interest in certain important measures is in serious conflict with the interests of teachers. Teachers join these bodies as an expression of their nebulous faith in the general values of organization and as a method of conforming to the wishes of their supervisory officers, rather than as an acceptance of an opportunity to participate effectively in the educational battles of the time.

Several constructive proposals to remedy these faults have been brought forward. Among these proposals the following may be mentioned as outstanding:

1. A desire and a technique for self-criticism should be developed by teachers' organizations. It should be cultivated into the most potent stimulant possible for making the associations effective. For example, a lively "Letters-to-the-Editor" column might be introduced into the journals, as one of several devices to encourage criticism.

2. The active interest of the members should be aroused, nurtured, and directed as a driving and guiding force in the associations. Teacher participation should be enlisted in both planning and working out the programs. As an illustration, consideration of issues which a teachers' organization faces should be carried down to all the members. At present many votes taken by the so-called legislative bodies are unanimous adoptions of committee reports and election of officers. The delegates who cast these unanimous votes often have no basis themselves for making an intelligent choice in the matter. The members back home are left in everlasting darkness.

3. The constitutions, bylaws, and existing practices of most associations need overhauling in the light of current theories in the field of political science. Domination by teachers rather than by administrators, for example, should be fostered.

4. Practical programs, which are both needed and desired by the teachers, should be formulated and then actually carried out. It is time for the plans of teachers' organizations to be brought out of the blue haze of uncertainty. The teachers of the nation

might plan and unite on a reasonable and needed specific program of permanent federal aid for public schools. Some such practical problem should be decided upon by each association as paramount at the moment, and then should serve as a focus for the major efforts of the organizational activities of all the teachers and the lay friends of education. At present many teachers are no more influential in shaping the educational structure than they are in causing changes in the weather.

5. Only the finest leaders in the profession should be tolerated as officers and executive secretaries. Petty politics, based on a desire to honor personal friends by electing them to office, irrespective of their fitness, prevails widely at present. This situation is strong evidence that teachers have not yet achieved high professional standards for their group activities.

6. A more effective integration of education organizations is needed. At present the national, state, and local associations, as well as various minority groups, seem to the ordinary teacher to be competing for his membership fee. One step to correct this has been taken by the Pennsylvania State Education Association. The membership blank of that organization is attached to the enrollment forms of the National Education Association and local association. Thus the suggestion is made to prospective members that these associations work together, and teachers can join all three at one time. There is no valid reason why state and local organizations should not lead the way toward complete integration by making their membership coinclusive with the larger organizations. Since 1921 the Maryland State Teachers Association has provided that any teacher who joins an affiliated county or city society automatically acquires membership in the state society. If this practice became widespread among the dominant local, state, and national organizations, the subsidiary associations might come to regard themselves as autonomous branches of the national society. Coordinated programs and united action would probably be fostered by such a plan of coinclusive membership. Care should be taken not to discourage minority groups, however, for they can be of great value. Places should be found for them within the general teachers' organization, and their autonomy not encroached upon. If militant

minorities are allowed no room within the dominant organizations, adjustment to new situations is greatly retarded and stagnation and eventual replacement become likely.

7. Organizations of teachers should assist public legislative bodies in providing the best possible education laws. Teachers are too often scared away at present by the cry, "Stay out of politics! You are seeking a selfish end!" If they would examine closely the activities of the groups which raise this cry, they would often discover that these groups are using these charges to divert attention from their own subtle and selfish control over government. The teachers' unions are not so timid here as the other teachers' associations.

8. The primary function of professional journalism is to keep members informed on all important developments which relate to their field of work. The present lack of effectiveness of teachers' association publications is attested by a widespread ignorance among teachers as to important news which affects their own profession.

9. Teachers' associations should study problems directly affecting the welfare of their members. Their type of leadership in the past has been largely responsible for the uninformed state of teachers concerning matters of tenure, salary laws and schedules, pensions, retirement plans, and the financing of education. It is significant that the organizations which have been most effective in these important fields are the teachers' unions and other classroom-teacher groups in which the influence of supervisory officers is at a minimum.

10. College teachers, as well as normal-school and college students who are planning to become teachers, need to be encouraged to participate actively in teachers' organizations. These groups are able to contribute much to the professional societies in leadership, research, planning, and action, and also in membership. If students were attracted to membership by special low student dues, and if membership were made to mean more than a subscription to a magazine which is already available in the school library, these students, when later joining the teaching staff of the nation, might function as a healthy leavening force for the entire profession.

In the past, teachers have judged their own organizations by the standards which they have used in evaluating their schools. In the first place, mere growth of the associations was often accepted as evidence of success, just as the growth of public education was looked upon as proof of adequate accomplishment in the schools. In the second place, the teachers have not participated in forming policies and in making other major decisions which vitally affected their associations. They have accepted, instead, whatever the officers of their organizations have chosen to do or not to do for them. Inside the schools, likewise, the teachers have been followers without any share in leadership. In the third place, the leaders in teachers' societies have, to a great extent, overlooked the peculiar professional needs and the special capabilities of many individuals. A similar situation prevailed in the schools, with the teachers largely unresponsive to differences among pupils that might have been capitalized advantageously.

None of these conditions need prevail in the future. With sufficient interest, intelligence, and use of existing knowledge and techniques, the teachers can transform their organizations into highly effective instrumentalities for the common advancement, in a multitude of different ways, of both their own welfare and the public good.

Suggested Readings

ALEXANDER, CARTER, *Some Present Aspects of the Work of Teachers' Voluntary Associations in the United States* (New York, Bureau of Publications, Teachers College, Columbia University, 1910).

Brooklyn Teachers Association, *Fiftieth Annual Report of the President, Including a History of the Association, 1874–1924* (September, 1924).

GRANRUD, J., *The Organization and Objectives of State Teachers' Associations* (New York, Bureau of Publications, Teachers College, Columbia University, 1926).

HOFFMAN, M. D., *Status of Voluntary Teachers' Associations in Cities of 100,000 Population or More*, U. S. Office of Education, Bulletin 1930, No. 36 (Washington, Government Printing Office, 1931).

MARSH, ARTHUR L., *The Organized Teachers* (National Association of Secretaries of State Educational Associations, 1936).

National Education Association, Educational Policies Commission, *A National Organization for Education* (March, 1937).

Progressive Education Association, *Progressive Education Advances* (New York, D. Appleton-Century Company, 1938).

SELLE, ERWIN S., *The Organization and Activities of the National Education Association* (New York, Bureau of Publications, Teachers College, Columbia University, 1932).

XXXIV

Public Attitude toward the Teaching Profession

Conduct outside the Classroom

THE conduct of American schoolteachers has always been a matter of public concern. From colonial days to the present time, teachers and ministers have been associated together in the minds of people, and the high character standards which have been imposed upon the latter have quite commonly been required of the former. Emphasis has been placed upon the peculiar nature of the vocation of teaching—the fashioning of human lives—and upon the importance of exemplary conduct on the part of teachers, both within and without the classroom. At no time in our history have lawyers, doctors, and other professional workers been expected to maintain a comparable level of righteousness with that required of schoolteachers. Parents apparently want their children to associate during the day with individuals whose personal conduct is elevated above the standards common to the homes from which the children themselves emanate.

Teachers were especially restrained in their activities up to the World War. Then came a breakdown in social controls; many of the old conceptions of morality were scrapped and a period of disillusionment followed. Authoritarian religion declined and a number of the former taboos were removed. In the large cities especially, teachers were accorded a degree of freedom in their personal habits which would have formerly been decried. While the war was not wholly responsible for the increased freedom granted to teachers, it furnished the occasion for them to escape from traditional bonds.

Beale [1] reports that before the war teachers in many small

[1] Beale, Howard K., *Are American Teachers Free?* (New York, Charles Scribner's Sons, 1936), pp. 374–75.

communities of the Middle West and South dared not go to a theater. Card playing and dancing were even more rigidly forbidden than the drama. In fact, as late as 1929 a Kansas board of education dropped eleven high-school teachers because they had attended a dance at a local country club.

Smoking has until recently been considered a cardinal sin for teachers, and in many sections of the country they must still confine their use of tobacco to their own private homes or dormitories.[2] In cities of more than a million population, both men and women teachers may now smoke freely away from school.

Drinking has been even less tolerated in the past than smoking and when discovered has frequently led to the dismissal of the offender. The temperance movement had a marked influence on the activities of teachers. In many states, the schools were employed to promote the interests of temperance societies and teachers were among the most active members in the campaigns against the saloon and the sale and use of intoxicating liquors. For a long period of time, therefore, drinking was almost universally denied to members of the teaching profession. Prohibition and the World War brought about a remarkable change in the attitude of the American people toward the use of alcohol. It made drinking more respectable and nearly three fourths of the teachers in the Northeast reported to Beale in 1935 that they could imbibe with impunity away from the schools.[3] It appears that women teachers are as free to drink as men. However, in spite of a more tolerant attitude on the part of the public toward the rights of teachers to take a drink, contracts in many sections of the country still forbid drinking and a common question put to applicants for teaching positions is, "Do you drink?" As a group, the teaching profession are not disposed to partake freely of alcoholic beverages, and even if all bans were lifted the vast majority of American schoolteachers would remain equally as temperate as they have been compelled to be in the past.

Sex immorality among schoolteachers has never been countenanced by the public except in a few sections of the South

[2] According to Beale, as late as 1923 Tennessee still had a law requiring teachers to teach the evils of "smoking cigarettes"; Indiana, the evils of "nicotine"; and Alabama and California, the evils of "tobacco."

[3] Beale, Howard K., *op. cit.*, p. 379.

where white school boards ignore it in Negro teachers. In all state tenure laws immoral conduct is a legitimate ground for dismissal and is so considered by the courts. While size of community does not necessarily alter the attitude of the public toward questions of morality, teachers in large cities undoubtedly feel fewer restraints with respect to their own conduct than those in the smaller communities. The personal life of the city teacher is more certainly detached from her school life than is that of teachers in villages and rural towns. It does not necessarily follow, however, that immorality among teachers is more prevalent in large cities than in small communities.

Public attitude toward divorce has changed perceptibly in the United States during the past quarter century and its influence on the appointment or retention of divorced teachers has been clearly observable. Except in cases where the publicity is a bit unsavory, and in small communities where gossip has magnified the circumstances causing the separation, the matter of divorce is much less likely to be an important factor in teacher selection than during earlier periods of our history. While scarcely a matter of conduct, marriage on the part of women teachers has been one of the most frequent grounds for their dismissal. The problem is primarily an economic one, although the sociological aspects of the situation have received some attention. As soon as teacher-training institutions were able to furnish an adequate supply of technically qualified teachers for the public schools, there was a movement instituted to oust married women in order to make room for their "more needy" sisters who were graduating from the normal schools. The argument commonly advanced was that two incomes in one family, with one coming from public taxation, were deemed unfair. As early as 1903 the New York Board of Education enacted a bylaw forbidding a woman teacher to marry.[4] Hundreds of school boards have taken similar action, calling for immediate resignation either upon marriage or at the end of the school year for which the offending teacher is employed.[5]

[4] "Married Women as Teachers," in *Educational Review*, February, 1903 (Vol. XXV), p. 213, and Woody, Thomas, *A History of Women's Education in the United States*, Vol. I, pp. 509–10, in Beale, Howard K., *op. cit.*, p. 384.

[5] A study of 1473 representative city school systems made by the Research Divi-

The states have not legislated on marriage, and the principles upon which the courts have laid down their decisions have not been altogether clear and consistent. The attitude of boards of education toward married women teachers has been increasingly antagonistic since the depression of 1929. The prejudice against them is so deep-seated that facts demonstrating equal efficiency [6] with single women teachers have been totally ignored, and the merit principle lost sight of completely in an effort to divide the salary budget according to the economic needs of applicants.

The social life of teachers is often restricted by local attitudes and regulations. In many small communities, men friends must be chosen carefully by women teachers. In Virginia, a recent contract is reported to have contained the stipulation that a teacher should not "keep company" with "young men." Beale reported a regulation of an Ohio County Board that teachers who "go with" other teachers shall be dropped at the end of the year. He also cited the case of a high-school principal in a New York State village who was dismissed in 1927 because he walked home every afternoon with a high-school teacher.[7] In some communities teachers are afraid to "go out" on school nights, and in others they can only preserve their good reputation by being in by ten or eleven o'clock.

In a few school districts, the trustees even dictate where teachers shall board and how many week ends they are expected to spend in the community. Teachers are called upon to be extremely generous with their time outside of school hours in promoting civic affairs and satisfying the whims of parents. Church attendance, Sunday-school teaching, and Christian Endeavor activities are commonly expected of teachers, even though the

---

sion of the National Education Association shows that in 1931 approximately 77 per cent of the cities employed no married women as new teachers and that in 62 per cent single women teachers who marry are required to resign either at once or at the end of the school year. (National Education Association, *Administrative Practices Affecting Classroom Teachers*, Research Bulletin, No. 1, January, 1932 [Vol. X], p. 19.)

[6] Studies have repeatedly shown married women teachers to be equally as efficient as single women, and in some respects superior to them. See Peters, David W., *The Status of the Married Woman Teacher* (New York, Bureau of Publications, Teachers College, Columbia University, 1934).

[7] Beale, Howard K., *op. cit.*, p. 389.

responsibility for such work is not written down officially in the rules and regulations of the board. While teachers are expected to be civic-minded, they are not allowed to be active in political affairs. From a fourth to a half of the teachers who reported to Beale [8] indicated that they were not permitted to campaign actively for a political cause or run for political office. As was pointed out elsewhere, except in large industrial cities there is considerable opposition to teachers joining unions. This attitude appears to have been more pronounced during the first two decades of the century than in recent years. In 1914 the teachers in Cleveland who attempted to organize a union were defeated and forced to sign a "yellow dog" clause in their contracts to the effect that they would not join a union. Similarly in St. Louis in 1920, the Board of Education demanded the dismissal of any teacher who joined a union and refused to employ any who belonged to one.

In certain other large cities, of which Chicago is perhaps the most notable example, efforts to break up teacher organizations have failed. Sixty-eight teachers were dropped in this city for violation of the Loeb rule, a regulation of the Board of Education adopted in 1916 against membership in teachers' unions and organizations affiliated with labor. When taken to Superior Court the teachers won their case. It was later reversed by the Supreme Court, but with the passage of a tenure law the rights of teachers to join unions were fully guaranteed.

From the foregoing discussion the reader may be inclined to feel that public-school teachers are compelled to lead a very restricted life, similar in many respects to that of a sister in a convent or a monk in a monastery. In many parts of the country such conditions prevail, and the effect of them has tended to deter many competent individuals from choosing teaching as a vocation. The profession generally, however, enjoys more personal freedom now than at any time in its history. It is the judgment of the author that this is due in part to the greater tolerance which has followed the decline of authoritarian religions and in part to the increased security accompanying teacher-

[8] *Ibid.*, p. 396.

tenure legislation.[9] The church in recent years has become more liberal and humane in its point of view. Some of the old hypocrisy which dominated the Christian church for centuries has disappeared, and for it there has been substituted a genuine effort to improve mankind and to elevate society to greater heights. Less emphasis is placed on dogma and creed and more attention is focused upon the great social problems of modern life. The effect of this change on churchgoing people generally has been rather profound. As a result, the latter have tended to dwell less upon the sinful nature of their brethren and more upon the opportunities for improving the world in which they move and have their being.

At least, this seems to be a rational explanation for the increased tolerance of the more sensitive citizens toward the personal conduct of their fellows. It is conceivable, of course, that what appears to be a more enlightened public attitude toward the outside activities of teachers is a mere shift in emphasis. Where dancing, card playing, gambling, drinking, staying out late at night, and failing to attend church were once frowned upon by the town fathers, perhaps these one-time offenses no longer seem important enough to warrant extended debate. It is possible that their place has now been taken by such matters as political affiliation, reputed beliefs, and "subversive" activities. It is the author's judgment, however, that the facts warrant the conclusion that genuine progress has been made in freeing teachers from the taboos to which they were formerly subjected, that teachers in large cities are approaching emancipation from the chains which enslaved them at the turn of the century, and that another generation of teachers will enjoy a degree of freedom in the rural districts which is not unlike that now achieved by their city sisters.

The importance of this increase in public tolerance toward the personal conduct of teachers cannot be overemphasized, for, as Beale has so succinctly put it, "not until they are allowed to lead normal lives, determine their own rules of conduct, and play a respected and self-respecting part in community life will individ-

---

[9] Tenure legislation has tended to give all teachers in a state as much freedom in their conduct as is now commonly accorded to those who teach in the largest cities.

uals who love freedom and have ideas and abilities stay in the teaching profession. Only then will many men again enter the profession." [10]

FREEDOM IN TEACHING

During the nineteenth century the matter of freedom in teaching was not a problem of pressing importance in the public schools. For the most part, teachers were uneducated and untrained, and occasion for conflicting opinions seldom arose in the classroom.[11] Teaching consisted almost entirely of passing on to pupils elementary facts that were in no way controversial in nature. Textbook instruction predominated, and by careful scrutiny of the basal texts the oversensitive town fathers could protect their offspring against the intrusion of any radical ideas, with full confidence that teachers would not add or subtract materially from the author's conclusions. During this whole century (nineteenth) there was little emphasis upon teaching pupils how to think. Education consisted in filling pupils' minds with subject matter. Furthermore, administrators and teachers were so busy during these earlier days keeping the schools going and trying to place the public-school enterprise on a sound footing that there was little time or energy left for conflicts of opinion. It is not surprising, therefore, that the problem of academic freedom was a relatively minor one among public-school teachers prior to the twentieth century.

Perhaps the most disturbing factor to parents before the World War was the new view of science and modernist religion which teachers brought directly to the classroom from their college and university experiences. New interpretations of biology led immediately to controversy because of their implications for the old-time religion.[12] The teaching of evolution has been con-

[10] Beale, Howard K., *op. cit.*, p. 406.

[11] There were occasions when teachers were attacked for their interpretation of the issues involved in the Civil War, for their attitude on slavery, and for failure to teach the harmful effects of alcohol upon the human system and the evils of cigarette smoking. Isolated cases comparable to most present-day interferences could be cited.

[12] The emotional response of the fundamentalists to the new science was so extreme that in one state an attempt was made to prescribe by law that pi should be changed from 3.1416 to 3.000, partly because it was simpler to use, but mostly be-

tested since the origin of the theory and is still discouraged in many states by law.[13] In fact, any theories which run counter to the more common interpretations of the Bible must be withheld from pupils. One writer has summed up the situation as follows: "Nothing can be taught in 70 per cent of the secular schools of this Republic today not sanctioned by the hosts of Fundamentalism." [14]

Next to religious issues, social and economic questions have constituted the chief sources of controversy in teaching. The role of government in the alleviation of poverty, public taxation, the tariff, peace and internationalism, patriotism, and politics are topics which have proved embarrassing to many teachers because of parental objections to the point of view assumed by the instructor or the facts presented for the pupils' consideration. In some instances the objectors are not parents, but societies or organizations whose platforms may have been criticized indirectly by a frank discussion by pupils of current questions.

There are many pressure groups, including business, religious, and patriotic organizations, which are still attempting to use the schools for propaganda purposes. Teachers unprotected by tenure are particularly susceptible to the influence of one or more of these agencies. Parents and the public generally have not understood the necessity of academic freedom in the interests of the civic education of youth. They have lost sight of the rights of children to the free use of their intelligence, to reach independent conclusions, and to examine old beliefs and attitudes. They forget that democracy is a distinctive way of life, as well as a political conception. It is difficult to see how the school can provide experiences in democratic living for pupils without freedom in teaching.

Practically, of course, the profession can move no faster in the

---

cause the Bible described the Vases of Solomon as three times as far around as across. (Lindsay, E. E., and Holland, E. U., *College and University Administration*, p. 460. Jordan, Royce, "Tennessee Goes Fundamentalist, "in *New Republic*, April 29, 1925 [Vol. XLII], p. 259.)

[13] Laws, resolutions, or official administrative edicts designed to ban or discourage the teaching of evolution have been passed in Florida, Mississippi, Arkansas, Tennessee, North Carolina, and Louisiana. (Beale, Howard K., *op. cit.*, pp. 227–28.)

[14] Shipley, Maynard, "Growth of the Anti-evolution Movement," in *Current History*, May, 1930 (Vol. XXXII), p. 330.

direction of academic freedom than the public is willing for it to go. Even today, however, the freedom which teachers enjoy in many communities depends to a large degree upon their intelligence, information, and tact. Until teachers win the respect and confidence of the leaders in the communities in which they work, it will be futile to press claims for larger grants of freedom. This comes only to those who are trusted and respected. The task ahead of the profession is twofold if academic freedom is to become a reality rather than a dream: first, to elevate the position of the American schoolteacher through high standards of training and scholarship and, second, to educate the public with respect to the importance of freedom in teaching. These achievements, together with a growing realization on the part of citizens generally of the true meaning of democracy, are likely to result in a larger degree of academic freedom than the profession has ever experienced.

Teacher Participation in School Administration

The story of the teaching profession in America would not be complete without mention of the changes which have been brought about in the nature of the teacher's responsibilities. In the days when teachers were chosen directly from the student body of colleges, universities, or high schools, without any special preparation for their jobs, it was obviously impractical to free them from supervision. The reader will have observed that school committees first attempted to exercise this function, then delegated it to principals and, later, to superintendents of schools. Education borrowed its administrative and supervisory machinery in part from business. Employees had to be supervised; their work appraised, and an accounting made to the stockholders. Teachers were hired, told what and what not to do, and fired when, in the judgment of their superior officers, their work was unsatisfactory. This procedure was refined as cities grew and school populations increased in size. General and special supervisors were added toward the end of the last century and the beginning of the twentieth, to relieve principals and superintendents of the multifarious duties which surrounded them. The quality of the supervision ranged from very bad to excellent.

But as long as teachers had no special stock in trade, these foremen were obviously necessary if the social heritage were to be faithfully passed on. Few teachers, even with the help of supervisors, could be expected to enrich this heritage, but they might at least be entrusted to hand it down undiminished to their pupils.

Then came higher certification standards and the great trek to teacher-training institutions. Teachers often surpassed their superiors in scholarship, professional knowledge, and in the amount of training which they had taken. With these advanced qualifications teachers became more critical of school policies and practices. The old line and staff organization which had been copied from the army, and to some extent from industry, was subjected to attack, partly because authority frequently emanated from incompetent persons and partly because, as originally conceived, it did not allow for democratic participation in the formulation of policies. The latter were usually determined by school officers, superintendents, supervisors, and principals, without the aid of the rank and file in the teaching corps. According to this type of organization, it was unethical for a classroom teacher to go over the head of her immediate superior officer. If she did not like his brand of supervision, she could resign and look elsewhere for a job. In only a few instances were teachers consulted about school problems, except possibly in a paternalistic way. The prevailing conception seemed to be that the teacher's job was to teach and that all other matters were extraneous to this end, therefore, no particular concern of hers.

School superintendents were no more responsible for this procedure than the teachers themselves. Boards of education expected the administrative staff to attend to administration, to propose policies, and to "govern" the schools as they would any other business enterprise. The tenure of superintendents of schools was always uncertain and in most instances brief. If he succeeded in pleasing the teachers, he probably antagonized the board of education; if he satisfied the board, he aroused the enmity of the teachers. In either case he lost out eventually, because the support of both groups was necessary. There were numerous exceptions to this rule, the personality of the executive head being the determining factor in some situations. School administrators, however, as a group have been in a most vulnerable position because of the size and nature of the responsibilities which they have had to shoulder.

While the line and staff organization has not been demonstrated to be inherently bad, the evils accompanying it have aroused considerable criticism on the part of teachers. As an administrative device, the arrangement is highly efficient; but, as commonly used, no provision is made for utilizing the intelligence and enthusiasm of classroom teachers in planning the work and operation of the school system. As long as teachers were untrained, an authoritarian administrative machine ran relatively smoothly. The progressive teacher, however, demands freedom from exploitation and control and wants a share in planning the work of the enterprise in which she is engaged.

Paralleling the advances in teacher qualifications were the passage of teacher-tenure laws (1909–1937) in many states, and the removal of the big stick from the hands of school administrators and board members. Teachers now began to assert their opinions to resist policies which they deemed detrimental to their own interests and those of the school system. Their increased training gave them confidence in their ability to contribute to the formulation of school policies, and their security provided them with courage to voice their sentiments. In some instances, their enthusiasm has been superior to their judgment and the results have been disastrous for the welfare of children. In most of the large school systems, there are a few politically minded teachers who are seeking to promote their own individual interests by professing to champion the cause of teacher and pupil welfare. These demagogues have misled thousands of professionally minded teachers who were unacquainted with the ways of politics.

Apart from this self-seeking group, however, there has been a growing resentment on the part of teachers generally to what they deem to be a class distinction among the educational workers in a school system. This is comparable in some ways to the development of class consciousness in other walks of life, such as capital and labor, rich and poor, young and old, men and women, and certain other groups which seem to be increasingly arrayed against each other in the struggle for power. To bridge this gap between the administrators and supervisors, on the one hand, and the rank and file of the teaching personnel, on the other, is one of the most pressing problems confronting education today. A few school systems are making headway, but the problem in most communities is still acute.

Some of our most thoughtful educators are looking for the solution in the direction of more participation by teachers in the determination of school policies. It is their belief that any adequate interpretation of democratic administration must allow teachers a large share in making decisions, many of which are of greater concern to teachers than to any other group in the school system. Teachers want and should have a voice in matters which concern the curriculum, teaching load, salaries, operation of buildings, supervision, textbooks, and supplies—in fact, in all matters in which their work is affected and in which their judgments may contribute to the development of a more adequate program of education.

To achieve this goal will require some modifications in the administrative organizations of school systems. A policies commission of some kind, composed of representatives of the educational personnel, will have to be formed and made an integral part of the school machinery. This agency would have, presumably, as its major function the formulation of policies to be presented to the board of education for action. The superintendent of schools might appropriately serve as chairman of this commission and provide the continuity and integration which is essential for the smooth operation of any legislative body. In the matter of execution, the traditional line and staff organization would continue to function as in the past. Once a policy had been approved, it would be put into effect through ordinary administrative channels. If the method of carrying out an agreed-upon policy proved obnoxious, the representative commission might then formulate a policy of administration which would remove the objectionable features in the old procedure. In other words, teachers would share in planning and all the advantages of a division of labor would still be retained.

Teachers' councils bear a faint resemblance to the organization just outlined, except that they have never been really considered as an essential part of the school machinery, nor have they functioned successfully in many communities. These organizations have been primarily grievance committees with access to the board of education, working apart from the superintendent and his staff and frequently at cross purposes with them.

Unless Fascist principles gain supremacy over our democratic traditions, future teachers in America will play a much larger part in planning and working out public-school programs than have their pedagogical forebears. Trained professional workers will not long submit to a type of administration which was designed to serve the needs of school systems manned by ignorant and untrained individuals, and which continues to superimpose policies without regard to the wishes or rights of those most concerned.

A radical change in supervision has accompanied the improved professional status of teachers in progressive school systems. Whereas formerly it was a highly personal matter involving classroom inspection, it is now becoming more and more a cooperative service which aims to improve teaching indirectly. Supervisors are now frequently available on call, and seldom intrude in schools or classrooms where their aid has not been solicited. This theory is in harmony with the newer point of view about learning. Efforts on the part of supervisors to compel teachers to change their methods of instruction have been ineffective and harmful. The substitution of genuine leadership for the authoritarian procedures common to American school systems during the first two decades of the present century has won the confidence and respect of the more intelligent members of the profession. The time is rapidly approaching when the old hierarchy which placed the teacher in a position subservient to that occupied by principals, supervisors, and administrators will disappear. A division of labor will be maintained, but the freedom of the professional teacher to pursue her work without interference will constitute the crowning achievement of a long chapter in the history of the profession.

SUGGESTED READINGS

BEALE, HOWARD K., *Are American Teachers Free?* (New York, Charles Scribner's Sons, 1936).

EWING, STEPHEN, "Blue Laws for School Teachers," in *Harper's Magazine*, December, 1927.

Michigan Education Association, "Democratic Participation in Administration," in National Education Association, Department of Elementary Principals, *Eighth Yearbook* (Washington, National Education Association, 1935).

NEWLON, JESSE H., *Educational Administration as Social Policy* (New York, Charles Scribner's Sons, 1934).

XXXV

The Social Composition of the Teaching Population

IT would be exceedingly difficult, from the meager data available on the topic, to show any marked decline or improvement since 1865 in the social and cultural heritage of those who have chosen teaching as a career. To be sure, present-day teachers are better trained and better educated than the teachers of post-Civil-War days but, from the standpoint of the racial stock from which they spring or the class of society from which they have emerged, there is no reason for believing that any substantial changes have occurred.

In America, as in most of the European countries, elementary teachers in the past have been drawn largely from the lower economic classes. The educational requirements for this group have never been so high as those established for teachers in the upper levels of the school system. The result has been that those young people whose parents could afford to send them to college have elected to teach in high school in preference to the elementary school. While state universities have provided educational opportunities at rather nominal rates, the time required to complete the full course of study and the incidental expenses accompanying attendance at college have constituted economic barriers for the young man or woman who had no financial backing. Scholarships have always made it possible for a few prospective elementary-school teachers to secure the additional educational opportunities offered in college; but for the most part, until the advent of teachers' colleges, economic status was the determining factor as to whether or not one chose to attend a normal school or a college or university.

Because of the cultural advantages of the college and university over those available in normal schools, there has developed in

American education something of a caste system among teachers, not altogether unlike that prevailing in France, Germany, and England. While our American traditions of democracy have made the social gap between the teaching groups here less apparent than in other countries, it has been the subject of considerable concern to those who have been most directly interested in the improvement of elementary education. High-school teachers have been better paid and have enjoyed greater prestige than have their colleagues in the lower grades of the school system.

Neither high-school nor elementary-school teaching, however, has appealed strongly to the more favored economic groups, because teaching has offered no special opportunities for the improvement of their financial status, nor has it, like medicine, captured the imagination of youth. Able young men have for years looked upon public-school teaching as a woman's job and, except for temporary periods, the more intelligent male graduates of American colleges appear to have sought expression for their energies and abilities in such respected walks of life as law, medicine, engineering, and business.

There appear to be no comprehensive studies of the social composition of the teaching population prior to Coffman's investigation in 1911. This author summed up his description of the typical female teacher of that date as follows: [1]

. . . twenty-four years of age, having entered teaching in the early part of her nineteenth year when she had received but four years' training beyond the elementary schools. Her salary at her present age is $485 a year. She is native born of native-born parents, both of whom speak the English language. When she entered teaching both of her parents were living and had an annual income of approximately $800 which they were compelled to use to support themselves and their four or five children. The young woman early found the pressure both real and anticipated to earn her own way very heavy.

To the above description of the typical female teacher there might have been added a sentence to the effect that she was more likely to be the daughter of a farmer or a tradesman than of a professional man, for an unpublished investigation by

[1] Coffman, Lotus D., *The Social Composition of the Teaching Population* (New York, Bureau of Publications, Teachers College, Columbia University, 1911), p. 80.

Dr. George D. Strayer in 1908 showed clearly that the population preparing to teach was coming from the agricultural and trade classes.

In 1926 Clyde Hill [2] and, later, Mary Moffett [3] made rather comprehensive studies of the background of students in teachers' colleges. The findings were similar to those reported by Coffman fifteen or twenty years earlier. The typical teachers'-college student in 1926 to 1929 was one of a family of four or five children; she was native-born of native-born parents; her father was a farmer, skilled workman, or owner of a small business. The median parental income was two thousand dollars to twenty-five hundred dollars. The student had been reared in a rural community or small town.

As Moffett reported, she differed only in choice of vocation from her sister who became a stenographer, nurse, or business clerk. Her life had been lived in an area the radius of which had taken her not more than one hundred to two hundred miles from home. Her major contacts with art had been in school buildings, stores, or her own home. In half of the homes there were no copies of the masterpieces of art, and her contacts with music, beyond local talent, had been by means of the radio and the phonograph. Her reading consisted, in addition to the daily scanning of the newspaper, of the *American Magazine, Ladies' Home Journal,* and *Saturday Evening Post,* and the reading of a light novel or other literature in book form less often than once a month. [4]

This same author reported, however, that the homes from which these prospective teachers came were substantial and well furnished according to the standards of rural and small-town communities. The parents, since they were farmers or tradesmen, ordinarily had fewer books in their homes than did the professional men.

From the standpoint of intelligence, the American public-

[2] Hill, Clyde M., *A Decade of Progress in Teacher Training* (New York, Bureau of Publications, Teachers College, Columbia University, 1927).

[3] Moffett, Mary L., *The Social Background and Activities of Teachers College Students* (New York, Bureau of Publications, Teachers College, Columbia University, 1929), p. 98.

[4] *Ibid.,* p. 19.

Table 26. The Intelligence of Teachers Compared with Certain Other Selected Groups of Workers [1]

Group	Number of Cases	Combined Scale Mean	Percentile Rank
College groups reported by Yerkes			
Teachers in service..................	399	18.63	91.77
Men, twenty colleges................	3,175	18.19	89.80
College men and women..............	4,750	18.18	89.62
Teachers in training.....	4,204	18.18	89.62
Women, thirteen colleges	1,575	18.13	89.44
Army groups			
Officers above major................	159	19.30	94.29
Officers, two years of college..........	1,271	18.89	92.79
All white officers...................	15,544	18.84	92.65
Captains..........................	3,023	18.73	92.22
Officers, high school graduates........	1,275	18.72	92.07
Teachers in service.................	399	18.63	91.77
Officers and men, two years of college..	2,090	18.27	90.15
Teachers in training................	4,204	18.18	89.62
Officers and men, high school graduates	3,698	17.70	87.08
White draft, two years of college......	819	17.30	84.61
White draft, high school graduates.....	2,423	16.99	82.64
Ohio University, and superior high school seniors			
Graduate students..................	139	19.79	95.64
Seniors...........................	760	19.11	93.57
Juniors...........................	1,097	18.92	92.92
Sophomores.......................	1,346	18.72	92.07
All students.......................	5,950	18.67	91.92
Teachers in service.................	399	18.63	91.77
Freshmen.........................	2,545	18.31	90.49
Teachers in training................	4,204	18.18	89.62
High school seniors.................	1,387	18.11	89.36

Note: Grouping determined by presence or absence of significant differences is indicated by horizontal lines within the columns.

[1] Taken from Dix, Lester, *op. cit.*, p. 62.

school teacher compares favorably with most other vocational groups and appears to be well enough equipped intellectually to cope with the perplexing problems which confront the teaching profession.[5] Workers in medicine, law, and engineering are, in all probability, more intelligent on the average than the rank and file among the teaching population, but the differences are not nearly so great as one might be led to suppose. Dix's[6] findings, as shown in Table 26, on the intelligence of teachers compared with that of other groups should be most reassuring to those who have been disturbed about the innate capacity of teachers.

While a cursory glance at Table 26 reveals the fact that teachers are surpassed by a few other groups for which intelligence data are available, the figures do not warrant any defeatist attitude on the part of those who are interested in the potentialities of the teaching profession. Considering the fact that America requires approximately 850,000 public-school teachers, out of the 73,000,000 adults[7] residing in the United States, to carry on the public-school enterprise and that the rewards provided have been extremely modest in amount, the quality of mind purchased has been more than might legitimately have been expected.

MEN AND WOMEN IN THE TEACHING PROFESSION

Perhaps the most remarkable change in the composition of the teaching population since Civil War days has been the decline in the proportion of men teachers in the profession. As Table 27 shows, approximately 41 per cent of the teachers were men in 1870, whereas in 1934 only 19.1 per cent of the 847,120 teachers were males.

While there has been a slight upturn in the proportion of men teachers since 1920, female supremacy has in no way been seriously challenged, nor is there reason to believe that any rapid trend in this direction is likely to develop. Not only have women

[5] The findings of Learned and Wood in Pennsylvania point to a somewhat different conclusion with respect to the intelligence of students in training in that state. Whether their findings are peculiar to the Keystone State and limited to the years since the depression, or whether they are applicable to the country as a whole and to teachers in service generally, is a moot question. (Learned, W. S., and Wood, Ben D., "The Student and His Knowledge," in *The Carnegie Foundation for the Advancement of Teaching*, Bulletin No. 29 [1938].)

[6] Dix, Lester, *The Economic Basis for the Teacher's Wage* (New York, Bureau of Publications, Teachers College, Columbia University, 1931), p. 62.

[7] 1930 Census.

demonstrated their peculiar fitness for the task of teaching, but their services can be secured at substantially lower cost to the taxpayers than an equal number of competent men instructors.

Table 27. Distribution of Teachers in the United States by Sex from 1870 to 1934 [1]

Year	Number of Men	Number of Women	Total Number of Teachers	Percentage of Men
1870	——	——	——	41.0 (estimate)
1880	122,795	163,798	286,593	42.8
1890	125,525	238,397	363,922	34.5
1900	126,588	296,474	423,062	29.9
1905	110,532	349,737	460,269	24.0
1910	110,481	412,729	523,210	21.1
1915	118,449	485,852	604,301	19.6
1920	95,654	583,648	679,533	14.1
1925	131,164	646,781	777,945	16.9
1930	141,771	712,492	854,263	16.5
1934	161,949	685,171	847,120	19.1

Note: With the exception of the last date, figures are from "Statistics of State School Systems, 1929–1930," in *Biennial Survey of Education in the United States, 1928–1930,* U. S. Office of Education, Bulletin 1931, No. 20, p. 28. Data for 1934 are from "Statistics of State School Systems, 1933–1934," in U. S. Office of Education, Bulletin 1935, No. 2, p. 66.

[1] Adapted from Chamberlain, L. M., and Meece, L. E., *Women and Men in the Teaching Profession* (Lexington, Ky., The University of Kentucky, 1937), p. 12.

While the gains made by women in other walks of life since 1870 have not been so pronounced as in teaching, they have, nevertheless, been substantial. In 1870, according to the United States Census, the proportion of women ten years old and over gainfully occupied was 13.1 per cent. By 1930 it had increased to 22 per cent. The gains made by the men during this same period were negligible, the proportion for 1930 being only 1.4 points above the figure for 1870.[8] Women have assumed a new role in the work of the world, and public-school teaching appears to have been the first successful invasion of women into the professions.[9]

Teachers have suffered certain losses from this rapid mortality

[8] In 1870 the proportion of males ten years and over gainfully occupied was 74.8 per cent; in 1930 it was 76.2 per cent.

[9] In 1930 the percentages of men in the recognized professions were as follows: physicians and surgeons, 95.6; clergymen, 97.8; lawyers, judges, and justices, 97.9; dentists, 98.2; technical engineers, 100.

among the men. In the first place, wages are lower than they would have been had a larger proportion of men remained in the profession. Except in equal-pay states, men have universally commanded higher salaries than women; and while this situation does not imply that women's wages would have been higher as a result, there are some reasons for believing that this would have been the case.

Men have always been closer to the taxpaying public than women. Through their affiliations with Rotary, Kiwanis, and Lions Clubs, fraternal orders, and Chambers of Commerce, they have had excellent opportunities of winning the confidence and support of the more influential citizens. The characterization of teaching as a woman's vocation has not enhanced the salary status of teachers. As times change and women more and more establish themselves in what has been until recently a man's world, there will be less discrimination against them, and the absence of any substantial proportion of men may not constitute a serious barrier.

The extent to which the cultural background of teachers will be elevated in the future depends almost entirely on the opportunities provided by educational institutions. The environmental limitations surrounding prospective teachers are the most serious handicaps confronting the profession. Coming as they do mostly from the lower middle class, they bear all the marks of this relatively unfavored social and economic group. To fill in these cultural gaps in the experiences of teachers is a task of considerable magnitude. If it is to be done, the teacher-training institutions will have to assume the major responsibility. The hope of attracting into teaching any sizable group of individuals from the higher economic classes in American society seems futile. The task before the profession is the selection of individuals, regardless of the particular layer of social and economic strata from which they happen to spring, who possess the intellectual and personal potentialities essential for teaching success, then to surround them with an environment which reeks with cultural opportunities and experiences. Through such a process of osmosis, American teachers may achieve a professional and cultural level beyond the dreams of present-day educators.

SUGGESTED READINGS

CHAMBERLAIN, L. M., and MEECE, L. E., *Women and Men in the Teaching Profession* (Lexington, Ky., The University of Kentucky, 1937).

COFFMAN, LOTUS D., *The Social Composition of the Teaching Population* (New York, Bureau of Publications, Teachers College, Columbia University, 1911).

HILL, CLYDE M., *A Decade of Progress in Teacher Training* (New York, Bureau of Publications, Teachers College, Columbia University, 1927).

MOFFETT, MARY L., *The Social Background and Activities of Teachers College Students* (New York, Bureau of Publications, Teachers College, Columbia University, 1929).

INDEX

INDEX